DI003940

Legal Issues in
Child Abuse
and Neglect
Practice
Second Edition

Interpersonal Violence: The Practice Series

Jon R. Conte, Series Editor

In this series...

LEGAL ISSUES IN CHILD ABUSE AND NEGLECT PRACTICE, Second Edition
by John E. B. Myers

CHILD ABUSE TRAUMA: Theory and Treatment of the Lasting Effects
by John N. Briere

INTERVENTION FOR MEN WHO BATTER: An Ecological Approach
by Jeffrey L. Edleson and Richard M. Tolman

COGNITIVE PROCESSING THERAPY FOR RAPE VICTIMS: A Treatment Manual
by Patricia A. Resick and Monica K. Schnicke

GROUP TREATMENT OF ADULT INCEST SURVIVORS
by Mary Ann Donaldson and Susan Cordes-Green

TEAM INVESTIGATION OF CHILD SEXUAL ABUSE: The Uneasy Alliance
by Donna Pence and Charles Wilson

HOW TO INTERVIEW SEXUAL ABUSE VICTIMS: Including the Use of Anatomical Dolls
by Marcia Morgan, with contributions from Virginia Edwards

ASSESSING DANGEROUSNESS: Violence by Sexual Offenders, Batterers, and Child Abusers
Edited by Jacquelyn C. Campbell

PATTERN CHANGING FOR ABUSED WOMEN: An Educational Program
by Marilyn Shear Goodman and Beth Creager Fallon

GROUPWORK WITH CHILDREN OF BATTERED WOMEN: A Practitioner's Manual
by Einat Peled and Diane Davis

PSYCHOTHERAPY WITH SEXUALLY ABUSED BOYS: An Integrated Approach
by William N. Friedrich

CONFRONTING ABUSIVE BELIEFS: Group Treatment for Abusive Men
by Mary Nõmme Russell

TREATMENT STRATEGIES FOR ABUSED CHILDREN: From Victim to Survivor
by Cheryl L. Karp and Traci L. Butler

GROUP TREATMENT FOR ADULT SURVIVORS OF ABUSE: A Manual for Practitioners
by Laura Pistone Webb and James Leehan

WORKING WITH CHILD ABUSE AND NEGLECT: A Primer
by Vernon R. Wiehe

TREATING SEXUALLY ABUSED CHILDREN AND THEIR NONOFFENDING PARENTS:
A Cognitive Behavioral Approach
by Esther Deblinger and Anne Hope Heflin

HEARING THE INTERNAL TRAUMA: Working With Children and Adolescents Who
Have Been Sexually Abused
by Sandra Wieland

PREPARING AND PRESENTING EXPERT TESTIMONY IN CHILD ABUSE LITIGATION:
A Guide for Expert Witnesses and Attorneys
by Paul Stern

TREATMENT STRATEGIES FOR ABUSED ADOLESCENTS: From Victim to Survivor
by Cheryl L. Karp, Traci L. Butler, and Sage C. Bergstrom

HOMICIDE: THE HIDDEN VICTIMS—A Guide for Professionals
by Deborah Spungen

TECHNIQUES AND ISSUES IN ABUSE-FOCUSED THERAPY: Addressing the Internal Trauma
by Sandra Wieland

Legal Issues in Child Abuse and Neglect Practice

Second Edition

John E. B. Myers

WITHDRAWN

Interpersonal Violence:
The Practice Series

SAGE Publications
International Educational and Professional Publisher
Thousand Oaks   London   New Delhi

For permission to reprint copyrighted material the author and publisher gratefully acknowledge the following:

Goodman, G. S., & Clarke-Steward, A. (1991). Suggestibility in children's testimony: Implications for child sexual abuse investigations. In J. Doris (Ed.), *The suggestibility of children's recollections.* © 1991 by the American Psychological Association. Reprinted by permission.

Spencer, J. R., & Flin, R. (1990). *The evidence of children: The law and the psychology.* © 1990 by The Blackstone Press, London. Reprinted with permission.

For information:

SAGE Publications, Inc.
2455 Teller Road
Thousand Oaks, California 91320
E-mail: order@sagepub.com

SAGE Publications Ltd.
6 Bonhill Street
London EC2A 4PU
United Kingdom

SAGE Publications India Pvt. Ltd.
M-32 Market
Greater Kailash I
New Delhi 110 048 India

Printed in the United States of America

Library of Congress Cataloging-in-Publication Data

Myers, John E. B.
    Legal issues in child abuse and neglect practice / by John E. B. Myers. — 2nd ed.
      p. cm. — (Interpersonal violence)
    Includes bibliographical references and index.
    ISBN 0-7619-1665-2 (cloth : acid-free paper) — ISBN 0-7619-1666-0 (pbk. : acid-free paper)
      1. Child abuse—Law and legislation—United States—Trial practice. I. Title. II. Series.
    KF9323 .M94   1998
    344.73′03276—ddc21   98-9022

This book is printed on acid-free paper.

01 02 03 04 10 9 8 7 6 5 4 3 2

Acquiring Editor:	C. Terry Hendrix
Editorial Assistant:	Dale Mary Grenfell
Production Editor:	Astrid Virding
Editorial Assistant:	Denise Santoyo
Typesetter/Designer:	Rose Tylak
Cover Designer:	Candice Harman

Contents

1. Prevalence and Effects of Child Maltreatment   1
   Physical Abuse   2
      Definition of Physical Abuse   2
      Prevalence and Effects of Physical Abuse   2
      Corporal Punishment   3
   Neglect   7
   Sexual Abuse   8
      Prevalence and Characteristics of Sexual Abuse   8
      Short- and Long-Term Effects of Sexual Abuse   10
      Psychological Treatment For Sexually
         Abused Children   17
      The Long Tradition of Disbelieving Women and
         Children Who Claim to Be Victims of Sexual Abuse   18
      Research on Fabricated Allegations of
         Child Sexual Abuse   30

2. The Child Protection System   36
   A Brief History of Child Protection in the United States   37
      The Colonial Period   37
      The 19th Century: Birth of Organized Child Protection   38
      The 20th Century: Transformation From
         Private to Government Child Protection   41
      Contemporary Child Protection   42

The Adversary System of Justice   43
Overview of the American Legal System   45
    The Government Interest in Child Protection   45
    The U.S. and State Constitutions   46
    Federal and State Statutes Relating to
        Child Abuse and Neglect   47
    Regulations   47
    Common Law   48
    The Judicial System   48
The Criminal Justice System   51
    The Reddings' Story   52
Child Protective Services and the Juvenile Court   68
    Child Protective Services   68
    The Juvenile Court   68
Family Court: Divorce and Child Custody   70
    Is An Attorney Necessary to Get a Divorce or Custody?   70
    The Legal Effect of a Divorce   71
    A Word of Caution   78
    Future Modification of Child Custody or Visitation   78
Three Laws Intended to Protect Children   79
    Sex Offender Registration Laws   79
    Megan's Law: Public Notification
        of Sex Offenders Living in the Community   80
    Involuntary Psychiatric Hospitalization of
        Dangerous Sexual Predators   81

3. Child Abuse Reporting Laws   82
    Who Is Required to Report?   83
    Mandatory Reporting: No Discretion   84
    Permissive Reporting: Discretion Allowed   84
    Definitions of Abuse and Neglect   85
    What Level of Suspicion Triggers Mandatory Reporting?   85
    Do Mandated Reporters Report?   88
    Factors Influencing the Decision to Report   89
        Is The Evidence Sufficient?   89
        Will Reporting Do More Harm Than Good?   90
        Will Reporting Undermine Therapy?   90
        How Serious Is the Maltreatment?   92
        What Kind of Abuse Is It?   92
        How Clear Is the Law in This Case?   92
        How Old Is the Child?   92
    Informed Consent, Confidentiality, and Forewarning   93

Liability Related to Reporting Suspected
   Child Maltreatment   93
    Liability for Failure to Report   94
    Liability for Reporting   96
   General Guidelines Regarding Reporting   98
   Are There Alternatives to Universal Mandatory Reporting?   98
   Two Problems for Your Consideration   100
    Five-Year-Old Sally   100
    Bill's Confession   101

4. Investigative Interviewing Regarding Child Maltreatment   102
   The Attack on the Interviewer   103
   Interviewing   105
    Children's Memory Capacity   105
    Suggestibility   114
    The Vocabulary of Investigative Interviews   123
    Recreating Context: Props and
      Anatomically Detailed Dolls   126
    Proper Interview Practices   129
    The Interviewer's Dilemma   136
    Interview Practices to Be Avoided   142
    Effect of Multiple Interviews on Memory   143
    Cognitive Interview, Narrative Elaboration, and
      Criteria-Based Content Analysis   148
    Documentation of the Child's Competence
      to Be a Witness   152

5. Investigating Suspected Child Abuse   153
   Hearsay: Gathering Verbal Evidence of Abuse   153
    Defining Hearsay   154
    Exceptions to the Rule Against Hearsay   157
    The Importance of Documentation   166
    Summary   168
   Multidisciplinary Investigation: Specialized
    Centers to Interview Children   168
    Research on Multidisciplinary Investigation   169
   Videotaping Investigative Interviews   172
    Arguments for Videotaping   173
    Arguments Against Videotaping   175
    Summary   177
   Bizarre, Fantastic, Ritual, and Satanic
    Allegations of Abuse   178

Satanic Conspiracies? 179
Children's Allegations That Are Bizarre,
  Improbable, or Impossible 181
Investigating Multiple-Victim Cases 191

6. Balancing the Need for Confidentiality and
   the Requirements of Disclosure 192
   Defining Confidentiality 193
   The Importance of Confidentiality 194
   Three Sources of Confidentiality 194
     The Ethical Duty to Protect Confidential
       Client Information 195
     Laws Making Client Records Confidential 196
     Privileges in Legal Proceedings 197
   Confidentiality When the Client Is a Child 203
   Confidentiality and Privilege in Group Therapy 204
   Informed Consent 206
     Children and Informed Consent 207
     Explaining the Limits of Confidentiality
       Is Part of Informed Consent 207
     Raw Psychological Test Data 208
     Managed Care, Informed Consent, and Confidentiality 209
   Disclosure of Confidential and Privileged Information 209
     Client Consent 209
     Subpoenas 211
     A Criminal Defendant's Constitutional
       Right to Confidential Records 213
     Reviewing Client Records Before Testifying 214
     Education Records 214
     Child Abuse Reporting Laws 215
     The Dangerous-Client Exception to Confidentiality 215
     Emergencies 219
     Court-Ordered Psychological Evaluation 219
     The Patient-Litigant Exception to Privilege 219

7. Expert Testimony 221
   Lay and Expert Witnesses 222
   Therapy vs. Forensic Evaluation: Avoiding
     Avoidable Dual Relationships 222
   Evidence Defined 228
   Substantive Evidence and Credibility Evidence 229
     Substantive Evidence 229

Credibility Evidence 229
Expert Testimony in Criminal and Noncriminal
    Proceedings 231
Metaprinciples of Expert Testimony 231
    Honesty 232
    Evenhandedness 232
    Limits of Expertise 233
    Preparation 234
Qualifying to Testify as an Expert 234
The Form of Expert Testimony 235
    Opinion Testimony 235
    The Hypothetical Question 237
    Expert Testimony Providing Background Information 238
    Combining Forms of Expert Testimony 238
Information on Which Experts May Rely for Testimony 239
Expert Testimony Based on Novel Scientific Principles 239
    General Acceptance—*Frye* 239
    Relevance Analysis—*Daubert* 240
    Does *Frye* or *Daubert* Apply to
        Mental Health Testimony? 241
Physical Abuse 242
    Expert Medical Testimony on Cause of Injury 243
    Battered-Child Syndrome 243
    Shaken-Baby Syndrome 244
    Munchausen Syndrome by Proxy 244
Neglect 245
    Medical Neglect 246
    Psychological Neglect 248
    Nonorganic Failure to Thrive 248
    Mentally Retarded Parents 249
    Psychiatrically Disabled Parents 249
    Physically Disabled Parents 249
    Drug Abuse as Neglect 249
    General Neglect—"Filthy Home" Cases 250
    Abandonment 251
    Educational Neglect 251
Sexual Abuse 251
    Medical Evidence of Child Sexual Abuse 251
    Expert Testimony Based Largely on
        the Psychological Effects of Sexual Abuse 251
    Expert Testimony Regarding Developmental
        Differences Between Children and Adults 270
    Expert Testimony Regarding the Alleged Perpetrator 271

Expert Testimony About Psychological Syndromes 274
Conclusion 278
Two Cases of Expert Testimony for Your Consideration 278
Commonwealth v. Spring 279
Commonwealth v. Milton 280

8. Cross-Examination and Impeachment:
Special Accommodations When Children Testify 282
Impeachment of Lay Witnesses 284
Impeachment With the Witness's Prior
Inconsistent Statements 284
Bias 284
Evidence That the Witness Has a
Character Trait for Untruthfulness 285
Conviction of Certain Crimes 285
Defects in Capacity 285
Inadequate Opportunity to Observe Events 285
Impeachment of Expert Witnesses 286
Avoid the Frontal Attack 286
Conduct a Positive Cross-Examination 286
Raise Doubts About the Expert's Testimony, and Save
Those Doubts for Closing Argument to the Jury 287
Undermine the Expert's Assumptions 290
Impeach an Expert With a "Learned Treatise" 292
Raise the Possibility of Bias 292
Summary 293
Limits on Cross-Examination 294
Reviewing Client Records in Preparation for Testifying 294
Special Accommodations for Children Who Testify 294

9. Liability of Professionals 298
Settings for Legal Action Against Professionals 299
Civil Actions Against Professionals 299
Administrative Law Proceedings 300
Criminal Prosecution 301
Malpractice and Negligence 301
Breach of Professional Responsibility 301
Negligence 302
Malpractice 309
State Law as a Basis of Civil Liability 316
Constitutional Rights 317
Parental Rights Under the Constitution 319

Sources of Government Authority to
    Intervene in the Family 321
How U.S. Constitutional Rights Are Enforced in
    Court: Section 1983 321
    Immunity From Liability 323

Analysis of Problems 334
  Sally's Case (Chapter 3) 334
  Bill's Confession (Chapter 3) 335
  Commonwealth v. Spring (Chapter 7) 335
  Commonwealth v. Milton (Chapter 7) 336
  Smith v. Allred and Jones (Chapter 9) 337

Appendix A: American Professional Society on the
  Abuse of Children, Practice Guidelines, Use of
  Anatomical Dolls in Child Sexual Abuse Assessments 339

Appendix B: Sample Protective Order for Videotapes
  of Investigative Interviews on Child Abuse 352

Appendix C: American Professional Society
  on the Abuse of Children, Guidelines for
  Psychosocial Evaluation of Suspected
  Sexual Abuse in Young Children 354

Appendix D: ABCs of Coping with Cross-Examination 364

References 367

Index 399

About the Author 412

For Willie and Eric

You're the greatest!

Also for David L. Corwin, M.D.,

a pioneer in child protection, and

the guy who got me started in this field

Last, but by no means least,

this book is for Lucy Berliner, M.S.W.,

friend, mentor, counselor, inspiration,

and very cool woman

1

Prevalence and Effects
of Child Maltreatment

Child abuse is a scourge on children that inflicts incalculable suffering. What's more, child abuse is ugly. It makes us wince and avert our eyes. During the past 35 years, however, society has stopped closing its eyes to the reality of child abuse. Citizens from all walks of life—politicians, professionals, parents—have said, "We've got to do something about this. Our kids deserve better." They're right, of course. Kids deserve love, support, encouragement, and friendship, not apathy, violence, ridicule, and abuse.

As I said, during the past 35 years, society has come to take child abuse seriously. But have we eliminated abuse? Hardly. If the efforts of the past three decades had succeeded completely, you could toss this book in the trash and go for a walk. Unfortunately, the book is still relevant. Child abuse remains a serious social ill.

This book is about law. The law cannot solve the problem of child abuse. The solution, if there is one, lies in classrooms and clinics, not courtrooms. Nevertheless, the law plays many roles in making life

1

better for children. The judges, lawyers, police officers, and probation and parole officers administering the legal system share goals with the social workers, nurses, physicians, educators, mental health professionals, and others laboring to protect children. Too often, however, a gap separates legal professionals from helping professionals. My goal in this book is to bridge that gap by giving nonlawyers information that will help them interact effectively with the legal system. Effective communication and cooperation between helping professionals and the legal system goes a long way toward child protection.

A book on legal issues is not the place for extensive analysis of the prevalence and effects of child abuse. Yet no book on child abuse is complete without some discussion of the scope of the problem. This chapter, therefore, briefly reviews the literature on the prevalence and impact of child abuse and neglect.

❏ Physical Abuse

Physical abuse is common. "Parental maltreatment is a severe social problem that affects children all over the world" (Cerezo, 1997, p. 215).

DEFINITION OF PHYSICAL ABUSE

Physical child abuse is nonaccidental physical injury. Legal definitions of physical abuse are found in three places: (a) criminal codes, (b) statutes governing the juvenile court, and (c) child abuse reporting laws (see Chapter 3).

PREVALENCE AND EFFECTS OF PHYSICAL ABUSE

Children are kicked, punched, clubbed, burned, starved, poisoned, and otherwise abused in every way you can imagine and some you can't. It is difficult to know the true prevalence of physical abuse.

Physically abused children are at increased risk of mental health problems as they grow up (Fergusson & Lynskey, 1997; Styron &

Janoff-Bulman, 1997). As Whipple and Richey (1997) observe, "The impact of a physically abusive childhood is profound" (p. 432). Some physically abused children batter their own children (Malinosky-Rummell & Hansen, 1993). Bower and Knutson (1996) state that "a history of abuse has become acknowledged as a risk factor for child maltreatment" (pp. 696-697).

Every year, more than a thousand children die from abuse or severe neglect (Daro & Lung, 1996). "Although such deaths are relatively infrequent, the rate of child maltreatment fatalities confirmed by CPS [child protective services] agencies has risen steadily over the past eight years" (Daro & Lung, 1996, p. 7). Official reports probably underestimate the scope of fatal abuse and neglect (Ewigman, Kivlahan, & Land, 1993). The actual number of children killed each year in the United States may be closer to 5,000 (Levitt, Smith, & Alexander, 1994). Fatal child abuse is particularly common among very young children and babies (Brewster et al., 1998; Kirshner & Wilson, 1994). Approximately 50% of fatalities are children under age 1 (McClain, Sacks, Froehlke, & Ewigman, 1993).

CORPORAL PUNISHMENT

Most American parents use corporal punishment (Edwards, 1996; Graziano, Lindquist, Kunce, & Munjal, 1992). More than 90% of children are physically punished at some time (Flynn, 1996). The rate of corporal punishment against adolescents is between 33% and 50% (Graziano & Namaste, 1990; Straus & Kantor, 1994). Corporal punishment is less prevalent in some countries than others (Fergusson & Lynskey, 1997). The situation in the United States was summarized by Graziano and Namaste (1990):

> Slapping, spanking, paddling and, generally, hitting children for purposes of discipline are accepted, pervasive, adult behaviors in U.S. families. In these instances, although physical attack and pain are involved between two people of vastly different size, weight, and strength, such behavior is commonly accepted as a proper exercise of adult authority over children.
>
> With the exception of warfare, self-defense, and the often necessary use of force by the police, no human interactions other than adult-child interactions carry such clear social supports for the unilateral use of

physical punishment by one party on another. Similar behavior between, for example, an employer and an employee carr[ies] clear
proscriptions and can readily provide the basis for civil and/or criminal actions brought by the victim. Children, it seems, have been
singled out from among all groups in American society as the recipi-
ents of such treatment. (p. 450)

In 1996, the American Academy of Pediatrics published a consensus statement on the short- and long-term consequences of corporal
punishment. According to this statement,

> Spanking is not recommended in infants and children under 2 years
> of age because escalation, should it occur, carries a greatly increased
> risk of causing physical injury.
>
> There are no data bearing on the effectiveness of spanking to control
> misbehavior short-term in the average family. Limited data on
> preschool-children with behavior problems suggest that spanking
> may increase the effectiveness of less aversive disciplinary techniques.
> Data relative to the long-term consequences of spanking of preschool
> children are inconclusive. . . .
>
> Currently available data indicate that corporal punishment . . . , when
> compared with other methods of punishment, of older children and
> adolescents is not effective and is associated with increased risk for
> dysfunction and aggression later in life. . . .
>
> Concerning forms of corporal punishment more severe than spank-
> ing in infants, toddlers, and adolescents, the data suggest that the risk
> of psychological or physical harm outweigh any potential benefits.

In 1998, the American Academy of Pediatrics moved beyond the
1996 consensus statement (Committee on Psychosocial Aspects of
Child and Family Health, 1998). In a report titled "Guidance for
Effective Discipline," the Academy states:

> Despite its common acceptance, and even advocacy for its use, spank-
> ing is a less effective strategy than time-out or removal of privileges
> for reducing undesired behavior in children. Although spanking may
> immediately reduce or stop an undesired behavior, its effectiveness
> decreases with subsequent use. The only way to maintain the initial
> effect of spanking is to systematically increase the intensity with which
> it is delivered, which can quickly escalate into abuse. Thus, at best,
> spanking is only effective when used in selective infrequent situations.

> Because of the negative consequences of spanking and because it
> has been demonstrated to be no more effective than other approaches
> for managing undesirable behavior in children, the American Acad-
> emy of Pediatrics recommends that parents be encouraged and
> assisted in developing methods other than spanking in response to
> undesirable behavior. (p. 726)

The law allows parents to use "reasonable" corporal punishment
against their children. Although the term *reasonable corporal punishment* sounds like an oxymoron to some, it is widely used. According
to the Iowa Supreme Court, "Parents do have a right to inflict
reasonable corporal punishment in rearing their children" (*Hildreth
v. Iowa Department of Human Services*, 1996, p. 159). A California
statute states that physical abuse "does not include reasonable and
age appropriate spanking to the buttocks where there is no evidence
of serious physical injury" (Cal. Welfare and Institutions Code § 300).

When does corporal punishment exceed "reasonable" limits and
become abuse? Whipple and Richey (1997) observe that "despite
decades of research on physical child abuse, remarkably little is
known about where to draw the line between permissible forms of
physical punishment and actual abuse" (p. 431). In *People v. Whitehurst* (1992), the California Court of Appeals stated:

> A parent who wilfully inflicts *unjustifiable* punishment is not immune
> from either civil or criminal prosecution. . . . Corporal punishment is
> unjustifiable when it is not warranted by the circumstances, i.e., not
> necessary, or when such punishment, although warranted, was exces-
> sive. "Both the reasonableness of, and the necessity for, the punish-
> ment is to be determined by a jury, under the circumstances of each
> case." (pp. 35-36)

As the court stated in *Whitehurst*, cases turn on their unique facts
(see Whipple & Richey, 1997). Judges consider the child's age, the
type of discipline inflicted, the means used, the degree of injury or
pain, and the number of episodes (Whipple & Richey, 1997).

Corporal punishment has harmful long-term effects for some children (Flisher et al., 1997). According to Flynn (1996), "Recent studies
have suggested that a host of potentially harmful behavioral and
psychological consequences may result from so-called 'ordinary'

physical punishment. These negative outcomes include alcohol abuse, depression, suicidal thoughts, behavioral problems, low achievement, and future economic insecurity" (pp. 59-60). On the other hand, Fergusson and Lynskey (1997) found that "occasional or mild use of physical punishment" is unlikely to have "either beneficial or detrimental effects on longer term adjustment" (p. 628).

Adults who were physically punished as teenagers were more likely to think about suicide and more likely to abuse alcohol.

In a study of 6,002 American families, Straus and Kantor (1994) examined the association between corporal punishment during adolescence and later mental health problems. They concluded that "corporal punishment in adolescence is associated with a significantly increased probability of depressive symptoms as an adult" (pp. 550-551). Adults who were physically punished as teenagers were more likely to think about suicide and more likely to abuse alcohol (see Wagner, 1997). Straus and Kantor (1994) found that "the more corporal punishment the subjects experienced when they were teenagers, the greater the risk that they will go beyond ordinary corporal punishment to acts that are severe enough to be classified as physical abuse" of their own children (p. 555).

In his classic 1978 paper titled "The Myth of Classlessness," Pelton (1985) described "substantial evidence of a strong relationship between poverty and child abuse and neglect" (p. 24) and asserted that "abusing and neglecting families are the poorest of the poor" (p. 28). Recent research by Fergusson and Lynskey (1997) confirm the relationship between severe physical punishment/abuse and socioeconomic circumstances. These authors reported "clear differences in childhood environments" in subjects who had different exposures to physical punishment or maltreatment:

> In general, those reporting overly frequent punishment, harsh, or abusive treatment more frequently came from demographically disadvantaged homes, experienced a higher rate of other childhood and family adversities, and were more often exposed to childhood sexual abuse. These results clearly suggest that the elevated rates of adjustment problems in this group may have been largely or wholly due to

the social environment and context in which physical punish-ment/maltreatment occurred, rather than to the traumatic effects of such treatment on longer term adjustment. Subsequent analysis sup-ports this conclusion to the extent that adjustment for prospectively measured childhood, family, and social circumstances substantially reduced the associations between reported physical punishment/maltreatment and adjustment at age 18. Nonetheless, even after such adjustment, those reporting overly frequent, harsh, or abusive treat-ment during childhood were at increased risk of involvement in self-inflicted or interpersonal violence (suicide attempt, violent crime, victim of assault) and were more prone to alcohol abuse/dependence. (p. 627)

When corporal punishment occurs in a psychologically and eco-nomically impoverished home, it is difficult to sort out the cause or causes of long-term adjustment problems. But in light of mounting evidence that corporal punishment does more harm than good, Judge Leonard Edwards (1996), one of America's leading legal authorities on child abuse, has asserted that "it should be illegal to use corporal punishment on all children under five years of age" (p. 1021).

❏ Neglect

Child neglect is common. Erickson and Egeland (1996) state that

although the bruises and scars of physical abuse are more readily apparent, the quiet assault of child neglect often does at least as much damage to its young victims. Typically defined as an act of omission rather than commission, neglect may or may not be intentional. It is sometimes apparent (as in the unkempt appearance of the child who comes to school without a bath or adequate clothing) and sometimes nearly invisible until it is too late. Neglect is often fatal, due to inadequate physical protection, nutrition, or health care. Sometimes, as in the case of "failure to thrive," it is fatal because of a lack of human contact and love. In some cases, neglect slowly and persistently eats away at children's spirits until they have little will to connect with others or explore the world. (p. 4)

Eight types of neglect are discussed in Chapter 7.

❏ **Sexual Abuse**

Child sexual abuse emerged from secrecy in the late 1970s and is today a major focus of concern.

PREVALENCE AND CHARACTERISTICS OF SEXUAL ABUSE

Child sexual abuse is common in the United States and other countries (Finkelhor, 1994; Goldman & Padayachi, 1997; Gorey & Leslie, 1997). The true prevalence of sexual abuse is unknown because such abuse occurs in secret and because most incidents are not reported to authorities (Russell, 1984). Finkelhor (1994), in a review of the prevalence literature, observed that "because sexual abuse is usually a hidden offense, there are no statistics on how many cases actually occur each year" (p. 34). However, research supports an estimate of 500,000 new cases of child sexual abuse every year in the United States (Finkelhor, 1994).

Approximately 20% of girls experience some form of sexual abuse during childhood, ranging from relatively minor touching to brutal rape and incest that goes on for years.

Both girls and boys are sexually abused (Finkelhor, 1986; Friedrich, Brambsch, Broughton, & Beilke, 1991). Approximately 20% of girls experience some form of sexual abuse during childhood, ranging from relatively minor touching to brutal rape and incest that goes on for years (Finkelhor, Hotaling, Lewis, & Smith, 1990; Flemming, 1997). Finkelhor (1994) concluded that "at least one in five adult women in North America experienced sexual abuse (either contact or noncontact) during childhood" (p. 37). Reece (1997) observes that "this 20 percent figure keeps recurring in all the studies from the US, UK and its former colonies, as well as in studies from western Europe" (p. 15).

Boys appear to be sexually abused at a lower rate than girls (Finkelhor, 1994). Research discloses that approximately 5% to 10% of boys are sexually abused.

In a nationwide survey of sexually abused children, "The median age at time of abuse was 9.9 years for boys and 9.6 for girls" (Finkelhor, Hotaling, Lewis, & Smith, 1989, p. 381). Sexual abuse occurs at all ages, however, from infancy through adolescence (Gold, Hughes, & Swingle, 1996).

Most victims of child sexual abuse know their perpetrator (Anderson, Martin, Mullen, Romans, & Herbison, 1993). Finkelhor (1994) states that

> abusers can be classified by their relationship to the child victim into three categories: family, acquaintances, or strangers. Sexual abuse is committed primarily by individuals known to the child, unlike the child molester stereotype that prevailed until the 1970s. In adult retrospective surveys, victims of abuse indicate that no more than 10% to 30% of offenders were strangers, with the remainder being either family members or acquaintances. (p. 45)

Girls are more likely than boys to be abused by a family member (Kendall-Tackett, Williams, & Finkelhor, 1993). According to Finkelhor (1994), "A major difference between boy victims and girl victims is that boys are less likely to be abused within the family" (p. 47).

Some older children and adolescents sexually abuse younger children (Becker, 1994; Sanders & Ladwa-Thomas, 1997). A high percentage of adult sex offenders began their deviance during adolescence (Murphy & Smith, 1996). One study of 411 adult sex offenders reported that 58% became sexually interested in children during adolescence (Abel, Mittleman, & Becker, 1985). In another study, 60% to 80% of adult offenders acknowledged that they began their deviant sexual careers as teenagers (Groth, Longo, & McFadin, 1982).

Adults sometimes shrug off sexual contact between a teenager and a younger child as "innocent sex play" or a "normal" part of growing up. This is a mistake. Sexual activity between teenagers and younger children is sometimes clearly abusive (Kaufman, Hilliker, & Daleiden, 1996). Such deviant behavior is a clear sign of trouble ahead. The teenager may be developing a deviant sexual interest that will last a lifetime (Becker, 1994). Although teenage sex offenders are often resistant to treatment, there is better hope for therapeutic success when offenders are young than when they are adults with a chronic pattern of sexual deviance.

SHORT- AND LONG-TERM
EFFECTS OF SEXUAL ABUSE

Sexual abuse has immediate, short-term effects as well as long-term effects (Finkelhor et al., 1989; Kendall-Tackett et al., 1993). Former Surgeon General C. Everett Koop (n.d.) described the consequences of child sexual abuse as "overwhelming." Briere and Elliott (1994) add that "research conducted over the past decade indicates that a wide range of psychological and interpersonal problems are more prevalent among those who have been sexually abused than among individuals with no such experiences" (p. 54).

Not all sexually abused children exhibit outward symptoms of harm or distress (Conte & Berliner, 1988; Kendall-Tackett et al., 1993). Of course, the fact that a child does not demonstrate observable symptoms does not mean that the child is not suffering. Some children cope with sexual abuse by trying their best not to think about it. The majority of sexually abused children manifest symptoms (Mian, Marton, & LeBaron, 1996).

There are several theories to account for the harm caused by sexual abuse. Among the theories, the conceptual framework articulated by Finkelhor and Browne (1985) is the most widely accepted. Their model describes four trauma-causing factors ("traumagenic dynamics"): traumatic sexualization, stigmatization, betrayal, and powerlessness. These may occur in other kinds of trauma besides sexual abuse, but only sexual abuse involves all four.

Traumatic sexualization is "a process in which a child's sexuality (including both sexual feelings and sexual attitudes) is shaped in a developmentally inappropriate and interpersonally dysfunctional fashion as a result of the sexual abuse" (p. 531). *Betrayal* is "the dynamic in which children discover that someone on whom they are vitally dependent has caused them harm" (p. 531). *Powerlessness*, also termed *disempowerment*, or "the dynamic of rendering the victim powerless," is "the process in which the child's will, desires, and sense of efficacy are continually contravened" (p. 532). Finally, *stigmatization*

> refers to the negative connotations—for example, badness, shame, and guilt—that are communicated to the child about the experiences and that then become incorporated into the child's self-image.... They can come directly from the abuser, who may blame the victim for the activity, denigrate the victim, or, simply through his furtiveness, convey a sense of shame about the behavior. When there is pressure for secrecy from the offender, this can also convey powerful messages of shame and guilt. But stigmatization is also reinforced by attitudes that the victim infers or hears from other persons in the family or community. (pp. 530-533)

The authors explained that these dynamics

> alter the child's cognitive and emotional orientation to the world, and create trauma by distorting a child's self-concept, worldview, and affective capacities. For example, the dynamic of stigmatization distorts children's sense of their own value and worth. The dynamic of powerlessness distorts children's sense of their ability to control their lives. (p. 531)

Short-Term Effects of Sexual Abuse

The immediate or short-term effects of sexual abuse vary from child to child (Deblinger, Lippmann, & Steer, 1996). The more severe the abuse, the more likely the child will be symptomatic. Kendall-Tackett et al. (1993) concluded from their review of the literature on the impact of sexual abuse that "molestations that included a close perpetrator; a high frequency of sexual contact; a long duration; the use of force; and sexual acts that included oral, anal, or vaginal penetration lead to a greater number of symptoms for victims" (p. 170).

Short-term symptoms of abuse are typically the result of the anxiety, stress, and fear caused by sexual abuse (Mian et al., 1996). Before describing specific symptoms, it is important to note that children react in many ways to sexual abuse. Few children demonstrate all the symptoms discussed below. Indeed, with the exception of post-traumatic stress disorder (PTSD), symptoms of which appear in approximately half of sexually abused children, no single symptom or group of symptoms is seen in a majority of sexually abused children. Kendall-Tackett et al. (1993) concluded from their review that across all studies of the effects of sexual abuse, "the percentage of victims with a particular symptom was mostly between 20% and 30%. It is important to note that, with the exception of PTSD, no symptom was manifested by a majority of victims" (p. 167).

Anxiety. Many abused children suffer anxiety-related symptoms (Berliner & Saunders, 1996). According to Briere and Elliott (1994),

> Child abuse is, by its nature, threatening and disruptive, and may interfere with the child's developing sense of security and belief in a safe, just world. Thus, it should not be surprising that victims of such maltreatment are prone to chronic feelings of fearfulness or anxiety. Elevated anxiety has been documented in child victims of sexual abuse as well as in adults who were molested as children. (p. 57)

Fear. Perpetrators of sexual abuse often threaten their victims in order to maintain silence (see Chapter 4, the section "Interviewing," subsection "The Interviewer's Dilemma," sub-subsection "The Disclosure Process in Child Sexual Abuse"). The fear induced by threats causes anxiety (Kendall-Tackett et al., 1993).

Nightmares and Sleep Problems. Quite a few sexually abused children have nightmares (Kendall-Tackett et al., 1993). Sometimes the nightmare is a terrifying reenactment of the abuse. More often, however, the child has generalized dreams involving monsters or other frightening events.

Acting out and General Misbehavior. All children misbehave, of course, but many sexually abused children are seriously distressed, and their unhappiness can lead to misbehavior at home and school. The academic performance of abuse victims may suffer (Kendall-Tackett et al., 1993). Older children and adolescents may run away, abuse drugs or alcohol, become promiscuous, or engage in illegal conduct, including prostitution (Brannigan & Van Brunschot, 1997; Fergusson, Horwood, & Lynskey, 1997).

Withdrawal. Whereas some children act out, others withdraw emotionally and socially (Kendall-Tackett et al., 1993).

Regression. A child regresses when the child reverts to an earlier stage of development. For example, a child who is toilet trained may wet the bed. Sexual abuse sometimes causes regression (Kendall-Tackett et al., 1993).

Encopresis. Encopresis is "incontinence of feces not due to organic defect or illness" (*Dorland's Illustrated Medical Dictionary,* 1994, p. 94). "Encopresis is a relatively uncommon disorder, occurring in 1.0%-1.5% of boys 7 to 12 years of age. It is three times as common in males as females," and it "may be a marker of sexual abuse" (Morrow, Yeager, & Lewis, 1997, p. 15).

Poor Self-Concept. The stigmatization described by Finkelhor and Browne (1985) accounts for sexually abused children's poor self-concept. Many abused children think the abuse was their fault and that they are bad, dirty, worthless, or "damaged goods" (Swanston, Tebbutt, O'Toole, & Oates, 1997).

Depression. Sexual abuse makes children sad. Clinical depression, however, goes beyond transitory sadness and is a serious psychiatric problem. Preschool-aged children can become clinically depressed. Among sexually abused children and adolescents, depression is common, and quite a few victims think about suicide (Briere & Elliott, 1994; Bryant & Range, 1997).

Developmentally Inappropriate Sexual Behavior. Certain kinds of sexual behavior are normal during childhood (e.g., masturbation), and normal sexual behavior is described in Chapter 7 (the section "Sexual Abuse," subsection "Substantive Evidence," sub-subsection "Symptoms That Can Provide Relatively Strong Evidence of Sexual Abuse"). Young sexually abused children, however, have experienced developmentally inappropriate sexual acts. It is not surprising that some sexually abused children demonstrate developmentally inappropriate sexual behavior (Kendall-Tackett et al., 1993).

Post-Traumatic Stress Disorder. The fourth edition of the *Diagnostic and Statistical Manual of Mental Disorders* (*DSM-IV*; American Psychiatric Association, 1994) lists PTSD as an anxiety disorder. According to the *DSM-IV,*

> The essential feature of Posttraumatic Stress Disorder is the develop-
> ment of characteristic symptoms following exposure to an extreme
> traumatic stressor involving direct personal experience of an event
> that involves actual or threatened death or serious injury, or other
> threat to one's physical integrity.... The person's response to the event
> must involve intense fear, helplessness, or horror (or in children, the
> response must involve disorganized or agitated behavior). The char-
> acteristic symptoms resulting from the exposure to the extreme
> trauma include persistent reexperiencing of the traumatic event, per-
> sistent avoidance of stimuli associated with the trauma and numbing
> of general responsiveness, and persistent symptoms of increased
> arousal. The full symptom picture must be present for more than 1
> month, and the disturbance must cause clinically significant distress
> or impairment in social, occupational, or other important areas of
> functioning.
>   Traumatic events that are experienced directly include . . . violent
> personal assault (sexual assault, robbery, mugging). . . . For children,
> sexually traumatic events may include developmentally inappropri-
> ate sexual experiences without threatened or actual violence or injury.
> (p. 424)

Most sexually abused children do not have all the symptoms of PTSD. Nevertheless, a majority of victims have some or many PTSD symptoms (Briere & Elliott, 1994, p. 56). Famularo, Fenton, Kinscherff, and Augustyn (1996) observe that "the type, duration, and frequency of trauma determines the likelihood of PTSD devel-opment, and as such Post Traumatic Stress Disorder may result from a single or repeated traumatic event exposure" (p. 954). PTSD in children can persist for years (Famularo, Fenton, Augustyn, & Zuckerman, 1996).

Young sexually abused children with PTSD symptoms may repeti-tively act out the abuse in their play. Many PTSD sufferers have difficulty sleeping and experience nightmares. They may have stom-achaches and headaches. Some children have an intense emotional reaction when they are reminded of the traumatic experience. Children with PTSD may try to avoid people and things that remind them of the abuse. For example, a child who was raped in a field might not want to go near fields. Because of their desire to avoid thinking about what happened, some children with PTSD are reluctant to talk about their abuse. Such reluctance makes it difficult to interview these children (see Chapter 4).

Finkelhor (1987) emphasizes that not all abused children develop PTSD. Moreover, it is a mistake to assume that a child who lacks PTSD symptoms has not been sexually abused.

Some *parents* of sexually abused children exhibit symptoms of posttraumatic stress disorder. Timmons-Mitchell, Chandler-Holtz, and Semple (1996) report that mothers whose children disclosed sexual abuse were more likely to have PTSD symptoms. Mothers who themselves were sexually abused as children are particularly likely to be symptomatic. (For discussion of expert testimony on PTSD, see Chapter 7, the section "Sexual Abuse," subsection "Expert Testimony About Psychological Syndromes," sub-subsection "Post-Traumatic Stress Disorder.")

Somatic Complaints. Somatic complaints associated with sexual abuse include stomachaches and headaches.

Summary. Child sexual abuse causes short-term psychological symptoms in many children. Symptoms vary from child to child, depending on the kind of abuse, the child's coping style, and the presence or absence of parental support. Symptoms may last days, months, or years. Moreover, symptoms may abate temporarily only to reappear later on.

Long-Term Effects of Child Sexual Abuse

An extensive literature documents the long-term harmful effects of child sexual abuse (e.g., Banyard, 1997; Berliner & Elliott, 1996; Choquet, Darves-Bornoz, Ledoux, Manfredi, & Hassler, 1997; McCauley et al., 1997; Robin, Chester, Rasmussen, Jaranson, & Goldman, 1997; Sarwer, Crawford, & Durlak, 1997; Wyatt & Powell, 1988). Many victims suffer long after their abuse, and some adults never fully recover (Salter, 1995). A substantial number of adult psychiatric patients were sexually abused during childhood (Briere & Zaidi, 1989). Yet despite what Salter (1995) poignantly described as the "footprints on the heart" left by sexual abuse, most adult survivors lead productive lives. Coffey, Leitenberg, Henning, Turner, and Bennett (1996) conclude that "childhood sexual abuse does not inevitably lead to adult disorders" (p. 447). Chandy, Blum, and Resnick (1996) add that "one of the remarkably positive aspects of populations that are vulnerable due to a variety of risk factors is that, in spite of their vulnerability, a large majority of them grow up normally and do well in life" (p. 503).

In his book on treatment for adult survivors of child sexual abuse, Briere (1992) described seven psychological disturbances found in adolescent and adult survivors of child sexual abuse: PTSD, cognitive distortions, altered emotionality, dissociation, impaired self-reference, disturbed relatedness, and avoidance. Briere described such cognitive distortions as feelings of helplessness, a chronic sense of danger, self-deprecation, and pessimism about the future and such altered emotional states as depression, fear, and anxiety. *Dissociation* was defined as "a defensive disruption in the normally occurring connections among feelings, thoughts, behavior, and memories, consciously or unconsciously invoked in order to reduce psychological distress" (p. 36). Multiple-personality disorder is a rare and extreme form of dissociation. Concerning impaired self-reference, Briere wrote that "it is the impression of many clinicians who work with survivors of early and/or severe child abuse that such individuals often suffer from difficulties in how they relate to self" (p. 42). In the category of disturbed relatedness, Briere discussed problems with interpersonal relationships, especially intimate and sexual relationships. Finally, Briere described psychological avoidance. Some adult survivors attempt to avoid the pain of sexual abuse by engaging in behaviors that consciously or unconsciously lessen their distress. Among the avoidance strategies are alcohol and drug abuse, self-mutilation, compulsive sexual behavior, and eating disorders.

The more severe the sexual abuse, the more likely it is that the victim will experience long-term adjustment problems (Kendall-Tackett et al., 1993). In particular, penetration is associated with adverse short- and long-term effects.

As discussed by Briere (1992), adult survivors are at increased risk of a broad range of mental health problems. Survivors have increased levels of somatic symptoms; low self- esteem; depression; anxiety disorders; PTSD; substance abuse; sexual dysfunction, including high-risk sexual behavior; conversion reaction; suicidal tendencies; self-mutilation; dissociation; multiple-personality disorder; border-line personality; psychosis; and eating disorders (see Gutierres & Todd, 1997; Read, 1997; Rodriguez, Ryan, Vande Kamp, & Foy, 1997).

> *Many runaway teenagers were abused at home.*

A history of childhood sexual abuse is found in a large percentage of adolescent prostitutes (Brannigan & Van Brunschot, 1997; Fergusson et al., 1997). Many runaway teenagers were abused at home. Rotheram-Borus, Mahler, Koopman, and Lanabeer (1996) write that "runaway and homeless youths have often been physically or sexually abused by their parents, with estimates ranging from 25% to 75%. Sexual abuse, in particular, is often mentioned as a precipitant of runaway behavior" (p. 390).

PSYCHOLOGICAL TREATMENT FOR SEXUALLY ABUSED CHILDREN

Finkelhor and Berliner (1995), in their review of the treatment literature, concluded that "taken as a whole, the studies of sexually abused children in treatment show improvements that are consistent with the belief that therapeutic intervention facilitates children's recovery" (p. 1414). Reeker, Ensing, and Elliott (1997) analyzed literature on group therapy and found that "effective group treatments for sexually abused children do exist" (p. 675).

Professionals differ in their approach to treatment, and there is no single "correct" way to treat sexually abused children. Many therapists use abuse-specific treatment (Cohen & Mannarino, 1998). The common elements of abuse-specific treatment are

(1) encouraging expression of abuse-related feelings (e.g., anger, ambivalence, fear), (2) clarifying erroneous beliefs that might lead to

negative attributions about self or others (e.g., self-blame), (3) teaching abuse prevention skills, and (4) diminishing the sense of stigma and isolation through reassurance or exposure to other victims (e.g., group therapy). (Finkelhor & Berliner, 1995, pp. 1418-1419)

Although sexual abuse is "associated with a range of emotional and behavioral problems for child victims" (Berliner & Saunders, 1996, p. 294), treatment can help children on the road to recovery (Deblinger et al., 1996; Monck, 1997).

THE LONG TRADITION OF DISBELIEVING WOMEN AND CHILDREN WHO CLAIM TO BE VICTIMS OF SEXUAL ABUSE

In Western society, there is a long tradition of disbelieving women who claim that they were raped or sexually assaulted (Brownmiller, 1975). This tradition of disbelief extends to children. But why? Summit (1988) has argued that society has a blind spot for child sexual abuse—a collective desire to avert our eyes from this ugly reality. Out of sight, out of mind (Gordon, 1988). Until recently, society was quite successful at ignoring child sexual abuse (Summit, Olafson, & Corwin, 1993). Yet the problem just won't go away. Olafson, Corwin, and Summit (1993) observe that "sexual abuse of children has repeatedly surfaced into public and professional awareness in the past century and a half, only to be resuppressed by the negative reaction it elicits" (p. 8). A useful way to understand the remarkable tenacity of skepticism regarding allegations of sexual abuse is to examine how the issue has surfaced and submerged over time.

Cycles of Recognition and Denial

In 1813, the influential French physician Ambrose Tardieu (1873) published a book entitled *A Medico-Legal Study of Assaults on Decency.* In this book, Tardieu discussed many instances of child sexual abuse. Later, Tardieu reviewed cases of attempted and completed sexual assault in France between 1858 and 1869. In the 11,576 cases studied, an astonishing 80% of the victims were children from 4 to 12 years of age. Tardieu's revelations sparked brief interest in the study of child sexual abuse. According to Summit (1988), "Tardieu generated an oasis of concern for children in a generally indifferent, adult-preoccupied society. Challenging the tradition that children typically lied about sexual assault, a few clinicians dared to argue for the truth and reality of those complaints" (p. 46).

Generally, however, Tardieu's work was met with skepticism. Despite Tardieu's stature as a leader in French medicine, his successors rejected his discoveries about child sexual abuse. Barely a year after Tardieu's death, Alfred Fournier gave a speech at the French Academy of Medicine entitled "Simulation of Sexual Attacks on Young Children" (cited in Summit, 1988, p. 46). Fournier warned that respectable men are targeted for blackmail by depraved children and their lower-class parents. Another successor to Tardieu stated, "Girls accuse their fathers of imaginary assaults on them or on other children in order to obtain their freedom to give themselves over to debauchery" (Brouardel, quoted in Masson, 1984, p. 44). This critic argued that 60% to 80% of children's complaints of sexual abuse are false. In the end, Tardieu's effort to open French eyes to the reality of child sexual abuse was suppressed and forgotten.

The second important recognition of child sexual abuse occurred in 1896, with the issue being raised by none other than Sigmund Freud. In April 1896, Freud presented a paper at the Vienna Society for Psychiatry and Neurology entitled "The Aetiology of Hysteria" (see Summit, 1988). In this paper, Freud theorized that the neurotic symptoms that he observed in his adult female patients were caused by sexual abuse during childhood (Kuhn, 1997). Freud described this as the "seduction theory." The seduction theory received a chilly reception from Freud's senior psychiatric colleagues, and not long after he presented the theory, Freud wrote to a friend, "I am as isolated as you could wish me to be: The word has been given out to abandon me, and a void is forming around me" (quoted in Masson, 1984, p. 10).

Rather than defending the seduction theory, Freud abandoned it in favor of the Oedipus complex, which explains neurotic symptoms in terms of sexual *fantasy* during childhood rather than actual sexual abuse. Thus, Freud bowed to criticism of his initial beliefs. Of course, sexual abuse of children did not stop, but society once again closed its eyes.

The third notable recognition of child sexual abuse occurred in the early 1930s with the work of Sandor Ferenczi. Like Freud, Ferenczi was a member of the psychiatric inner circle. Unlike Freud, however, Ferenczi did not abandon his belief that child sexual abuse was responsible for adult neurosis. In 1932, he presented a paper entitled "The Passions of Adults and Their Influence on the Sexual and Character Development of Children." In it, he explored the subject of deeply repressed memories of child sexual abuse. According to Summit (1988),

> Like Freud 36 years before, Ferenczi hoped to change entrenched beliefs by presenting outrageous discoveries. And like his mentor before him, Ferenczi was banished from kinship. Unlike his teacher, Ferenczi did not recant his beliefs, so he remains an awkward footnote in the chronicle of scientific thought. (p. 49)

We are now living in the fourth, most widespread, and longest-lasting era of acknowledgment of child sexual abuse. Hopefully, the current era of recognition is sufficiently well established that we will not repeat the mistakes of the past. Society appears less willing today to close its eyes to sexual abuse. Nevertheless, the blind spot for sexual abuse has staying power. One continues to hear statements such as "Sexual abuse is rare," "You can't trust kids," and "All this fuss about sexual abuse is nothing but hysteria."

The Contribution of the Professional Literature
to the Tradition of Skepticism

Throughout the first six decades of the 20th century, relatively little was written about child sexual abuse in psychiatric, psychological, medical, or sociological journals. As late as 1977, Henry Kempe (1978) gave a speech to the American Academy of Pediatrics in which he described child sexual abuse as a "hidden pediatric problem and a neglected area" (p. 382). Before the mid-1970s, much of the professional writing about sexual abuse was dominated by four themes: (a) Children are responsible for their own molestation, (b) mothers are to blame, (c) child sexual abuse is rare, and (d) sexual abuse does no harm (Reid, 1995). A few examples from professional journals of the time illustrate these themes.

Children Are Responsible for Their Own Molestation. A common theme in pre-1975 writing on child sexual abuse, particularly incest, is that children are responsible for the molestation. According to Finkelhor (1979),

> In the field of "victimology," there is a tradition of theories . . . that try to understand the ways in which victims contribute to their own victimization. The process is usually called "victim precipitation," and it highlights the fact that victims frequently contribute to their own murders—by striking a first blow or hurling an insult—or to their own robberies—by leaving doors unlocked and valuable possessions in plain sight.
>
> What is unusual in the case of sexual abuse of children is the degree of importance that the victim precipitation analysis has assumed. The idea that murder victims bring on their own demise developed fairly late in the field and had a moderate effect on our understanding of homicide. In contrast, the idea that children are responsible for their own seduction has been at the center of almost all writing on sexual abuse since the topic was first broached. (p. 23)

An example of this attitude is Bender and Blau's (1937) description of their work with 5- to 12-year-old incest victims:

> The few studies that have been made of this subject have been contented to consider it an example of adult sex perversion from which innocent children must be protected by proper legal measures. Although this attitude may be correct in some cases, certain features in our material would indicate that the children may not resist and often play an active or even initializing role. . . . The history of the relationship in our cases usually suggested at least some cooperation of the child in the activity, and in some cases the child assumed an active role in initiating the relationship. . . . It is true that the child often rationalized with excuses of fear of physical harm or the enticement of gifts, but these were obviously secondary reasons. Even in the cases in which physical force may have been applied by the adult, this did not wholly account for the frequent repetition of the practice. (p. 513)

Similarly, a 1975 textbook on psychiatry stated that "the daughters collude in the incestuous liaison and play an active and even initiating role in establishing the pattern" (Henderson, 1975, p. 1536), and Kinsey wrote in 1953 that "in many instances, [incestuous experiences] were repeated because the children had become interested in the sexual activity and had more or less actively sought repetitions of their experience" (p. 118). Thus, in pre-1975 professional writing on incest, children were often blamed for the abuse.

Mothers Are to Blame. In pre-1975 journal articles, children were not the only ones responsible for sexual abuse. Mothers shared the blame. Reid (1995), in a review of the early literature, concluded:

> Mother-blaming is as common as victim-blaming in the psychological and sociological literature. Mothers of incest victims are routinely referred to as frigid, hostile, unloving women. As women who are so cold and rejecting that they cause their husbands to seek sexual satisfaction elsewhere. (pp. 13-14)

Child Sexual Abuse Is Rare. Some early writers claimed that child sexual abuse was rare. In 1955, a sociologist wrote that "the problem of incest is peculiar in several respects. Statistically its occurrence is negligible. Because of this infrequency the extent of its disruptive effect on human group life is minor" (Blumner, introduction to Weinberg, 1955, p. xi). The textbook on psychiatry referred to earlier stated that father-daughter incest occurs at a rate of one girl in a million (Henderson, 1975).

Sexual Abuse Does No Harm. In addition to claiming that sexual abuse is uncommon, contributors to the early professional literature sometimes asserted that abuse does little harm. In 1952, Bender and Grugett wrote that "in contrast to the harsh social taboos surrounding such relationships, there exists no scientific proof that there are any resulting deleterious effects" (p. 827). In 1953, Kinsey advanced the theory that incest is seldom inherently harmful:

> It is difficult to understand why a child, except for its cultural conditioning, should be disturbed at having its genitalia touched, or dis-

turbed at seeing the genitalia of other persons, or disturbed at even more specific sexual contacts. . . . Some of the more experienced students of juvenile problems have come to believe that the emotional reactions of parents, police officers, and other adults who discover that a child has had such contact, may disturb the child more seriously than the sexual contacts themselves. (p. 121)

Similarly, Brunhold (1964) asserted that "lasting psychological injury as a result of sexual assaults suffered in infancy is not very common" (p. 8). Pomeroy (1976) stated that "when we examine a cross-section of the population as we did in the Kinsey Report we find many beautiful and mutually satisfying relationships between fathers and daughters. These may be transient or ongoing, but they have no harmful effects" (p. 13). And in 1979, a professor stated that incest "may be either a positive, healthy experience or, at worst, neutral and dull" (quoted in DeMott, 1980).

Summary. Before the mid-1970s, much of the psychiatric, psychological, medical, and sociological writing on child sexual abuse downplayed the seriousness of the problem. Herman (1981) reviewed the early literature and discovered "a vastly elaborated intellectual tradition which served the purpose of suppressing the truth about incest, a tradition which, like so many others, originates in the works of Freud" (p. 9).

The Legal Literature

A tradition of skepticism is not limited to mental health and medical journals. When we shift to early writing by lawyers, we find a level of skepticism that is, if anything, higher. (For more detailed analysis of the legal literature see Myers, Diedrich, Lee, & McClanahan-Fincher, 1998.)

Unless you are an attorney, you may not realize that law libraries are filled with thousands of articles written by law professors, law students, and practicing attorneys. These articles are contained in journals called law reviews. Hundreds of law review articles appear yearly. I examined law review articles on rape and sexual assault back to the late 1880s. Articles were located through the *Index to Legal*

Periodicals and Books (1997), which is the legal profession's equivalent of *Index Medicus* or *Psychological Abstracts*. The *Index to Legal Periodicals and Books* lists law review articles by subject and year. It began publication in 1888.

Today, the *Index to Legal Periodicals and Books* has a subject heading for "child sexual abuse." This was not always the case, however. "Child sexual abuse" was added as a separate subject in 1991. Before 1991, sexual abuse was listed under "child abuse." The subject heading "child abuse" appeared in 1970. Before 1970, *physical* child abuse was listed under the crime of "assault and battery." What few articles there were on child sexual abuse were listed under "rape." Thus, to locate articles on child sexual abuse before the 1970s, it was necessary to use the subject heading "rape" in the *Index to Legal Periodicals and Books*. As it turns out, it was useful to read law review articles on rape of adults as well as articles on child sexual abuse. The attitude of law review authors toward adult rape victims was nearly identical to their attitude toward child victims.

Before approximately 1975, very little was written in law reviews about rape of adult women. Even less was written about child sexual abuse. Of the few articles on child sexual abuse, most dealt with statutory rape. Almost nothing was written about incest. Of the hundreds of law review articles published annually, only a handful each year discussed rape or sexual abuse. By contrast, many articles every year discussed theft, murder, and other crimes. In the mountainous law review literature before 1975, the fact that so few pages were devoted to sexual assault speaks volumes. The silence of legal scholars is further evidence of society's blind spot for sexual abuse (Summit, 1988).

Interestingly, of the relatively few pre-1975 law review articles on rape or sexual abuse, most were written by law students, not law professors. Before roughly 1975, law professors virtually ignored rape and sexual abuse as topics worthy of scholarly research and writing.

Reading the relatively few pre-1975 law review articles on rape and sexual abuse, one is struck by the skepticism expressed toward women and girls (sexual abuse of boys was rarely discussed).

Throughout pre-1975 law review articles, the level of disbelief is remarkable.

The best way to get a feel for the skepticism pervading pre-1975 law review articles is to let the authors speak for themselves. A dominant theme in pre-1975 law review articles is fear of fabricated claims of rape or sexual abuse. Ploscowe, a law professor, cautioned in 1960 that "prosecuting attorneys must *continually* be on guard for the charge of sex offenses brought by the spurned female that has as its underlying basis a desire for revenge, or a blackmail or shake-down scheme" (p. 223). A 1938 law student article in the *Virginia Law Review* stated that "the rape statute affords promising fields for extortion and malicious prosecutions" (Note, 1938, p. 338). In 1970, a law student writing in the *University of Pennsylvania Law Review* stated:

> The incidence of false accusations and the potential for unjust convictions are perhaps greatest with sexual offenses. Women often falsely accuse men of sexual attacks to extort money, to force marriage, to satisfy a childish desire for notoriety, or to attain personal revenge. Their motives include hatred, a sense of shame after consenting to illicit intercourse, especially when pregnancy results, and delusion. (Note, 1970, p. 460)

In 1952, a law student warned in the *Yale Law Journal* that "the sexual nature of the crime is conducive to false accusations" (Note, 1952, p. 56). He continued:

> False reports may also stem from other sources. A rape accusation is so potent a weapon against a man that a woman may deliberately and maliciously distort her report of the sexual encounter to secure for herself money, marriage, or revenge. (p. 69)

In 1925, Puttkammer wrote that

> in its very nature rape is a crime which is peculiarly open to false accusations and is difficult of defense. For generations, judges have been repeating Lord Hale's statement that "it is an accusation easily

to be made and hard to be proved, and harder to be defended by the party to be accused though never so innocent." (p. 421)

Related to concern about fabricated allegations was fear of "crazy women." According to Ploscowe (1960),

> Complaints of sex offenses are easily made. They spring from a variety of motives and reasons. The psychiatrist and the psychoanalyst would have a field day were he to examine all complaints of rape, sexual tampering with children, incest, homosexual behavior with young boys, deviant sex behavior, etc., in any given community. He could find that complaints are too often made of sexual misbehavior that has occurred only in the overripe fantasies of the so-called victims. Frequently, the more or less unconscious wish for the sexual experience is converted into the experience itself. (pp. 222-223)

The *Yale Law Journal* student article, cited above, warned that "more serious [than the deliberate fabrication] is the problem of the psychopathic woman. She may completely fabricate a forceful sexual act yet be unaware of the fanciful origin of her complaint" (p. 69). In 1966, a law student wrote in the *Stanford Law Review* that

> masochistic tendencies seem to lead many women to seek men who will ill-treat them sexually. The problem becomes even greater when one recognizes the existence of a so-called "riddance mechanism." This is a phenomenon where a woman who fears rape unconsciously sets up the rape to rid herself of the fear and to "get it over with." (Note, 1966, p. 682)

Pre-1975 law review articles on rape were preoccupied with the issue of consent. Several authors discussed the idea that "no" really means "yes." The *Stanford Law Review* article mentioned above addressed this issue by quoting from a 1965 book:

> Although a woman may desire sexual intercourse, it is customary for her to say, "no, no, no" (although meaning "yes, yes, yes") and to expect the male to be the aggressor. . . . It is always difficult in rape cases to determine whether the female really meant "no." (Slovenko, 1965, quoted in Note, 1966, p. 682)

The *Yale Law Journal* student author stated that "many women . . . require as a part of preliminary "love play" aggressive overtures by the man. Often their erotic pleasure may be enhanced by, or even depend upon, an accompanying physical struggle" (Note, 1952, p. 66). Further, "A woman's need for sexual satisfaction may lead to the unconscious desire for forceful penetration, the coercion serving neatly to avoid the guilt feelings which might arise after willing participation" (p. 67). Indeed, "The feminine wish to be subjected to a sexual attack may become the subject of an hallucination" (p. 69). A 1954 student article similarly reported that "resistance during preliminary love-making greatly increases the sexual pleasure of some women" (Note, 1954, p. 728).

Before adoption of rape shield laws in the 1970s, defense attorneys routinely put rape victims "on trial" by offering evidence of the woman's lack of "chastity." Pre-1975 law review articles reflect nearly unanimous support for this defense strategy. For example, a 1938 law student article stated that "it is everywhere conceded that in a prosecution for rape by force and against the will of a female, her previous unchastity may be shown as rendering it more probable that she consented to the act" (Note, 1938, p. 336). Even in statutory rape cases, in which the victim was a child, law review authors favored evidence of unchastity. Ploscowe (1960) wrote that "it is imperative that the lack of chastity of the young woman be deemed a defense to a charge of statutory rape. It is ridiculous for the police to charge with rape every male who may have had sexual contact with a promiscuous young woman or a young prostitute" (p. 222). A 1960 article stated that "it is not always justifiable to punish a male as a felon for succumbing to the lures of an immoral, underage female" (Note, 1960, p. 213; see also Note, 1938; Note, 1952; Tonry, 1965).

If we change the focus from law review articles to books about law, one treatise stands out. John H. Wigmore, a law professor at Harvard, was one of the most famous legal scholars in the United States. In 1904, he published the first edition of his monumental 12-volume treatise on the law of evidence. Although Wigmore was brilliant, his thinking about sex offense victims was remarkably negative. Yet because he was so influential among judges and attorneys, he contributed mightily to the tradition of skepticism. According to Wigmore (1904/1974),

> Modern psychiatrists have amply studied the behavior of errant young girls and women coming before the courts in all sorts of cases. Their psychic complexes are multifarious, distorted partly by inherent defects, partly by diseased derangements or abnormal instincts, partly by bad social environments, partly by temporary physiological or emotional conditions. One form taken by these complexes is that of contriving false charges of sexual offenses by men. The unchaste mentally (let us call it) finds incidental but direct expression in the narration of imaginary sex incidents of which the narrator is the heroine or the victim. On the surface the narration is straight-forward and convincing. The real victim, however, too often in such cases is the innocent man. . . . No judge should ever let a sex offense charge go to the jury unless the female complainant's social history and mental makeup have been examined and testified to by a qualified physician. It is time that the courts awakened to the sinister possibilities of injustice that lurk in believing such a witness without careful psychiatric scrutiny. (pp. 736-737, 740)

Summary

During the first six decades of the 20th century, the legal, mental health, and medical literatures contributed to a legacy of disbelief about allegations of rape and child sexual abuse. Then, quite suddenly in the middle of the 1970s, professional writing changed dramatically. Before discussing this change, however, I want briefly to describe my concern about the skepticism of the pre-1975 literature. My concern is not that authors were skeptical of women and children. I have no quarrel with skepticism qua skepticism. Indeed, I believe a healthy measure of skepticism is important to any inquiry. My concern with the pre-1975 literature is not the skepticism but the level of skepticism—a level that was exaggerated and inaccurate. Skepticism, like most things, is useful in moderation but can be destructive when taken to extremes. I believe that the skepticism of the pre-1975 literature on rape and child sexual abuse abandoned moderation and crossed the line into a dangerous and destructive demagoguery.

1975—The Continental Divide in Professional Writing

As far as professional writing about child sexual abuse is concerned, 1975 is the continental divide. Before that year, professional writing, although not monolithic, was largely skeptical. Beginning in the early 1970s, however, there was a virtual explosion of writing that was more sympathetic to victims of rape and sexual abuse. What caused this dramatic shift in professional writing? The feminist movement of the 1960s and 1970s was largely responsible.

In law review articles, the more positive post-1975 tone can be traced directly to authorship. Most law review articles are written by law students and law professors. It was not until the 1970s that substantial numbers of women began studying law and entering the ranks of law professors. Before that time, the vast majority of law students and law professors were men. Much of the post-1975 legal literature on rape and child sexual abuse is written by female law students and professors, as well as by male students and professors with feminist leanings. One of the groundbreaking post-1975 law review articles, for example, was Vivian Berger's 1977 article entitled "Man's Trial, Woman's Tribulation: Rape Cases in the Courtroom," which asserted that "the singularity of the law of rape stems from a deep distrust of the female accuser" (p. 10). (see also Giles, 1976; LeGrand, 1973; McDermott, 1975; Note, 1972; Welch, 1976; Wesolowski, 1976; Wood, 1973).

The women's movement was not the only factor influencing writing on rape and child sexual abuse. The modern era of child protection coincided with the women's movement (see Chapter 2, the section "A Brief History of Child Protection in the United States"). The modern child protection movement got seriously under way in the mid-1960s and was firmly entrenched by 1975. In addition, the 1970s witnessed the birth of the victim's rights movement and the first important research aimed at understanding the prevalence and harmful effects of child sexual abuse (see the pioneering research of Finkelhor, 1979, and Russell, 1983, 1986).

Despite the impressive gains of the 1970s and 1980s, the long tradition of skepticism continues to influence the thinking of some judges, attorneys, journalists, doctors, and mental health professionals. Indeed, throughout the United States and Europe, the level of skepticism may once again be on the rise (Beckett, 1996; Letourneau & Lewis, in press; Myers, 1994, 1995).

RESEARCH ON FABRICATED ALLEGATIONS
OF CHILD SEXUAL ABUSE

In light of the tradition of skepticism regarding child sexual abuse, it is useful to review research on fabricated allegations (Everson, Boat, Bourg, & Robertson, 1996). Before discussing this research, however, it is important to note that several terms are used to describe "false" reports of abuse. The most common terms are *false, fabricated, unfounded,* and *unsubstantiated.* Unfortunately, there is no generally agreed-on definition of these terms, and lack of definitional consensus sometimes leads to confusion.

In this book, the term *false report* is avoided because the word *false* is ambiguous. Is a false report a deliberate lie? Is it a good-faith report that turns out to be untrue? Is it both? Neither? Sink (1988) observed that

> the broadly defined category of "false allegations" includes almost any situation in which an abuse report cannot be substantiated. The term fails to differentiate situations of intentional falsification from situations of misunderstanding or situations where inadequate information is available to determine the true or false nature of a report. (p. 38)

The wiser course is to eschew the term *false.*

Throughout the following discussion, the term *fabricated report* means a deliberate, intentionally untrue report or claim of abuse. A fabricated report may be made by a child or an adult, although research suggests that most fabricated reports are by adults and adolescents, not young children (Jones & McGraw, 1986).

The terms *unfounded* and *unsubstantiated* are treated here as synonyms. An unsubstantiated report of abuse occurs when a report is made to child protective services or the police and some form of investigation follows, but no determination is reached. The unsubstantiated category is important because a significant percentage of reports wind up in the unsubstantiated column. In some cases, a report is unsubstantiated because the investigation is inadequate. In other cases, the investigation is adequate, but there is not enough evidence to reach a conclusion. Perhaps the child is too young to describe what happened, or witnesses move away or refuse to cooperate. In the final analysis, some unsubstantiated reports are undoubtedly fabricated. It is probable, however, that most unsubstantiated reports are made in good faith, whether or not they are accurate. Unfortunately, some individuals erroneously equate unsubstantiated reports with fabrications. Building on this error, these individuals conclude that the country is awash in a flood of fabricated allegations of child abuse.

Before leaving the realm of definition, it is important to introduce the term *misperception report*. In an undetermined number of cases, parents operating in good faith misperceive information about their child, thereby coming to a suspicion of sexual abuse where none exists. The likelihood of misperception may be particularly high among estranged, separated, or divorced parents, some of whom are ready to assume the worst about each other (see Myers, 1997b). For example, consider a divorced couple who fought a bitter and protracted battle for custody of their 3-year-old daughter. Eventually, the mother won custody and the father received liberal visitation. One Sunday afternoon, the father returned the child to the mother's home following a weekend visit. While giving her daughter a bath, the mother noticed that the little girl's genital area was irritated. The mother said, "How did you get all red in your private parts?" The child responded, "Owie. Daddy finger." Alarmed, the mother suspected sexual abuse. In fact, however, there was no abuse. On Saturday, while visiting her father, the child said, "Daddy, my privates hurt." The father noticed the irritation and used his finger to apply soothing ointment. If the mother files a report of suspected abuse, she will be acting in good faith. Her report is not fabricated. When she is unable to prove the abuse, she should not be branded a "false accuser." Misperception reports are responsible for confusion, recrimination, and heartache.

In custody disputes, the belief is widespread that mothers raise nearly all allegations of child sexual abuse. Research does not support this belief. Thoennes and Tjaden (1990), in a study of allegations of sexual abuse in custody cases, found that such allegations were uncommon. When the allegation of sexual abuse was made, mothers accused biological fathers in 48% of Thoennes and Tjaden's cases. In another 6% of cases, women accused second husbands of molesting children from the woman's prior marriage.

> However, in 10% of the cases, fathers alleged that a child was sexually abused by the mother's new male partner, while in 6% of the cases the mother herself was accused of abuse. Moreover, nearly 20% involved accusations by mothers (13%) or fathers (6%) against other relatives and family friends. Finally, in 11% of the cases the allegation of sexual abuse originated with someone other than a parent. (Thoennes & Tjaden, 1990, p. 154)

Although women file a majority of accusations of sexual abuse in family court, the belief that women raise almost all such accusations is untrue. Moreover, it is not surprising that women file most allegations: Most perpetrators of sexual abuse are men.

Turning now to research on fabricated reports of child sexual abuse, it should be noted that studies fall into two categories: (a) studies that focus on fabricated reports in family court child custody disputes and (b) studies that do not focus on custody disputes but that have a broader concentration.

In research that does not focus specifically on custody, two studies stand out. In 1983, Jones and McGraw (1986) evaluated 576 reports of suspected sexual abuse made to the Denver Department of Social Services (DSS) during that year. The researchers defined *fictitious reports* to include "deliberate falsifications, misperceptions, and confused interpretations of nonsexual events" (p. 29). Jones and McGraw did not differentiate between what I refer to as fabricated reports and misperception reports. Eight percent of the reports were probably fictitious. Among the small number of fictitious reports, most were by adults. Very few of the fictitious reports were by children. The researchers concluded that "fictitious allegations are unusual" (p. 38).

The second important study is a replication of the 1983 study described above. During 1995, Oates et al. (in press) evaluated 551 reports of child sexual abuse made to the Denver Department of

Social Services. Oates and his colleagues found that children made fictitious reports in only 2.5% of the total sample.

The two Denver studies are important because of the large number of cases and the rigor of the assessment process. Other research discloses rates of fabrication similar to the Denver studies, although it is difficult to compare studies because individual researchers use different definitions and methodologies (Everson & Boat, 1989; Faller, 1988; Goodwin, Sahd, & Rada, 1982; Peters, 1976).

Although the rate of deliberately fabricated reports appears to be low—2% to 10%—it is important to remember that quite a few good-faith (i.e., nonfabricated) reports are nevertheless unsubstantiated. In the second Denver study, described above, for example, Oates et al. (in press) found that 34% of good-faith reports were not "true": That is, in 34% of good-faith reports there was no abuse. Another 21% of the good-faith reports were inconclusive. Poole and Lindsay (1998) note:

> For many years, it was frequently claimed that about 5%-8% of sexual abuse allegations were false. . . . This estimate of the false allegation rate is misleadingly low because of the practice of counting only intentionally false allegations. . . . When these other mechanisms were included (e.g., honest misunderstandings of children's statements or problems caused by reliance on presumed indicators of abuse followed by suggestive interviewing), rates of false allegations rose considerably (e.g., from 6% to 23% in Jones & McGraw, 1987; from 8.8% to 35% in Faller, 1991). (p. 2)

Thus, among all reports of child sexual abuse, a substantial percentage are unsubstantiated. Either there was no abuse, or abuse is unascertainable.

When the focus of research narrows to custody cases in family court, several authors report high rates of fabricated allegations. Green (1986) evaluated 11 suspected victims and concluded that 4 of the allegations were probably fabricated (36%). Benedek and Schetky (1985) were unable to document abuse in 10 of 18 cases (55%). Regarding these studies, Quinn (1988) comments that "these are very small clinical samples with a selective pattern of referrals" (p. 181). Berliner (1988) adds that these and similar studies "describe a limited number of cases referred for evaluation. . . . In most of the cases described, there were multiple evaluations and conflicting opinions among professionals. Ultimately, there is no way of knowing that the authors' assessments are accurate" (p. 52).

Jones and Seig (1988) evaluated 20 cases in which sexual abuse allegations arose in custody disputes. The researchers found that 20% of the allegations probably were fictitious. Jones and Sieg concluded that

> the setting of the divorce and custody dispute does seem to raise the likelihood that clinicians will find an increased number of fictitious allegations. However, in the study nearly ¾ (70%) were reliable, arguing strongly against the practice of dismissing allegations in custody disputes contexts as most likely false. (p. 29)

An additional ingredient in the fabricated-allegations problem is the appearance of opportunism that attaches when allegations of sexual abuse arise for the first time in custody litigation (Myers, 1997b). It is tempting to think that if sexual abuse really occurred, the nonabusing parent would discover it sooner. Charges of sexual abuse that coincide with custody litigation are intuitively suspicious. Couple this suspicion with the perception that angry parents will "stoop to anything" to gain custody, and the stage is set for disbelief.

Although the stakes involved in custody litigation push some parents into dishonesty, the fact that an allegation of abuse arises for the first time when a family breaks up does not mean the allegation is false (Corwin, Berliner, Goodman, Goodwin, & White, 1987). Some children disclose or experience sexual abuse for the first time when their parents separate. As Corwin et al. point out,

> There are several reasons abused children may be more likely to disclose abuse by a parent and to be believed by the other parent following separation or divorce. With the breakup of the parents comes diminished opportunity for an abusing parent to enforce secrecy as there is increased opportunity for the child to disclose abuse separately to the other parent. Decreased dependency and increased distrust between parents increases willingness to suspect child abuse by the other parent.

> Additionally, the losses, stresses, and overall negative impact of separation and divorce may precipitate regressive "acting out" by parents, including child sexual abuse. (p. 102)

There is no evidence that the number of fabricated allegations in custody cases has reached flood stage. The fact that fabricated allegations occur in custody cases should not degenerate into unfounded statements such as "the vast majority of children who profess sexual abuse are fabricators" (Gardner, 1987, p. 274).

Fabricated allegations occur inside and out of custody litigation. Nevertheless, research suggests that fabricated allegations are uncommon. When fabrication occurs, the responsible party usually is an adult, not a young child.

The party accused of child sexual abuse may wish to offer expert testimony related to fabricated allegations. Such testimony is allowed in some cases. In *United States v. King* (1992), the Court of Appeal for the Armed Forces wrote that expert testimony about "the age at which children normally develop the 'capability' of 'fabricating' is often quite germane and precisely the sort of thing" an expert could describe (p. 341). On the other hand, the same court observed in *United States v. Ingham* (1995), that testimony "regarding the percentage of false allegations of child sexual abuse [is] not admissible just because somebody with a diploma says it is so. First, basic foundations of scientific validity have to be met" (p. 226). In a similar vein, the Idaho Supreme Court rejected defense expert testimony on the percentage of fabricated allegations (*State v. Purkinson*, 1996). The Idaho court observed that there was no evidence in the record that such testimony is reliable.

2

The Child Protection System

Professionals from social work, psychology, medicine, nursing, education, and related disciplines carry the lion's share of responsibility for responding to child abuse and neglect. The law plays an important secondary role. The purpose of this chapter is to describe the system of child protection used in the United States, with particular emphasis on law. Increased understanding of the law helps professionals interact more effectively with the legal system and lowers the communication barriers that sometimes separate judges, lawyers, and law enforcement officers from members of the helping professions. In light of the shared goals of all professionals working to protect children, increased communication is essential.

This chapter is divided into seven sections. The first section offers a brief history of America's child protection system. The second section describes the adversary system of justice. The third section provides a broad overview of the American legal system. The fourth section discusses the specifics of the criminal justice system. The fifth section describes child protective services and juvenile court. The sixth section discusses the family court. The last section describes three laws intended to protect children from dangerous sexual predators.

❏ A Brief History of Child Protection in the United States

Throughout history, children have been battered, abandoned, sexually abused, and neglected (deMause, 1974; Radbill, 1987). Yet since earliest times, concerned adults have intervened to rescue children from maltreatment (Boswell, 1988). For example, in many of Charles Dickens's novels, such as *Oliver Twist*, children are sorely abused by many but lovingly protected by a few. Thus, neither child abuse nor efforts to stop it are new.

THE COLONIAL PERIOD

Although physical abuse by parents occurred during the colonial period, documentation is sparse. Then, as now, the law allowed parents to use "reasonable" force to correct their children, and authorities rarely interfered with parental discipline (Blackstone, 1765/1915). (For discussion of "reasonable" corporal punishment, see Chapter 1.) An occasional master was prosecuted for cruelty to a servant. Thus, in 1655, Robert Latham of Massachusetts was convicted of causing the death of his 12-year-old servant. As punishment, Latham's goods were confiscated, and it was ordered that he be "burned in the hand" (Bremner, 1970).

Children living in poverty posed special problems. In colonial days, little effort was made to distinguish poverty from neglect. The colonists created few specialized institutions to care for destitute, orphaned, neglected, or abandoned children. "Prior to 1800 orphan homes or asylums for unfortunate children were rare" (Bremner, 1970, Vol. 1, p. 262). Destitute parents who were deemed "worthy" by local overseers of the poor could receive meager financial assistance to provide in-home care for young or disabled children. In-home support was called "outdoor relief" to contrast it with "indoor relief" provided in almshouses. Not all young children remained at home, however. Regardless of parental wishes, some poor children were sent to live with other families at town expense. When children who were dependent on public aid were old enough to work, they were indentured to merchants or farmers "on the best terms that could be arranged" (Bremner, 1970, Vol. 1, p. 64). Indenture lasted until the child attained adulthood. In some communities, the primitive vendue system was used, in which care of the poor was auctioned off to the *lowest* bidder, with the town paying the expense (Bremner, 1970).

THE 19TH CENTURY: BIRTH OF ORGANIZED CHILD PROTECTION

Little progress was made during the first half of the 19th century. The practice of indenture for poor children remained popular (Bremner, 1970). Even the loathsome vendue system persisted in some communities. In the 1830s, orphanages and children's asylums began to appear, although the demand for care always outstripped the supply (Bremner, 1970; Tiffin, 1982). By midcentury, eastern cities were growing rapidly, swelled by waves of immigration. The Industrial Revolution was steaming ahead, fueled by an army of poorly paid laborers, including thousands of children. As cities expanded, more and more children fell on hard times.

One outspoken midcentury critic of conditions facing city children was Charles Loring Brace. In 1852, Brace graduated from Union Theological Seminary and began work with the poor in New York's slums. Brace was struck by the plight of poor children. With help from interested clergy, Brace founded the New York Children's Aid Society in 1853 and served as its secretary until his death in 1890 (Bremner, 1970; Leiby, 1978).

Brace's solution for children trapped in urban squalor was to wrench them away from their poverty-stricken parents and send them "out west" to grow up as foster children in "wholesome" midwestern communities. During Brace's administration, the Children's Aid Society placed more than 90,000 children (Leiby, 1978; Radbill, 1987). Brace was never short of critics, particularly Catholics, who argued that his hidden agenda was converting poor Catholic children by placing them in Protestant foster homes. Brace was also criticized for lax supervision of his far-flung foster children.

Charles Loring Brace and a cadre of social reformers, primarily women, generated wider concern for children. This stirring of conscience set the stage for what was unquestionably the galvanizing event in U.S. child protection: the case of little Mary Ellen (Bremner, 1970; Lazoritz, 1992). In December 1873, Etta Wheeler was a missionary in New York's slums. She learned of Mary Ellen, who was cruelly abused by her foster mother. Wheeler turned to the police and children's societies, but to no avail. In desperation, she approached the influential Henry Bergh, founder of the New York Society for Prevention of Cruelty to Animals (SPCA). Bergh was moved, and asked Elbridge Gerry, an attorney, to obtain a court order removing Mary Ellen from her foster mother. Gerry did so, and Mary Ellen was rescued. The foster mother was convicted of assault. Eventually, Mary Ellen was adopted by Etta Wheeler's sister, in whose home she thrived (Lazoritz, 1990).

The public was captivated by Mary Ellen's story and by the irony that New York had a society to protect animals but not children. Efforts were soon under way to remedy the situation, with Elbridge Gerry playing a leading role, assisted by Henry Bergh of the New York SPCA. On December 28, 1874, the first meeting of the New York Society for Prevention of Cruelty to Children (SPCC) convened (Bremner, 1970; Lazoritz, 1992). Gerry served as legal counsel to the New York SPCC until 1879, when he became its president, a position he held until 1901.

From its origin in New York, the concept of nongovernmental child protection spread quickly, and by 1900, more than 150 nongovernmental child protection societies dotted the national map. Although employees of child protection societies were private citizens, they had powers not unlike those of the police (Gordon, 1988). For example, society agents investigated cases, took children before judges, and initiated prosecution of abusive caretakers.

From the dawn of organized child protection, a debate raged that continues to this day. Should the primary mission of child protection be rescuing children from dangerous and unwholesome environments? Or should removal be the last resort, with primary effort concentrated on preventing maltreatment and keeping abused and neglected children at home? The New York SPCC favored the rescue model, whereas the equally influential Boston SPCC emphasized prevention (Williams, 1980). Of course, none of the societies pursued a purist philosophy, and child protection has always combined prevention, service, and removal.

During the last half of the 19th century, the courts took a more active role in protecting children. For example, in 1858, a California man was convicted of raping an 8-year-old child (*People v. Bernal*, 1858). In 1862, an Iowan was charged with "inhumanly whipping and beating" his 3-year-old son (*State v. Bitman*, 1862, p. 486). In 1874, a North Carolina woman was charged with murdering her baby by throwing the child into a river (*State v. Thorp*, 1875). In 1880, a Pennsylvania court ruled that a father "shamefully neglected" his children by failing to get medical care needed to save their lives (*Heinemann's Appeal*, 1880). The 1890s witnessed an increase in prosecutions for sexual abuse of children (e.g., *Davis v. State*, 1891; *Grimes v. State*, 1895; *State v. Juneau*, 1894; *State v. Washington*, 1897; *Trent v. State*, 1892; *White v. Commonwealth*, 1894).

The most important legal landmark of the late 19th century was the creation of the nation's first juvenile court in Chicago in 1899 (Hurley, 1907). The idealistic reformers who created the juvenile court thought it would be the savior of troubled youth. The court was responsible not only for abused and neglected children but also for children in trouble with the law. As the creators of the juvenile court saw it, the fatherly judge would take boys and girls under his protective arm and prescribe just the right "social medicine" to set each child on the path to safe and productive adulthood (Mack, 1909).

The most important legal landmark of the late 19th century was the creation of the nation's first juvenile court in Chicago in 1899.

The juvenile court was immediately popular and spread across the country (Fox, 1996). Of course, the creators of the juvenile court were naive about the ability of a judge to ameliorate the deep-seated social ills responsible for juvenile delinquency, child abuse, and neglect. Nevertheless, the juvenile court was a brilliant humanitarian idea, and the court continues to play an important and positive role (Sagatun & Edwards, 1995).

THE 20TH CENTURY: TRANSFORMATION FROM
PRIVATE TO GOVERNMENT CHILD PROTECTION

During the first 30 years of the 20th century, a consensus emerged that child protection is properly a function of government rather than of private charitable societies. In 1914, the secretary of the Pennsylvania SPCC asserted that child protection "is, after all, the job of the public authorities. The public ought to protect all citizens, including the children, from cruelty and improper care" (American Humane Association, 1914, p. 25). Carl Carstens, the influential director of the Child Welfare League of America, favored government child protection, and in 1924, he gave an important speech advocating increased government involvement in child protection (Bremner, 1970; Gordon, 1988). The Great Depression, from 1929 through the 1930s, contributed to the demise of privately funded child protection because charitable giving dried up (DeFrancis, 1968). In 1933, the *Social Work Yearbook* described "the growing acceptance of states, counties, and municipalities of the responsibility for protective work" (Hubbard, 1933, p. 79).

While the United States staggered through the Great Depression, the spotlight shifted from child protection to economic survival. As the Depression lifted, the rise of European fascism gripped public attention, soon to be followed by the United States' entry into World War II. As these political events played themselves out on the world stage, the transformation to government child protection continued behind the scenes. By midcentury, government child protective services (CPS) agencies were firmly entrenched.

Unfortunately, the nascent government CPS system suffered a shortcoming that plagues it to this day: chronic underfunding. In 1968, Vincent DeFrancis, director of the Children's Division of the American Humane Association, discussed a nationwide study of child welfare services and lamented that "most disturbing was the finding that no state and no community has developed a Child Protective Service program adequate in size to meet the service needs of all reported cases of child neglect, abuse and exploitation" (p. 25). Juvenile court judges came to a similar conclusion. In 1949, the

Council of Juvenile Court Judges noted that "our juvenile courts are not well equipped with probation, psychiatric, and other essential services, except in certain large centers, and even there they fall far short of the desirable" (p. 20). Lack of resources was and is an obstinate obstacle to effective child protection.

Through the first five decades of the 20th century, many people were prosecuted for physical or sexual abuse of children (Myers et al., 1998). Although the rate of prosecution during the first half of the 20th century was modest by today's standard, the law did not ignore child abuse.

CONTEMPORARY CHILD PROTECTION

Until the 1960s, child abuse was not a focus of national attention. But that soon changed. The civil rights movement of the 1960s stirred the national conscience. Resurgent feminism forced Americans to open their eyes to the harsh reality of woman abuse and child abuse. The medical profession finally acknowledged physical child abuse as a serious problem (see Chaffey, 1946, 1972, 1974; Lazoritz, Baldwin, & Kini, 1997; Williams, 1980). One physician in particular, pediatrician Henry Kempe, kindled interest in child abuse. In 1962, Kempe, Silverman, Steele, Droegmuller, and Silver published their landmark article describing the battered-child syndrome. In the same year, the Children's Bureau of the U.S. Department of Health, Education, and Welfare (now Health and Human Services) sponsored an important conference on child abuse. The conferees, including Kempe, recommended adoption of laws requiring professionals to report suspected child abuse. Beginning in 1963, state legislatures enacted reporting laws, and in the remarkably short span of 4 years, all states had reporting laws on the books. (See Chapter 3 for detailed discussion of reporting laws.)

As reporting laws went into effect, the frightening dimensions of child abuse came slowly into focus. By 1976, there were 416,000 reports of abuse and neglect. By 1982, reports climbed to nearly a million, and by 1998, the number soared to the neighborhood of 3 million. The U.S. Advisory Board on Child Abuse and Neglect (1990) declared that "child abuse and neglect in the United States now represents a national emergency" (p. 3). Today, the reality of child abuse is painfully evident.

The remainder of this chapter explores the legal structure designed to protect children from abuse and neglect. Before we examine the legal components of the child protection system, however, it is important to explain a dimension of American law that is difficult for many professionals to understand: why the legal system is so adversarial.

❑ The Adversary System of Justice

Disputes between individuals and disputes between individuals and government are resolved in many ways. The vast majority of disagreements are disposed of informally through negotiation and compromise. Formal litigation in court "is society's last line of defense in the indispensable effort to secure the peaceful settlement of social conflicts" (Hart & McNaughton, 1958, p. 51). In the United States, litigation is based on the adversary system developed in England (Spencer & Flin, 1993). The adversary system is founded on the belief that the most effective way to

> *In the United States, litigation is based on the adversary system developed in England.*

arrive at just results in court is for each side of a controversy to present the evidence that is most favorable to its position and to let a neutral judge or jury sift through the conflicting evidence and decide where the truth lies. In other words, the truth emerges from a clash of adversaries in the controlled environment of a courtroom.

Medical and mental health professionals often wonder at the adversary process and find themselves saying, "These lawyers are a strange lot. How do they expect to find the truth when they seem to spend half their time hiding it from each other and the other half obfuscating the facts with squabbles over inconsequential details?" There is a kernel of truth in this criticism. Nevertheless, the adversary system, for all its shortcomings, has stood the test of time and leads to the truth in most cases.

A useful way to understand the gulf that sometimes separates attorneys from other professionals is to consider two hypothetical college graduates, Ms. Jones and Ms. Smith, both with the same major—psychology, for example—and similar interests, temperaments, and backgrounds. One goes to law school, and the other seeks a Master's in social work. From the first day of graduate school, the neophyte lawyer and social worker arc embarked on very different journeys.

Ms. Smith's first social work class is "Introduction to Social Theory." The first 10 minutes consist of introductions to allow the students and teacher to get to know one another and share a little of their backgrounds. The remainder of the hour is a lecture.

Across campus at the law school, the first class is "Contract Law," and the first words out of the professor's mouth are, "Ms. Jones, what are the facts in the case of *Hawkins v. McGee*?" For the next 50 minutes, the law professor grills the terrified Ms. Jones with questions she cannot comprehend and points out the flaws in each of her answers. When the professor finally asks the class, "Are there any questions?" no one has the temerity to speak. There is no lecture—just dialogue between the professor and Ms. Jones. After class, Ms. Jones is supported by new friends who say, "You did a wonderful job." To themselves, the friends thank heaven that Ms. Jones was the target, not them.

Ms. Smith's experience in the social work department was very different from Ms. Jones' in the law school. Ms. Jones and her colleagues got their first taste of the adversary system. They learned that their professor will force them to think critically under pressure, analyze, question, argue, challenge, debate, and respond to criticism—in short, "to think like a lawyer." As a social worker, Ms. Smith has the same need for critical thinking and rigorous analysis, but she learns these skills from a different perspective. The emphasis in the social work program is on cooperation rather than competition, on building bridges rather than confrontation. From the first days of their professional training, the social worker and the lawyer march to different drummers. Little wonder that at graduation, Ms. Smith, MSW, and Ms. Jones, JD, speak different languages.

Ms. Smith and Ms. Jones love children and decide to devote their careers to helping victims of child abuse and neglect. Ms. Smith, the social worker, takes the plunge into CPS, whereas Ms. Jones, the attorney, joins the child abuse unit at the district attorney's office. Not only must these young professionals struggle with the complexities of their new callings, but they must learn to communicate with each other. Communication may be difficult, but communicate they must, because neither of them can achieve the goal of child protection without the cooperation and assistance of the other.

❏ Overview of the American Legal System

Law is the social institution through which society provides order and protection for its members. Two sources of power underlie the legal system: the police power and the *parens patriae* authority. The police power authorizes government to stop people from harming one another. State legislatures rely on the police power to enact laws prohibiting child abuse and neglect. Law enforcement and CPS professionals rely on the police power to take abused and neglected children into emergency protective custody.

The police power is supplemented by the *parens patriae* authority, which is the state's inherent authority to protect people, including children, who cannot protect themselves. The Latin term *parens patriae* comes from English law. The English king was *parens patriae*, or father of the country, and had authority to protect children. When the United States gained independence from England, the *parens patriae* authority was vested in state legislatures. Through the combined authority of the police and *parens patriae* powers, states have ample authority to protect abused and neglected children.

THE GOVERNMENT INTEREST IN CHILD PROTECTION

The government has a compelling interest in the welfare of children. The U.S. Supreme Court described this interest in *Prince v. Massachusetts* (1944), in which the Court wrote that the state's assertion of authority to protect children "is no mere corporate concern of official authority. It is the interest of youth itself, and of the whole community, that children be both safeguarded from abuses and given opportunities for growth into free and independent citizens" (p. 165). The government's interest in child welfare is particularly compelling in the context of child abuse. The U.S. Supreme Court has characterized the government's interest in protecting children as an "objective of surpassing importance" (*New York v. Ferber*, 1982, p. 757). (The government's authority to protect children is discussed in greater detail in Chapter 9, the section "Constitutional Rights," subsection "Sources of Government Authority to Intervene in the Family.")

THE U.S. AND STATE CONSTITUTIONS

The U.S. Constitution is the fundamental source of law in the United States. The U.S. Constitution establishes the federal government and distinguishes the federal government from state governments. The U.S. Constitution divides the federal government into three branches: the legislative branch (Congress), the executive branch (the President), and the judicial branch (the federal courts). Amendments to the original U.S. Constitution make up the Bill of Rights, and the U.S. Supreme Court has ruled that the Bill of Rights extends important rights to parents, children, and families. For example, parents have a constitutional right to freedom from unwarranted government intrusion into the privacy of the family. (For further discussion, see Chapter 9, the section "Constitutional Rights," subsection "Parental Rights Under the Constitution.")

Every state has its own constitution and bill of rights. Like the U.S. Constitution, state constitutions create three branches of government: the state legislature; the executive branch, led by the governor; and the state court system. State bills of rights are very similar to the federal Bill of Rights, although a few state constitutions contain rights that are not found in the U.S. Constitution.

If a state legislature passes a law that is inconsistent with the U.S. Constitution or a federal statute enacted by Congress, the U.S. Constitution or the federal statute prevails. Within the sphere of its authority, federal constitutional and statutory law is supreme and takes precedence over conflicting state law.

FEDERAL AND STATE STATUTES RELATING TO CHILD ABUSE AND NEGLECT

Laws relating to child abuse and neglect come from three sources: statutes, regulations promulgated by agencies of the executive branch of government, and court decisions. On the federal level, Congress has enacted several laws that affect child protection efforts. In 1974, Congress passed the Child Abuse Prevention and Treatment Act, which, among other things, created the National Center on Child Abuse and Neglect. Another important federal statute was the Adoption Assistance and Child Welfare Act of 1980, commonly known as Public Law 96-272, which required states to make reasonable efforts to prevent removal of maltreated children from parental custody. In 1997, Congress passed the Adoption and Safe Families Act, which made the safety of abused and neglected children the top priority for professionals working in the child protection system. The 1997 law makes it easier to terminate the rights of abusive parents so that children can be placed for adoption.

State legislatures are constantly at work on legislation relating to child abuse and neglect. State criminal codes define child abuse and neglect and establish punishments. Reporting laws exist in every state (see Chapter 3). State statutes create CPS agencies, juvenile courts, and other social agencies.

REGULATIONS

Enacting statutes is the exclusive province of the legislature. Professionals working with abused and neglected children know, however, that statutes are not the only laws affecting practice. Agencies of the executive branch of government have authority to promulgate administrative regulations. Federal administrative regulations are compiled in the Code of Federal Regulations, which consists of some 200 volumes dealing with everything from railroads to rodents and from trees to turnips. State administrative regulations are contained in state administrative codes. Administrative regulations have the same force of law as statutes enacted by the legislature.

An example may help illustrate the complex web of federal and state statutes and regulations that govern many programs for children. In 1975, Congress enacted the Individuals With Disabilities Education Act (Public Law 94-142) to provide handicapped children with appropriate educational opportunities. Congress appointed the U.S. Department of Education to administer the act. In its turn, the Department promulgated regulations to implement the Act. As is often the case, the agency regulations actually have a more important impact on day-to-day practice than the statute itself. The layers of law do not end with the federal statute and its implementing regulations, however, because states promulgate their own statutes and administrative regulations regarding special education. And that's not all! Added to the labyrinth of federal and state statutes and regulations are mountains of agency policies, protocols, and procedures. Sometimes it takes a lawyer just to *find* the applicable law, let alone understand it.

COMMON LAW

Although much of the law affecting practice with abused and neglected children takes the form of statutes and regulations, another important source of law requires mention. Appellate courts have limited authority to make law. Law created by judicial decision is called *common law.* Decisions of the U.S. Supreme Court and state appellate courts create legally binding precedents, some of which are very important for professionals working with children. For example, in *Maryland v. Craig* (1990), the U.S. Supreme Court ruled that certain traumatized children may testify without having to face the person accused of sexually abusing them. In *DeShaney v. Winnebago County* (1989), the Supreme Court ruled that a CPS agency did not violate little Joshua DeShaney's constitutional rights when the agency failed to protect the child from vicious attacks by his father.

THE JUDICIAL SYSTEM

The work of American courts is divided between criminal and civil cases. Criminal litigation is instituted by federal, state, county, and city prosecutors against individuals charged with violating criminal statutes.

Turning to civil cases, a wide variety of legal proceedings fall under the category of civil litigation. Examples include divorce, child custody proceedings, personal injury litigation, and proceedings in juvenile court to protect abused and neglected children.

Federal Courts

In the United States, there are two distinct, although sometimes overlapping, court systems: federal courts and state courts. The federal court system divides the United States into 13 judicial circuits. Circuits are subdivided into federal judicial districts. Every state has at least one federal judicial district, and populous states have two or three. In the federal system, trial courts are called *federal district courts*, and trial judges are *U.S. district judges*. District judges are assisted by U.S. magistrates. Magistrates exercise limited judicial authority under the supervision of district court judges (see Figure 2.1).

When the United States is a party to litigation, the government is represented by the U.S. attorney. There is one U.S. attorney for each federal judicial district, assisted by a staff of lawyers known as *assistant U.S. attorneys*. Although most criminal prosecution of child abuse occurs in state court, a substantial amount of prosecution occurs in federal court.

After a trial in federal district court, an appeal may be taken to the appropriate U.S. circuit court of appeal. Judges of the U.S. circuit courts are called *circuit court judges*. The federal circuit courts of appeal have decided a number of very important child abuse cases (e.g., *Morgan v. Foretich*, 1988; *United States v. Iron Shell*, 1980; *United States v. Rouse*, 1997).

At the pinnacle of the federal court system is the U.S. Supreme Court, which is the appellate court of last resort in the federal court system. The U.S. Supreme Court's appellate authority is not limited to the federal courts, however. The Supreme Court has the final word on the meaning of the U.S. Constitution, and to implement its authority as final arbiter of the U.S. Constitution, the U.S. Supreme Court has power to review state appellate court decisions interpreting the U.S. Constitution. When a state court misinterprets the U.S. Constitution, the U.S. Supreme Court has authority to correct the mistake.

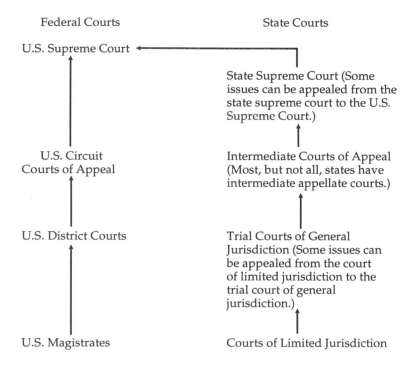

Figure 2.1. The American Judicial System

The U.S. Supreme Court's authority to review state court decisions interpreting the U.S. Constitution explains why the U.S. Supreme Court, which is a federal court, sometimes renders the final decision in cases originating in state court. The U.S. Supreme Court's decision in *Maryland v. Craig* (1990) is a good example. Ms. Craig was prosecuted and convicted in a Maryland state court for sexual abuse. At trial, several children testified via closed-circuit television. In her state court appeal, Ms. Craig's lawyer argued that permitting the children to testify outside Ms. Craig's physical presence violated the U.S. Constitution. Specifically, defense counsel argued that Ms. Craig's right to confront accusatory witnesses, guaranteed by the Sixth Amendment of the U.S. Constitution, was violated. The Maryland Court of Appeals agreed and reversed Ms. Craig's conviction. Because the state court interpreted a provision of the U.S. Constitution, the U.S. Supreme Court had authority to review the case. The U.S. Supreme Court determined that the Maryland court misinterpreted the U.S. Constitution and consequently reversed the state court's decision. Thus, a *federal* court reviewed and reversed a *state* court decision.

State Courts

Every state has a system of trial and appellate courts. Trial courts are the workhorses of the legal system, handling hundreds of thousands of cases every year. Every county or parish has a trial court of general jurisdiction that handles a wide variety of civil and criminal cases. Depending on the state, this court is called a *superior court, district court, circuit court, county court, court of general sessions,* or some other name. In rural areas, the court of general jurisdiction may have one judge, whereas a court located in a major city may have scores of judges.

The trial court of general jurisdiction is often complemented by a trial court of limited jurisdiction, which handles less serious criminal cases, such as misdemeanors, and civil cases involving relatively small amounts of money. The limited-jurisdiction trial court may be called a *city court, municipal court,* or *magistrate's court.* In this book, the term *magistrate's court* is used to describe the court of limited jurisdiction. In addition to conducting trials of misdemeanor cases, the judges of the magistrate's court play an important role in felony cases. In some felony cases, there is a preliminary hearing before a magistrate, who decides whether there is sufficient evidence to proceed to trial in the court of general jurisdiction (see the section "The Criminal Justice System," subsection "Roger's Preliminary Hearing," later in this chapter).

❏ The Criminal Justice System

The criminal justice system plays an important role in protecting children from abuse. When allegations of abuse arise, the police are often notified, and, in most cases, an investigation ensues. If the investigation turns up sufficient evidence, the police contact a prosecuting attorney, who decides whether to file criminal charges against the person suspected of abuse. When charges are filed, most suspects either confess or are found guilty following a trial. When the perpetrator is convicted or confesses, the judge imposes punishment to fit the crime.

Most readers of this book have had little contact with police, prosecutors, and criminal court. Nevertheless, if you work with abused children or their families, you should know something of the criminal justice system. I could fill these pages with dry discussion of criminal law and procedure, but I'd bore you. Instead of a lengthy dissertation, I'll tell you the story of one family, the Reddings, and what they experienced in the criminal justice system. What happened to the Reddings is typical of the procedures in the criminal justice system and should give you a useful introduction.

THE REDDINGS' STORY

Diane Redding is the 10-year-old daughter of Beth and Roger Redding. The Reddings live in a comfortable middle-class neighborhood. Both parents work full time. Roger is a computer engineer and travels a lot. Beth is a kindergarten teacher.

The Secret Is Disclosed

Not long ago, Diane was staying the night with her best friend. It was then that Diane whispered to her friend, "My dad is molesting me. It's got to be a secret, so promise not to tell anybody." Although Diane's friend promised not to tell, she couldn't keep the promise and soon told her own mother, who telephoned Beth Redding.

Beth was shocked and confused. She scooped Diane up and drove to the pediatrician's office. The doctor examined Diane and found medical evidence of sexual abuse. Once the doctor assured Diane that it was "okay to talk about it," Diane tearfully described a year-long history of molestation by her father. Roger Redding had begun by touching Diane and had slowly progressed to full sexual intercourse.

This progression from inappropriate but relatively minor touching to more serious abuse is common and is often called *grooming*. Diane told the doctor that her father said, "If you ever tell, I'll go to jail. The family will break up, and you will be taken away from your mother and me forever."

The doctor telephoned CPS, as she was required to do by the state child abuse reporting law (see Chapter 3). The doctor told Beth to plan on visits from a CPS social worker and the police. Beth told the doctor she and Diane would stay with Beth's brother until Beth could figure out what to do. That night, Roger returned home from a business trip to an empty house and no note from his wife.

The Visit From Child Protective Services

The same evening, a CPS social worker interviewed Diane and her mother at the brother's home. The social worker believed Diane's story. Beth told the social worker that she would keep Diane away from Roger. The social worker decided that Diane was safe with her mother and that there was no need for CPS or the juvenile court to get involved. The social worker told Beth that the police would contact her.

The Police Investigation

The next morning, there was a knock on the brother's door. Beth opened the door to find a uniformed police officer. Beth invited her in, and the officer told Beth that CPS had called the police. The officer interviewed Diane, who repeated what her father had done. Beth said, "I can't understand how my husband could do such a thing, but I believe my daughter." The officer called the pediatrician, and the doctor told the officer about the medical evidence of sexual abuse.

Roger Redding Is Arrested

The investigating officer returned to the police station and discussed the case with a detective from the police department's child abuse unit. The detective and the officer decided that they had enough evidence to arrest Roger. The next step was to get a warrant for his arrest. The detective went to the courthouse and asked a judge called a *magistrate* to issue an arrest warrant. Armed with an arrest warrant, the detective and the investigating officer arrived at the Redding home, where Roger was frantically trying to find his family. The detective said, "Are you Roger Redding?" Roger replied, "Yes. What do you know?" The detective handed Roger the arrest warrant and said, "Mr. Redding, you are under arrest for sexual abuse of your daughter. You will need to come with us to the police station." Roger slumped into a chair, dropped his head into his hands, and said, "Oh, no. How did you find out?" The detective replied, "Find out what?" Roger said, "You know, about my daughter? I'm just sick about this." The detective carefully wrote down what Roger said while the uniformed police officer told Roger that he had a right to remain silent and a right to an attorney and that anything he said could be used against him in court. Roger was handcuffed, searched, and taken to the police station. At the station, Roger was "booked"—that is, fingerprinted, photographed, and put in a jail cell.

When the uniformed police officer informed Roger of his right to remain silent, the officer gave Roger the famous *Miranda* warning, which takes its name from *Miranda v. Arizona* (1966). Under the Constitution, statements by suspects in police custody are admissible in court only if the suspect received the *Miranda* warning before speaking. When police question a suspect in custody, the application of *Miranda* is clear. But does *Miranda* apply when social workers question adults suspected of child abuse? Do social workers have to give the *Miranda* warnings? Generally, the answer is no. Social workers are not law enforcement officers, and social workers do not take adults into custody (see *Commonwealth v. Berrio*, 1990 [MA]; *Fain v. State*, 1985 [AL]; *Gresh v. State*, 1990 [FL]; *People v. Battaglia*, 1984 [CA]; *State v. Hathorn*, 1981 [LA]; *State v. Holden*, 1987 [MN]; *Hennington v. State*, 1997 [MS]; *State v. Nations*, 1987 [NC]; *State v. P.Z.*, 1997 [NJ]; *State v. Sprouse*, 1996 [SC]; *Wicker v. State*, 1987 [TX]). Some courts rule that if an adult is already in police custody, a social worker who is working in conjunction with law enforcement must give the *Miranda* warnings before interviewing the adult (*State v. Helewa*, 1988).

The Prosecutor's Decision to File Charges

The next step in the criminal process was the prosecutor's decision to file formal criminal charges. Many people believe that criminal charges cannot be filed unless the victim agrees, presses charges, or signs a complaint. Generally, this is not true. With serious crimes such as child sexual abuse, the prosecutor has the authority to file charges whether the victim agrees or not. Of course, if the victim or the victim's protective parent is uncooperative, the prosecutor may decline to file. In the final analysis, however, the decision to file criminal charges is made by the prosecutor, not the victim or the victim's family.

Prosecutors have the authority—called *prosecutorial discretion*—to decide whether to file criminal charges. In child sexual abuse cases, prosecutors consider several factors in deciding whether to file charges. The prosecutor wants to know how serious the abuse is and how strong the evidence is. When the evidence is strong, the prosecutor is more likely to file charges than when the evidence is weak. The prosecutor makes a judgment about whether the child will be a good witness if there is a trial. In most child sexual abuse cases, the child is the most important witness, and if the child is quite young, the prosecutor may decide that the child will not be a good witness. In addition to considering whether the child will be a good witness in court, the prosecutor evaluates what the child said about the abuse to parents, social workers, teachers, doctors, friends, and others. If the child's story remained basically consistent over time, the prosecutor is more likely to file charges. If the child's story changed with each telling, the prosecutor may hesitate because inconsistencies can be used to undermine the child's credibility as a witness (see Chapter 7, the section "Sexual Abuse," subsection "Credibility Evidence"). In addition to what the child said, the prosecutor considers whether there is evidence to corroborate the child's story. For example, if there is medical evidence of sexual abuse, the prosecutor is more likely to file charges. It should be mentioned, however, that medical evidence exists in only a small percentage of cases (see Brewer, Rowe, & Brewer, 1997).

If the prosecutor decides *not* to file criminal charges, parents may feel frustrated and angry. On learning that charges will not be filed, it is common for protective parents to ask, "How can you make a decision not to prosecute? My child said he did it! Isn't that enough? Don't you believe my child? Are you going to let that child molester get away with it?" Unfortunately, there are quite a few cases in which prosecutors *do* believe children and are convinced that abuse happened but nevertheless decline to file charges because there is not enough evidence to prove the abuse in court. In criminal cases, a prosecutor has to produce enough evidence to meet a very high burden of proof called *proof beyond a reasonable doubt.* If there is not enough evidence to prove the abuse beyond a reasonable doubt, there is little point in filing charges in the first place. Thus, it is not uncommon for prosecutors to tell protective parents, "I'm sorry, I can't file charges. I believe your child was molested, but there just isn't enough evidence to prove it in court." Prosecutors do not enjoy disappointing protective parents, and they do not like it when offenders escape justice. Nevertheless, prosecutors have an ethical as well as a legal duty to file charges only when evidence of guilt is strong.

Several hours after Roger's arrest, the detective dropped by the office of the prosecutor responsible for child abuse cases. The prosecutor reviewed the papers in the case and chatted with the detective. The prosecutor agreed with the detective that the evidence against Roger was strong, and the prosecutor decided to file charges. The prosecutor prepared a document called a *complaint* and filed it with the court. The complaint started the formal criminal court process.

*Roger Redding's Initial Appearance
in Court and His Release on Bail*

A person who is arrested and charged with a crime has a right to be taken before an impartial magistrate as soon as possible. Roger Redding's first appearance in court was on the morning following his arrest. Roger was in court along with his lawyer. The prosecutor who filed the charges was there too. Diane and Beth were not in court. Roger's first court appearance was brief. The magistrate informed

Roger of the charges against him and told him his preliminary hearing would be in 2 weeks. After some discussion between the magistrate and the attorneys, the magistrate set bail at $50,000 and told Roger that if he was released from jail on bail, he was not to live at home or have any contact with his daughter until the criminal charges were resolved. In less than 15 minutes, the hearing was over and Roger was escorted back to jail by a sheriff's deputy. Later that day, Roger's attorney arranged bail, and Roger was released from jail.

Roger's Preliminary Hearing

In many states, a person charged with crime has a right to a court proceeding called a *preliminary hearing*. The purpose of a preliminary hearing is to enable a judge to decide whether there is enough evidence of guilt to require the accused person, now called a *defendant*, to stand trial. Although a preliminary hearing is less formal than a trial, the hearing is adversarial. The defendant is present with an attorney. The prosecutor must introduce enough evidence of guilt to convince the magistrate that a trial should be held. In some cases, the child testifies at the preliminary hearing, and this is usually the child's first experience in court. If the magistrate decides there is enough evidence for a trial, the child will probably have to testify again at the trial, if there is one. There is no jury at a preliminary hearing.

In some states, a person accused of crime has a right to grand jury indictment. A grand jury is a group of citizens from the community who are responsible for deciding whether formal criminal charges should be filed against individuals suspected of crime. The prosecutor meets with the grand jury behind closed doors and presents evidence of the suspect's guilt. If the grand jury decides that the prosecutor's evidence is sufficient, the grand jury issues a document called an *indictment*. The indictment charges the defendant with specific crimes.

A grand jury does not decide guilt or innocence in individual trials. Rather, the grand jury serves as a screening device early in the criminal justice process to ensure that innocent people are not charged with violating the law. The jury that decides an individual case is called a *petit jury*, not a grand jury, and it is the petit jury that we are used to seeing on television.

Returning to the Redding case, Roger's preliminary hearing was 2 weeks after his initial appearance in court. The prosecutor decided not to ask Diane to testify at the preliminary hearing because the prosecutor believed that there was enough evidence to convince the magistrate that Roger should stand trial without putting Diane through the ordeal of appearing in court. The doctor testified for the prosecution and told the magistrate about the medical evidence of sexual abuse. The investigating police officer testified and told the magistrate what Diane had said. Although Roger's attorney had the right to call witnesses—including Diane and her mother—at the preliminary hearing, the defense attorney decided against calling witnesses. The magistrate ruled that the testimony of the doctor and the police officer was sufficient to require Roger to stand trial.

Pretrial Diversion

In many communities, individuals charged with certain crimes may be eligible for a program that diverts them away from prosecution and into some form of rehabilitation or treatment (LaFave & Israel, 1991, p. 645). Participation in pretrial diversion depends on the nature and seriousness of the crime, whether the individual is a first-time offender, and the likelihood the individual will participate in and benefit from treatment. If the individual successfully completes treatment, the criminal charges are dropped. Failure to complete treatment allows the prosecutor to proceed with prosecution on the original charges.

Roger Redding's attorney attempted to persuade the prosecutor to allow Roger to participate in the pretrial diversion program operating in Roger's community. Because of the seriousness of the charges, however, the prosecutor refused to authorize diversion for Roger. As is usually the case with diversion programs, the prosecutor has considerable discretion on whether to divert or prosecute.

Pretrial Motions

When a case looks as if it will proceed to trial, the opposing attorneys often file pretrial motions requesting the judge to resolve selected legal issues before the trial. Pretrial motions are often called *motions in limine*. For example, the prosecutor may file a pretrial motion requesting the judge to permit a child to testify via closed-circuit television so that the child does not have to face the alleged perpetrator. Defense counsel might ask the judge to order a psychiatric evaluation of the child.

Preparation for Trial: Discovery

During the weeks before the trial, the attorneys prepare. The defendant's attorney interviews witnesses, talks to potential expert witnesses, and plans trial strategy. In addition, defense counsel engages in pretrial discovery. Discovery is a process that permits each party to litigation to learn about evidence possessed by the other party. The parameters of pretrial discovery vary from state to state. In general, the defense is allowed fairly broad discovery of documents and evidence under the control of the prosecutor. Under the U.S. Constitution, the prosecutor is obliged to disclose evidence that could exculpate the defendant. In some states, the defendant's attorney sends the prosecutor a document called a *bill of particulars*, which requests the prosecutor to provide details about the charges against the defendant.

In addition to gaining access to records under the direct control of the prosecutor, the attorney for the person accused of abuse may have a right to inspect records created by mental health and medical professionals. For example, the defense attorney may seek access to a child victim's psychotherapy records. The defense attorney's need to inspect a professional's client records is particularly great when the professional will testify at trial as a witness for the prosecution. The complex rules governing defense access to confidential client information are beyond the scope of this book (see Myers, 1997a). For advice on responding to requests for client information, see the information provided below as well as in Chapter 6.

The prosecutor's right to pretrial discovery from the defense is generally narrower than the defendant's right to discovery from the prosecution. Limitations on discovery by the prosecutor arise primarily from the defendant's constitutional right against self-incrimination (LaFave & Israel, 1991, p. 860).

Professionals who interviewed or treated a child may be contacted by defense counsel or by investigators working for the defense. Before discussing a case with *anyone,* professionals should be clear about the affiliation of the individual seeking information.

If the individual wishing to discuss a case is a representative of the defense, the professional should consider several factors before agreeing to discuss the matter. Generally, professionals are under no legal obligation to communicate with the defense over the telephone, in person, or by letter. The defense attorney can obtain a subpoena that compels the professional to testify at a formal deposition or a trial, but unless subpoenaed, the professional has the right to decide whether to communicate with defense counsel. (For discussion of subpoenas, see Chapter 6, the section "Disclosure of Confidential and Privileged Information," subsection "Subpoenas.")

In deciding whether to talk to defense counsel, the professional should consult with the child if the child is mature enough to assist in decision making. In addition, parents or caretakers should be consulted. A word of caution is appropriate. If the professional decides against speaking with defense counsel before the trial, it should come as no surprise at trial when the defense attorney asks, "I called you about this case before the trial, but you refused even to talk to me, didn't you?" The purpose of this question, of course, is to give the jury the impression that the professional is not objective. Following such a question, the professional may provide an explanation for the decision not to communicate with defense counsel.

The professional should consider whether discussing a case with the defense might inadvertently reveal information about the child that is protected from disclosure by a privilege such as the psychotherapist-client privilege or by the ethical obligation of professionals to safeguard confidential client information. (See Chapter 6 for discussion of confidentiality.)

There are times when it is appropriate and in a child's best interest for a professional to communicate with defense counsel. For example, following consultation with the treating therapist, the defendant's attorney may be persuaded that the best course is for the defendant to plead guilty and seek treatment as an alternative to prison.

When considering whether to communicate with defense counsel, professionals should proceed with caution and should keep in mind that the defense attorney has *one* responsibility: to provide zealous representation for the accused. Many defense attorneys are sensitive to the child's welfare, but the defense attorney does *not* represent the child, and if the child's needs conflict with the rights of the accused, defense counsel is ethically bound to protect the defendant at the expense of the child.

Before communicating with defense counsel, the professional might contact the prosecutor assigned to the case. Prosecutors are not supposed to discourage witnesses from talking to the defense. The prosecutor may, however, give advice about the consequences of communicating with defense counsel.

If the professional is acquainted with an attorney in private law practice, a quick telephone call can dispel doubts about talking to defense counsel. Professionals employed by government agencies can consult with supervisors before discussing cases with representatives of the defense.

Most professionals working with children feel more comfortable discussing a case with the prosecutor than with defense counsel. But here too a degree of forethought is advisable. Generally, professionals who treat children are not at liberty to disclose confidential information to a prosecutor without permission from someone in a position to authorize disclosure.

Prosecutors are sensitive to the welfare of child victims. Indeed, many prosecutors view the child as their second client—the first client being the citizens of the community. Nevertheless, the prosecutor in a criminal case is not the child's attorney, and cases arise in which the prosecutor's strategic decisions are not in the child's best interest. Thus, although professionals working with abused and neglected children are usually justified in the ease with which they interact with prosecutors, it is advisable, especially for professionals treating children, to maintain a degree of professional distance from both sides of the adversarial struggle. Naturally, when a professional is retained to testify as an expert for the prosecution or the defense, a close working relationship with the attorney is necessary and appropriate. (For discussion of expert testimony, see Chapter 7.)

Professionals who provide treatment for individuals accused of child abuse are careful to protect confidential information about their clients. When the professional is contacted by the defense attorney or the prosecutor, the advice outlined above is, for the most part, applicable. The client should be consulted about communication with attorneys and release of confidential information.

As part of trial preparation, the defense attorney may seek to interview the child. Is the child required to submit to an interview with defense counsel? If so, will the interview occur in the defense attorney's office or in some more neutral location? Finally, does the defendant have a right to attend the interview? These are difficult questions. On the one hand, the child is often the prosecution's most important witness, and the defense attorney's ability to prepare for trial may be handicapped if the attorney is not permitted to interview the child. Exclusion of the defendant from a pretrial interview may interfere with the defense attorney's ability to ask effective questions. On the other hand, an interview by the defendant's attorney may be difficult for the child, and seeing the defendant may be quite upsetting. In some states, the judge in charge of the case has authority to permit the defense to interview the child before the trial. The judge may impose conditions on the interview to ensure that the child is not harassed or traumatized. In quite a few states, an adult responsible for the child may refuse to allow the child to be interviewed before the trial (Myers, 1997a).

Roger's Attorney Tries to Negotiate a Plea Bargain With the Prosecutor

With Roger on his way to trial on serious charges, his attorney telephoned the prosecutor to begin plea negotiations, or, as it is usually called, *plea bargaining*. Plea bargaining is a process of back-and-forth negotiation between a prosecutor and a defense attorney. Reduced to its essentials, the defense attorney's goal in plea bargaining is to get the best possible "deal" for the defendant. In exchange for the deal, the defendant promises to plead guilty. In some cases, the defendant pleads guilty to the original charges, and the prosecutor agrees to ask the judge to be lenient when the judge decides what punishment the defendant should receive. In other cases, the defendant pleads guilty to reduced charges in exchange for a lighter sentence.

There is nothing unethical or improper about plea bargaining. Indeed, plea bargaining is common in nearly all kinds of criminal cases, including child abuse. As a result of plea bargaining, the vast majority of criminal cases do not go all the way to a trial in court. In fact, between 70% and 90% of all criminal cases end in guilty pleas before the trial. Thus, trials are the exception rather than the rule.

In the Redding case, Roger's attorney and the prosecutor discussed the possibility of Roger's pleading guilty to a less serious crime, but Roger insisted that he was not guilty of anything, and the lawyers could not strike a bargain that Roger would accept.

Roger's Trial in Criminal Court

A defendant charged with a serious crime such as child sexual abuse has the right to a jury trial. If the defendant does not want a jury, the judge performs the job normally carried out by the jury.

In jury trials, the first step is for the lawyers to pick a petit jury from a pool of potential jurors. The judge or the lawyers question individual jurors to gauge if they will evaluate the evidence fairly and follow the law. There are two ways to excuse potential jurors from the jury: (a) for cause and (b) by peremptory challenge. When there are serious doubts about a juror, or when serving on the jury would pose significant hardship for a juror, the judge may excuse the juror for cause. A peremptory challenge is a lawyer's privilege to excuse a small number of potential jurors without offering any explanation for doing so. In exercising peremptory challenges, a lawyer excuses jurors who the lawyer thinks will be unsympathetic to the lawyer's side of the case.

Once a jury is selected, the lawyers make their opening statements. The prosecutor goes first and explains to the jury what the prosecutor believes the evidence will prove. The opening statement gives the prosecutor an opportunity to paint a verbal picture of what is to come. Following the prosecutor's opening statement, the defense attorney makes an opening statement. Needless to say, the defense attorney paints a different picture than the prosecutor.

With opening statements complete, the prosecutor begins presenting evidence of the defendant's guilt. The portion of the trial during which the prosecutor presents evidence of guilt is called the prosecution's *case-in-chief.* The prosecutor's most important evidence is usually testimony from the child. Indeed, in most cases, the child is the prosecution's "star" witness. In addition to the child, the prosecutor may ask the protective parent to testify. Finally, the prosecutor may offer testimony from medical or mental health professionals (see Chapter 7). The one person that the prosecutor cannot call as a witness is the defendant. The defendant in a criminal trial has a constitutional right not to testify.

A person who testifies in court takes an oath to tell the truth. Following the oath, the attorney who requested the person to testify asks questions. This part of the testimony is called *direct examination.* The purpose of direct examination is to give the witness an opportunity to tell the jury what the witness knows about the case. For

Testifying is seldom easy for children. Yet when children are prepared for what to expect in court, and when they have the support of a loving parent, they cope well with testifying.

example, when a child testifies on direct examination, the child tells the jury about the abuse. Obviously, describing sexual abuse to a group of unfamiliar adults in a large and forbidding courtroom is difficult for children, especially when the defendant is sitting there too. Nevertheless, you would be encouraged by how well most children do on the witness stand.

Testifying is seldom easy for children. Yet when children are prepared for what to expect in court, and when they have the support of a loving parent, they cope well with testifying (Goodman et al., 1992; Myers, Goodman, & Saywitz, 1996; Oates, Lunch, & Stearn, 1995; Runyan, 1993; Runyan, Everson, Edelsohn, Hunter, & Coulter, 1988; Whitcomb, Goodman, Runyan, & Hoak, 1994). Moreover, psychological research indicates that when children receive support from parents, testifying is unlikely to cause lasting harm (Goodman et al., 1992; Myers et al., 1996; Oates et al., 1995;

Runyan, 1993; Runyan et al., 1988; Whitcomb, Goodman, et al., 1994). Children do not enjoy testifying, but once it is over, they bounce back. In fact, after they testify, some children report that although it was "scary," they were glad to have an opportunity to "tell the jury what happened."

After direct examination, the other attorney has the right to cross-examine. When a child testifies, the defense attorney usually cross-examines the child. The defense attorney may try to make the child look like an unreliable witness or even a liar. For example, if the child did not say anything about the abuse for a long time, the defense attorney may ask the child questions about the delay (see Chapter 7, the section "Sexual Abuse," subsection "Credibility Evidence"). The defense attorney focuses on delay in an effort to convince the jury that the abuse never happened and that the child is lying. Another way to cross-examine a child is to catch the child saying inconsistent things about the abuse.

To many parents and professionals, cross-examination of a child by a defense attorney seems unfair. After all, how is a 6- or 10-year-old supposed to cope with the tricks of an experienced attorney? But don't be too hard on defense attorneys. The cross-examining defense attorney is just doing his or her job. In our adversary system of justice, the defense attorney owes loyalty to one person, the defendant. If the case goes to trial, the defense attorney is duty bound to attack the prosecution's witnesses, including the child. After all, the child is usually the prosecution's most important witness.

When the prosecution has presented all its witnesses and other evidence, the prosecution rests its case-in-chief. Next, the defense presents its case-in-chief. The defense calls witnesses to poke holes in the prosecutor's evidence. The defendant may testify during this part of the trial. If the defendant testifies, the prosecutor may cross-examine. Finally, the defense rests.

Following the defense case-in-chief, the prosecutor may put on a case-in-rebuttal to respond to issues raised by the defense. The case-in-rebuttal, if there is one, is usually brief.

When both sides have rested, the prosecutor and defense attorney make their closing arguments to the jury. Each lawyer uses closing arguments to summarize the evidence and persuade the jury to vote for the attorney's side.

The judge instructs the jurors on the law that they must follow to decide whether the defendant is guilty. The jury then retires to decide the defendant's fate. If the jury decides that the defendant is not guilty, the case is over. The prosecution is not allowed to appeal an acquittal to a higher court. If the jury decides that the defendant is guilty, however, the defendant *is* allowed to appeal to a higher court. The responsibility of the appellate court is to decide whether serious mistakes were made at the trial. If serious mistakes occurred, the appellate court may order a new trial.

Let's get back to the Reddings. At Roger's trial, Diane testified against her father. As you can imagine, testifying was very difficult. Like many incest victims, Diane was torn between love for her father and the desire to stop the abuse. The detective testified and told the jury the incriminating things that Roger said on the day he was arrested. The pediatrician testified and described the medical evidence of sexual abuse.

Roger's attorney vigorously cross-examined Diane to attack her credibility. The defense attorney asked Diane, "Why did you wait so long to tell?" "You could have told your mother, couldn't you?" and "Did your mother put you up to this testimony here in court?" The defense attorney tried to convince the jury that Diane was lying and that she had been coached by Beth.

Roger testified on his own behalf and denied that he had touched Diane in a sexual way. Roger testified that Diane had been coached into a false story by her mother.

The jury deliberated for 2 days and still could not reach a verdict. Such lengthy deliberation is not unusual. The hours dragged like years as everyone waited on pins and needles. Finally, on the third day, the jury sent a note to the judge: It had reached a verdict. Everyone rushed back to court. Roger sat stony faced and pale next to his attorney. Beth sat in the public area of the courtroom wringing her hands. Diane was at her grandmother's home in another city, anxiously waiting. The judge turned to the jury and said, "Ladies and gentlemen of the jury, have you reached a verdict?" The forewoman of the jury stood and said, "Yes, your honor, we have a verdict." The judge said, "What is your verdict?" The forewoman nervously fingered the slip of paper clenched in her hand. Slowly, she opened the paper and read, "We the jury find Roger Redding guilty as charged."

Roger put his head on the table. Beth sobbed quietly. When Beth telephoned the news to Diane, the child nestled in her grandmother's arms and cried tears of grief and relief.

Roger Redding Receives His Punishment

When a defendant pleads guilty or is found guilty after a trial, the judge decides what punishment the person deserves. Depending on the seriousness of the crime and the defendant's prior criminal record, the judge may sentence the defendant to prison. In some cases, the judge suspends the prison sentence and places the person on probation. With probation, the defendant lives in the community under the supervision of a probation officer. In some child sexual abuse cases, the defendant is placed on probation and ordered to get psychological treatment.

In Roger Redding's case, the judge sentenced Roger to 5 years in state prison. The judge suspended all but 6 months of the prison sentence. Roger served 6 months in the county jail and was released on probation. Roger was required to move out of the family home. He was ordered to have no contact with his family until he had completed a treatment program for child molesters. At last report, Roger was working hard in therapy. Diane was in therapy too. Somehow, Beth found the courage to bring her daughter through this difficult experience. Beth has not decided what the future holds. For now, she is content to help her daughter heal.

Epilogue

Roger Redding's conviction was bittersweet for Diane and her mother, and the same is true for thousands of other families afflicted by incest. On the one hand, involvement in the criminal justice system is difficult for everyone. Careers and reputations are ruined, and families fly apart at the seams. On the other hand, conviction sends a clear message: Child sexual abuse is wrong. Sexual abuse is an extraordinary betrayal of trust that will not be tolerated. Moreover, for many offenders, the brutal reality of a criminal conviction supplies the motivation they need to make meaningful progress toward controlling their deviant behavior (Salter, 1995).

❏ Child Protective Services and the Juvenile Court

Every community has a government system to protect children from abuse and neglect. The system has three main components: (a) CPS; (b) the courts, including the juvenile court; and (c) law enforcement. This section focuses briefly on CPS and the juvenile court. The criminal courts are described earlier in this chapter, and the family court is described later in this chapter.

CHILD PROTECTIVE SERVICES

The government agency with primary responsibility for protecting children from abuse and neglect is CPS. CPS is normally a branch of the county social services or welfare department. In some communities, CPS investigates all allegations of child abuse, whether the suspected offender is a parent, another family member, an acquaintance, or a stranger. More often, however, the mission of CPS is limited to protecting children from abuse within the family, particularly abuse by parents. In many communities, CPS is not involved when abuse is committed by adults outside the family.

THE JUVENILE COURT

Every county has a court that is responsible for two types of cases involving young people: juvenile delinquency cases and child abuse and neglect cases. Juvenile delinquency is criminal activity by minors, primarily teenagers. Although juvenile delinquency is an important social issue, delinquency is beyond the scope of this book.

The juvenile court is charged with responsibility to protect children from abuse and neglect (Hardin, 1996; Sagatun & Edwards, 1995). For the most part, the juvenile court's authority is limited to abuse and neglect occurring within the family. The juvenile court does not typically exercise authority over maltreatment by strangers, teachers, coaches, or relatives who do not live with the child. Maltreatment by outsiders is handled in criminal court.

The juvenile court judge has broad authority over parents who abuse or neglect their children. For example, the judge can remove the child from the parents' custody and establish conditions that the parents must fulfill to regain custody. The juvenile court judge can order maltreating parents to attend counseling or parenting classes. If efforts to reform an abusive parent fail, the juvenile court has the power to terminate the legal relationship between the abusive parent and the child, although this drastic measure is used only as a last resort.

In some cities, the juvenile court is housed in a separate courthouse with one or more judges and a staff of probation officers and social workers. In small communities and rural areas, one or two judges are responsible for all court work, including criminal, civil, and juvenile court cases.

CPS receives reports of child abuse from parents, neighbors, doctors, teachers, and others. When a report is received, a CPS social worker decides whether an investigation is warranted. If so, a social worker is dispatched to interview the child, the parents, and others who may have relevant information. If the social worker believes that a crime has been committed, the police are notified.

When a CPS investigation uncovers evidence of abuse or neglect, the social worker has several options. If only one parent is responsible for the abuse or neglect, and if the maltreating parent is willing to move out or there is little likelihood of further maltreatment, the social worker may leave the child at home under the protection of the nonabusive parent. If the abusive parent poses an immediate threat to the child and refuses to vacate the family home, the social worker or a police officer may take the child into emergency protective custody. When one parent is abusive and the other parent cannot or will not protect the child, protective custody may be necessary.

When a child is taken into emergency protective custody by a social worker or the police, the child is placed with relatives or in a foster home or children's receiving home. As soon as the child is removed, CPS is required to commence proceedings in juvenile court. Within a day or two, a juvenile court judge decides whether the child should remain in protective custody or return home.

When CPS believes that abuse or neglect occurred and that the child needs protection, CPS requests the appropriate government attorney to commence legal proceedings in juvenile court. The attorney, who is typically the local district attorney, files a document called a *petition* with the juvenile court. The parents may retain an attorney to contest the allegations of maltreatment. If parents cannot afford an attorney, the county pays for the parents' attorney.

In most juvenile court cases, the parents, with the assistance of their lawyer, work out an agreement with the government attorney and CPS. For example, the parents may agree to get counseling. Thus, most juvenile court cases do not proceed all the way to a trial on the allegations of abuse. Social workers employed by CPS or the juvenile court monitor the parents to ensure that progress is being made. The ultimate goal is usually to reunite the family and help the parents avoid further maltreatment.

When parents are embroiled in child custody or visitation litigation in family court, CPS may be reluctant to get involved. CPS social workers may assume that the family court will protect the child without assistance from CPS or the juvenile court. Of course, in many cases this conclusion is warranted. In other cases, however, it is appropriate for CPS to be involved even though the family court is also playing a role. Each case should be decided on its own merits, with the focus on the safety of the child (Edwards, 1987).

❏ Family Court: Divorce and Child Custody

This section discusses the family court, or, as it is called some places, domestic relations court. The family court handles divorce, child custody, and related matters. A divorce is started when the attorney for one spouse files a document in court called a *complaint* or *petition*. The complaint or petition is the first of many documents that are filed in the typical divorce. The last document, and the one that officially ends the marriage, is the judge's decree or judgment of divorce.

IS AN ATTORNEY NECESSARY TO GET A DIVORCE OR CUSTODY?

This is one of the most commonly asked questions. Attorneys are expensive, and people want to know if they really need an attorney to get divorced. The law does not require divorcing spouses to be represented by attorneys, and some couples obtain a divorce without the assistance of lawyers. Usually, however, proceeding without a lawyer is wise only in limited circumstances in which the legal issues are clear-cut. Consider, for example, Mary and Tom, who have been married 1 year. Both want a divorce, and they agree on how to divide what little property they have. There are no children. Mary and Tom are young, and both work. For this divorcing couple, lawyers may be unnecessary.

For couples who do not fit Mary and Tom's simple situation, a lawyer is often necessary. Clearly, if a couple has children and if there is any dispute about custody or visitation, legal assistance is critical. Moreover, if one parent suspects the other of abusing their child, legal help is *indispensable*.

People getting divorced sometimes ask whether both spouses need a lawyer. An individual may say, "My spouse already has a lawyer. I don't have the money to pay for one. Can't I let my spouse's lawyer draw up the legal papers?" Again, if there are children, and if custody or visitation is contested, the answer is clear: Each parent should have a lawyer.

THE LEGAL EFFECT OF A DIVORCE

A divorce accomplishes five things.

End of the Marriage

The divorce ends the marriage and returns the former spouses to the legal status of single persons.

Division of Property

The second important issue resolved in a divorce is the division of property, including the family home, furniture, cars, investments, and pensions. In most cases, the couple, with the assistance of lawyers, work out an agreement regarding property division. Following negotiation, the lawyers prepare a document called a *stipulation* or *marriage settlement agreement* describing the property division. The spouses sign the final agreement, and it is incorporated into the divorce decree, making the agreement enforceable as a court order.

If the spouses cannot agree on some aspect of dividing their property, a trial on that issue may be necessary. Every state has a complex set of laws governing property division on divorce.

Spousal Support

The third aspect of divorce concerns spousal support, or, as it used to be called, alimony. Spousal support is not provided in all divorces. For example, if the marriage was relatively short and both spouses are employable, the judge is unlikely to order spousal support. When spousal support is ordered, it may be for a limited time. The law concerning spousal support is complex. It will suffice for our purposes to say that spousal support is most likely when one spouse has financial need (e.g., lacks employment skills) and the other spouse has the ability to pay.

Child Support

The fourth component of divorce concerns child support. When a marriage ends, both parents remain financially responsible for the children. If one parent receives primary or sole custody of the children, the noncustodial parent is typically ordered to make monthly child support payments to the custodial parent.

In blended marriages, there is a biological parent and a stepparent. During the marriage, both "parents" pool their resources to support the family. When blended marriages end, however, the stepparent has no further financial obligation to the stepchild unless the stepparent adopted the child or agreed to provide continuing support. For financial purposes, an adopted child is treated the same as a biological child.

Child Custody and Visitation

The fifth aspect of divorce concerns child custody and visitation. In family law, the word *custody* is used several ways to describe postdivorce child rearing:

- *Sole legal custody* means that one parent has the right to make important decisions for the child. For example, the parent with sole legal custody has authority to decide where the child goes to school and whether the child should receive medical care.
- *Sole or primary physical custody* means that one parent has the primary right to physical control of the child. The parent with sole physical custody—called the *custodial parent*—is the parent with whom the child lives most of the time. The custodial parent does most of the day-to-day parenting, including getting the children up and ready for school, taking them to the doctor, driving them to lessons, and tucking them in at night. The parent with sole physical custody often, although not invariably, has sole legal custody as well. In some cases, one parent has sole physical custody, and the parents share joint legal custody.
- *Joint legal custody* means that parents share the right and the responsibility to make decisions relating to the health, education, and welfare of their child.
- *Joint physical custody* means that each parent has significant periods of physical custody.
- *Joint legal and physical custody* means that the parents share physical and legal custody.

Joint custody in one form or another is a good solution for divorced parents who can cooperate. When there is friction and animosity between parents, however, joint custody seldom works. When one parent accuses the other of child abuse, the chances of successful joint custody are small.

In the typical divorce, one parent gets primary custody and the other gets visitation. Visitation is a legally enforceable *right*, not a mere privilege. Visitation is granted automatically unless the noncustodial parent has engaged in serious misbehavior such as child abuse or criminal activity.

The divorce decree usually describes the visitation schedule of the noncustodial parent. The custodial parent has no right to change the schedule unilaterally. If, for some reason, the custodial parent believes that visitation should be stopped, the parent must return to court and ask a judge to modify the visitation schedule. A custodial parent cannot simply cut off visitation.

Until 15 or 20 years ago, many states had custody laws that favored mothers of young children. This maternal preference was called the "tender years presumption." The belief was that young children are usually better off with their mother. Today, the law has changed. The fundamental rule of child custody law today is that a child's mother and father have *equal* rights to custody. Thus, in a dispute over custody, the parents begin on equal legal footing. Neither parent has an advantage over the other. The equal right to custody applies whether or not the parents ever married.

Most divorcing parents work out a custody and visitation arrangement that suits their needs and the needs of their children. The lawyers write up the parents' agreement and present it to the judge. So long as the agreement is in the best interest of the children, the judge approves it. When parents cannot agree on custody or visitation, however, a trial may be necessary, and the judge determines who should have custody and what visitation is appropriate.

Contested custody litigation is extremely difficult for parents and children alike. Most divorcing couples are not on the best terms anyway, and when child custody becomes an issue, things can turn very ugly. The degree of hostility in some custody battles defies description. Although bitterness, anger, frustration, and hurt feelings are not inevitable by-products of custody litigation, they are the norm rather than the exception.

As stated above, when divorcing parents cannot agree on custody, the judge decides. To determine custody, the judge applies a legal rule called the *best-interest-of-the-child standard*. Under this standard, the judge evaluates all available evidence about the parents and the child and makes the custody decision that serves the child's best interests. In many cases, the best-interest decision boils down to this: Which parent is better equipped and more likely to meet the child's needs?

The best interest of the child standard sounds simple, and sometimes it is. For example, suppose mother is a doting parent who struggles with a limited budget to meet her child's emotional, educational, and other needs. Father, by contrast, is an alcoholic who regularly drinks his paycheck, beats his wife, and yells at the child. Custody is easy. Mother gets sole custody, and father will be lucky to get visitation. As you can imagine, most custody cases are not so simple. More often than not, both parents are decent people and loving parents. Many times, there is no clear right answer, and judges agonize over these decisions.

In some communities, parents battling over custody are urged or required to consult a professional mediator who is trained to help divorcing parents work out their differences and reach a friendly—or at least not openly hostile—custody and visitation arrangement (see Kenney & Vigil, 1996). When mediation succeeds, there is no need for an adversarial custody battle in court.

When parents cannot agree on custody, and a judge must decide, the judge needs as much information as possible about each parent's strengths and weaknesses. In the adversary system of justice, the judge does not conduct an independent investigation of the parents. Rather, the judge holds a trial at which the lawyers do what lawyers are trained to do: win. Thus, the mother's attorney presents evidence designed to convince the judge that the mother is the better parent. The mother's attorney also points out the father's weaknesses. The father's attorney returns the favor by presenting evidence that puts the father in a good light and casts a shadow over the mother. If a parent has skeletons in the closet—and who among us does not—expect the other side to rattle them. After listening to all the evidence, the judge decides the child's best interest.

When a judge uses the best-interest-of-the-child standard, the judge considers a wide range of evidence, including the factors listed below.

The Primary Caretaker Presumption In many families, one parent does most of the day-to-day parenting. For example, the mother may be a full-time homemaker while the father holds down a 40-hour-a-week job. When young children are involved and mother and father are both good parents, judges often decide that custody should be awarded to the primary caretaker.

In many states, there is a legal presumption that the primary caretaker should have custody. To overcome or rebut the presumption favoring the primary caretaker, the other parent tries to prove that the primary caretaker has some rather serious faults. If the judge is convinced that the child's best interest will be fostered by awarding custody to the nonprimary caretaker, the judge may do so.

If both parents are primary caretakers, neither one has the advantage of the primary caretaker presumption.

Which Is the Better Parent? Most contested custody cases boil down to this: Who is the better parent? Which parent is more likely to provide the love, guidance, discipline, support, and nurturance that children need to develop into happy and well-adjusted adults? Custody is awarded accordingly.

After the Divorce, Which Parent Is Most Likely to Encourage the Child's Relationship With the Other Parent? When parents divorce, it is usually in the child's best interest to have regular contact with the parent who does not receive custody. Of course, this is not the case when child abuse is involved: Then contact with the abuser may be unwise. Apart from abuse cases, however, judges consider which parent is more likely to encourage the child's postdivorce relationship with the other parent. The parent who is most likely to foster continued contact with the other parent has an advantage in court.

Mental Illness. The fact that a person has mental health problems does not make the person a bad parent. Many people struggling with mental illness are wonderful parents. It is also true, however, that some parents with serious mental illness are not up to the demands of day-to-day parenting. Judges consider the mental health and stability of both parents, and if one parent has a mental illness that could seriously interfere with the parent's ability to care for children, the judge may decide that the other parent should have custody.

Alcohol and Drugs. Drinking in moderation is generally not important in custody cases. Problem drinking and alcoholism, on the other hand, are definite black marks. If a judge has to choose between an alcoholic and a parent who does not drink or who drinks responsibly, the choice is clear.

Drug abuse is illegal, and judges unquestionably frown on such behavior. For many judges, so-called recreational drug use is a clear indication of irresponsibility that is inconsistent with good parenting. Parents who are addicted to drugs such as cocaine or heroin cannot take care of children and should not have custody.

Suppose a Parent Has an Extramarital Affair? Many divorces start because one spouse is unfaithful. An extramarital affair does not necessarily make a person a bad parent. Thus, the affair itself is usually not crucial, especially if it is over.

Although marital infidelity is usually not decisive, the way that the unfaithful partner handles the situation can influence the judge's thinking. Suppose, for example, that the father had an affair with a woman at the office. The children knew nothing about the affair and, as far as they were concerned, everything was normal. The affair ended 6 months ago. In this situation, the father's affair probably will not count against him in the custody case. Suppose, however, that the father handled things differently. While he was still married, he spent weekend nights at his lover's apartment. Moreover, he insisted that the children sleep there too. In this case, the judge may well conclude that the father's behavior sets a bad example for the children.

Spousal Abuse. A man who beats or sexually assaults his wife does not deserve custody of children, and judges take spousal abuse very seriously.

A Parent's Religious Beliefs. A parent's religious belief or lack of belief usually does not play a major role in custody decision making.

The Child's Wishes. The law in most states requires judges to consider the child's wishes about custody, at least by the time children reach age 8 or 9. Judges give little weight to the wishes of young children. Indeed, some judges do not consider young children's wishes at all. By the time children approach adolescence, however, most judges consider their preference. Although judges listen to older children, they are not required to go along with the child's wishes.

Child Abuse. Physically abusing a child is grossly inappropriate, and a physically abusive parent has two strikes against him or her. Of course, a parent who hit a child may argue that he or she was disciplining, not abusing, the child. You will recall from Chapter 1 that the law allows parents to use "reasonable" corporal punishment.

Thus, in a custody case, the question may be whether a parent crossed the line that separates reasonable corporal punishment from abuse. Child sexual abuse is inconsistent with a child's best interests.

A WORD OF CAUTION

Suppose you have a client who is the parent of a young child. Your client tells you that she thinks the father is sexually abusing the child. She says that she is thinking about a divorce or, if she is already divorced, cutting off visits. Take heed! In family court today, *any* allegation of child sexual abuse is likely to be met with extreme skepticism. A parent who alleges child sexual abuse in family court and fails to prove it can be in for an unbelievable nightmare. The woman (it usually happens to women) who makes the allegation and cannot prove it may be labeled a hysterical false accuser who is unfit for custody. The mother who sought to protect her child in family court ends up losing the child to the man she believes is a molester!

Alleging sexual abuse in family court is a topic that is so troubling, so emotional, so complicated, and so likely to end in disaster that I have written an entire book on the subject. If you have a client who suspects sexual abuse and who is thinking of going to family court, *your client needs expert legal help immediately!* Although my book on this subject is no substitute for expert assistance, the book may be a useful resource. The book is entitled *A Mother's Nightmare: Incest: A Practical Legal Guide for Parents and Professionals* (Myers, 1997b).

FUTURE MODIFICATION OF CHILD CUSTODY OR VISITATION

A judge's final decision is usually just that: final. Consider, for example, a criminal case in which the jury finds the defendant innocent and the judge makes a final judgment acquitting the defendant. The prosecutor cannot put the defendant on trial again for the same crime. The prosecutor gets only one bite at the apple. The judgment of acquittal is final, or, as lawyers say, *res judicata* (a thing decided). Similarly, in most kinds of civil cases, the final judgment is *res judicata*.

In family court, *res judicata*—the finality of judgments—is complex. Two aspects of a divorce judgment are *res judicata* and cannot be relitigated: the divorce itself and the property division. When it comes to child custody, visitation, child support, and spousal support, however, different rules apply (see Myers, 1997b, pp. 112-116). Judgments regarding custody, visitation, and support *can* be modified in the future if circumstances change substantially.

The family court has continuing authority over children of divorce until they reach the age of majority. If circumstances change substantially, a family court judge can modify custody or visitation.

❏ Three Laws Intended to Protect Children

All states criminalize child sexual abuse, and incarceration of convicted sex offenders plays an important role in protecting children. Nevertheless, incarceration lasts only so long, and the vast majority of convicted sex offenders eventually return to the community. In recent years, a growing number of states have adopted new approaches to protecting children from convicted sex offenders. These approaches include (a) laws requiring convicted sex offenders to register with authorities, (b) laws authorizing public notification when sex offenders move into a community—so-called Megan's laws, and (c) laws permitting involuntary civil commitment of dangerous sexual predators at the end of their prison terms. Each of these legislative innovations promises increased child protection. Yet these laws constitute significant invasions of the liberty and privacy of sex offenders who, though at risk of reoffending, have "paid their debt to society."

SEX OFFENDER REGISTRATION LAWS

Laws requiring convicted sex offenders to register with local law enforcement authorities are nearly universal in the United States. Although registration laws vary from state to state, similarities outnumber differences. Convicted sex offenders must register with law enforcement, providing name, address, fingerprints, photograph, and vehicle license number. Changes in address must be reported, and failure to register is a crime.

Law enforcement officers use registry information to assist investigations. Most states allow prospective employers to determine whether job applicants are registered.

Sex offenders have challenged registration laws in court, arguing that the laws violate privacy and subject offenders to unfair and unequal treatment. Nearly all court challenges have failed, however, and registration laws are on firm legal ground (*Doe v. Poritz*, 1995).

MEGAN'S LAW: PUBLIC NOTIFICATION OF SEX OFFENDERS LIVING IN THE COMMUNITY

Under sex offender registration laws, law enforcement knows the whereabouts of convicted offenders. Is it wise to extend such knowledge to schools, parents, and even the general public? On the one hand, parents are in the best position to protect their children from a sex offender living across the street. On the other hand, public notification is a major invasion of privacy. Moreover, loss of privacy is not the only concern: Public notification under Megan's law has led to scattered acts of vigilantism against sex offenders (Freeman-Longo, 1996).

A study in Washington State found that community notification did not appear to lower recidivism, although "offenders who were subjects of community notification were arrested for new crimes much more quickly than comparable offenders who were released without notification" (Washington State Institute for Public Policy, 1995, p. ii). Perhaps offenders subjected to community notification are watched more closely and caught more quickly.

Megan's laws were the target of vigorous legal challenge. New Jersey's law, for example, was assailed as a violation of the constitutional guarantees of equal protection and privacy, as well as an affront to the constitutional prohibitions against cruel and unusual punishment, ex post facto laws, double jeopardy, and bills of attainder. In 1995, New Jersey's Megan's law was upheld by the state supreme court, which ruled that "the Constitution does not prevent society from attempting to protect itself from convicted sex offenders. . . . To rule otherwise is to find that society is unable to protect itself from sexual predators by adopting the simple remedy of informing the public of their presence" (*Doe v. Poritz*, 1995, pp. 372,

422). Most courts to date have rejected constitutional challenges to Megan's laws (*Doe v. Pataki*, 1997; *E.B. v. Verniero*, 1997; *In re B.G.*, 1996; *Opinion of the Justices to the Senate*, 1996; *Russell v. Gregoire*, 1997). An occasional court has struck down a version of Megan's law (*State v. Myers*, 1996).

INVOLUNTARY PSYCHIATRIC HOSPITALIZATION OF DANGEROUS SEXUAL PREDATORS

A few particularly dangerous sexual predators simply are not safe at large. Recidivism is high among these offenders (Furby, Weinrott, & Blackshaw, 1989; Hall, 1995; Prentky, Knight, & Lee, 1997; Salter, 1995). For especially dangerous offenders, jail is the only safe place. Yet, when a sexual predator completes his prison term, he is entitled to release. One solution to the dangers posed by sexual predators living in the community is to hospitalize the offenders in secure psychiatric institutions. Unfortunately, most sexual predators cannot be hospitalized under traditional civil commitment laws because the offenders lack the psychiatric diagnoses required for involuntary commitment.

In 1990, Washington State took the bull by the horns with a new law permitting involuntary civil commitment of "sexually violent predators" (Washington Revised Code § 71.09.010). Other states followed suit, including Arizona, California, Colorado, Connecticut, Illinois, Iowa, Kansas, Massachusetts, Minnesota, Nebraska, New Jersey, New Mexico, Oregon, Tennessee, Utah, and Wisconsin.

Individuals civilly committed as sexual predators lost no time challenging the constitutionality of the new laws. In *Kansas v. Kendricks* (1997), however, the U.S. Supreme Court ruled that the Kansas law is constitutional. Similar commitment laws will withstand constitutional challenge.

To summarize, no one wants a return to the pillory, where minor offenders were publicly humiliated in the town square. Child sexual abuse, however, is anything but minor, and society has a right to defend itself from criminals that prey on children. The laws described in this section undoubtedly infringe on the liberty and privacy of sex offenders. The question is whether that infringement is justified by the benefit that such laws bring to society.

3

Child Abuse Reporting Laws

The modern era of child protection began in 1962, the year that pediatrician C. Henry Kempe et al. published their landmark article describing the battered-child syndrome. Kempe et al.'s article focused national attention on the plight of physically abused children. Also in 1962, the federal government sponsored an important conference on child abuse. The conferees recommended laws requiring physicians to report suspected physical abuse to authorities. By 1965, the American Medical Association (1965), the American Humane Association (1963), the Council of State Governments (see Meriwhether, 1986), and the Children's Bureau of the U.S. Department of Health, Education, and Welfare (Children's Bureau, 1963) had all published model child abuse reporting laws.

Beginning in California in 1963, state legislatures enacted reporting laws, and in the remarkably short span of 4 years, every state had reporting legislation on the books (Goodpaster & Angel, 1975). Early reporting laws were, for the most part, limited to physical abuse. Other forms of maltreatment were added later. The majority of early reporting laws were limited to physicians and, to a lesser extent, nurses. Today, reporting laws embrace all professionals working with children. A few reporting laws followed the early advice of the American Medical Association and permitted but did not require professionals to report (Paulsen, 1967). Six states—Alaska, Missouri, New Mexico, North Carolina, Texas, and Washington—had permissive reporting laws. "The person or persons cited in the law 'may report' rather than 'shall report' " (DeFrancis, 1968, p. 26). Today, however, mandatory reporting for professionals is universal in the United States.

Since the enactment of reporting laws nearly 40 years ago, a great deal has been learned about child abuse and neglect. The reporting laws played a key role in accumulating that knowledge. In particular, the reporting laws provided essential data on the prevalence of maltreatment (Daro & Wang, 1997). In 1962, before enactment of reporting laws, the American Humane Association conducted a survey of the prevalence of maltreatment. To gather data, the association was forced to turn to the only source of information available at the time—newspaper accounts! The survey revealed a total of 662 cases. With enactment of reporting laws, data emerged on the true prevalence of abuse and neglect. The reporting laws wrenched the secret of abuse and neglect out of the dark and into the light of day, where it could not be ignored.

❑ Who Is Required to Report?

Professionals who come in contact with children are required to report suspected abuse or neglect to designated child protection or law enforcement authorities. In this book, the individuals required to report are called *mandated reporters.* The list of mandated reporters is long: "Across states, there are nearly 40 different professions specifically named in mandatory reporting laws" (Kalichman, 1993, p. 24). The list includes educators, physicians, dentists, nurses, coroners, mental health professionals, social workers, law enforcement officers, and child care providers. Some reporting laws include pharmacists, firefighters, paramedics, and "commercial film and photographic processors" (California Penal Code § 11166(e), 1997). Some states require clergy members to report. In California, for example, a clergy member must report suspected abuse unless the suspicion arises out of a "penitential communication," which is defined as "a communication, intended to be in confidence, including but not limited to, a sacramental confession, made to a clergy member who . . . has a [religious] duty to keep those communications secret" (California Penal Code § 11166(c)(2)).

Researchers can be mandated reporters. "Contrary to the common belief that researchers are not mandated reporters, state laws do not make this exclusion" (Kalichman, 1993, p. 47).

In a small number of states, *every person,* whether professional or layperson, is a mandated reporter. The "everyone reports" states are Florida, Indiana, Kentucky, Mississippi, Nebraska, New Hampshire, New Jersey, New Mexico, and North Carolina.

❏ Mandatory Reporting: No Discretion

When suspicion of child abuse or neglect rises to the level specified in the reporting law, mandated reporters *must* report. "Professionals who have attained a level of reasonable suspicion of child abuse are not afforded professional judgment and legal flexibility in reporting" (Kalichman, 1993, p. 153). If the triggering level of suspicion exists, a mandated reporter has *no* discretion in the matter: A report must be made whether or not the professional believes that reporting is wise.

❏ Permissive Reporting: Discretion Allowed

In most states, only mandated reporters are required to report suspected child maltreatment. Laypersons generally are not mandated reporters and may decide for themselves whether to report suspected abuse or neglect.

❏ Definitions of Abuse and Neglect

Each state's reporting law contains definitions of physical abuse, sexual abuse, neglect, and other forms of reportable maltreatment. Definitions vary slightly from state to state, and professionals should familiarize themselves with applicable law. Although definitions vary, common themes can be distilled from the reporting laws. Physical abuse is generally defined as nonaccidental physical injury (see Chapter 1). Sexual abuse is typically defined by reference to definitions contained in criminal laws against such abuse (see Chapter 1). Neglect is a protean concept that defies precise definition. Generally, it includes failure by caretakers to provide minimally adequate nutrition, nurturance, clothing, shelter, or medical care (see Chapter 7).

Several states (California, Florida, Illinois, Indiana, Iowa, Massachusetts, Minnesota, Missouri, Nevada, Oklahoma, and Utah) require reporting newborn infants who show signs of drug exposure or fetal alcohol syndrome. Many states require reporting suspicious deaths.

❏ What Level of Suspicion Triggers Mandatory Reporting?

For many professionals, the question "What level of suspicion triggers the duty to report?" is the most important yet the most perplexing issue under the reporting law. Basically, the reporting duty is triggered when a professional possesses a prescribed level of suspicion that a child may be abused or neglected. The phrases used to describe the triggering level of suspicion vary slightly from state to state and include "cause to believe," "reasonable cause to believe," "known or suspected abuse," and "observation or examination which discloses evidence of abuse." Despite shades of difference, the basic thrust of the reporting laws is the same across the United States. Reporting is triggered when a professional has evidence that would lead a competent professional to believe that abuse or neglect is reasonably likely. According to the California reporting law,

> Reasonable suspicion means that it is objectively reasonable for a person to entertain a suspicion, based upon the facts that could cause a reasonable person in like position, drawing, when appropriate, on his or her training and experience, to suspect child abuse. (California Penal Code § 11166(a))

The Wisconsin Court of Appeals (*State v. Hurd*, 1986) shed light on the meaning of *reasonable suspicion:*

> Whether a person possesses a reasonable suspicion that child abuse has occurred . . . examines the totality of the facts and circumstances actually known to, and as viewed from the standpoint of, that person. Thus, the test becomes whether a prudent person would have had a reasonable cause to suspect child abuse if presented with the same totality of circumstances as that acquired and viewed by the [professional].
>
> The phrase "reasonable cause to suspect" is a readily ascertainable and understandable standard that involves a belief, based on evidence, but short of proof, that an ordinary person would reach as to the existence of child abuse. (p. 46)

Still not clear? I'm not surprised. The "reasonable certainty" standard is inherently vague. Unfortunately, ethics codes and professional writing on the subject (including this chapter) provide little insight into the meaning of *reasonable certainty.* Kalichman (1993) observes that "it is widely known that legal standards for reporting do not translate to standards of professional practice. As a result, professionals are left to define their own personal standards for what constitutes reasonable suspicions of child abuse" (pp. 146-147). In the final analysis, reasonable suspicion depends on the facts of each case, as interpreted through experience and judgment.

All that is required is reasonable suspicion of maltreatment. The law requires reporting of suspicion, not certainty.

It is important to note that the duty to report does *not* require the professional to "know" that abuse or neglect occurred (Committee on Professional Practice, 1995). All that is required is reasonable *suspicion* of maltreatment. The law requires reporting of suspicion, not certainty. A mandated reporter who postpones reporting until doubt is eliminated violates the reporting law. The law deliberately leaves the ultimate decision about maltreatment to investigating officials, not mandated reporters. Thus, Kalichman (1993) advises professionals "not to investigate the occurrence of child abuse by engaging in activities outside of ordinary professional roles" (p. 154). Zellman and Faller (1996) add that

> reporting laws ask professionals to be reasonably vigilant and to report their suspicions or beliefs that maltreatment occurred or is occurring. The laws are clear that no more is required: Indeed, professionals are precluded explicitly from conducting any further investigation, a prohibition reinforced by the short latency period before a report is required. (p. 365)

This is not to say that professions should ask no questions and consider no alternatives to abuse. The point is that in-depth investigation is the bailiwick of law enforcement and social services, not mandated reporters.

Consider this hypothetical case: You are a therapist, and you recently started treating a 7-year-old boy. The boy's parents are married, and the family seems stable. Until recently, the boy's school performance was satisfactory. A few weeks ago, however, things deteriorated precipitously. The boy became a discipline problem at school, and his academic work fell off the bottom of the chart. You are told by a school guidance counselor that a week ago the boy took a little girl behind the school building and forcibly touched her breasts. What should you do? First, is the boy a perpetrator who must be reported? Second, does the boy's sexual aggression and other behavior indicate that he may be a victim?

If I were the therapist, I would ask a few questions before filing a report. I would contact the guidance counselor to double-check my understanding of what happened behind the school building. If the boy admits to me that he touched the girl's breasts, I would make a report. Even if the boy denies the incident, I would report. It seems to me the evidence about the little girl rises to the level of reasonable suspicion and that a report is required. (In some states, a case is not reportable unless the perpetrator is a number of years older—for example, 5 years older—than the victim.)

Regarding the possibility that the boy himself is a victim of sexual abuse, I confess that I cannot figure out the answer to my own hypothetical. The literature tells us that sexual aggression in a 7-year-old child is a red flag (see Chapter 7, the section "Sexual Abuse," subsection "Substantive Evidence," sub-subsection "Symptoms That Can Provide Relatively Strong Evidence of Sexual Abuse"). Moreover, the sudden deterioration in the boy's school performance indicates that *something* is going on. But what? If I ask the boy and he describes being abused, then it is easy: I report. But what if the boy says nothing happened? (Cases like this make me happy that I'm just a professor, hiding safely in the ivory tower, and not a professional treating children in the real world.) So what would I do if the boy denied being abused? I think I would start by talking to the boy's mother. Perhaps she would have some ideas. If not, I believe I would report to CPS. My gut reaction is that the boy may have been sexually abused. I may be wrong, but I'll go with my gut feeling.

As the foregoing hypothetical makes clear, uncertainty about when to report causes considerable anxiety. (The hypothetical certainly made me uncomfortable.) Fortunately, the law does not require professionals to be "right." Thus, professionals do not violate the reporting law when they report suspected abuse that turns out not to exist. All the law requires is good faith and reasonable professional judgment.

❑ Do Mandated Reporters Report?

Professionals who are aware of the duty to report sometimes do not (Zellman, 1990). According to Finkelhor and Zellman (1991), "Large numbers of professionals fail to report suspected child abuse" (p. 335). Zellman and Faller (1996) report that although most professionals try to comply with the reporting law, "almost 40% of respondents [to a survey] admitted that at some time in their careers they had suspected abuse or neglect but had decided not to make a report" (p. 364) and that "a majority of children who are recognized as abused or neglected by mandated reporters do not enter the CPS report base. Most cases of suspected maltreatment known to professionals are not reported or investigated" (p. 364).

❑ Factors Influencing the Decision to Report

Reporting laws require the reporting of reasonable suspicion. Yet as we have seen, reasonable suspicion is a vague concept that provides little guidance. A more helpful approach is to consider factors that influence decision making about reporting.

IS THE EVIDENCE SUFFICIENT?

The stronger the evidence of abuse, the more likely a professional is to report (Zellman, 1990). In research studies, "The most frequently endorsed reason for failing to report was a lack of sufficient evidence that maltreatment had occurred" (Zellman & Faller, 1996, p. 365). Kalichman (1993) notes that "when abuse seems highly probable, almost all professionals appear likely to report" (p. 67). Thus, bruises and other physical signs are especially likely to instigate reporting. The same is true for verbal disclosures of abuse: "Studies have repeatedly shown that the majority of professionals will report when a child makes a specific statement alleging physical or sexual abuse" (p. 67). Kalichman concluded from his review of the literature that

> disclosures of child abuse can be interpreted as evidence of maltreatment and should surpass reporting thresholds. Disclosures of abuse or neglect by a child or perpetrator invariably warrant investigation. It is beyond the role of human services professionals to discern the credibility of a disclosure when the costs of undetected maltreatment are so high. Disclosures by persons other than the victim or perpetrator are more complex given the potential motives for accusations of child abuse. However, all disclosures or allegations of abuse warrant child protective system investigation to verify the occurrence of alleged abuse. (pp. 149-150)

When evidence of maltreatment hovers at or just below the level of reasonable suspicion, professionals sometimes opt against reporting. As the evidence gains strength, and especially as it surpasses the threshold of reasonable suspicion, professionals generally report.

WILL REPORTING DO MORE HARM THAN GOOD?

Professionals occasionally fail to report because they think reporting will do more harm than good. A study by Zellman (1990) found that

> mandated reporters do weigh potential efficacy in making decisions about reporting. Since in many cases would-be reporters believe that a report is more likely to harm than to help the child or family, concerns about efficacy put professionals in a bind. While they are required under the law to report suspected abuse and neglect, they often must do so believing that their report will not be helpful to anyone, and may in fact be harmful. (p. 334)

Some professionals doubt the ability of child protective services to intervene effectively. In Zellman's (1990) survey of mandated reporters, "Sixteen percent considered the poor quality of CPS services an important reason for not having reported" (p. 14). An anecdote illustrates doubts about CPS:

> One pediatrician who provides primary health care to extremely impoverished families spoke out publicly at a recent national conference in San Diego about her reasons for breaking the law. Based on her experience, families often failed to return for essential health services after a report was filed, but only in the most serious cases did child protective services (CPS) provide any assistance. Thus, the family lost health services, and she lost the opportunity to monitor the child's welfare and possibly intervene to improve family functioning. (Finkelhor & Zellman, 1991, p. 336)

WILL REPORTING UNDERMINE THERAPY?

Some mental health professionals worry that mandatory reporting deters sex offenders from seeking therapy. Berlin, Malin, and Dean (1991) examined the impact of mandatory reporting on the rate of self-referral to the Johns Hopkins Sexual Disorders Clinic. During the 10 years prior to institution of mandatory reporting, 73 adults self-referred to the Clinic for treatment of sexual deviance involving child victims. When mandatory reporting went into effect, self-referrals dropped to zero. Berlin et al. also examined the rate at which men in treatment admitted incidents of child sexual abuse. "Mandatory reporting deterred patients' disclosures about child sexual abuse that occurred during treatment. In 1988 the disclosure rate during treatment dropped from approximately 21 per year to zero" (p. 449).

Many mental health professionals believe that mandatory reporting undermines the therapist-client relationship (Kalichman, 1993). In point of fact, however, little research supports this concern, and some professionals argue that successful treatment and mandatory reporting are not mutually exclusive. Watson and Levine (1989) state that "it is possible . . . that it is trust, not absolute confidentiality, that is essential for the psychotherapeutic relationship. Trust may develop or be maintained even though confidentiality can not be guaranteed or has been breached" (p. 255). Harper and Irvin (1985) opine that in some cases therapy can benefit from reporting. Kalichman (1993) adds that

> relative positive and negative effects of reporting on treatment most likely relate to the manner in which clients are informed of the limits of confidentiality, the sources of information leading to the suspicion, the quality of therapeutic alliance prior to reporting, and the degree to which the reporting process was integrated into therapy. (p. 54)

Steinberg, Levine, and Doueck (1997) surveyed 907 psychologists regarding the effects of reporting on the therapeutic relationship. Their findings echo those of Kalichman. Steinberg et al. reported that "a strong therapeutic alliance established prior to a mandatory report appears to be predictive of better outcome following the report, with respect to client reactions and client retention in treatment" (p. 119) and that

> the degree of explicitness with which the therapist presented the mandatory reporting requirement and the concomitant limits on confidentiality were related to client reactions. The more explicit the therapist was with the client, the more positive was the client's emo-

tional response. Further, there was a trend in the findings suggesting that explicitness may have resulted in better retention in treatment, although that outcome did not reach statistical significance. (p. 119)

Steinberg et al. concluded that

mandatory reporting does not necessarily do irrevocable damage to a therapeutic relationship. Although some 25% of clients may drop out, most are retained in treatment and many are able to overcome the negative feelings elicited by the report. Further, there are beneficial outcomes of reporting. In the present study, most of the therapists who had filed reports believed that their reporting resulted in at least the temporary cessation of the abuse. (p. 120)

HOW SERIOUS IS THE MALTREATMENT?

The more serious the maltreatment, the more likely it is that a report will be filed (Zellman, 1990). According to Kalichman (1993), "Signs of abuse that are indicative of severe abuse are also related to higher rates of reporting. Visible signs of maltreatment, therefore, generally constitute reasonable suspicion and exceed most professionals' thresholds for reporting" (p. 67).

WHAT KIND OF ABUSE IS IT?

Zellman (1990) found that professionals were more likely to report sexual abuse than physical abuse or neglect.

HOW CLEAR IS THE LAW IN THIS CASE?

When the reporting law clearly indicates that a report is required, professionals are likely to report (Zellman, 1990).

HOW OLD IS THE CHILD?

A report is more likely when a child is young (Zellman & Faller, 1996).

❑ Informed Consent, Confidentiality, and Forewarning

Informed consent is a requirement for medical and mental health treatment (Reed, 1992). Informed consent is discussed in Chapter 6. A vital component of informed consent is informing clients of the limits of confidentiality. Prospective clients should understand that the duty to report child abuse *overrides* confidentiality (Crenshaw & Lichtenberg, 1993). According to a committee of the American Psychological Association, "It is advisable at the outset of treatment to inform your clients that the usual rule concerning confidentiality does not apply when the duty to report child abuse arises" (Committee on Professional Practice, 1995, p. 378). Further, according to Smith and Meyer (1984),

> The fact that the therapist is required to report any patient disclosure of child abuse would be an important part of a patient's or client's determination of whether or not to enter therapy or to tell the therapist about the abuse. (p. 361)

Taylor and Adelman (1989) suggest the following language to inform teenagers and children of the limits of confidentiality:

> Although most of what we talk about is private, there are three kinds of problems you might tell me about that we would have to talk about with other people. If I find out that someone has been seriously hurting or abusing you, I would have to tell the police about it. If you tell me you have made a plan to seriously hurt yourself, I would have to let your parents know. If you tell me you have made a plan to seriously hurt someone else, I would have to warn that person. I would not be able to keep these problems just between you and me because the law says I can't. (p. 80)

❑ Liability Related to Reporting Suspected Child Maltreatment

This section discusses two liability issues arising from reporting laws: liability for *failure* to report and liability *for* reporting.

LIABILITY FOR FAILURE TO REPORT

If a professional fails to report suspected abuse and a child is abused or killed as a result, the professional can be sued for malpractice. General principles of malpractice are discussed in Chapter 9, and you may wish to review that material. In addition to broad principles of malpractice, which apply in every state, a few states have laws specifically authorizing lawsuits against professionals who willfully fail to report. A New York statute, for example, provides that "any person, official or institution required by [law] to report a case of suspected child abuse or maltreatment who knowingly and willfully fails to do so shall be civilly liable for the damages proximately caused by such failure" (N.Y. Social Services Law § 420(2)). Similar laws exist in Arkansas, Colorado, Iowa, Michigan, and Rhode Island.

The leading American case on malpractice liability for failure to report is *Landeros v. Flood,* decided by the California Supreme Court in 1976. Gita Landeros was born on May 14, 1970. In Gita's lawsuit against Dr. Flood, Gita's lawyer claimed that Gita was brutally beaten by her mother and stepfather. On April 26, 1971, when Gita was 11 months old, her mother took her to a hospital, where Gita was examined by Dr. Flood. The child was suffering from spiral fractures of both bones in her lower right leg, for which the mother had no explanation. Gita's back was covered with bruises, and she had scratches on other parts of her body. In addition, Gita had a healing skull fracture. Gita had the classic signs of battered-child syndrome (see Chapter 7, the section "Physical Abuse," subsection "Battered-Child Syndrome").

Unfortunately, Dr. Flood failed to diagnose child abuse. Because he did not diagnose abuse, he did not report to the authorities. Gita was released from the hospital and taken home, where she was further brutalized with blows to her eye and back, puncture wounds to her leg and back, bites on her face, and second- and third-degree burns on her hand. On July 1, 1971, a little more than 2 months after her examination by Dr. Flood, Gita was taken to a different hospital, where a different doctor immediately diagnosed battered-child syndrome and notified the authorities. Gita was placed in foster care. Gita's parents fled but were captured and convicted of child abuse.

Gita sued Dr. Flood, claiming that his failure to diagnose and report the abuse was medical malpractice. Essentially, Gita's lawyer argued that if Dr. Flood had properly diagnosed battered child syndrome and reported to authorities, Gita would not have suffered the second round of abuse. Thus, according to Gita's claim, even though Dr. Flood did not himself inflict the second round, he was legally obligated to compensate Gita for the second round of injuries. The California Supreme Court agreed, ruling that if the facts turned out to be as Gita's lawyer claimed, then Dr. Flood's failure to diagnose and report child abuse was malpractice.

The lesson of *Landeros v. Flood* is simple. Professionals who fail to diagnose and report suspected maltreatment may be financially liable if a child suffers further abuse (e.g., *Stecker v. First Commercial Trust*, 1998). This is true for sexual abuse and neglect as well as for physical abuse.

In addition to civil liability along the lines of *Landeros v. Flood*, failure to report may spur state licensing officials to take administrative action against a professional. In *Matter of Schroeder* (1988), for example, a psychologist's license was restricted because he failed to report known child sexual abuse committed by two of the psychologist's clients.

Deliberate failure to report is a crime, and in a small number of cases, professionals who fail to report are prosecuted. *State v. Hurd* (1986) is a straightforward example. Hurd was the administrator of a private youth ranch and school and thus was a mandated reporter. Six boys lived at the ranch. Also living at the ranch was a man who sexually abused a number of the boys. Hurd knew of the abuse but did not report it. Hurd was convicted of willfully failing to report suspected child abuse.[1]

Also instructive is *People v. Cavaiani* (1988), in which a woman suspected that her husband was sexually abusing their 9-year-old daughter. The woman contacted a therapist named Cavaiani, who began treating the family. During individual therapy sessions, the child told Cavaiani that her father fondled her breasts. When Cavaiani questioned the father, the father stated that if he touched the child, it was accidental and nonsexual. Cavaiani did not report. Some time later, the child disclosed her father's conduct to a counselor at school, who reported to CPS. When the prosecutor learned that Cavaiani had failed to report, Cavaiani was charged with a misdemeanor. As the case against Cavaiani made its way slowly through the legal system, the Michigan Court of Appeals had the opportunity to write:

> In this case, the victim told defendant [Cavaiani], and the victim's father did not deny, that the abuse occurred. Therefore, defendant had more than a "reasonable suspicion" of its occurrence. The Legislature intentionally used "reasonable cause to suspect" as the threshold for requiring a report in the belief that public policy is better served by investigating possibly unfounded reports of child abuse than by failing to investigate where abuse may prove to have occurred.
>
> Defendant, in the course of exercising professional judgment, might have concluded that the information supplied to him indicating that the victim was being abused was inaccurate or some kind of fantasy. That hardly makes the [reporting] statute vague or overbroad. Defendant had reasonable suspicion of child abuse, but concluded that his suspicions were not factually founded. With respect to defendant's legal obligations under [the reporting law], it was not for him to make this determination, but for the responsible investigative agencies, such as the Department of Social Services, to make. While defendant is free to decide that the victim's allegations are untrue for purposes of rendering professional treatment, he is not free to arrogate to himself the right to foreclose the possibility of a legal investigation by the state. (pp. 412-413)

LIABILITY FOR REPORTING

Lawsuits for *failure* to report are rare. Lawsuits *for* reporting, on the other hand, are more common, although far from ubiquitous. In the typical case, the subject of a report, usually an angry parent, brings a lawsuit against the reporter. The parent claims that the report was baseless and that reporting triggered an unwarranted investigation.

In discussing lawsuits against reporters, it is essential to mention the immunity provided by reporting laws. In one form or another, all reporting laws provide reporters with immunity from liability. The Rhode Island law is typical: "Any person participating in good faith in making a report pursuant to [the reporting law] shall have immunity from any liability, civil or criminal, that might otherwise be incurred or imposed" (R.I. General Laws § 40-11-4).

It is important to understand what immunity provisions do *not* do. Immunity does not prohibit angry parents from suing. What immunity does is give professionals a way out of lawsuits *after* the suits are filed. (For more on the limits and benefits of immunity, see Chapter 9, the section "Constitutional Rights," subsection "Immunity From Liability.")

> *It is important to understand what immunity provisions do not do. Immunity does not prohibit angry parents from suing.*

Immunity provisions of reporting laws vary from state to state. In a few states, immunity is absolute, affording reporters a very early escape from a lawsuit and, in many cases, discouraging lawsuits altogether. Most states, however, grant qualified rather than absolute immunity. In qualified-immunity states, immunity extends only to reports made in good faith. In many qualified-immunity states, the law gives the reporter an advantage by creating a legal presumption of good-faith reporting (e.g., N.Y. Social Services Law § 419). When the law presumes good faith, the reporter does not have the burden in court of proving good faith. Rather, the burden of proof falls on the person suing to rebut the presumption and establish that the reporter acted in bad faith. Basically, the presumption of good faith gives the reporter a leg up in court.

Immunity clearly covers the act of reporting. In many states, immunity extends beyond the report to acts leading up to the report and, after the report is filed, to communication with investigators and testifying in court (*May v. Southwest Wyoming Mental Health Center*, 1993; *Thomas v. Chadwick*, 1990).

Quite a few states have laws that penalize deliberately fabricated reports. Iowa law, for example, provides that

> a person who reports or causes to be reported to the department of human services information regarding an alleged act of child abuse, knowing that the information is false or that the act did not occur, commits a simple misdemeanor. (Iowa Code § 232.75(3))

❏ General Guidelines Regarding Reporting

In his excellent book on reporting, Kalichman (1993) offers the following guidelines:

- Knowledge of state laws regarding requirements to report suspected child maltreatment is necessary for all mandated reporters.

- Treatment and research professionals need standard informed-consent procedures that clearly detail the conditions under which confidentiality is limited.

- Disclosures of child abuse can be interpreted as evidence of maltreatment and should surpass reporting thresholds.

- Suspicions of child maltreatment based on behavioral or physical indicators that do not appear to warrant reporting require close evaluation before reporting can be completely dismissed.

- Professionals operate within their areas of competence and defined professional roles and should not overstep their limitations to verify the occurrence of child abuse.

- It is necessary to inform parents or guardians of a report before it is filed unless doing so would endanger the welfare of the child or children. ·

- Professionals should keep thorough and detailed records of information released in a report.

- Professionals are expected to follow up on reports to the child protection system.

- When professionals do not report suspected child maltreatment because they have caused a report to be filed by someone else, it is necessary to follow up on the case and verify that a report was filed with the child protection system.

- Cases of suspected child abuse that do not surpass reporting criteria should be discussed with a colleague to achieve some degree of objective reliability in reporting decisions.

- Training in recognizing signs of child maltreatment should be obtained by all human service professionals to the degree to which they have potential contact with abused children or abusive adults. (pp. 149-151)

❏ Are There Alternatives to Universal Mandatory Reporting?

Professionals in the United States tend to take mandatory reporting for granted, as if it were inevitable. It comes as a bit of a surprise to learn that not everyone thinks mandatory reporting is a great idea, and that not all countries require reporting (Thompson-Cooper, Fugere, & Cormier, 1993). Belgian child psychiatrist Catherine Marneffe (1996) has criticized the current child protection system, including mandatory reporting, and argued for what she perceives to be a more empathic and caring approach:

> *It comes as a bit of a surprise to learn that not everyone thinks mandatory reporting is a great idea, and that not all countries require reporting.*

Parents and children would be free to choose their therapist and always be involved in each decision process. Help should be and stay an offer, not an obligation, which implies a voluntary participation system and not a mandatory reporting system. . . .

Therefore, treatment of abused and neglected children must be based on a clear separation from the judicial system, which is a necessary condition to establish a trustful relationship with the families. How can treatment be successful if parents are not provided with an assurance of privacy and a sense of trust, which permits the most open and intimate expression of thoughts and feelings? (pp. 381-382)

Marneffe has asserted that

successful therapeutic responses to child abuse and neglect are perfectly possible if a new model in child protection is offered based on empathy, trust, and encouragement for those who fail in raising their children instead of the traditional approaches, based on mandatory reporting, control, judgment, and sanctions. (p. 383)

Short of abandoning mandatory reporting, Finkelhor and Zellman (1991) offer a provocative proposal that they call "flexible reporting options." Under their proposal, certain highly skilled professionals would have reporting options that are not currently available in the United States. "One option might be to defer the report until a later time. Another option might be to make the report in confidence, deferring an investigation until later, or indefinitely" (p. 337).

It is worth remembering that mandatory reporting did not come down from the mountaintop with Moses. Rather than assuming that mandatory reporting is etched in stone, ask yourself whether Finkelhor, Zellman, and Marneffe may be on to something.

❏ Two Problems for Your Consideration

In the following two cases, would you report suspected child abuse?

FIVE-YEAR-OLD SALLY

Sally attends kindergarten at her neighborhood school. It is near the end of the school year. Earlier in the school year, Sally's mom and dad separated, and they are now locked in a bitter divorce and custody battle. Sally lives most of the time with her mother but spends 1 or 2 days a week at her dad's apartment. Both parents take an interest in Sally's education. Until her mother and father separated, Sally was doing well in school. She is a bright little girl who seemed to shine at school and was well liked by her classmates. Recently, however, Sally's teacher noticed that Sally was increasingly subdued and withdrawn. No longer was she the spontaneous, bubbly little girl that she had been. Worried, the teacher took Sally aside and asked, "Sally, are you okay?" No reply. The teacher continued, "Lately you seem worried. Is there anything I can do?" Still no reply. The teacher asked, "Is there anything you would like to tell me?" Sally looked at the floor and said, "No. I'm just sad, I mean, um, I'm just tired." A few days later, the teacher noticed Sally and 5-year-old Eric hiding in the back of the classroom kissing on the mouth. The teacher gently intervened and said, "Children, it's not okay to kiss here at school. I'm glad you two are friends, but you can show your friendship in other ways." Sally ran from the room. When the teacher caught up with her, Sally was crying hysterically.

Question: If you are Sally's teacher, will you report Sally to CPS? If so, what persuades you that there is reasonable suspicion of some kind of child maltreatment? What kind of maltreatment do you suspect? For my thoughts on Sally's case, see page 334.

BILL'S CONFESSION

Bill, aged 45, entered psychotherapy for treatment of depression. Although Bill has a long history of depression, he has maintained steady employment as a computer programmer. Bill never married. During the 10th week of therapy, Bill said,

> There is something I want to tell you. It's been eating away at me for years, but I've never told anyone. About 8 years ago, I molested a teenage boy. Well, to be honest, he wasn't a teenager. He was only 11 at the time. He's 19 now and is away at college. He lived down the block, and he used to stop by my place once in a while to admire my sports car. One day I was washing the car and he stopped by on his bike. After I finished the car I invited him in to watch TV. One thing led to another, and eventually, well, I took off his clothes and put his penis in my mouth. It only happened once, and I felt terrible. I've felt terrible ever since. It's just that I was so depressed and lonely at the time. I was desperate for human contact. Lately I've been lonely again. There's nobody in my life. I keep thinking about that time 8 years ago. I feel guilty, but I have to confess, I fantasize about it over and over. I've never touched another kid, but I just can't stop thinking about it.

Question: If you are Bill's therapist, will you report the 8-year-old molestation to CPS? Remember, the victim is now an adult. See page 335.

❏ Note

1. Hurd's conviction was reversed on appeal because the trial judge made a mistake in instructing the jury.

4

Investigative Interviewing Regarding Child Maltreatment

Investigating suspected child abuse and neglect is a difficult responsibility requiring skill and patience. In sexual abuse cases, the child is usually the only eyewitness. Medical and corroborating evidence are often unavailable, and the child's credibility takes center stage, raising complex questions about memory, suggestibility, and, in particular, the ways that children are interviewed (McGough, 1994). In physical abuse cases, the investigation usually focuses on medical evidence of abuse and identifying the perpetrator. Interviewing and the child's credibility play a less central role in physical abuse and neglect cases.

Interviewing children about possible maltreatment is an extremely important and challenging task (Morgan, 1995; Perry & Wrightsman, 1991). This chapter emphasizes investigative interviews designed to determine whether abuse occurred. The chapter is directly relevant to CPS social workers, law enforcement officers, and mental health and medical professionals who interview children about abuse and neglect.

At first glance, this chapter, with its emphasis on investigative interviewing, may seem only tangentially relevant to medical and mental health professionals who treat abused and neglected children. Nothing could be further from the truth. Important legal issues arise *whenever* professionals interact with children who may be victims of maltreatment, whether the interaction occurs in a police station or a clinic. The legal implications of talking to children cut across all settings.

Important legal issues arise whenever professionals interact with children who may be victims of maltreatment, whether the interaction occurs in a police station or a clinic. The legal implications of talking to children cut across all settings.

Chapter 4 is divided into two main sections. The first examines the increasing criticism directed at professionals who interview children. The second goes into detail about interviewing, with an emphasis on children's memory and suggestibility, as well as proper and improper interview practices.

Chapter 5 continues the discussion of investigation with in-depth analysis of the vitally important but poorly understood role of professionals in documenting *verbal* evidence of abuse and neglect. Chapter 5 also discusses key issues such as videotaping investigative interviews, multidisciplinary investigation, and evaluation of bizarre and fantastic allegations of abuse by young children.

❑ The Attack on the Interviewer

During the 1980s, when child sexual abuse charges were filed, who was the primary target of the defense attorney? The child. The defense asserted that young children are incompetent witnesses, have poor memories, cannot differentiate fact from fantasy, and do not understand the need to tell the truth. The attack on older children and adolescents sometimes centered on charges that these children were seeking revenge.

The child is usually the state's most important witness, and it is not improper for the defense attorney to undermine the child's credibility. Some children, after all, are not competent to testify, and an occasional child lies or distorts the truth. What is interesting today, however, at the end of the 20th century, is a change in strategy among defense attorneys. Increasingly, defense attorneys take aim not only at children but also at the professionals who interview or treat them.

Until the 1990s, interviewers were seldom the target of defense efforts to prove that sexual abuse did not occur. Not so today. The new rallying cry of the defense is "attack the interviewer." Defense attorneys accuse interviewers of tainting children's memories with leading questions. The defense argues that interviewers coerce malleable young minds into believing things that never happened. The goal of this defense strategy is to undermine the child's credibility by attacking the adults who talked to the child.

There is no denying that defective interviewing exists. Indeed, there is reason to believe that poor interviewing was relatively common during the 1980s. Despite the assertions of some critics, however, there is no concrete evidence that indefensible interviewing was or is the norm. Moreover, serious efforts are underway to improve the skills of interviewers (Myers, 1996). Books and articles on interviewing proliferated after 1990 (see Hewitt, 1998; Poole & Lamb, 1998; Saywitz & Elliott, 1999). Interviewing is a regular topic at national and regional conferences. Many state and local agencies have increased training for interviewers. Pat Schene, the former director of the American Humane Association's Children's Division, observed that during the past 10 years, "Numerous forces have moved the training agenda forward" (personal communication, July 20, 1994). Although bad interviewing persists, concerted efforts to train interviewers have borne fruit. Indeed, the increased attention to forensically defensible interviewing is one of the most important and positive accomplishments of the past decade.

❑ Interviewing

This section discusses interviewing. The section begins with analysis of children's memory and suggestibility. From there, we turn to some of the practical problems faced by interviewers, including proper and improper interviewing practices.

Dr. Gail S. Goodman of the University of California at Davis and Dr. Karen J. Saywitz of the University of California at Los Angeles are two of the world's leading authorities on children's memory and suggestibility. They are also experts on interviewing. This section draws heavily on their wisdom and research. Portions of this section were published as Myers, Goodman, and Saywitz (1996).

CHILDREN'S MEMORY CAPACITY

A child's ability to provide accurate information during interviews depends on the child's capacity to remember. Scientists have yet to unlock all the secrets of memory. There is general agreement, however, that memory is not like a videotape that is simply replayed (Jones, 1992). Rather, memories of specific events are reconstructed through complicated cognitive processes that mature with age (Fivush, 1993).

A large body of psychological research exists on children's memory (Cassel & Bjorklund, 1995; Fivush & Hudson, 1990; Goodman & Bottoms, 1993; Nelson & Ross, 1980; Zaragoza, Graham, Hall, Hirschman, & Ben-Porath, 1995). Overall, research establishes that children, including preschool-age children, have substantial memory capacity. "Children have good memories. Even children as young as two and three years old can accurately recall information about personally experienced events over extended periods of time" (Berliner, 1997, p. 8). Generally, as children get older, they can provide more information about events they have experienced. Regarding children's general memory capability, Lamb (1994) stated, "It is clear that young victims are able to provide reliable and accurate accounts of events they have witnessed or experienced" (p. 1024). Fivush and Shukat (1995) add that "research over the last decade has amply demonstrated that even quite young children are able to recall personally experienced events accurately over extended periods of time" (p. 6). Finally, Baker-Ward, Gordon, Ornstein, Larus, and Clubb (1993) report that "recent investigators of preschoolers' long-term retention of selected personal experiences have successfully challenged earlier views of young children's recall abilities as being quite restricted. . . . Young children's reports of personally experienced events can be extensive and accurate" (p. 1530).

Memory is not perfect in children or adults, but "it is important not to exaggerate the fallibility of human memory. Memory is often wonderfully detailed and accurate" (Lindsay & Reed, 1994, p. 293). In the final analysis, when the question is whether to believe children, memory capacity is not the issue. Children as young as 2 and 3 can remember events that they have experienced (Bauer & Mandler, 1990).

If memory capacity is not the issue, what is? Suggestibility. The truly worrisome issue is not basic memory capacity, which is good, but the possibility that memory can be distorted by suggestive questioning. Before turning to suggestibility, however, it is useful to describe five types of memory: free recall, cued recall, recognition, script memory, and so-called repressed or recovered memory. Understanding these types of memory will be helpful when we turn to the practical obstacles faced by interviewers.

Free Recall

A child uses free recall when he or she recalls an event without assistance from external cues or stimuli to trigger memory. With free recall, the child relies on internal memory strategies to bring forth recollection. Free recall "is the most complex form of memory. It requires that previously observed events be retrieved from memory with few or no prompts" (Perry, 1987, p. 489).

One of the most consistent findings of research on children's memory is that young children are not as adept at free recall as older children, adolescents, and adults. As Spencer and Flin (1993) summarize,

To date, research has shown clearly that the most salient and consistent age difference in witnessing is found when the memory test is free recall. This means that the subject is asked to recount everything he or she remembers without prompting, such as "Describe everything you saw." In response to this type of questioning, younger children typically report less information than older children and adults, but most significantly, the information they do recall is generally accurate. (p. 289)

As reported by Spencer and Flin, one of the most stable findings of research on children's memory is that when young children are asked open-ended questions such as "What happened?"—requiring free recall—they spontaneously recall less information than older children and adults (Goodman, Rudy, Bottoms, & Aman, 1990). Young children's answers to free-recall questions are often very short, on the order of three or four words (Davies, 1996). Pipe, Gee, and Wilson (1993) observe that "when children are simply asked to describe something that has happened, their accounts are frequently very brief" (p. 25). Goodman, Quas, Batterman-Faunce, Riddlesberger, and Kuhn (1994) add that "one of the most reliable findings in the memory-development literature is that young children have difficulty retrieving detailed episodic memories on their own" (p. 271). Saywitz, Snyder, and Lamphear (1996) reported that "young children's free-recall responses are typically incomplete and brief ('We played')" (p. 201).

The dilemma caused by young children's brief answers to open-ended free-recall questions is particularly pronounced with some timid 2- and 3-year-olds. It is not unusual for a very young child to answer "Nothing" to the question "What happened?" even though the child remembers the incident. It can be very difficult to determine, solely on the basis of a young child's responses to open-ended questions, what, if anything, happened.

Although young children often provide frustratingly short answers to open-ended questions, the information they provide in response to such questions is likely to be accurate (Batterman-Faunce & Goodman, 1993; Carter, Bottoms, & Levine, 1996; Roberts & Blades, 1996). According to Cassel et al. (1995), "Although young children's free recall of events is typically low, it is usually accurate" (p. 508).

Of course, free recall is not error-free. In particular, free recall can be contaminated by suggestive questioning (Brainerd & Poole, 1997; Leichtman & Ceci, 1995; Poole & Lindsay, 1998; Poole & White, 1995).

Because young children are not proficient in free recall, they are not adept in responding to open-ended questions such as "What can you tell me about that?" According to Pipe et al. (1993), "Free recall alone is therefore seldom likely to be a satisfactory basis for obtaining children's testimony" (p. 26). Consequently, interviewers often find it necessary to ask young children suggestive and even mildly leading questions to trigger their memories. Saywitz et al. (1996) reminded us that "young children rely on adult questions to trigger retrieval of additional information" (p. 201). According to Lamb, Sternberg, and Esplin (1995),

> Even the most skillful investigators use direct and leading questions when interviewing young children and the inclusion of such questions does not invalidate the testimony, provided that steps are taken to limit potential damage by framing focused questions carefully, avoiding coercive repetition, and by pairing direct or leading questions with open-ended prompts so as to return the child to recall. (p. 439)

Cued Recall

A child uses cued recall when some stimulus reminds the child of something from the past. The stimulus "brings back the memory." With cued recall, the memory-jogging stimulus is something *other than* the reappearance of the precise thing remembered. Something triggers a mental association in the child's mind between the stimulus and the thing—person, place, or event—that is stored in memory. Thus, a child may see a car that reminds the child of the car driven by the kidnapper.

In many cases, the cue that triggers memory is a question. Because young children have a relative deficit in free recall when compared to older children and adults, interviewers often rely on cued recall to learn what children remember (Fivush, 1993). A child who says very little in response to open-ended questions may supply vital information when questions tap cued recall. Lamb et al. (1995) describe some of the difficulties facing interviewers:

In general, young children tend to provide briefer accounts of their experiences than do older children and adults, but their accounts are quite accurate. . . . When prompted for more details ("Did he have a beard?"), however, . . . the probability of error rises dramatically, albeit alongside an increase in the number of details provided . . . . Children's responses are often very brief, and interviewers must thus probe further to signal that they are interested in detailed descriptions of specific incidents. . . . Although open-ended questions are most likely to encourage accurate accounts of events children have experienced, these accounts are often incomplete, especially when preschoolers are being interviewed. As a result, it is often necessary to begin asking more focused questions quite early in the interviews of young children. . . . Suggestive utterances should be avoided whenever possible. When a child does not address certain issues in response to open-ended and directive prompts, however, it may be necessary for investigators to ask leading or suggestive questions. (p. 439)

Cued recall develops early in life. By age 4, children are generally quite proficient at cued recall.

Recognition

With cued recall, a child's memory is jogged by a stimulus that is different from the thing remembered. With recognition memory, in contrast, a child who experienced something or observed someone in the past is presented with the same thing or person again, and the subsequent presentation triggers the child's memory. A classic example of recognition memory is a police lineup. If the perpetrator is in the lineup, the perpetrator triggers recognition memory. Bjorklund (1995) describes recognition memory as "the most basic form of retrieval . . . , in which a person remembers a familiar stimulus upon being presented with it again" (p. 233).

Recognition memory develops early in life, and 3- and 4-year-olds are good at recognition.

Script Memory

Script memory is common in adults and children. Events that are repeated a significant number of times form a mental script. Many children, for example, have a script memory of an outing to

McDonalds. The child might not remember what happened on a specific McDonalds visit, but the child has a script for what generally happens at the Golden Arches.

Mental scripts take on legal significance when a child is asked to describe a specific episode of an event that happened numerous times. Fivush (1993) notes that "when trying to recall a specific instance of an event that has been experienced many times, both children and adults have difficulty distinguishing any one occurrence from all other occurrences" (p. 19). Memory for specific instances can blur into a generic script of the repeated event.

Recovered or Repressed Memories

People occasionally remember events that have been long forgotten (Corwin & Olafson, 1997). Most of us have said, "Gosh, I haven't thought of that in years!" Sometimes, memories of bygone events are accurate, sometimes not. Adults occasionally "recover" long-dormant memories of abuse during childhood (Williams, 1998). Controversy exists over the reliability of adult recovered or repressed memories of childhood sexual abuse (Freyd, 1996; Loftus, 1997; *Ramona v. Superior Court*, 1997). In this chapter, however, we are interested not in *adult* memory, but in *children's* memory. The issue before us is the reliability of children's memories of relatively recent events, not adult memories of events that may have happened decades earlier.

To the extent that doubts exist about recovered memories in adults and, in particular, about psychotherapeutic techniques sometimes used to elicit such memories, such doubts should be confined to adults and should not be allowed to undermine confidence in children's general memory capacity. For the most part, the controversy swirling around adult recovered memories is not directly relevant to children's recall.

Although psychological literature on adult recovered memory for abuse during childhood is only marginally relevant to children's memory, it is useful to be aware of the literature regarding recovered and repressed memories.

Research by Williams (1994) sheds light on adult forgetting of sexual abuse during childhood. Williams studied 129 adult women who had documented evidence of sexual abuse during childhood.

The author located and interviewed the women 17 years following their abuse. Thirty-eight percent of the women had no recollection of their abuse during childhood. "Women who were younger at the time of the abuse and those who were molested by someone they knew were more likely to have no recall of the abuse" (p. 1167).

Of the 129 women interviewed by Williams (1995), 80 (62%) remembered their abuse. Among those who remembered being sexually abused as children, 1 in 10 stated that at some time in the past they had forgotten the abuse. Thus, 16% of women who recalled abuse occurring 17 years earlier had periods during which they did not remember. Williams (1995) concluded:

> This examination of recovered memories of child sexual abuse relied on a small sample and thus the statistical analyses must be considered preliminary. But these findings are important because they are based on a prospective study of all reported cases of child sexual abuse in a community sample. Because the abuse was documented in hospital and research records this is the first study to provide evidence that some adults who claim to have recovered memories of child sexual abuse recall actual events which occurred in childhood. These findings also are not limited to a clinical sample of women in treatment for child sexual abuse. The findings document the occurrence of recovered memories. There is no evidence from this study of child sexual abuse experienced in this community sample of women that recovery of memories was fostered by therapy or therapists. For this sample of women memories resurfaced in conjunction with triggering events or reminders and an internal process of rumination and clarification
>
> Regarding the accuracy of accounts, this study suggests that while the women's reports of some details have changed . . . the women's stories were in large part true to the basic elements of the original incident. . . . While these findings cannot be used to assert the validity of *all* recovered memories of child abuse, this study does suggest that recovered memories of child sexual abuse reported by adults can be quite consistent with contemporaneous documentation of the abuse and should not be summarily dismissed by therapists, lawyers, family members, judges or the women themselves. (pp. 669-670)

Some adults claim to remember being abused as infants or very young children. The phenomenon of infantile amnesia (discussed later in this chapter) casts doubt on such memories. According to Williams (1995),

Much of the literature on memory would bolster a hypothesis that there is an association between age at time of abuse and recall of the event in adulthood. Adult memories for events of very early childhood may be limited by what has been called "infantile amnesia." Empirical research on memory for events of childhood has suggested that the earliest recall does not go back to before the age of 3 or 4. (p. 651)

Elliott and Briere (1995) describe research on a national random sample of 724 individuals who responded to a questionnaire regarding delayed recall of trauma. The researchers state that

as has been found in other studies, a significant number of subjects reported delayed recall of childhood sexual abuse. Although less frequent than in clinical samples, 42% of sexually abused subjects reported some level of amnesia for the abuse, with 20% of sexual abuse victims describing a period of time when they were completely amnestic for the abuse. (p. 640)

(See also Widom & Shepard, 1996.)

Forgetting

Memory can fade. One child put it this way: "My memory is the thing I forget with." Forgetting is normal in adults and children (Koocher et al., 1995). Some research suggests that young children forget certain events more quickly than adults (Goodman et al., 1994). Moreover, it is important to add that

traumatic and stressful events can be retained over significant periods of time by young children. . . . For salient features of an event to which children attend, consider important, and thus encode well, children may at times be no more susceptible to forgetting, memory impairment, and suggestibility effects than adults. (Koocher et al., 1995, p. 213)

Whatever the resolution of research on forgetting, there is general agreement that it is a good idea to interview children (and adults) promptly. Moreover, although time takes its toll, children can accurately remember salient events months and years later. Fivush and Schwarzmueller (1995) report that "children as young as 2½ years of age are able to remember accurate details of their past experiences, and they can retain these memories even over a period of 1 to 2 years" (p. 563).

Childhood or Infantile Amnesia

Events that occur before the second or third birthday are often lost to later memory. The term *childhood or infantile amnesia* is used to describe this normal developmental phenomenon (Bauer, 1994). Freud (1916-1917/1966) described the "remarkable amnesia of child-hood . . . the forgetting which veils our earliest youth from us and makes us strangers to it" (p. 326).

The fact that adults seldom remember events from very early childhood does not mean that 2- and 3-year-old children lack the ability to remember recent events. Bauer (1994) describes psychological research on memory in very young children, writing that "children as young as three years of age already have well-organized representations of familiar events. . . . Children as young as two-and-a-half can provide verbal reports on past events" (p. 31).

The effect of infantile amnesia warrants skepticism when older children or adults describe "memories" of abuse during infancy or very early childhood.

Stress and Memory

Abuse is stressful. Thus, it is important to describe the impact of stress on memory (Berliner & Briere, 1998; Williams, 1998). "The nature and reliability of traumatic memories have been controversial in psychiatry for over a century" (van der Kolk & Fisler, 1995, p. 505). Until recently, most research on children's memory did not examine the effects of stress. In the past few years, however, a small number of studies examined children's and adults' memories for stressful events (Peterson, 1996; Peterson & Bell, 1996).

At one time, the dominant thinking in psychological circles was that stress had a debilitating effect on memory, and some researchers remain committed to this view. Recent research, suggests, however, that core features of stressful events can be durably retained in memory, whereas peripheral details may or may not be well remembered (Goodman, Bottoms, Schwartz-Kenney, & Rudy, 1991; Goodman, Hirschman, Hepps, & Rudy, 1991; Koocher et al., 1995).

Studies of children's memory for stressful events support the view that core features of such events can be well remembered. Goodman, Hirschman, et al. (1991) found that distress was associated with more complete recall and greater resistance to suggestion. Warren-Leubecker (1991) reports that children who were more upset about the space shuttle Challenger disaster remembered the event better than children who were less upset. Steward and Steward (1996) compared the memory reports of children who were less distressed during a painful medical procedure to memory reports of children who were more upset. As a group, children who were more upset reported a greater amount and more accurate information at an interview 6 months after the event, although a few of the highly upset children were particularly inaccurate. On the other hand, some researchers report decrements in memory for stressful experiences (Bugental, Blue, Cortez, Fleck, & Rodriguez, 1992; Merritt, Ornstein, & Spiker, 1994; Peters, 1991).

Several researchers studied children's memories for horrifying events such as witnessing homicides of loved ones, kidnappings, and sniper attacks at schools (Jones & Krugman, 1986; Pynoos & Eth, 1984; Pynoos & Nader, 1989; Terr, 1991). As one would expect, children traumatized in these ways demonstrate accuracies and inaccuracies of memory.

Summary

Children have good memory capacity. Children as young as 2 and 3 remember with sufficient accuracy to be credible reporters of events. Thus, children do not have a general memory deficit.

SUGGESTIBILITY

"Suggestibility refers to the susceptibility of memory to distortion or error" (Berliner, 1997, p. 10). Children's suggestibility has concerned professionals for years (Davis, 1998). Early in the 20th century, European writers cast a shadow over children's credibility. In 1910, German physician Baginsky opined "that children are the most dangerous of all witnesses" and argued that children's testimony should "be excluded from [the] court record whenever possible" (quoted in Whipple, 1911, p. 308). In 1911, Belgian psychologist Varendonck asked, "When are we going to give up, in all civilized nations, listening to children in courts of law?" (quoted in Goodman, 1984b, p. 9). In 1926, Brown wrote, "Create, if you will, an idea of what the child is to hear or see, and the child is very likely to hear or see what you desire" (p. 133). Freud added to skepticism of children's credibility with his theory that women and girls fantasize sexual assault (see Chapter 1, the section "The Long Tradition of Disbelieving Women and Children Who Claim to Be Victims of Sexual Abuse," subsection "Cycles of Recognition and Denial"). Yet, occasional endorsements of children's testimony lie scattered through the historical record. Blackstone (1769), the famous English judge of the 18th century, wrote that children "of very tender years often give the clearest and truest testimony" (p. 214).

Although a small amount of empirical study of children's suggestibility occurred during first half of the 20th century, it was not until the late 1980s that the modern era of psychological research on suggestibility commenced (Ceci & Bruck, 1993, 1995; Goodman, 1984b). What began as a small amount of research grew into a sizable corpus of empirical study. Today, although much remains to be learned, significant strides have been made to increase our understanding of children's suggestibility (Ceci & Huffman, 1997; Myers, Goodman, & Saywitz, 1996; Poole & Lamb, 1998; Warren & McGough, 1996).

There Is No Simple Relationship Between Age and Suggestibility

Psychological studies do not converge on a simple relationship between age and suggestibility (Garbarino & Scott, 1990; Zaragoza, 1987). Children are not invariably more suggestible than adults (Goodman, 1984a; Goodman et al., 1990). Suggestibility depends on the interaction of cognitive, developmental, emotional, and situational factors, including the child's interest in the event. Despite the complexity of the issue, modern research supports the following conclusions.

Older Children. By the time children reach age 9, 10, or 11, they approach adult levels of suggestibility (Cole & Loftus, 1987). This is not to say, of course, that children of this age are not suggestible: Given the right circumstances, everyone is suggestible. The point is that suggestibility in older children and adolescents is not appreciably greater than it is in adults.

Young Children, Particularly Young Preschoolers. Young children, particularly those age 5 and younger, appear to be more suggestible than older children and adults (Bruck, Ceci, Francoeur, & Barr, 1995; Ceci & Huffman, 1997). Ceci, Huffman, Smith, and Loftus (1994) state that "although even adults are suggestible, there appears to be a reliable age-related vulnerability to suggestive postevent questioning, with preschoolers disproportionately more vulnerable to these forms of suggestion than older children and adults" (p. 388). Consequently,

> There appears to be no useful purpose served by attempting to gainsay what is surely a scientifically robust conclusion, namely, that preschoolers present a special reliability risk if the postevent context has been riddled with repeated, erroneous suggestions. Young children's suggestibility proneness, while probably reduced for bodily events, is by no means nonexistent or negligible.
>
> Having said the above, it is important for the sake of balance to also say that children, no matter how much more suggestible they are than adults, are nevertheless capable of recollecting large amounts of forensically accurate information when the adults who have access to them have not engaged in repeated erroneous suggestions. In many of the studies that have reported age-related differences in suggestibility, young children perform quite well—until and unless an interviewer persists in making repeated erroneous suggestions or subtly rewards the child for inaccurate answers. Short of this, the children do quite well. (p. 389)

What about children who are beyond the preschool years but who are have yet to attain the age—9 to 11—when suggestibility approaches adult levels? Children in this range, like older children and adults, can be suggestible, and concern is warranted when leading questions are asked of such children. Research discloses, however, that children beyond the preschool years are able in many cases to resist misleading suggestions (Berliner, 1997).

As stated above, children, including preschoolers, are not invariably suggestible. Children can resist being misled by suggestive questions (Merritt et al., 1994). In some psychological studies that involve a single interview regarding potentially abusive actions, children who are 5 years old or older demonstrate considerable resistance to false suggestion. Even when children are questioned twice with misleading questions about possibly abusive acts, inaccuracies do not necessarily increase (Goodman & Aman, 1990). Berliner (1997) noted that

> in most laboratory studies, a majority of even young children successfully resist intentional efforts to mislead them, especially about the central aspects of personally experienced and emotionally relevant events. Errors about peripheral or irrelevant details are common among both children and adults. (p. 10)

As Melton et al. (1995) concluded, "Age does have some relation to suggestibility, but probably less than often has been assumed" (p. 59). Although young children are suggestible, they do not deserve the epithet "the most dangerous of all witnesses."

When studying children's suggestibility, it is important not to lose sight of the fact that adults are also suggestible (Lindsay, 1994). Too often in discussions of children's suggestibility, the suggestibility of adults is downplayed or ignored, leaving the inaccurate impression that children have cornered the market on suggestibility. Although concern regarding children's suggestibility is warranted, concern about children has been magnified out of proportion to reality. Suggestibility exists across the life span. Adults do not leave suggestibility behind to gather dust with the playthings of childhood.

Please, No More Indefensible Statements
About Children's Credibility!

During the 1980s, some professionals were under the mistaken impression that children are not suggestible, at least not about sexual abuse. Moreover, some professionals thought children do not lie about abuse. People said things such as "Children can't be misled about sexual abuse," "Children may be suggestible about some things, but not abuse," and "If the child said it, it has to be true." Is anybody out there still saying such things? If so, please pull them aside and talk some sense into them! Children *are* suggestible—not as suggestible as many adults believe, but suggestible nonetheless. Children do not lie very often about abuse, but it happens. Indefensible statements about children's suggestibility and truthfulness— meant to strengthen children's credibility—actually do just the opposite. Moreover, such statements make *all* professionals, not just the speakers, look stupid.

Trends in Psychological Research on Children's Suggestibility

As stated above, early psychological research on children's suggestibility painted a bleak picture. During the mid-20th century, psychologists devoted little attention to suggestibility (Ceci & Bruck, 1993; Goodman, 1984b). The 1980s witnessed the birth of the modern era of research. Although studies conducted during the 1980s established that young children are more suggestible than older children and adults, the research of the 1980s exploded the myth that children are invariably suggestible. Thus, from the standpoint of children's credibility, the 1980s was a high-water mark.

Beginning in the early 1990s, there was a resurgence of skepticism regarding children's credibility and, in particular, children's suggestibility. During the 1990s, a number of prominent researchers designed experiments to highlight children's suggestibility. Studies designed to illustrate children's weaknesses are legitimate and important. Such research sheds light on how *not* to interview children. Nevertheless, studies that focus disproportionately on children's weaknesses and that ignore their strengths have the potential to exaggerate children's suggestibility and unfairly undermine their credibility. Marxsen, Yuille, and Nisbet (1995) express concern about the increasingly negative psychological literature, which has tended to concentrate on the suggestibility of children and to neglect other topics relevant to those who investigate suspected cases of child sexual abuse.

That young children are more suggestible than adults is well-established. This does not mean that the investigative interviewing of children is impossible, only that it requires skill and care. However, the literature's overemphasis on suggestibility can give the police, the judiciary, the media, and the general public the mistaken impression that children are inherently unreliable. This is an issue of considerable moment because such an impression can be the basis for social decisions with far-reaching consequences.

The suggestibility problem is a complex one, but the literature [gives] the impression that children are simply untrustworthy witnesses. This is simply not true. (pp. 450-451)

Children do not have a monopoly on suggestibility. As Spencer and Flin (1993) note, "Whilst there is no doubt that children can be influenced by suggestion, it must be emphasised that adults too are notoriously susceptible to suggestive and leading questions" (p. 303). Lamb et al. (1995) caution that "we cannot continue holding children to a higher standard than adult witnesses" (p. 445). Although children have weaknesses, they have strengths too. Remember what Blackstone (1769) said so long ago: Children "of very tender years often give the clearest and truest testimony" (p. 214).

Suggestibility Is Multiply Determined

Suggestibility is not simply a matter of age. Thus, it is wrong to conclude that a 4-year-old is invariably more suggestible than a 40-year-old. "Knowing a child's age in itself is not enough" (Goodman & Schwartz-Kenney, 1992, p. 31). Suggestibility on a particular occasion depends on situational, developmental, and personality factors, including the type of event, how well it is remembered, the type of information sought by the interviewer (e.g., central details vs. peripheral details), the way the interview is conducted, whether the interviewer intimidates the child, and a host of other influences before and during the interview (Ceci & Huffman, 1997; Pezdek, Finger, & Hodge, 1997).

Questioning by Authority Figures and Social Demands of Interviews

Children are sometimes more suggestible when questioned by an authority figure (Ceci, Ross, & Toglia, 1987). Moreover, young children, particularly preschoolers, appear less able than older children to withstand the social demands of the interview (Cassel, Roebers, & Bjorklund, 1996). Thus, because they find it difficult to "stand their ground" in the face of suggestive questions, young children are at greater risk of going along with adult suggestions.

Suggestibility Regarding Central Details
Versus Peripheral Details; Participant Versus Bystander

Children, like adults, are more likely to give incorrect reports and to be more suggestible about peripheral details than about central, salient, memorable details (Dent, 1992). Child abuse is often highly salient, and a child who is questioned about abuse is likely to be less suggestible than a child questioned about an innocuous or poorly remembered event (Goodman & Saywitz, 1994).

Participation in an event, as opposed to mere observation, sometimes lowers suggestibility (Goodman et al., 1990; Tobey & Goodman, 1992). Participation may make the event more memorable.

The Effects of Stereotypes and Accusatory Atmosphere

An interviewer can create an atmosphere that is accusatory regarding a particular person, typically a suspect. In addition, an interviewer might describe an individual—again, usually a suspect—in negative terms. It comes as no surprise that negative stereotypes and an accusatory atmosphere cause some interviewees—children and adults—to be suggestible regarding the object of the unflattering commentary.

A study by Tobey and Goodman (1992) examined the effect on nonabused 4-year-olds of questioning by a police officer. The children experienced a staged, nonabusive event. The children played with a research assistant who was described to the children as a "baby-sitter." Eleven days later, the children were interviewed about the experience. Some of the children were interviewed in a neutral fashion by a research assistant; other children were interviewed by a police officer who said,

> I am very concerned that something bad might have happened the last time that you were here. I think that the babysitter you saw here last time might have done some bad things, and I am trying to find out what happened the last time you were here when you played with the babysitter.

The researchers compared the two groups of children in terms of their answers to interview questions put by the research assistant or the police officer. Questioning by the police officer had a deleterious impact on some children's accuracy, although "it is worth noting that only two children in the police condition seemed to be decisively misled by the police officer's suggestion that the babysitter may have done some bad things" (p. 790).

Leichtman and Ceci (1995) conducted research designed to highlight the danger of negative stereotypes during interviews of young children. In their study of nonabused preschool-aged children, one group of children was told on several occasions about a man named Sam Stone, who, according to the story, was very clumsy. Thus, the children were inculcated with the stereotype of a clumsy Sam Stone. Other children in the study did not receive this stereotyping information. Some time later, Sam Stone visited the children's preschool classroom. He stayed about 2 minutes but did nothing clumsy or unusual. Following Sam Stone's uneventful visit to the classroom, the children in both groups were interviewed once a week for 4 successive weeks—some with leading questions—about Sam Stone's visit. The leading questions contained an implication that Sam had ripped a book and soiled a teddy bear. Finally, at a fifth interview, the researchers examined the impact of leading questions on the children who had been told in advance that Sam Stone was clumsy. Children who had received the stereotyping message about Sam were more likely than other children to provide inaccurate information in response to leading questions. This study underscores the importance of avoiding questions that stereotype possible perpetrators.

Suggestibility Regarding Ambiguous Events

In some cases of suspected child sexual abuse, the touching of the child's body is ambiguous. For example, touching a young child's genitals may be proper caretaking or a crime, depending entirely on the adult's intent. Research indicates that young children may be especially susceptible to suggestion regarding ambiguous acts (Goodman & Clark-Stewart, 1991; Lepore & Sesco, 1994; Thompson, Clarke-Stewart, & Lepore, 1997).

> *Research indicates that young children may be especially susceptible to suggestion regarding ambiguous acts.*

When touch is ambiguous, a young child may not know how to interpret the touch: Was it a "good touch" or a "bad touch"? Because the child does not know what to make of it, the child may readily acquiesce in an interviewer's interpretation. On the other hand, if a child has a clear understanding of what happened and what it meant, the child will probably be less suggestible (see Pezdek & Roe, 1997). Clearly, when touch is ambiguous, interviewers must avoid questions that suggest one interpretation over another.

It should be added that although children may go along with suggestive questions about the *meaning* of ambiguous events, children are less suggestible regarding *what* they observed. A child might be led astray about the meaning of an ambiguous touch, but the child could probably describe the touch itself.

Lowering Suggestibility

Suggestibility can be lowered by preparing children for interviews (Pezdek & Greene, 1993; Siegal & Peterson, 1995; Warren, Hulse-Trotter, & Tubbs, 1991). Children can be told to pay close attention and to report only what "really happened." The interviewer can inform the child that certain questions may be difficult to understand and that the child should not guess or make up answers. Dent (1991) advises telling children that the interviewer does not know what happened and that children are free to say, "I don't know."

Saywitz, Geiselman, and Bornstein (1992) suggest that children be given instructions such as the following:

> 1. "There may be some questions that you do not know the answers to. That's okay. Nobody can remember everything. If you don't know the answer to a question, then tell me 'I don't know,' but do not make anything up. It is very important to tell me only what you really remember. Only what really happened."
> 2. "If you do not want to answer some of the questions, you don't have to. That's okay. Tell me 'I don't want to answer that question.' "
> 3. "If you don't know what something I ask you means, tell me 'I don't understand' or 'I don't know what you mean.' Tell me to say it in new words."
> 4. "I may ask you some questions more than one time. Sometimes I forget that I already asked you that question. You don't have to change your answer, just tell me what you remember the best you can." (p. 756)

THE VOCABULARY OF INVESTIGATIVE INTERVIEWS

Professionals use several words to describe types of questions, including *open-ended, focused, specific, suggestive,* and *leading,* to name the most common. There is no universally agreed-on meaning of these terms. Nevertheless, employing the terms consistently is helpful, and, to that end, definitions are offered below.

The greatest concern focuses on suggestive questions. *Webster's Ninth New Collegiate Dictionary* (1985) defined *suggestive* as "indicative," "stimulating thought," and "stirring mental associations" (p. 1180). Given this expansive definition, nearly any question can be suggestive. "As Binet (1900) was the first to point out, all questions are intrinsically suggestible in that they imply there is a right answer" (Davies, 1996, p. 241). Whether a question is suggestive depends on how the question is asked, by whom, and where the question fits into the entire socio-psycho-linguistic context of the interview. Suggestiveness is plainly a matter of degree and context, with some questions highly suggestive and others barely so.

It is useful to think of suggestiveness as a continuum and to array our descriptive words along this continuum (see Figure 4.1). *Open-*

Open-Ended ⟶ Focused ⟶ Specific ⟶ Leading

Figure 4.1. The Continuum of Suggestiveness

ended questions reside at the least suggestive—and least worrisome—end of the continuum. Open-ended questions include general inquiries such as "Can you tell me about that?" and "Did anything happen?" Often open-ended questions are little more than invitations to speak.

Moving along the continuum from left to right, we encounter *focused questions.* A focused question may be defined as one that focuses a child's attention on a particular topic, place, or person but that refrains from providing information about the object of the question. For example, "Shall we talk about preschool now?" focuses the child on preschool but does not suggest that the questioner wants any particular information about preschool.

Many of the "Wh" questions common to interviews are focused. Thus, questions such as "Where did that happen?" "Who was there?" and "When did that happen?" are often focused.

When a child describes abuse, avoid "why" questions. From a child's perspective, "why" questions can sound like attributions of blame. Although the interviewer may not see it that way, the child's interpretation is reasonable. Place yourself in a child's shoes and consider these "why" questions: "Why did you go with the man?" "Why did you get in his car?" "Why didn't you ask him to stop?"

There is no bright line separating focused from *specific questions.* In many cases, a specific question is simply a question that probes for greater detail following a child's answer to open-ended or focused questions. Frequently, although not invariably, specific questions have greater potential for suggestivity than questions that simply focus a child's attention.

Specific questions sometimes call for short answers. Thus, "What color was his jacket?" is a specific question. Specific questions such as "Was the jacket red?" sometimes require "yes-no" answers.

Whether such questions are suggestive or leading can depend on the context in which the questions are asked. If the child has not mentioned someone wearing a jacket, then such questions suggest that someone was dressed in a jacket. By contrast, if the child has already mentioned someone in a jacket, such questions are less suggestive.

A *leading question* is a question that, to one degree or another, suggests that the questioner is looking for a particular answer. The California Evidence Code definition is typical: "A leading question is a question that suggests to the witness the answer that the [questioner] desires" (1998, § 764). Of course, leading questions come in black and white and innumerable shades of gray. Few would disagree that "He touched your pee-pee, isn't that right?" is not only leading but highly so. Linguists use the term *tag question* to describe such questions (Walker, 1994). A tag question is essentially a statement of fact followed by a request for agreement. A further example of a tag question is "He took you there three times. Isn't that right?" Separating this question into two sentences allows us to see the statement of fact followed by the request for agreement "tagged" on at the end.

Compare the foregoing with a situation in which a child spontaneously describes an act of abuse and the interviewer follows up with "How many times did that happen?" Clearly, this is not as suggestive as a tag question. Some might argue that the question is not suggestive at all. Others would disagree, arguing that the question is mildly leading because it suggests that the interviewer believes that more than one episode of abuse occurred.

One useful method of evaluating questions is to ask whether the question builds on information provided spontaneously by the child. If so, concern about suggestivity is lessened. On the other hand, if a question introduces new information not previously mentioned by the child, concern about suggestivity increases.

In the final analysis, labels such as *focused, specific,* and *leading* provide little more than a starting place for analysis of suggestivity. Accurate analysis requires consideration of each question in turn, along with analysis of the questions that precede it. Each question is a thread in a tapestry. To see the pattern, it is necessary to stand back and gaze on the whole.

RECREATING CONTEXT: PROPS AND
ANATOMICALLY DETAILED DOLLS

Recreating the context of an event can influence memory and
suggestibility (Spencer & Flin, 1993). Children's memories may be
influenced more strongly by contextual factors than the memories of
adults. During interviews, it is sometimes useful to use props to
create context and help children remember (Pipe et al., 1993). According to Koocher et al. (1995),

> It is well known that young children's reports of events are often less
> complete than those of older children and adults. It is also well known
> that cues and reenactment can at times result in elicitation of more
> complete information from children. (p. 200)

Pipe et al. (1993) similarly state that

> context cues have been found to be effective in prompting children's
> recall in natural environments and may be especially important for
> very young children, for whom memory may be strongly tied to
> context. Taking children back into the situation in which an event
> occurred or providing very specific physical cues related to the event
> may therefore provide stimulus support for children's recall. . . .
> Despite the potential benefits of cues and props, there may also be
> disadvantages when they are used to obtain testimony from children.
> In particular, there is the danger that irrelevant cues will have a
> suggestive function and mislead children into making errors in their
> reports. (p. 26)

Pipe et al. conclude that

> there is now clear evidence that cues and props can help children
> provide more complete event reports than they would normally pro-
> vide in a free-recall account. Cues and props may also help when
> children are questioned quite specifically if the questions relate di-
> rectly to the cue items. Interviewers must, of course, always be aware
> of the risk that these retrieval techniques might reduce the accuracy of
> reports. The effect on accuracy appears to depend on the nature of the
> cues and props, the way they are presented, and how children are
> instructed to use them. We are cautiously optimistic that there will be
> few adverse effects on accuracy when children are interviewed with

props in view or when props are used in conjunction with specific questions. (pp. 42-43)

The interview prop that has generated the most concern is the anatomically detailed doll (Boat & Everson, 1988a, 1988b; Everson & Boat, 1990, 1994). There is agreement that anatomical dolls are not a test for sexual abuse. Guidelines on use of anatomical dolls published by the American Professional Society on the Abuse of Children (APSAC, 1995) state:

> The use of anatomical dolls as a diagnostic test for child sexual abuse is not supported by the empirical evidence. Specifically, it is not appropriate to draw definitive conclusions about the likelihood of abuse based solely upon interpretation of a child's behavior with the dolls. There is no known behavior with the dolls that can be considered a definitive marker of sexual abuse in the absence of other factors, such as the child's verbal account or medical evidence. (p. 6)

The APSAC doll guidelines are reproduced in full as Appendix A.

In 1995, Koocher et al. reviewed the literature on anatomical dolls and concluded that "the requisite information is simply unavailable and not known to be forthcoming to allow [anatomically detailed] dolls to be used as a test" (p. 202).

Although anatomical dolls are not a test for sexual abuse, research generally indicates that nonabused children seldom engage in explicit sexual behavior with anatomical dolls (Dawson, Geddie, & Wagner, 1996; Everson & Boat, 1994). When a young child places anatomical dolls in what appear to be sexual positions, further investigation is warranted (Jampole & Weber, 1987). As Boat and Everson (1993) summarized,

> Available research indicates that explicit sexualized play with anatomical dolls, including enactment of sexual intercourse, cannot be considered a *definitive* marker of sexual abuse in the absence of a clear verbal account of abuse by the child. However, the fact that anatomical dolls are not a definitive diagnostic test for sexual abuse does not negate their clinical usefulness as a tool in sexual abuse evaluations. Evidence of explicit sexual knowledge in a young child warrants careful evaluation of the source of such knowledge. (p. 64)

Some research discloses "increased sexual interaction with [anatomical dolls] among low-income, African-American preschoolers, when compared with middle-income, White preschoolers" (Dawson et al., 1996, p. 375; see also Boat & Everson, 1994; Geddie, Dawson, & Weunsch, 1998).

The APSAC guidelines on anatomical dolls (APSAC, 1995) summarize the primary concerns raised about the dolls:

> Concern has been expressed about possible harm through the use of anatomical dolls [during interviews]. One concern is that anatomical dolls may suggest sexual material, encouraging false reports from non-abused children. Another is that the dolls may be overstimulating or even traumatizing to non-abused children by introducing them prematurely to sexual ideas and body parts. A final concern is that interviewers using the dolls may be poorly trained and overzealous in their search for sexual abuse, eliciting unreliable, if not erroneous, evidence of abuse. (p. 2)

Clearly, anatomical dolls, like all props, can be misused (Boat & Everson, 1996; Bruck, Ceci, Francoeur, & Renick, 1995). In the hands of trained and objective interviewers, however, the dolls are a useful adjunct to the interview process (Goodman & Aman, 1990). In particular, anatomical dolls are useful (a) to stimulate memory, (b) to allow children to demonstrate what they have difficulty putting into words, and (c) to confirm that the interviewer correctly understands the child's vocabulary and meaning for various terms.

The APSAC guidelines (APSAC, 1995) state that

> the majority of available research does not support the position that the dolls are inherently too suggestive and overly stimulating to be useful in sexual abuse investigations and evaluations. Specifically, there is little empirical evidence that exposure to the dolls induces non-abused, sexually naive children to have sexual fantasies and to engage in sex play that is likely to be misinterpreted as evidence of sexual abuse. (p. 2)

In a research study, parents of nonabused children interviewed with anatomical dolls did not report that their children were traumatized by exposure to the dolls (Boat, Everson, & Holland, 1990).

There is general agreement that caution is necessary before using anatomical dolls with children under age 5 (DeLoache, 1995). Indeed, some experts believe that dolls should not be used at all with preschoolers. A very young child may be distracted by the dolls. In addition, it can be difficult to tell whether a young child is simply playing with a doll or is using the doll to describe an actual event. Many 3-year-olds lack the cognitive sophistication required to use a doll to represent a person. A very young child's lack of "representational capacity" can lead to breakdowns in understanding between the child and the interviewer. DeLoache (1995), in a review of the research on use of anatomical dolls with young children, concluded that

> *There is general agreement that caution is necessary before using anatomical dolls with children under age 5.*

> research on the use of anatomical dolls to interview young children should allay the worst fears of high rates of false negatives and false positives. However, the research offers meager support for the supposition that dolls enhance children's reports.
>
> Although anatomically correct dolls are widely believed to facilitate the investigation of child abuse, there is extremely meager empirical or theoretical support for using dolls to interview very young children, that is, children of 3 years of age or less. (pp. 167, 177)

During investigative interviews and courtroom testimony, toys and other props, including anatomical dolls, are often used to help children describe events.

PROPER INTERVIEW PRACTICES

As you consider interview practices, keep in mind that every child is unique. There is no single correct way to interview children. There is no gold standard, no one protocol that professionals must always follow. Interviewers improvise as the interview unfolds, and flexibility is the order of the day. According to Jones (1992),

Flexibility to change direction should be incorporated into the "style" of the interviewer, so that allowance can be made for the child's special needs. There is no "cookery book" of predictable questions and answers, nor a particular order in which they would be put. (p. 19)

There are numerous books and articles on interviewing. Hewitt (1998), Poole and Lamb (1998), and Saywitz and Elliott (1999) should be required reading for every interviewer.

The Interviewer's Knowledge of the Facts of the Case

Some professionals recommend that interviewers know little about a child or the facts of a case before an interview (White, Strom, & Quinn, 1987). Cantlon, Payne, and Erbaugh (1996) found that interviewers who did not know the facts of the case before the interview began obtained more disclosures from children than interviewers who possessed background information.

Most interviewers obtain background information before the interview begins. Davies et al. (1996) suggest that interviewers "gather relevant history pertaining to the current allegations from both the referring agency and the child's caretakers" (p. 191). The utility of background information is apparent in light of the fact that focused and specific questions are often necessary during investigative interviews. Interviewers may have difficulty formulating such questions without some background data.

Although professionals are justified in gathering background information before an interview begins, the professional should avoid giving the child the impression that the professional already knows what happened. For example, the professional should not say, "You can tell me about it, I know who hurt you." A child who believes that the interviewer already knows what happened may be at increased risk of providing inaccurate information in response to suggestive questions (Warren et al., 1991).

Rapport Building

It is important to build rapport with children (Bull, 1995). Sternberg et al. (1997) state that "from a child's perspective, the investigative interview is a unique and possibly puzzling context in which he or she is expected to overcome reticence about interacting with unfamiliar adults" (p. 1134). The rapport-building phase helps children relax and feel comfortable (Jones, 1992). Toward the end of the rapport phase, interviewers familiarize children with what will follow.

During the rapport-building phase, Sternberg et al. (1997) recommend that interviewers maximize the use of open-ended questions. In research with actual forensic interviews, children whose rapport-building sessions were dominated by open-ended questions "provided two and a half times as many details and words in response to the first substantive question as children" whose rapport sessions were filled with closed-ended, suggestive questions (p. 1141). Using open-ended questions to build rapport creates an expectation that the child "does the talking." (For detailed discussion of the importance of rapport building, see Poole & Lamb, 1998.)

Preparing a Child for Questioning

The interviewer helps the child understand the nature of the interview and the need for accuracy. Such instruction is important because children may have misconceptions about the interview process. According to Warren, Woodall, Hunt, and Perry (1996),

> Interviewers should take greater care to establish the ground rules of the interview [to] counter the child's predictable assumptions. Research has shown that these assumptions may include: (a) every question must be answered, even if I don't understand it; (b) every question has a right or wrong answer; (c) the interviewer already knows what happened, so if he or she says something that differs from what I remember, I am wrong; and (d) I am not allowed to answer "I don't know," or to ask the interviewer to clarify a question. (p. 234)

Sternberg et al. (1997) add:

> In most social contexts, adults "test" children's knowledge by asking questions to which the adults already know the answers. In forensic interviews, by contrast, children are often unique sources of novel information. Because children are unused to being treated as impor-

tant informants, interviewers must clearly communicate their expectations regarding the children's roles and responsibilities. Specifically, they need to explain the informant's role, motivate children to provide detailed and complete accounts of experienced events, highlight the importance of telling the truth, and encourage children to correct inaccurate statements made by the interviewers. (p. 1134)

Children should be informed of the interviewer's expectations. Depending on the child's age, the interviewer can explain limits on confidentiality. Saywitz, Nathason, Snyder, and Lamphear (1993) suggest motivating instructions such as "Try your hardest" and "Do your best." Warren et al. (1996) add that "interviewers may wish to explicitly state that they do not already know exactly what happened, or everything that has happened to the child, and that they need the child to provide some answers" (p. 234). Warren et al. also recommend that children be told that some questions might be tricky, that "I don't know" is an acceptable answer, and that children should describe only what they truly remember. Further recommendations are given below.

Be Supportive, Yet Professional

Children should feel as comfortable as circumstances allow. Children are more likely to perform well when the interviewer is nice (Carter et al., 1996; Davis & Bottoms, in press; Goodman, Hirschman, et al., 1991). "Social influences, such as 'reinforcement'—which presumably make the interviewer less intimidating—can have an important effect in optimizing children's performance" (Goodman & Schwartz-Kenney, 1992, p. 22). Young children are likely to be less suggestible when the interviewer is friendly and supportive, yet professional.

Carter et al. (1996) examined the influence of supportive versus intimidating interview styles on the memory and suggestibility of 5- to 7-year-old children. They found that "children interviewed in a supportive manner were more accurate about nonabuse-relevant details than children interviewed in an intimidating context" (p. 346) but that the two groups did not differ in accuracy of responses to abuse questions or in likelihood of (falsely) reporting that abusive events had taken place during the play event. Children given social support were better able to resist misleading suggestions than children who were interviewed in an intimidating way. Thus, "Social support did not lead to a marked increase in suggestibility feared by some critics of socioemotionally supportive interviewing techniques" (p. 350). The authors explained these results by citing "past research . . . illustrat[ing] that social support decreases anxiety and increases self-confidence in subjects facing a complex cognitive task and that decreased intimidation leads to increased resistance to suggestion" (p. 350). The authors concluded that "perceived social support led children in our study to feel less anxious, more empowered, and in turn, less intimidated and better able to resist misleading suggestions from the interviewer" (p. 351).

It is appropriate to praise children for trying their best. Simple compliments such as "You are working hard" or "Good job," which are completely normal—indeed, expected—in any other child-adult interaction, do not undermine the integrity of the interview. Children should be treated like children, even in the important context of investigative interviews.

Initial Questioning

Once rapport is established, initial questions should be as non suggestive as possible. According to Dent (1992), "When accuracy is the prime consideration, the interviewer should make use of free recall or general questions, at least in the first instance" (p. 11). Begin with open-ended questions that invite narrative responses. Moreover, persist as long as you can with open-ended, nonsuggestive questions. Lamb and his colleagues report that interviewers have a tendency to abandon open-ended questions too quickly and to turn prematurely to suggestive questions (Lamb et al., 1995, 1996; Lamb, Sternberg, & Esplin, 1994). As the interview progresses, keep thinking to yourself, "Is there some way I can come up with at least one more open-ended question?" and "Are there any possible open-ended questions I haven't asked yet?" Open-ended questions are not only forensically defensible but also productive. Children sometimes disclose more information in response to open-ended questions than in response to specific or leading questions (Lamb et al., 1996; Stern-berg et al., 1996).

When a child does not respond to open-ended questions—and many children do not—the interviewer moves cautiously along the continuum of suggestivity described in Figure 4.1. The interviewer may begin with questions that focus the child's attention on a particular topic and then, when necessary, move gradually to more specific questions, some of which cross the line into suggestive and mildly leading.

Saywitz and Geiselman (in press) note that although "a number of researchers have advocated that interviewers avoid specific questions completely, which they define as inherently leading," such an approach is neither necessary nor particularly useful:

> Unfortunately, the exclusive use of general questions does not guarantee accuracy any more than using leading questions guarantees contamination. For example, in the study of children's recall for a physical examination . . . , children were asked if the doctor put something in their mouths. Many incorrectly answered, "No." When asked more specifically if the doctor put a thermometer in their mouths to take their temperature, the same children answered, "Yes," offering the correct response. The more general question was perhaps less leading, but it also elicited the greater number of incorrect responses.

These authors suggested that

> interviewers begin with open-ended questions and proceed with the most nonleading approaches first. Then, . . . specific follow-up questions begin with category questions, then short answer questions regarding facts revealed in the initial narrative. . . . Category questions focus children's attention on the kind of information that is relevant to the forensic context. They include questions beginning with Who, What, When, Where, or How. Studies of the development of organizational strategies, cuing, and story recall suggest that categorical prompts might focus children's attention on the forensically relevant categories and increase memory performance. Particularly useful might be 'wh' questions regarding the participants (e.g., "What clothes were the people wearing?" "What did their hair look like?"), the setting (e.g., "What was the weather like that night?" "Was it inside or outside?"), and the conversations (e.g., "What did he say?"). . . . These

category questions can be followed with requests for elaboration ("Tell me more"), clarification ("I do not understand"), or justification ("What makes you think so?"). Such prompts elicit additional information from the child's perspective rather than the adult's.

Testing Alternative Hypotheses

Throughout the interview, the professional tests two alternative hypotheses: that abuse occurred and that it did not. Keeping an open mind on whether abuse occurred is vital (Ceci & Bruck, 1993, 1995). As Jones (1992) cautioned, "The over-riding general principle is that of open-mindedness. We are not interviewing sexually abused children, but children who *may* have been sexually abused" (p. 19).

"Yes-No" Questions and Multiple-Choice Questions

Questions in the "yes-no" and multiple-choice formats are not necessarily suggestive, although they can be. Moreover, answers to "yes-no" and multiple-choice questions are often difficult to interpret. Children's answers to such questions should be clarified by asking children to elaborate in their own words or to explain their responses.

Questions Regarding Particular Persons

During investigative interviews, children are asked about particular people, including suspects. There is no universally agreed-on way to direct a child's attention to a particular person. Saywitz and Geiselman (in press) suggest that individuals not mentioned by the child be introduced with open-ended or short-answer questions rather than yes-no or multiple-choice questions (e.g., "Was someone else there?" "Yes." "Who?" rather than "Was John there?" or "John was there, wasn't he?"). When it comes to discussing suspects, the critical point is not whether the interviewer names names but how the subject is handled.

Repeating Questions Within a Single Interview

Interviewing children who may be traumatized, frightened, confused, timid, or embarrassed requires skill and patience. Not infrequently, an interviewer must ask about something more than once. Perhaps the first time a question is asked, the child does not understand, gives an ambiguous or partial answer, or simply declines to respond. Of course, there are risks in repeating questions. Children who are asked the same question more than once may assume that they gave the "wrong" answer the first time and feel pressure to provide the "right" answer when the question is repeated (Fivush & Schwarzmueller, 1995; Memon & Vartoukian, 1996). Young children are more likely than older children to succumb to the social demands of the interview and to go along with leading questions asked by authoritative adults (Cassel et al., 1996). With these risks in mind, it is useful to inform children that some questions may be repeated and that repetition does not mean the child's first response was wrong.

In the final analysis, the danger of repetition lies not so much in covering the same territory twice but in how the interviewer handles the situation. Interviewers sometimes change the wording of questions, and skillful interviewers take care to ensure that children do not feel pressure to change or invent answers.

THE INTERVIEWER'S DILEMMA

If it were possible to interview children without suggestive questions, everyone would happily agree to ban such questions. But unfortunately, it is not that simple. Interviewers are on the horns of a dilemma. If they limit themselves to open-ended, nonsuggestive questions, they will miss some abused children. But if they ask suggestive questions, they increase the probability of inaccuracy (Bruck, Ceci, Francoeur, & Barr, 1995). There is no escaping this dilemma, and good interviewers have it in the back of their mind as they weigh the risks and benefits of questions.

It is often necessary to ask focused, specific, and, yes, even mildly leading questions. Spencer and Flin (1993) observe that "in a typical forensic context, free recall and very general questions are of limited use, and interviews need to use more specific questions in order to elicit the maximum amount of information" (p. 290). The goal in forensic interviewing is to reduce the number of suggestive and mildly leading questions while respecting the need to ask such questions.

To understand the need for cautious and sparing use of suggestive and mildly leading questions during interviews, it is necessary to discuss three issues: (a) the process by which children disclose abuse, (b) young children's difficulty responding to open-ended questions that require free recall, and (c) the impact on interviewing of children's emotional development.

Before turning to these issues, it is important to state that when an interviewer asks a suggestive or mildly leading question, the interviewer should follow up with an open-ended question. Bull (1995) describes this technique:

> If a leading question is used because the child seems to need to be led, and it produces an evidentially related response (particularly one that contains relevant information not led by the question), then the interviewer should *immediately* refrain from asking further leading questions but revert to one of the nonleading [questioning techniques]. In this way, the interview can avoid being one composed largely of leading questions. (p. 187)

The Disclosure Process in Child Sexual Abuse

The first reason for suggestive and, when necessary, mildly leading questions during forensic interviews relates to the psychological pressure felt by victims—pressure that can result in halting, piecemeal disclosure. Goodman and Schwartz-Kenney (1992) observe:

> Children who suffer sexual abuse may fail to report it for many reasons: for example, they may be embarrassed about what happened, they may not remember the event or may not have interpreted it as abuse, or they may have been instructed not to tell. For such children, an open-ended, free-recall question may fail to elicit a report. (p. 22)

Some abused children are threatened into silence. Others are too embarrassed to tell (Arata, 1998). Some abused children suffer psychological trauma that interferes with disclosure (Chaffin, Lawson,

Selby, & Wherry, 1997). When a child finally discloses abuse, the child may tell a friend, parent, teacher, school counselor, or other professional. With young children, "The most common disclosure of sexual abuse . . . is the direct, though often unintentional or 'accidental,' statement of the child victim to a parent, older sibling, or pre-school teacher" (Steward & Steward, 1996, p. 2).

Sorensen and Snow (1991) studied the disclosure process in 116 sexually abused children receiving psychotherapy. During early therapy interviews, nearly 80% of the children denied their abuse or were tentative about disclosing.

Bradley and Wood (1996) studied disclosure in 234 sexual abuse cases validated by child protective services. Bradley and Wood found a disclosure rate during investigative interviews that was considerably higher than the rate reported by Sorenson and Snow:

> Ninety-six percent of victims in the present study made a partial or full disclosure of abuse during at least one interview with [CPS] or police. . . . Six percent of victims initially denied to [CPS] or police that abuse had occurred. . . . Ten percent of victims in the present study displayed reluctance to discuss the topic of abuse, or specific aspects of the abuse, during one or more interviews with [CPS] or police. . . . Three percent of victims in the present study recanted their allegations. (Bradley & Wood, 1996, p. 885)

In a study by Elliott and Briere (1994), 84% of children revealed abuse during the first forensic interview. Similarly, Sternberg et al. (1997) found a disclosure rate of more than 90% in forensic interviews. Sternberg and her colleagues suggest that their rate, as well as Bradley and Wood's (1996), and Elliott and Briere's (1994) rates were higher than the rate reported by Sorenson and Snow (1991) because rates of disclosure may be higher in front-line investigations than in clinical settings.

Dubowitz, Black, and Harrington (1992) evaluated 28 children who had abnormal medical findings indicative of sexual abuse. During interviews, 25% of the children did not disclose any information regarding abuse.

Lawson and Chaffin (1992) studied 28 children with sexually transmitted diseases. The children were interviewed by a social worker who was trained in forensic interviewing. Only 43% of the children disclosed sexual abuse during the initial interview. Thus, more than half of these abused children did not disclose. Lawson and Chaffin commented:

> Surveys of adult survivors indicate that they rarely reported sexual abuse when they were children, and the child abuse field has continued to struggle with questions regarding "hidden victims." The present findings provide additional reason to be concerned about under-identification of sexual abuse in the current generation of young child victims. Even when directly interviewed by a trained specialist who was sure the child had been molested, the majority of these . . . victims did not make even minimal disclosure. (p. 539)

A study by Saywitz, Goodman, Nicholas, and Moan (1991) illustrates the need for direct questions when interviewing young children about embarrassing topics such as genital touch. The authors studied nonabused 5- and 7-year-old girls who had experienced a routine medical examination by a pediatrician. As part of the examination, half the girls received an external inspection of the vaginal and anal areas. The other half did not receive the vaginal and anal examination. Some time later, all the children were questioned about the entire examination. Questioning began with open-ended questions such as "What happened?" Then the children were asked focused and mildly suggestive questions, including whether their vaginal and anal areas were examined.

Most of the children who experienced the vaginal or anal examination did not disclose the examination in response to open-ended questions such as "What happened?" The majority of children revealed the vaginal or anal examination only when they were asked mildly suggestive questions such as "Did the doctor touch you there?"

Of the children who did *not* receive a vaginal or anal examination, the great majority (92%) resisted suggestive questions about such an examination. Only three children (8%) said they received a vaginal or anal examination when they did not. Saywitz et al.'s research supports the conclusion that although there is a risk of obtaining inaccurate information when mildly suggestive questions are asked, there is a greater risk that potentially embarrassing but truthful information will not be disclosed when such questions are *not* asked.

In a similar study involving reports of genital contact and use of leading questions, Bruck, Ceci, Francoeur, and Renick (1995) reported that 2- and 3-year-old children produced a rate of false reports of genital touch that was higher than the number of false reports found by Saywitz et al. (1991) in older children.

The secretive and embarrassing nature of child sexual abuse can inhibit disclosure. Many young victims cannot provide detailed and spontaneous descriptions of abuse without some degree of specific questioning (Spencer & Flin, 1993). When a child finally discloses, the child may begin by revealing a small part of the abuse. The child tests the water to determine how adults will react to "the secret." If adults are accepting, the child feels safe to reveal a little more until, eventually, the entire story is disclosed. Because disclosure is difficult for many sexually abused children, interviewers sometimes have to exert gentle pressure.

Young Children's Difficulty Responding to Questions That Require Free Recall

The second reason for suggestive and mildly leading questions during interviews is grounded in principles of memory development. As explained earlier in this chapter, young children, particularly preschoolers, are not very good at responding to open-ended questions such as "Can you tell me about that?" Open-ended questions require free recall, and young children have not mastered the cognitive skills required for efficient free recall.

Young children frequently provide very little information in response to free-recall questions and often need "many questions and prompts in order to recall both recently and distantly experienced events" (Fivush, 1993, p. 6). Because of their developmental immaturity, then, young children often need suggestive and mildly leading questions to unlock memory. Although suggestive and mildly leading questions carry the risk of error, such questions are often necessary for developmental reasons when interviewing young children. According to Berliner (1997),

One of the most important differences between younger children and older children is that, although what younger children report in response to open-ended questions is as likely to be accurate, it is less complete. While younger children remember a great deal, they require far more external assistance to retrieve information. Young children rarely provide more information that what is directly requested. They rely on questions to trigger and organize recall and need prompts and cues to a greater extent than older children and adults. In order to obtain sufficient information to learn whether a crime was committed and what exactly happened to a child, especially a young child, it will invariably be necessary to ask questions and prompt memory. (p. 9)

Children's Emotional Development and the Need for Suggestive and Mildly Leading Questions

A third reason that interviewers sometimes ask suggestive and mildly leading questions relates to children's emotional development and the psychological effects of trauma. Saywitz and Elliott (1999) note that among young children, avoidance is a common strategy for coping with anxiety. With young children, avoidance is often the first inclination in response to an unfamiliar adult who raises anxiety-provoking topics. The more painful the topic, the more the effort to avoid it, and the interviewer may have to gently prod the child with suggestive questions.

The problem of avoidance is compounded when children suffer from PTSD, a psychiatric disorder seen in many victims of sexual assault (see Chapter 1). One of the hallmarks of PTSD is persistent avoidance of reminders of the trauma. Victims of child abuse may use silence, distraction, or other methods to avoid discussing the subject.

Summary

Suggestive and mildly leading questions should be avoided when possible. Interviewers should begin with open-ended questions that require free recall. Suggestive questions are justified only when nonsuggestive techniques are exhausted. Competent interviewers, however, ask suggestive and mildly leading questions. In the final analysis, cautious use of suggestive and mildly leading questions is necessary and justified.

INTERVIEW PRACTICES TO BE AVOIDED

Although there is no one right way to interview, there are some things to avoid. Highly leading questions come immediately to mind. It is difficult to envision a case in which it would be proper to ask questions such as "He touched your vagina, isn't that right?"

Children should not receive praise only when they give answers the interviewer wants to hear. As discussed earlier in this chapter, professionals can maintain neutrality while being supportive.

Interviewers should not criticize a child's answers or interrupt a child unnecessarily. Don't suggest that a child should know the answer to a question. A condescending attitude or comments such as "I bet you don't remember the color of his hair" undermine children's confidence.

It is usually improper to tell a child what other people have said about a suspect. Shaw, Garven, and Wood (1997) use the term *co-witness information* to describe situations in which an interviewer tells a child what someone else said. Shaw and his colleagues found that co-witness information had an adverse impact on children's accuracy. When children

> received incorrect information about co-witnesses' responses to a question just before [the children] provided their own response to that same question, the [children] were more likely to give the same incorrect responses as the co-witness (or co-witnesses) than they were if they received no co-witness information. (p. 516)

This research supports the consensus that children should not be told such things as "Some of the other kids already told me what happened, so you can tell me" or "Your mother told me all about what he did to you. Now you tell me."

Children must not be coerced, frightened, or threatened into answering questions. For example, telling children that they cannot have a break until they answer certain questions can be construed as coercive.

Although it is unrealistic to expect interviewers to be completely objective, competent interviewers do not approach cases with their mind already made up. The purpose of investigative interviewing is to determine *whether* abuse occurred, not to confirm abuse.

EFFECT OF MULTIPLE INTERVIEWS ON MEMORY

Considerable attention has focused on reducing the number of times children are interviewed (see Chapter 5, the section "Multidisciplinary Investigation"). Reducing interviews is important for at least seven reasons. First, multiple interviews are thought to add stress to already vulnerable children. Second, if children are required to repeat their descriptions of abuse many times, they "may begin to relate their experience in a nonemotional, rote fashion, thus weakening the believability of their testimony" (Steward & Steward, 1996, p. 6). Third, "Over time children may become reluctant to talk repeatedly about material that is emotionally distressing for them and withhold information" (Steward & Steward, 1996, p. 6). Fourth, young children are often inconsistent across interviews, and inconsistency can undermine credibility (see Chapter 7, the section "Credibility Evidence"). Fifth, repeated interviews may cause children (and adults) to be more confident in their memories without necessarily being more accurate (Shaw & McClure, 1996). Sixth, the higher the number of interviews, the greater the likelihood that an interviewer will ask unnecessarily suggestive questions. Seventh, multiple interviews may create or reinforce inaccurate memories, particularly when suggestive questions are used.

With the disadvantages of multiple interviews in mind, the solution seems obvious: one interview! There appears to be much to gain and little to lose by eliminating multiple interviews. Yet few things are as simple as they first appear, and preoccupation with reducing the number of interviews can become the tail that wags the dog. For the following reasons, multiple interviews are sometimes necessary. First, some sexually abused children reveal their abuse gradually. Some molested children cannot "tell the whole story" in one sitting. Second, multiple interviews often lead to new information. Third, repeat interviews can strengthen memory through repetition (Fivush &

Schwarzmueller, 1995). Fourth, although multiple interviews can produce inconsistencies, inconsistency can be explained. These reasons are discussed below.

The Disclosure Process

As discussed earlier in this chapter, quite a few sexually abused children hesitate to disclose. More than one interview may be necessary to learn what happened.

Obtaining Additional Information

Limiting the number of interviews sometimes results in loss of information. Children, like adults, do not necessarily recall everything in a single interview, and multiple interviews may yield additional details.

Strengthening Memory Through Repetition

Memory can be solidified by talking about an event more than once. From time immemorial, teachers have drilled students with the admonition, "Now, class, the more you practice, the better you'll remember for the test." On this theme, Poole and White (1995) state that "in terms of memory, . . . there is little doubt that discussing an experience can dramatically improve the ability of children and adults to recall it at a later time" (p. 27). According to Fivush and Schwarzmueller (1995), "The more frequently a personally experienced event is recalled, the more easily that event can be recalled on subsequent occasions and the more information can be recalled about the event" (p. 556). Warren and Lane (1995) add that

> one consistent finding of repeated testing research in the laboratory has been that material not recalled on initial tests can be "reminisced," or recalled on subsequent tests without additional study. In fact, the amount of information reminisced on later memory tests sometimes exceeds the amount forgotten, a phenomenon known as "hypermnesia." (pp. 45-46)

Children's accuracy during repeated questioning depends in part on whether questions are suggestive. A number of studies indicate that repeatedly interviewing children in a nonsuggestive fashion has little detrimental effect on memory and may actually improve recall through rehearsal or reminiscence (Brainerd & Ornstein, 1991; Dent, 1991). Inaccuracy can be more pronounced when repeated false suggestions are presented, especially to young children (Poole & White, 1995).

Inconsistency Can Be Explained

Children sometimes describe different aspects of remembered events at different times. Of course, describing different aspects of a single event can look like inconsistency, and inconsistency can undermine credibility. It is important, therefore, to understand why children, particularly little ones, are so often so inconsistent.

One explanation for inconsistency, of course, is prevarication. Children, like adults, lie. Another explanation is misleading or suggestive questioning. But as Fivush and Shukat (1995) point out, "Even when no misleading or suggestive information is provided, preschoolers are remarkably inconsistent in the information they recall on multiple trials even after relatively short delays" (p. 12), and "While the total amount of information recalled about specific events does not seem to change over time, children recall different information each time they recount an event" (p. 17). Inconsistency that is not related to lying or interviewer direction is caused by several factors, including (a) the nature of disclosure among abused children, (b) the impact on memory of multiple episodes of abuse, and (c) developmental immaturity.

The Disclosure Process. This is the third time that we have discussed the impact of the disclosure process on interviewing and children's credibility! The psychological pressures that inhibit disclosure explain why professionals have to ask suggestive questions, why multiple interviews are sometimes needed, and why some children are inconsistent across multiple interviews. When a child is interviewed more than once, each telling is a little different. For example, one interviewer may elicit information that the child is unwilling to share with another interviewer. Moreover, some abused children recant, and some recant their recantation. Needless to say, recantation is inconsistent. Understanding the disclosure process helps put children's inconsistency in psychological perspective.

By the way, we are not done talking about the disclosure process. We will return to the issue again in the discussion of videotaping in Chapter 5, and yet again in Chapter 7 on expert testimony.

The Impact on Memory of Multiple Episodes of Abuse. Children who have been molested repeatedly for months or years have understandable difficulty remembering particular episodes. Memory blurs. According to Fivush and Shukat (1995), "Everything we know about personal memories, from childhood through adulthood, would suggest that, the more frequently one experiences an event, the more difficult it is to recall a single specific experience of that event" (p. 18). (See the discussion of script memory earlier in this chapter.) Hudson (1990) similarly noted that "there is also evidence that highly routine episodes of familiar events are extremely difficult to recall because they have become fused into the generalized representations and are no longer available to recall as distinct episodes" (p. 168). When a child who has suffered repeated abuse is asked to recall specific episodes—as often happens in court—the child may become confused and, as a result, inconsistent. Thus, the nature of repetitive sexual abuse can generate inconsistency.

Developmental Reasons for Young Children's Inconsistency. There are developmental reasons for inconsistency in young children, particularly preschoolers. According to Gordon and Follmer (1994), "Developmental research suggests that young children may be less consistent than older children in what they remember over a series of interviews" (p. 284). There are five developmental reasons for inconsistency among young children.

• *Difficulty in Self-Editing for Error.* Young children are not proficient at monitoring their communications for error, omission, contradiction, and inconsistency (Fivush & Shukat, 1995). Thus, a young child may not realize that he or she is "not making sense." Adults, by contrast, continuously monitor their speech to ensure a smooth, coherent narrative. As I sit at the word processor, I think about each sentence before I write, and most of the stupid, inconsistent, and incoherent things that pop into my mind get edited out. As an adult, I am pretty good at self-monitoring for error. Young children, by contrast, are not adept at this skill, and their relative deficit in self-editing can lead to inconsistency.

• *Difficulty in Narrating*. Telling a story from beginning to middle to end is a learned skill, and preschoolers are not very good at it. You may recall that the public television program *Sesame Street* teaches the concepts of beginning, middle, and end. A preschooler who has not mastered this developmental task may begin in the middle, jump to the beginning, switch to the end, and, finally, return to the middle. The child's story may look inconsistent to an adult, especially an adult who does not understand the developmental reasons for the child's disjointed narrative.

• *Egocentricity*. Young children are egocentric. Regardless of how mixed up they may be, they are likely to assume that the adult understands precisely what they are saying.

• *Difficulty in Monitoring Understanding of Questions From Adults*. A fourth developmental reason for inconsistency is that little children have difficulty understanding when they do not understand. Children's ability to monitor how well they understand questions— called *comprehension monitoring*—develops gradually. Because of limited comprehension-monitoring skills, young children some-times think they understand questions when they do not, and their answers may not make sense or may look inconsistent.

Even when children realize that they do not understand a question, they seldom ask for clarification or admit confusion. It is up to adults to make sure children understand.

• *Difficulty in Organizing Memories*. The fifth developmental explana-tion for inconsistency in young children relates to memory develop-ment, as discussed by Fivush and Shukat (1995):

One possibility that has been suggested in the literature is that young children rely on adults' questions to guide their recall. Thus, if adults ask the same questions over time, young children will provide the same information, but if adults ask different questions over time, children's recall will seem inconsistent. While it certainly may be the case that young children will answer the same questions in the same way across recall trials, their inconsistent recall cannot be completely attributed to inconsistent questions.

Another possibility is that preschool children are inconsistent because their memories are not well organized. In particular, it has been argued that personal experiences are organized as canonical narratives and these narrative forms are learned during the preschool years. Before children have control over these narrative forms, their memories will not be coherently organized and therefore they will be inconsistent. (pp. 12-13)

It is important to understand the psychological and developmental reasons for inconsistency. Some degree of inconsistency is *normal* with children, including children victimized by abuse.

Summary

It is not my intent to downplay the drawbacks of multiple interviews. Warren and Lane (1995) remind us that "repeated questioning, even when it is completely neutral, can have unanticipated harmful consequences. . . . Memory reports appear to become more complete with repeated interviews, but both accuracies and inaccuracies increase" (p. 46). The point of this discussion is that there are benefits as well as drawbacks to multiple interviews.

COGNITIVE INTERVIEW, NARRATIVE ELABORATION, AND CRITERIA-BASED CONTENT ANALYSIS

This subsection briefly describes three innovative interview techniques.

The Cognitive Interview

The cognitive interview (CI) is a collection of memory retrieval techniques that, when properly used, can increase the amount of accurate information retrieved during interviews (Fisher & McCauley, 1995). The CI was pioneered by Fisher and Geiselman for use with adults (Geiselman, Fisher, MacKinnon, & Holland, 1985). The CI is used in practice by a substantial number of police departments and has been adapted for use with children (Geiselman, Saywitz, & Bornstein, 1993).

Geiselman et al. (1993) described the CI as being theoretically based on

> two factors that are integrally involved in the retrieval of memories. First, a memory is composed of several features, and the effectiveness of any technique to access a memory is related to the extent to which the features of the context created by the retrieval technique overlap with the features comprising the memory for the information that is sought. Second, there may be several retrieval paths to a memory for an event, so that information not accessible with one memory-retrieval technique may be accessible with a different technique that creates a different memory cue.

The CI is a memory-retrieval procedure whose techniques are borrowed from research in cognitive psychology:

> The cognitive interview consists of four general retrieval methods plus additional, more specific techniques. Of the four general methods, two attempt to increase the feature overlap between the memory for the event and the memory-retrieval mnemonic: (1) mentally reconstructing the environmental and personal context that existed at the time of the crime, and (2) reporting everything (being complete), even partial information, regardless of the perceived *importance* of the information. The other two methods encourage using multiple retrieval paths: (3) recounting the events in a variety of orders, and (4) reporting the events from a variety of perspectives. (p. 73)

In an interesting study, Geiselman et al. (1993) employed the CI with nonabused third-grade (8- and 9-year-old) and sixth-grade (11- and 12-year-old) children. Children in the study experienced a staged event at school. Two days later, the children were interviewed about the staged event by actual sheriff's deputies. For purposes of the sheriff interview, the children were divided into three conditions: (a) children who received a CI, (b) children who received a standard interview, and (c) a third group of children who received a CI plus a practice session on how to be interviewed. Children in the practice condition participated in a practice session shortly following the staged event. During the practice session, the children were instructed on how to respond during an interview. The children were familiarized with the CI, with what happens during an interview, and with "what it means to say, 'I don't know' " (p. 75).

Geiselman et al. found that regardless of the interview condition, the children in this study were quite accurate:

> The accuracy rates of the children's recall with the sheriffs were remarkably high, with cognitive interviewing with practice = 88%, cognitive interviewing without practice = 89%, and standard interviewing = 84%. These average absolute levels of accuracy provide another illustration of the capability of recollection by young children who are interviewed by experienced law-enforcement personnel. (p. 82)

Children who received the CI recalled more accurate information than children who received a standard interview. Geiselman et al. report that the CI

> led to significant improvements in the number of correct items recalled in comparison to standard procedures. Collapsing across grade levels, the percentage of improvement over standard procedures was 18% with cognitive interviewing without practice, and was 45% with cognitive interviewing with practice. (p. 85)

Geiselman et al. conclude that "(1) cognitive questioning techniques can enhance the completeness of recollections by children, and (2) it is advantageous for children to have practice with the cognitive questioning procedures prior to receiving a cognitive interview about the event of legal importance" (p. 88).

Studies of the CI generally indicate that when the interviewer is properly trained, the CI yields additional accurate information without an increase in inaccurate information.

Narrative Elaboration

Narrative elaboration (NE) is a technique pioneered by Saywitz and her colleagues (Saywitz et al., 1996; Saywitz & Snyder, 1996). Basically, it is a package of memory-enhancing techniques designed to maximize children's recall. According to Saywitz et al. (1996),

> Narrative elaboration is an intervention package extrapolated from laboratory studies of memory development. It incorporates six experimental procedures that have enhanced the memory performance of school-age children in the laboratory: memory strategy instruction, practice with feedback, rationales for strategy utility, organizational guidance according to category cues, external memory aids (e.g., pictorial cues), and reminders to use new strategies on subsequent events. (pp. 201-202)

Saywitz et al. (1996) conducted research on NE and found that "children in the narrative elaboration condition recalled significantly more correct information than the control group when given an opportunity to elaborate on their free recall with the use of visual cues, improving completeness by about one third" (p. 209).

Criteria-Based Content Analysis

Criteria-based content analysis (CBCA) is a technique designed to assess the validity of a statement describing abuse (Lamb et al., 1997). CBCA is the key component of an overall assessment process called *statement validity analysis.* To perform a criteria-based content analysis, a verbatim transcript of a child's statement is analyzed in light of a set of predetermined criteria. Raskin and Esplin (1991) explained that CBCA "consists primarily of a content analysis of a witness's statement based on the premise that accounts of self-experienced events differ in content and quality from statements based on invention or fantasy" (p. 154).

Research is underway on CBCA's ability to differentiate valid from invalid descriptions of abuse. At this writing, however, serious questions remain about the utility of CBCA (Anson, Golding, & Gully, 1993; Berliner & Conte, 1993; Rudy & Brigham, 1997; Wells & Loftus,

1991). Lamb et al. (1997) concluded from empirical research that they conducted on CBCA:

> Overall, the results reported here are quite sobering, particularly when viewed from the perspective of forensic application. . . . The level of precision [with CBCA] clearly remains too poor to permit the designation of CBCA as a reliable and valid test suitable for use in the courtroom. . . . CBCA scores should not yet—and perhaps should never—be used in forensic contexts to evaluate individual statements. (pp. 262-263)

DOCUMENTATION OF THE CHILD'S COMPETENCE TO BE A WITNESS

During interviews, it is useful to ask questions that demonstrate children's capabilities in the following areas:

- Capacity to observe events
- Sufficient memory to recall events
- Ability to communicate
- Ability to distinguish fact from fantasy
- Understanding of the difference between the truth and a lie and appreciation that it is wrong to lie

5

Investigating Suspected Child Abuse

This chapter builds on the material on interviewing in Chapter 4. This chapter devotes substantial attention to the role of professionals in gathering verbal evidence of maltreatment. The chapter also discusses multidisciplinary investigation, videotaping interviews, evaluating bizarre allegations of abuse, and, briefly, investigating cases with multiple victims.

❏ Hearsay: Gathering Verbal Evidence of Abuse

A child's statements to professionals, parents, teachers, and others may be powerful evidence of abuse. Professionals who investigate child abuse or treat abused children understand the importance of documenting the child's words. Many professionals, however, do not fully realize that documenting words is only half the battle. A child's words are usually hearsay, and hearsay cannot be used in court unless certain requirements are met. Professionals are uniquely situated to document the factors that *must coexist with words* to meet these requirements. Knowing what to watch for when children describe abuse opens the courtroom door to children's words and can spell the difference between peril and protection.

DEFINING HEARSAY

Before legal proceedings begin, much of what children say—and some of what they do—is hearsay. The intricacies of hearsay are among the most complex in the law. Indeed, many lawyers have only a limited understanding of hearsay. As we prepare to delve into the law of hearsay, you may find yourself saying, "Now wait just a minute here. I had the good sense not to go to law school. Why should I have to fiddle with the hearsay rule and its exceptions? Hearsay is for you legal beagles." I appreciate your sentiments. Like it or not, however, if you work with abused and neglected children, you cannot ignore hearsay. Why? Because children's hearsay statements play a critically important role in proving abuse, and the legal beagles depend on you *non*lawyers to document the factors that make it possible to use hearsay in court.

> *Like it or not, however, if you work with abused and neglected children, you cannot ignore hearsay.*

Fortunately, it is not necessary to master the nuances of hearsay to deal quite effectively with its implications for practice. It is helpful, however, to have an understanding of hearsay, so let us begin with a definition. The standard definition of hearsay is "an out-of-court statement offered for the truth of the matter asserted." The definition is not terribly helpful. It is more useful to break the definition into three components. A child's words are hearsay if all of the following exist:

1. The child described something that happened (e.g., abuse).
2. The child's words were spoken before the court proceeding at which an adult now proposes to repeat the child's words (e.g., 6 weeks before

the court hearing, the child told an interviewer about abuse; the interviewer is now in court to repeat what the child said).

3. The child's words are used in court to prove that what the child said really happened (e.g., the child's words are repeated in court to prove that the abuse happened).

To test your understanding of hearsay, consider the case of 4-year-old Sally Jones, who was allegedly molested by a neighbor named Bill. Immediately on her release by the offender, Sally burst into her home crying and blurted out, "Mommy, mommy, Billy played nasty with me. His pee-pee was big and hard, like a stick, and he pushed it in my mouth, and white stuff came out that tasted really yucky!" What powerful evidence of abuse!

Bill is charged with molestation, which he denies. At Bill's trial, Sally does not testify because she is too frightened to communicate. There is no medical or physical evidence of abuse. There are no eyewitnesses except Sally. The prosecutor has a problem. How can the prosecutor prove sexual abuse when the only eyewitness cannot testify? One way is to call Sally's mother, Mrs. Jones, as a witness and ask her to repeat Sally's graphic description of Bill's conduct. That is, the prosecutor uses what Sally said *to her mother* as proof that Sally was abused.

Mrs. Jones takes the witness stand. The prosecutor asks some preliminary questions and then comes to the point: "Mrs. Jones, what did Sally say to you when she ran into the house that day?" Before Sally's mother can repeat what her daughter said, the defense attorney says, "Your honor, I object. The prosecutor's question calls for inadmissible hearsay."

You be the judge. Is the defense attorney right? Are Sally's words to her mother hearsay? Go back to the three-part definition. First, Sally intended her words to describe something that happened. Second, Sally's words were uttered before Bill's trial, and at the trial, Sally's mother proposes to repeat what her daughter said. Third, the prosecutor is offering Sally's words to prove that what Sally said really happened: that is, to prove that what Sally said is true. All three elements of the definition are satisfied: Sally's words are hearsay.

Hearsay is generally not allowed in court. Although there are exceptions to the rule against hearsay, the law is clear that hearsay is inadmissible. Unless the prosecutor can convince the judge to apply one of the exceptions, the judge will sustain defense counsel's objection, and Sally's mother will not be permitted to repeat Sally's description of the abuse.

To expand on Sally's case, suppose that Sally's mother takes her to the hospital shortly after the initial disclosure. At the hospital, Sally is interviewed by a social worker. The interview takes place half an hour after Sally disclosed to her mother. By the time Sally talks to the social worker, she has stopped crying, although she is still visibly upset. In response to the social worker's questions about what happened, Sally points to her mouth and says, "Bill put his pee-pee in here." The social worker hands Sally an anatomical diagram of a little girl and asks Sally to circle the part of the girl's body where Bill touched Sally. Sally circles the mouth. Finally, the social worker hands Sally anatomical dolls and asks her to illustrate what happened. Sally says that the adult doll is Bill and the child doll is Sally. Sally places the adult doll's penis in the mouth of the child doll and pushes in and out.

At Bill's trial, the prosecutor calls the social worker as a witness and asks the social worker to repeat Sally's description of what Bill did, including Sally's gesture pointing to her mouth. The prosecutor also asks the social worker to describe what Sally did with the anatomical diagram and dolls. Once again, however, defense counsel says, "Your honor, I object. This question too calls for hearsay."

When Sally spoke to the social worker, Sally intended to describe what Bill did to her. Thus, Sally's words satisfy the first element of the hearsay definition. But that's not all. When Sally pointed to her mouth, she was describing something that happened. The same is true of Sally's drawing on the diagram and her positioning of the anatomical dolls. Sally used nonverbal communication to describe something that happened.

Is Sally's nonverbal communication hearsay? Nonverbal communication that is intended to describe something that happened can be hearsay. Consider a simple example. Suppose that shortly following the assault, Sally is taken to a police station to see whether she can pick her assailant out of a lineup. Seven men walk on stage, and the police officer says, "Now Sally, do you see the man who hurt you?"

Sally might say, "Yes, that's him. Right in the middle." Alternatively, Sally might say nothing but point to the man in the middle. The message is the same whether Sally uses words or gestures. Sally's pointing gesture is the equivalent of words. Like the words "That's him," Sally's gesture is hearsay if the police officer testifies at Bill's trial and describes Sally's pointing gesture at the lineup.

What Sally said to the social worker, along with Sally's nonverbal communication, occurred before the court proceeding at which they are offered as evidence; therefore, the second element of hearsay is satisfied.

Finally, if the prosecutor uses Sally's verbal and nonverbal communication with the social worker to prove that Sally was abused, then the final element of hearsay is satisfied. Unless the prosecutor can circumvent the hearsay rule, the judge will prohibit the social worker from describing what Sally said and did during the interview.

The prosecutor's ability to use Sally's hearsay in court depends on whether the hearsay meets the requirements of an exception to the rule against hearsay. Although there are more than 40 exceptions to the hearsay rule, only a handful play a day-to-day role in child abuse cases. Each hearsay exception has its own specific requirements, and professionals play a key role in documenting these requirements. In case after case, watchful professionals document the often fleeting and subtle information that is needed to meet the requirements of a hearsay exception. The professional's documentation turns out to be the key factor that allows a child's words—although hearsay—to be repeated in court.

EXCEPTIONS TO THE RULE AGAINST HEARSAY

Five hearsay exceptions are discussed below: (a) the excited utterance exception, (b) fresh complaint of rape, (c) the state-of-mind exception, (d) the medical diagnosis or treatment exception, and (e) the so-called child hearsay exceptions. All states have the excited utterance and state-of-mind exceptions. All states but one apply the fresh-complaint doctrine to children. A majority of states have some version of the medical diagnosis or treatment and child hearsay exceptions.

TABLE 5.1 Elements of the Excited Utterance Exception

1. The child experienced a startling event.
2. The child made a statement relating to the startling event.
3. The child's statement was made while the child was still experiencing
   excitement caused by the startling event.

The Excited Utterance Exception

An excited utterance is a hearsay statement that relates to a startling event. The excited utterance must be made while the child is still under the excitement caused by the startling event. Although an excited utterance is hearsay, it can be used in court. Three requirements must be fulfilled for a child's hearsay statement to be an excited utterance (see Table 5.1).

First, the child must experience a startling event that excites the child. Recall Sally's case, in which Sally was allegedly molested by the neighbor, Bill. The molestation easily qualifies as a startling event. Not all acts of sexual abuse startle or excite children, but Sally's experience was sufficiently startling for the excited-utterance exception.

Second, the child's hearsay statement must relate to the startling event. Sally's statement to her mother described the abuse and thus clearly meets the relationship requirement. The statement to the social worker also referred directly to the event and thus meets the relationship requirement.

Finally, the child's hearsay statement must be made while the child is still experiencing the excitement caused by the startling event. Sally reported the abuse to her mother shortly after it occurred and while she was still upset and crying. Thus, Sally's statement to her mother is an excited utterance and can be used in court even though it is hearsay. The judge will overrule defense counsel's objection, and Sally's mother *will* be permitted to tell the jury what Sally said that day.

But what about Sally's hearsay statement to the social worker at the hospital? Is the statement to the social worker, uttered at least half an hour after the sexual abuse and in response to the social worker's questions, an excited utterance? To answer this, we need to examine the factors that judges consider in evaluating hearsay offered under the excited-utterance exception:

- *Nature of the event.* Certain events are more startling than others. Judges consider the nature of the event and the likely impact that such an event would have on a child of similar age and experience.

- *Lapse of time.* The longer the delay between a startling event and a child's hearsay statement describing the event, the less likely it is that the child was still excited when the statement was made. Judges agree, however, that lapse of time is not dispositive on the issue of excitement, and delay is considered along with other factors indicating presence or absence of excitement. Judges have approved delays ranging from a few minutes to several hours.

- *Emotional condition.* A child's emotional condition is an important indicator of excitement. If a child was upset and crying when a statement was made, the judge is more likely to conclude that the statement is an excited utterance. On the other hand, if the child was calm when the statement was made, or if a period of calm or sleep intervened between a startling event and a child's statement relating to the event, the statement is less likely to qualify as an excited utterance. Of course, some highly traumatized children appear calm or even dazed.

- *Speech pattern.* The way that a child makes a statement may indicate excitement. For example, pressured or hurried speech indicates excitement.

- *The words themselves.* The child's words themselves may indicate excitement. Remember Sally, who said, "Mommy, mommy, Billy played nasty with me. His pee-pee was big and hard, like a stick, and he pushed it in my mouth and white stuff came out that tasted really yucky!" The fact that Sally's sentence ends in an exclamation point indicates excitement. In fact, Sally's statement nicely illustrates "Myers' exclamation point rule." If the appropriate punctuation for the end of a child's statement is an exclamation point, it is an excited utterance. Of course, you won't want to quote "Myers' exclamation point rule" in court, but the "rule" works 99% of the time. Try it.

> *The most important factor is whether the statement is a product of reflection and deliberation or a spontaneous response to a startling event.*

- *Physical condition.* A child's physical condition may indicate whether the child is excited. For example, statements from a child who is injured or in pain are likely to be excited utterances.

- *Spontaneity.* In evaluating a statement as a potential excited utterance, the most important factor is whether the statement is a product of reflection and deliberation or a spontaneous response to a startling event. The more spontaneous the statement, the more likely it is to meet the requirements of this hearsay exception.

- *Questioning.* Children often describe abuse in response to questions from an adult. The way a child is questioned has an impact on whether the statement is an excited utterance. Judges agree that questioning does not necessarily destroy spontaneity. For example, a few open-ended questions are unlikely to eliminate spontaneity. When questions are leading, however, spontaneity may be lacking.

- *First safe opportunity.* Most children are abused while under the physical control of the abuser. When the child finally escapes to a place of safety, the child may disclose. In some instances, however, a substantial amount of time elapses between the abuse and the disclosure, raising questions about the excited utterance exception. A number of court decisions state that when a child makes a hearsay statement at the first safe opportunity, the statement may qualify as an excited utterance even if quite a bit of time has elapsed.

- *Rekindled excitement.* Sometimes, after a child experiences a startling event, days or weeks go by until something triggers or rekindles the excitement of the original event. Such a lapse of time is normally much too long for the excited utterance exception. In a small number of cases, however, courts use the rekindled excitement idea to approve children's hearsay statements as excited utterances.

Professionals who interview or treat children can watch for and document the factors listed above and in Table 5.2. Documentation at the time of the interview or examination goes a long way toward convincing a judge that a child's hearsay statement is an excited utterance.

Now that we have examined the factors that judges look to in deciding whether hearsay is an excited utterance, let us return to Sally. We have already determined that Sally's statement to her mother is a slam-dunk excited utterance. But what about Sally's statement to the social worker, half an hour after the initial disclosure and in response to the social worker's questions? Is Sally's statement to the social worker an excited utterance? This is a close case. Frankly, I don't know how a judge would rule. Of one thing I am sure, however. If the social worker documented the factors described above, there is a much greater chance that the judge will conclude that Sally's words and acts at the hospital were excited utterances. Thus, in Sally's case, the ability to use what Sally said and did at the

TABLE 5.2 Factors Indicating Whether a Child Is Still Experiencing the Excitement Caused by the Startling Event

---

Nature of the event
Lapse of time
Child's emotional condition
Speech pattern
Words spoken
Child's physical condition
Spontaneity
Questioning by adults
Statement made at first safe opportunity

---

hospital as evidence in court depends not so much on the skill of a prosecutor as on the knowledge of the social worker.

Fresh Complaint of Rape

Under a venerable legal doctrine called "fresh complaint of rape," an adult rape victim's initial disclosure can be used in court to corroborate the victim's testimony at trial (Myers, 1997a). In all but one state, the fresh complaint doctrine applies to children as well as adults. Moreover, fresh complaint evidence is not limited to rape cases. Thus, regardless of the type of sex offense, a child's fresh complaint describing the offense may be admissible.

A child's description of sexual abuse that does not qualify as an excited utterance—perhaps because too much time elapsed—may be used in court as a fresh complaint. Indeed, a child's description of abuse may be a fresh complaint even if it was uttered weeks or months following the abuse.

The State-of-Mind Exception

The state-of-mind exception is the most theoretically complex exception to the rule against hearsay. The exception allows limited use in court of statements describing a person's emotions, sensations, or physical condition. Among the many states of mind allowed under this exception are statements indicating plan, intent, motive, pain, love, hate, and other emotions.

This book is not the place to unravel the mysteries of the state-of-mind exception. For our purposes, it will suffice to say that professionals can assist attorneys by documenting children's statements that describe their emotions, including feelings of affection, fear, and dislike. In addition, professionals should document statements describing bodily feeling. Finally, professionals should document the child's belief that abuse occurred.

The Medical Diagnosis or Treatment Exception

Most states have an exception to the hearsay rule for certain statements made to professionals providing diagnostic or treatment services. This exception—commonly called the *medical diagnosis or treatment exception*—allows use in court of a child's words describing medical history. The medical history "consists of data identifying the patient, the source of referral to the doctor, the name of the person providing the medical history, and chief complaint, a history of the present illness, past medical history, family history, psychosocial history, and a review of body systems" (Myers et al., 1989, p. 36). The medical diagnosis or treatment exception allows statements describing a child's past and present symptoms, pain, and other sensations. Finally, the exception allows a child's description of the cause of injury or illness.

The primary rationale for the diagnosis or treatment exception is that statements to treating professionals are likely to be reliable because the patient has an incentive to be truthful (Mosteller, 1989). After all, a patient's health—even life—may depend on the accuracy of information provided to a physician or nurse. This rationale is applicable for many older children and adolescents. Young children, however, may not understand the need for accuracy and candor with health care providers. When a child does not understand that his or her well-being can be affected by statements to a professional, the primary rationale for the diagnosis or treatment exception evaporates.

The diagnosis or treatment exception applies to statements made to medical professionals, such as physicians and nurses. In most states, the exception also applies, at least in some cases, to statements to mental health professionals.

To increase the probability that a child's statements satisfy the requirements of the diagnosis or treatment exception, professionals can take the following steps.

First, determine whether the child understands that the purpose of the interview or examination is to provide diagnosis and/or treatment. Document the child's understanding. In one case, for example, a pediatrician introduced herself to her 4-year-old patient with "I'm Dr. Bays, and I'm going to do a checkup to see how strong you are, how healthy you are, and if there's anything that needs to be done" (*State v. Logan*, 1991). The doctor's introduction informed the child of the purpose of the interview and examination and helped persuade the judge that the child's statements to the doctor met the requirements of the medical diagnosis or treatment exception.

If more than one professional interacts with a child during an assessment, the child may be informed that each professional is involved in the diagnostic or treatment process. Again, documentation is critical. In *State v. Logan*, mentioned above, Dr. Bays conducted her physical examination and initial interview of the child and then introduced the child to a nonmedical colleague who conducted a videotaped interview. Dr. Bays made sure that the child knew that the nonphysician was part of the assessment team.

Second, emphasize the importance of providing accurate and complete information. Document anything that indicates that the child understands the importance of accuracy.

Third, document how and why information disclosed during an interview is *pertinent* to effective diagnosis or treatment. The medical diagnosis or treatment exception does not include everything patients tell professionals; only statements that are pertinent to diagnosis or treatment are included.

Fourth, if a child identifies the perpetrator during an interview, document why knowing the identity of the perpetrator is pertinent for diagnosis or treatment. For example, an emergency room physician needs to know who abused a child so that the doctor can ensure the child's safety. Protecting a child from continued abuse is an essential element of treatment. With some forms of abuse, a physician needs to test for sexually transmitted disease, and the identity of the abuser is pertinent. A mental health professional providing treatment for a sexually abused child may need to know who abused the child.

The medical diagnosis or treatment exception plays an important role in child abuse litigation, and documenting the information outlined above increases the likelihood that a child's hearsay statements will satisfy the requirements of the exception.

Child Hearsay Exceptions

Many states have special hearsay exceptions for reliable statements that do not meet the requirements of one of the traditional exceptions such as excited utterance. These special exceptions are known as *residual* or *catchall exceptions.* A slim majority of states have a catchall exception especially for children's hearsay, and I call these *child hearsay exceptions.*

The key question under residual, catchall, and child hearsay exceptions is *reliability.* To evaluate reliability, judges consider the factors outlined below and in Table 5.3:

- *Spontaneity.* Spontaneity can be an indicator of reliability. The more spontaneous a child's statement, the less likely it is to be a product of fabrication or distortion.
- *Statements elicited by questioning.* The reliability of a child's statement may be influenced by the type of questions that elicit the statement. When questioning is leading, the possibility exists that the questioner influenced the child's statement, raising questions about reliability. As the U.S. Supreme Court pointed out in *Idaho v. Wright* (1990), however, use of leading questions does not necessarily render hearsay unreliable.
- *Consistent statements.* Reliability may be enhanced when a child's description of abuse remains consistent over time. When a child's story varies significantly each time, reliability may be questioned. This is not to say, however, that complete consistency is required for hearsay to be reliable. What is important is consistency regarding core details. Consistency about peripheral details is less important. The reasons for children's inconsistency were discussed in Chapter 4.
- *The child's state of mind and emotion.* A child may display affect or emotion that supports the reliability of hearsay. For example, an older child may demonstrate embarrassment or shame that one might expect on disclosure of sexual abuse. Of course, some abused children are not emotional as they describe abuse. For example, a child who has described abuse five times to five different interviewers may have a bland delivery. Furthermore, a child with dissociative symptoms may disclose without apparent emotion.

TABLE 5.3 Factors Related to the Reliability of Children's Statements

Spontaneity
Questioning
Consistent statements
Child's state of mind and emotion
Play or gestures that support the child's description of abuse
Developmentally unusual knowledge of sexual acts or anatomy
Idiosyncratic details about sexual abuse
Use of developmentally appropriate terminology
Child's belief that disclosure might lead to punishment of the child
Child's or adult's motive to fabricate
Child's correction of the interviewer

- *Play or gestures.* A young child's play or gestures while describing abuse may enhance the reliability of the child's statement. For example, if a child places the penis of an anatomical doll in the mouth of another doll or in the child's mouth while describing sexual abuse, the child's verbal statement may gain trustworthiness.

- *Developmentally unusual sexual knowledge.* Young children lack the experience required to fabricate detailed and anatomically accurate accounts of sexual acts (MacFarlane & Waterman, 1986). (See Chapter 7.) It is difficult to imagine a 4-year-old inventing a detailed and accurate account of fellatio, including ejaculation, unless the child has either experienced fellatio or seen it. Of course, care must be taken to rule out alternative explanations for a child's developmentally unusual sexual knowledge.

- *Idiosyncratic detail.* Presence in a child's statement of idiosyncratic details of sexual activity points toward reliability. Jones (1992) noted the diagnostic significance of a young child who knows what sex smells, tastes, or feels like. Lack of idiosyncratic detail does not make a description of abuse unreliable. Some forms of abuse lack unique detail. Fondling through clothing is an example. With young children, paucity of detail is sometimes a function of difficulty in responding to open-ended question that require free recall. (See Chapter 4 for discussion of free recall.)

- *Developmentally appropriate terminology.* When a young child describes abuse in words that one expects from a child of that age, reliability may be enhanced. By contrast, if a child's disclosure employs adult terminology, the possibility of coaching arises. A child's vocabulary is not a litmus test for reliability, however. Some children experience multiple interviews, and it is not uncommon for children to pick up terms such as *molest* or *penetration* during the course of interviews. A child who would not spontaneously use adult terminology may disclose abuse to a parent, who introduces a term that seems unusual coming from the child. An abused child with a sophisticated vocabulary might use adult terms. Thus, in considering a child's terminology, it is important to assess the child's developmental and linguistic level along with the number of times the child was interviewed and by whom.

- *Child's or adult's motive to lie.* Evidence that a child or an adult had a motive to lie affects reliability.
- *Correcting the interviewer.* Reliability may be enhanced when a child does not agree with everything the interviewer says or when a child corrects an interviewer. Disagreement and correction demonstrate that the child has a firm mental picture of what happened. Furthermore, disagreement indicates that the child is not simply responding unthinkingly or answering questions to please the interviewer.

The factors listed above are not the only indicators of reliability, and I urge you to write down *anything* that sheds light on the reliability of a child's statements describing abuse.

THE IMPORTANCE OF DOCUMENTATION

Professionals are in a peerless position to record children's hearsay statements *and* to document the factors that judges consider to determine whether hearsay meets the requirements of an exception. By taking a few moments to document the factors discussed above, professionals substantially increase the probability that a child's hearsay statements can be used in later legal proceedings. The Verbal Evidence Checklist in Figure 5.1 can be photocopied and used to document children's descriptions of abuse.

I cannot emphasize too strongly the importance of documentation. The legal proceeding at which a child's hearsay statements are offered as evidence may occur months or years after the child discloses abuse. Unless there is careful documentation of *exactly* what was asked and *exactly* what the child said, there is very little chance that the professional will remember when the time comes for the professional to get on the witness stand and repeat the child's hearsay. A vague recollection of what a child said will not do. Paraphrasing what children say may be acceptable in some circumstances, but more often than not, the law requires the exact words spoken by the child. Only detailed documentation holds any realistic promise of

Child's Name:_____ Date:_____ Your Name:_____ Case No.:_____

____ Document your questions. Don't paraphrase.
____ Document child's *exact* words. Don't paraphrase.
____ Did child tell anyone else? Who? When? Why? What?

All Professionals Document:

____ *Elapsed time:* How much time elapsed between the event and the child's description? (Be precise; minutes count.)
____ *Emotional condition:* Child's emotional condition when child described what happened. (Crying? Upset? Calm? Excited? Traumatized?)
____ *Physical condition:* Was child hurt, injured, in pain?
____ *Spontaneous?* Was child's description spontaneous? (E.g., Was child's description unprompted or in response to questions?)
____ *Consistency:* If child described the event more than once, are there consistencies across descriptions?
____ *Developmentally unusual sexual knowledge or conduct:* Document any developmentally unusual sexual knowledge or behavior, including idiosyncratic details (e.g., smells or tastes).
____ *Motive to lie:* Does anyone—child or adult—have a motive to lie?
____ *Reliability:* Document *anything* that sheds light on the reliability of the child's statement, i.e., anything that gives you reason to believe the child.

Ask Questions About and Document:

____ Child's memory for simple events (e.g., breakfast this morning? What was on TV today?)
____ Child's ability to communicate in a way adults can understand.
____ Child's understanding of the difference between truth and lies. (Don't ask children under age 9 to define "truth" and "lie." *Don't* ask kids to give examples of truth or lies. *Don't* ask kids to explain the difference between truth and lie. *Do* give examples of something that is true and something that is a lie. Then ask the child to identify which it is (E.g., hold up a blue pen and say "If someone said this is blue, would that be the truth or a lie?").
____ Child's understanding of the importance of telling the truth to you.

Clinical Professionals Providing Medical or Psychological Diagnosis or Treatment
____ Inform child of your clinical purpose. (E.g., "I'm going to give you a checkup to make sure you are healthy." "My job is talking to kids to help them with their problems.")

(continued)

Figure 5.1. Verbal Evidence Checklist

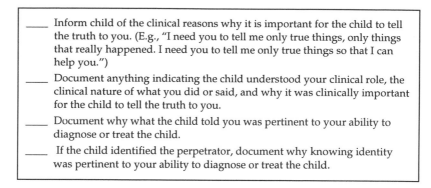

____ Inform child of the clinical reasons why it is important for the child to tell the truth to you. (E.g., "I need you to tell me only true things, only things that really happened. I need you to tell me only true things so that I can help you.")

____ Document anything indicating the child understood your clinical role, the clinical nature of what you did or said, and why it was clinically important for the child to tell the truth to you.

____ Document why what the child told you was pertinent to your ability to diagnose or treat the child.

____ If the child identified the perpetrator, document why knowing identity was pertinent to your ability to diagnose or treat the child.

Figure 5.1. Verbal Evidence Checklist (continued)

preserving the necessary detail. Moreover, documentation is needed not only of the child's words but also of the factors that indicate whether hearsay meets the requirements of an exception to the hearsay rule.

SUMMARY

What children say is often poignant and powerful evidence of abuse. Professionals from medicine, nursing, social work, psychology, education, and other disciplines play a key role in increasing the odds that what children say can be used in court to protect them.

❏ Multidisciplinary Investigation: Specialized Centers to Interview Children

When child maltreatment is suspected, several agencies may investigate. If abuse occurs in the child's home, social workers from CPS are involved. If the maltreatment constitutes a crime, law enforcement investigates. In either case, a public attorney, typically a prosecutor, may play a role. Medical and mental health professionals are often consulted. Although the investigatory needs of CPS and law enforcement overlap, their needs are not identical (Pence & Wilson, 1994).

With several agencies simultaneously investigating possible abuse, each professional may desire to interview the child, raising the possibility of disjointed investigation and multiple interviews. During the 1980s, a trend emerged toward coordinated, multidisciplinary investigation of child abuse, and today, more than 30 states and the federal government have laws mandating or authorizing joint law enforcement-CPS investigation.

An important goal of multidisciplinary investigation is to reduce the number of times that children are interviewed. To this end, a large number of communities have specialized child interview centers modeled on the Children's Advocacy Center pioneered in 1985 in Huntsville, Alabama. More than 300 specialized child interview centers operate around the United States.

RESEARCH ON MULTIDISCIPLINARY INVESTIGATION

Although multidisciplinary investigation is believed to be superior to the "traditional" approach, in which each agency goes its own way, there is relatively little empirical study of the effectiveness of multidisciplinary investigation.

In 1994, Tjaden and Anhalt completed a broad-based evaluation of the impact of joint law enforcement-CPS investigation. The three-and-a-half-year research project evaluated the impact of investigative practices on case processing in Colorado Springs, Denver, and Las Vegas. These locations varied in their approach to investigation, with one city using an interdisciplinary approach, another city using a traditional (independent) approach, and the third city in between. The authors found that "caseworker response time was significantly shorter in joint investigation cases than in independent investigation cases" (p. 15), with an average time lapse of 3.3 days from the report to the start of the CPS investigation in the independent cases and 1.6 days in the joint investigation cases. The authors suggest that the shorter time lapse in joint investigation cases occurred because these cases "involved more serious allegations and therefore received a higher priority" (p. 15).

Joint investigations were found to be significantly longer than independent investigations. Further, joint investigations were more thorough: "Caseworkers made twice as many contacts during joint investigations than during independent investigations" (p. 17). But the increased number of contacts in joint investigations cases "did not result in more repeat contacts with various parties involved in the case" (p. 17).

As for effects on case outcome,

> Joint investigations affected every one of the case outcome variables. . . . Cases with joint investigations were significantly more likely to result in custody removal, perpetrator departure from the home, victim corroboration, perpetrator confession, founded reports, treatment plan development, dependency filings, and criminal filings. Moreover, cases with joint investigations were significantly more likely to result in convictions when criminal charges were filed against the perpetrator. (p. 18)

Although joint investigation was related to increased conviction rates, it "[did] not necessarily result in a higher prosecution rate" (p. 24). The rate of prosecution depends on many factors, including the priorities of the prosecuting authority.

In Tjaden and Anhalt's study, police and social workers participating in joint investigations "universally agreed that joint investigations 'take more time' and 'are more thorough' than independent investigations" (p. 19). Professionals participating in the research believed that "the thoroughness of joint investigations leads to better outcomes for children and families experiencing child abuse" (p. 19).

Tjaden and Anhalt's research focused on joint law enforcement-CPS investigation. Research conducted in Chicago and Sacramento shifts the focus to specialized child interview centers. In Chicago, Jaudes and Martone (1992) compared investigation by a hospital-based multidisciplinary child interview center to traditional investigative practices. The child interview center's primary goal was "to reduce the number of interviews and the number of interviewers," and this goal was achieved. The authors reported that 80% of the children interviewed at the special center were interviewed only once, whereas before the center, 50% of children were interviewed three or more times. In addition, children interviewed at the special center were interviewed by fewer professionals.

Jaudes and Martone (1992) reported additional differences between the child interview center and the traditional approach. In cases handled through the center, there were "increases in (1) identification of the perpetrator; (2) charges pressed if identification of the perpetrator occurred, and (3) indicated cases of sexual abuse by the state child welfare agency" (p. 1166). The authors concluded that

> interdisciplinary evaluations of allegedly sexually abused children not only decreased the number of investigative interviews and interviewers a child faced, but also increased the likelihood of identification of the perpetrator, the indicated cases by the state agency, and the criminal charges being pressed by the police in conjunction with the State's Attorney's Office. We believe interdisciplinary evaluations of alleged sexual abuse cases are necessary, and we strongly recommend formation of interdisciplinary teams in regionalized centers to assess allegedly sexually abused victims. (p. 1167)

To turn from investigation to prosecution, Martone, Jaudes, and Cavins (1996) reported in a follow-up study that "at the prosecution stage, [the child interview center] did not affect prosecution variables such as trial outcome, indictments, and guilty pleas" (p. 463).

In 1989, the California Legislature funded a pilot project in Sacramento to operate a multidisciplinary child interview center (California Attorney General's Office, 1994). The Sacramento County Attorney's Office, in cooperation with CPS and law enforcement, established a multidisciplinary interview center staffed by highly trained "child interview specialists." To evaluate the effectiveness of the Sacramento center, children interviewed there were compared to children whose cases were handled before establishment of the center. Comparisons were possible between 177 children whose cases were handled before the center and 212 children handled through the center. The final report on the center pilot project stated:

> As implemented in Sacramento County, the multidisciplinary interview center was associated with a significant reduction in the number of interviews. A child whose case was investigated prior to implementation of the pilot project was eleven times more likely to experience multiple interviews than a child involved in an investigation conducted through the multidisciplinary interview center. The proportion of cases with multiple interviews was reduced from 48% prior to implementation of the pilot project to 4% after instituting the project ($p < .0001$). . . .

Analysis of data from Sacramento County indicates that the average number of interviewers who question children was significantly lower for children involved in the pilot project than for children involved in standard investigative procedures ($p < .0001$). . . .

The Sacramento pilot project was associated with significantly less interview time. (pp. 34-35)

The Sacramento multidisciplinary interview center, like the center in Chicago, reduced the number of interviews. Professionals in Sacramento "expressed the opinion that highly trained interviewers who use standardized interview protocols increased accountability and improved the quality of evidence" (p. 38).

Martone et al. (1996) found that the child interview center in Chicago did not affect prosecution variables such as rate of indictment, guilty pleas, or guilty verdicts at trial. A similar result was obtained in Sacramento. This is not to say that multidisciplinary child interview centers do not affect prosecution variables. The results obtained by Tjaden and Anhalt (1994), discussed earlier in this section, indicate that joint law enforcement-CPS investigation can influence prosecution. Until further research is conducted, however, we do not have enough data to conclude one way or another whether child interview centers affect prosecution outcomes.

Despite uncertainty regarding the impact of child interview centers on prosecution outcomes, such centers clearly can reduce the number of interviews and interviewers. Moreover, many professionals believe the child-friendly atmosphere of such centers reduces stress for children.

❑ Videotaping Investigative Interviews

Should investigative interviews be videotaped? This is a controversial issue in some communities. Credible arguments are possible for and against videotaping. This section briefly summarizes the arguments for and against videotaping.

ARGUMENTS FOR VIDEOTAPING

Videotaping Reduces the Number of Interviews

Videotaping reduces the need for multiple interviews. Professionals who are not present for an interview can watch the tape rather than reinterviewing the child.

Videotaping Preserves Evidence of Abuse

A child's videotaped interview may contain powerful verbal evidence of abuse, admissible under exceptions to the hearsay rule (see the discussion of hearsay earlier in this chapter). Videotaping memorializes exactly what the child said. Moreover, videotaping preserves the child's emotion, demeanor, and body language at the moment of disclosure. This nonverbal accompaniment is often as important as the child's words.

Videotaping Provides an Incentive for Interviewers to Use Proper Interview Technique

Videotaping puts the interviewer in the spotlight, increasing the incentive to use proper interview technique. Reducing inappropriate interviewing is not the only advantage of videotaping, however. When an interview is done properly, the videotape attests convincingly to the quality of the interview and makes it difficult to argue that the interviewer coached the child or asked unnecessarily leading questions. Davies et al. (1996) wrote that "the videotape can stand as a rebuttal to allegations that the interviewer coached, coerced, or intimidated a child into making abuse allegations" (p. 190).

The Videotape May Discourage Recantation

Once children disclose abuse, powerful forces may pressure them to recant (see Chapter 4, the section "Interviewing," subsection "The Interviewer's Dilemma," sub-subsection "The Disclosure Process in

Child Sexual Abuse"). A videotape is an irrefutable record of a child's words, and the tape can be used to help the child resist pressure to recant. Of course, the fact that a description of abuse is videotaped does not make it true. Defense counsel may argue that videotaping a false allegation sets it in stone and provides the prosecution improper leverage to coerce the child to adhere to a false story. Although this argument has appeal in some cases, the defense attorney is not without weapons to attack false allegations. In view of the documented pressure on actual victims to recant, the use of videotape to help children maintain disclosure appears justified.

Videotaping May Convince the Nonoffending Parent That Abuse Occurred

When sexual abuse occurs within a family, the nonoffending parent may or may not believe the child. A videotaped disclosure is sometimes useful to persuade a skeptical parent that abuse occurred.

A Videotape May Encourage Confession

Viewing a child's videotaped disclosure may persuade defense counsel that the child will be an effective witness and that the best course for the defendant is to negotiate a guilty plea. In some cases, the defendant views the tape and realizes, for the first time, the harm caused by abuse. A guilty conscience prompts a guilty plea.

A Videotape May Refresh a Child's Memory

Months or years may pass before a child testifies in court. A videotaped statement, made when the child's memory was fresh, is useful to help the child remember the details of the offense.

Expert Witnesses May Use the Videotape

If expert witnesses are to testify, they may view the videotape rather than interviewing the child.

ARGUMENTS AGAINST VIDEOTAPING

*Videotaping Places Exaggerated Emphasis on
Inconsistencies in Children's Descriptions of Abuse*

Critics of videotaping worry that defense counsel will exaggerate the importance of (a) the child's inconsistencies during the videotaped interview, (b) inconsistencies between the videotaped interview and the child's other statements describing abuse, and (c) inconsistencies between the videotaped interview and the child's testimony in court. Inconsistencies across time are inevitable, particularly about peripheral details and particularly among young children (see Chapter 4, the section "Interviewing," subsection "Effects of Multiple Interviews on Memory," sub-subsection "Inconsistencies Can Be Explained"). But with videotape in hand, defense counsel can magnify minor inconsistencies, unfairly undermining the child's credibility.

Proponents of videotaping respond, "Since when is it improper to focus on inconsistent statements?" Proponents of videotaping argue that the most effective way to deal with children's inconsistency is not to avoid videotaping but to explain inconsistency. For example, during the testimony of an older child, the child can explain the inconsistency. With younger children, the prosecutor can call as witnesses the adults to whom the child disclosed abuse. As the adults describe the gradual, halting disclosure that is common among abused children, jurors can see the reasons for inconsistency. Finally, if defense counsel focuses on inconsistency, the prosecutor may call an expert to explain the psychological and developmental reasons for inconsistency (see Chapter 7, the section "Sexual Abuse," subsection "Credibility Evidence").

Defense Counsel May Take Portions of the Videotape out of Context

Some sexually abused children disclose their abuse gradually, revealing further details over time. Due to the progressive nature of disclosure, an interview that is videotaped early in the investigation may provide an incomplete picture of the abuse. Moreover, in many cases, a child's most spontaneous and powerful statements are off camera. A child's initial disclosure to a parent or teacher, for example, may be compelling, but it is not videotaped. Yet, if a later interview is videotaped, the tape may take center stage, pushing the child's unrecorded statements into the background and deflecting attention from what may be compelling evidence.

Opponents of videotaping worry that when a videotape becomes the center of attention, the child may appear unconvincing. Indeed, defense counsel may concentrate on a lackluster videotape to distract the jury from the child's other, more compelling, statements.

Proponents of videotaping respond that the solution to defense efforts to focus misleading attention on the videotape lies in the judge's authority to ensure that matters are not distorted or taken out of context.

Defense Counsel Exaggerates Interviewer Error

A common defense tactic is to attack the way that children are interviewed. Opponents of videotaping argue that preserving an interview on tape encourages this strategy by handing the interview to the defense on a silver platter. The focus of litigation shifts away from what the child said and onto the questions asked. Defense counsel, perhaps assisted by an expert, dwells on the negative impact of suggestive questions and other questionable interview practices.

Proponents of videotaping respond that when interviews are done poorly, the defense *should* attack. The goal should not be to hide improper interviewing. Rather, when properly conducted video-taped interviews are attacked unfairly, jurors should be informed that children have sufficient memory capacity and are not as suggestible as many adults believe. Moreover, jurors can be informed of the reasons for children's inconsistency. Jurors can be told why competent interviewers ask suggestive questions. Equipped with this information, the jury can put defense counsel's attack in perspective.

Videotaping Everything That Children Say Is Neither Possible nor Desirable

The U.S. Supreme Court observed in *Idaho v. Wright* (1990) that "out-of-court statements made by children regarding sexual abuse arise in a wide variety of circumstances" (p. 818). Opponents of videotaping emphasize that it is not possible to videotape every contact with children. Yet if videotaping becomes the norm, children's statements that are not on tape may be viewed with unwarranted skepticism.

In some circumstances, it is inappropriate to videotape contact with a child. Psychotherapy is a prime example of adult-child interaction that should not be routinely videotaped. Privacy, confidentiality, and trust are indispensable to therapy, and videotaping may undermine all three.

Proponents of videotaping do not disagree with the foregoing observations. Rather, most proponents of videotaping favor limiting videotaping to formal investigative interviews, in which taping is usually feasible and in which the purpose is to gather evidence.

Videotaping Causes Stage Fright

Some opponents of videotaping argue that taping makes children uncomfortable, interfering with the interview. The video camera may inhibit older children, and young children may be distracted by the equipment.

Experience with videotaping rebuts these concerns. Many children quickly forget the camera. Moreover, in many communities, the camera is out of sight behind a one-way glass.

Videotapes May Fall Into the Wrong Hands

Opponents of videotaping worry about preserving the confidentiality of videotaped interviews. In particular, opponents are concerned that videotapes of children describing extremely embarrassing acts will show up on the six o'clock news. Although there is no way to guarantee security for videotapes, the protective order given in Appendix B, signed by a judge, goes far in the right direction.

SUMMARY

Who has the better argument about videotaping? I don't know. I confess, however, that I am a fan of taping. I can see little to lose and a lot to gain by videotaping interviews. Research in California lends support to the protaping camp (California Attorney General's Office, 1994). The California Attorney General sponsored two pilot projects designed to evaluate videotaping in the context of interviews conducted at multidisciplinary interview centers. Videotaping was evaluated using a "video-off/video-on" model of comparison. During the video-off portion of the project, 100 investigative interviews at each pilot project were conducted without videotaping. Following this, the next 100 interviews at each project were videotaped. "At the end of the process, comparisons were made between video-off and video-on cases" (pp. 57-58). The results of the pilot projects can be summarized as follows. Videotaping appeared to have no deleterious effect on investigation or prosecution. A large majority of prosecutors, police officers, and social workers involved in the pilot projects were enthusiastic about videotaping, stating that videotaping improves investigation and reduces stress for children.

> *Videotaping improves investigation and reduces stress for children.*

❏ Bizarre, Fantastic, Ritual, and Satanic Allegations of Abuse

Children describe many forms of physical and sexual abuse. Scattered among the thousands of "routine" allegations are a small number that contain elements of the fantastic and bizarre. A small number of children and adults describe ritual and even satanic abuse. According to Jones (1991),

> After some years of working with sexually abused children and their families many practitioners encounter children who have been subjected to sadistic, perverse, and sometimes bizarre practices. Some of the acts described are at the very reaches of human imagination, and because of this professionals may find it extremely difficult to maintain neutrality when faced with such histories. (p. 163)

SATANIC CONSPIRACIES?

During the 1980s, frightening stories of satanic abuse surfaced in the United States and Europe (Kelly, 1996). Children and adults described horrific satanic ceremonies, complete with human and animal sacrifice, drinking blood, and sadistic sexual abuse. Some people believe in well-organized, large-scale satanic conspiracies.

There is no doubt that some sex offenders engage in ritualistic practices and that a few perverts offend in the name of religion or the devil. When it comes to satanic conspiracies, however, the evidence just is not there. Lack of evidence is not for want of looking. Law enforcement professionals have investigated in vain for satanic conspiracies (Lanning, 1992b). In Utah, for example, the attorney general's office conducted an intensive statewide investigation into allegations of ritual child abuse (Utah Attorney General, 1995). According to the final report,

> Investigators statewide were told stories of bizarre sexual and physical abuse. They listened as victims recalled memories of rapes, torture, animal sacrifice and even murder. Victims spoke of bearing children, only to have them taken away for use in sacrificial ceremonies. Utah's police officers and their departments have dedicated thousands of hours as they followed up on allegations, searched hillsides for ritual sites, "staked-out" potential ceremonies, etc. Their combined efforts were unable to recover any physical evidence to support the claims of the existence of organized cults. Evidence has been uncovered to support the thought that individuals have in the past, and are now committing crime in the name of Satan or other deity. The allegations of organized Satanists, even groups of Satanists who have permeated every level of government and religion were unsubstantiated. (p. 47)

Of course, conspiracy theorists have a ready answer for the Utah report and others like it: "You didn't find the satanic conspirators because they're too smart for you. You see, the satanists have infiltrated every level of society, from the FBI to the church to the local police department." Kenneth Lanning of the FBI has heard these arguments many times. His response (Lanning, 1992b) makes sense to me:

Any professional evaluating victims' allegations of "ritual" abuse cannot ignore or routinely dismiss the lack of physical evidence (no bodies or physical evidence left by violent murders); the difficulty in successfully committing a large-scale conspiracy crime (the more people involved in any crime conspiracy, the harder it is to get away with it); and human nature (intragroup conflicts resulting in individual self-serving disclosures are likely to occur in any group involved in organized kidnaping, baby breeding, and human sacrifice). If and when members of a destructive cult commit murders, they are bound to make mistakes, leave evidence, and eventually make admissions in order to brag about their crimes or to reduce their legal liability.

Until hard evidence is obtained and corroborated, the public should not be frightened into believing that babies are being bred and eaten, that 50,000 missing children are being murdered in human sacrifices, or that Satanists are taking over America's day care centers or institutions. No one can prove with absolute certainty that such activity has NOT occurred. The burden of proof, however, as it would be in a criminal prosecution, is on those who claim that it has occurred. The explanation that the Satanists are too organized and law enforcement is too incompetent only goes so far in explaining the lack of evidence. For at least eight years American law enforcement has been aggressively investigating the allegations of victims of ritual abuse. There is little or no evidence for the portion of their allegations that deals with large-scale baby breeding, human sacrifice, and organized satanic conspiracies. Now it is up to mental health professionals, not law enforcement, to explain why victims are alleging things that don't seem to have happened. (pp. 39-40)

Lanning laid down the gauntlet for mental health professionals to explain what seem to be improbable claims of ritual abuse. Psychologists Bottoms, Shaver, and Goodman (1996) accepted Lanning's challenge: They conducted a large-scale survey of psychologists "to determine the number and nature of cases involving alleged ritualistic and religion-related child abuse" (p. 1). The survey disclosed no credible evidence supporting widespread ritualistic or satanic abuse of children. "Our results point to the possibility that some acts of child abuse qualify as 'ritualistic,' but not that highly organized, intergenerational, international child-abusing satanic cults exist" (p. 29). Bottoms et al. found that a small number of well-intended but misguided therapists unwittingly manufacture allegations of ritualistic abuse. Bottoms and Davis (1997) describe the survey findings:

Our results convinced us that the threat of satanic conspiracies was greatly exaggerated. First, relatively few therapists ever directly encountered a single case of alleged satanic abuse. Approximately 11% had seen a case reported by an adult survivor, 13% had seen a case reported by a child. An even smaller number of clinicians accounted for the vast majority of ritual abuse cases reported; for example 2% of our sample claimed to have encountered hundreds of cases each. Second, . . . therapists who reported cases were especially likely to have attended special workshops dealing with ways to identify and treat ritual abuse, to believe in the reality of satanic ritual abuse and repressed memories, to use suggestive "memory recovery" techniques such as hypnotic age regression which can produce false memories and iatrogenic symptoms in clients, and to diagnose their clients as suffering from controversial maladies such as multiple personality disorder (MPD, now known as dissociative identity disorder). Third, nearly all therapists believed their clients' claims about satanic practices even though there was little or no corroborative evidence for them. Finally, nearly all of the claims about satanic abuse arose in the context of psychotherapy. In general, it seems that only after the phenomenon was well known (after seminal public accounts such as *Michelle Remembers*) did many individuals outside of therapy decide that they too suffered from it.

What we learned from our surveys is largely supported by the research of others interested in ritual abuse and in the larger controversy over the reality of recovered, formerly repressed memories of childhood abuse. Combining these converging findings with the fact that police and FBI agents have never been able to find evidence of child abusing satanic cults, and adding in the fact that many alleged victims of such cults have now been discredited or have recanted their stories, one has to conclude that there probably never were any highly organized, intergenerational satanic cults. (pp. 114-115)

On the basis of what we know today, the evidence does not support widespread satanic abuse of children. What then should professionals do when a child's description of abuse contains elements that are bizarre or fantastic? This question is addressed below.

CHILDREN'S ALLEGATIONS THAT ARE BIZARRE, IMPROBABLE, OR IMPOSSIBLE

When a child's description of abuse contains elements of the fantastic, the bizarre, the sadistic, the ritualistic, the horrific, or the physically impossible, should the child's entire disclosure be discarded? No. Horrible child abuse happens, and it simply will not do to dismiss children's claims out of hand.

Lanning (1992b) pointed out that there is "no single, simple answer" to why children allege things that do not seem true. Lanning described seven possible explanations for bizarre and impossible allegations. First, some allegations may be caused by pathological distortion and pseudomemories: "The allegations in question may be errors in processing reality influenced by underlying mental disorders such as dissociative disorders, borderline or histrionic personality disorders, or psychosis" (p. 21). Second, fantastic allegations may be a product of traumatic memory. Some children who are subjected to severe physical or sexual abuse may experience memory distortions due to the enormity of the trauma. Third, some fantastic allegations may grow out of normal childhood fears and fantasy. Fourth, improbable allegations may be produced by misperception, confusion, and trickery:

> Some clever offenders may deliberately introduce elements of Satanism and the occult into the sexual exploitation simply to confuse or intimidate the victims. Simple magic and other techniques may be used to trick the children. Drugs may also deliberately be used to confuse the victims and distort their perceptions. (p. 23)

Fifth, some overzealous professionals may use suggestive interview practices to introduce fantastic ideas that children come to believe. Sixth, certain allegations (e.g., broad, multimember satanic conspiracies) may be the product of urban legend. Seventh, many allegations "probably involve a *combination* of the answers previously set forth, as well as other possible explanations unknown to the author at this time" (p. 24).

In an important article, Everson (1997) provides insight into possible sources of exaggerated, bizarre, and impossible allegations—especially those involving young children, in which "the accounts of abuse seem to contain the stuff of fantasy (or perhaps nightmares) rather than the credible, internally consistent, plausible descriptions of abuse that professionals are trained to expect in bonafide cases of abuse" (p. 134). Everson noted that "although this problem may be more prevalent and more severe in multivictim, multiperpetrator cases involving preschool-aged children, it is certainly not confined to such cases" (p. 134). Everson theorized that implausible descriptions of abuse arise from three potential sources: (a) the event itself— that is, what actually happened to the child; (b) the assessment process—interviewer error, miscommunication, and occasional deliberate fabrication; and (c) influences outside the assessment process. Each of these potential sources of error interacts with the child's unique personality to set the stage for exaggeration, fantasy, or distortion.

Everson subdivided his three sources of error into 24 specific "mechanisms to explain improbable elements in children's accounts of abuse" (p. 135). I urge careful study of Everson's article, which provides a thorough analysis of each mechanism, accompanied by numerous case examples. Because some readers of this book may not have ready access to Everson's article, his 24 mechanisms are summarized below.

The Event Itself: Whatever Actually Happened to the Child

Because of their youth and inexperience, children may misperceive the nature of what happened to them. Everson (1997) described 10 ways that such misperception can result in distorted or exaggerated descriptions of abuse.

The Child's Description Is Accurate. Although Everson's article is largely focused on improbable descriptions of abuse, Everson reminds us that truth is sometimes stranger than fiction. Some improbable descriptions of abuse are undoubtedly accurate. Everson cautioned that

> assessment of this possibility must rest on a consideration of the law of physical and biological science, the specifics of the case, and the corroborating evidence, and not on one's own sexual interests, sensibilities, or expectations about the world and how children should be treated. (p. 136)

Society has a tendency to close its eyes to the reality of child sexual abuse, and this tendency intensifies as allegations become more severe. Goodwin (1994) described the credibility problems encountered by individuals who claim to be victims of severe sadistic abuse:

> Human beings are always hoping for evidence that things are not as bad as we suspect. We are relieved to find anyone willing to tell us that the Holocaust was not really that bad nor Hiroshima.
>
> In the history of child abuse, this phenomenon manifests itself in the tendency for the most severe cases to be the least believed. (p. 480)

Although bizarre and improbable allegations of abuse should not be accepted at face value, neither should such allegations be rejected out of hand.

Deliberate Attempts by the Perpetrator to Confuse or Discredit the Child. Some perpetrators realize that a surefire way to undermine a child's credibility is to incorporate elements of the fantastic into the sexual abuse. Thus, a perpetrator might wear a robe, light candles, or chant. Lanning (1992b) noted that "some clever offenders may deliberately introduce elements of Satanism and the occult into the sexual exploitation simply to confuse or intimidate the victims" (p. 23). If the child works up the courage to tell, the description may be undermined by talk of robes, candles, chanting, and so forth.

Drug-Induced Misperception. Children are sometimes given drugs or alcohol to make them more docile. Intoxication can distort memory or perception.

The Child Incorporating Threats Into Memory. Threats are used to force children into sexual abuse and, following abuse, to silence them. With young children, threats of monsters can be quite effective. Everson (1997) suggests that "incorporation of threats may explain reports of animals or babies being killed in some accounts of abuse" (p. 137).

Memory Distortion Caused by Severe Trauma. Severe trauma and emotional distress can distort perception and memory. In extreme cases, trauma causes hallucinations. Some victims of severe trauma suffer PTSD. The psychological impact of extraordinary trauma accounts for some of the distortion and inaccuracy of children's reports of abuse.

Fantasy as a Coping Mechanism. When reality is too painful, children sometimes use fantasy as a coping mechanism. According to Everson (1997),

> A relatively common defense against strong feelings of anxiety and vulnerability in young children is to launch into a fantasy in which they play the role of a powerful, indestructible superhero. Clinical experience suggests that this phenomenon seems to occur more frequently among preschool-age boys, but it is also sometimes seen among girls. Typically, the child reaches a level of significant anxiety in his or her account of a disturbing event and switches roles from the helpless victim to an all-powerful, "don't tread on me," strongman who is readily able to defeat the victimizer. (p. 139)

Although fantasy helps children cope with anxiety, credibility may be undermined in the process.

Exaggeration as a Coping Mechanism. A severely traumatized child may lack the words to describe how horrible something was. Lacking appropriate words, the child may resort to exaggeration to convey "the depth of his or her fear, anxiety, or pain" (Everson, 1997, p. 139).

Misstatements to Shift Blame. Many abused children are reluctant to identify their perpetrator. A young child caught in this dilemma may invent a tall tale containing an imaginary offender.

Misstatements Caused by Developmental Immaturity. Young children's linguistic and experiential immaturity sometimes leads to inaccurate reporting. Everson (1997) suggested that "perhaps one of the most likely reasons for unusual and implausible material in accounts of abuse is that the child is attempting to describe events that are developmentally beyond his or her ability to understand or communicate" (p. 140).

Goodman, Quas, Bottoms, Qin, Shaver, Orcutt, and Shapiro (1997) studied children's developing understanding of religion, including the devil. They concluded that,

> at least until adolescence, the knowledge children obtain from their religious training, their families, and the media does not appear to be sufficient to allow them to concoct elaborate claims of satanic child abuse on their own. Pre-adolescent children have relatively little direct knowledge of information typically included in allegations of satanic child abuse. Even so, many children do have knowledge of satanism, the occult, and violence more generally. Although knowledge increases reliably with age, even young children possess some knowledge relevant to ritual abuse allegations. It is possible that this knowledge could lead children to make statements that an adult might interpret as the basis of a ritual abuse allegation, particularly if the questioner were unaware of conditions under which children are suggestible, or if he or she believed that ritual abuse happens and is common. (p. 1124)

Misstatements Caused by a Child's Effort to Understand New Phenomena. In the effort to make sense of a new experience, such as sexual abuse, a child draws on limited knowledge of the world. Because the child's understanding of how things work is incomplete, the child may be unable to assimilate and comprehend the novel experience in a way that makes sense to others. The result can be distortion of memory that plays out as an improbable allegation.

The Assessment Process: Interviewer Error,
Miscommunication, and Occasional Deliberate Fabrication

When sexual abuse is suspected, investigative authorities swing into action. The way that children are interviewed can cause distortion. Interviews contain numerous opportunities for miscommunication. The child may be describing apples, but the interviewer hears oranges. Once the child and the adult are unwittingly embarked on different paths of understanding, the stage is set for miscommunication and, at times, distortion. Finally, there is no gainsaying that some children deliberately fabricate allegations of abuse. Everson's 10 interview-related mechanisms are summarized below.

Every Telling Is a Little Different. Everson suggested that a child's original description of abuse can be distorted as it is passed from one adult to the next. (See the discussion of children's inconsistency earlier in this chapter.)

Miscommunication During the Interview. Miscommunication can lead to misunderstanding. Everson (1997) suggests that "some of the miscommunications in interviews with children occur not because of developmental limitations on their part, but because of an adult's error in asking questions or in tracking a child's responses" (p. 142).

Impact of Leading Questions. Children's suggestibility and the impact of leading questions are discussed in Chapter 4. An interviewer may introduce elements of fantasy, exaggeration, or distortion through use of improperly leading questions.

Use of Dolls and Props During Interviews. The benefits and risks of using dolls and other props during interviews are discussed in Chapter 4. Like any tools, dolls and props can be misused by incompetent or biased interviewers, leading to distortion.

Confabulation. Everson (1997) defined *confabulation* as "the process of filling in gaps in memory with information that is usually not true" (p. 143). The gap-filling material may be fantasy or exaggeration generated by the child or suggested by an interviewer.

Fatigue. Children have a limited attention span and limited tolerance for the give and take of an interview. When pressed beyond their endurance, young children may supply fanciful answers just to "get it over with." Everson (1997) wrote that "with mental fatigue may come mental confusion, memory lapses, confabulation, loosening of associations, [and] greater susceptibility to suggestive influences" (p. 144).

Exaggeration to Get Attention. An occasional child exaggerates or distorts to gain attention or approval. The child thinks, "Gee, the grownup is sure interested in what I have to say. I guess I'll make the story even more exciting!"

The "Little White Lie" That Got Away. What starts out as "a little white lie" sometimes turns into a whopper. At one time or another, most of us have told a minor fib, only to find that the fib takes on a life of its own and that we have to tell bigger and bigger lies to preserve the original deception. This process can occur with disclosure of sexual abuse. The child distorts something that seems inconsequential and finds it necessary to expand the lie, sometimes to extreme proportions.

Intentional Fabrication. Some children deliberately lie or exaggerate (Kirkpatrick, 1997). This worrisome problem appears to be most common among older children and adolescents. (See Chapter 1 for discussion of fabrication.)

A Penchant for Tall Tales. A few children have a penchant for spinning tall tales filled with fantasy. Everson (1997) noted that

> this phenomenon seems to be relatively uncommon among normal children. Identifying it as a factor in an abuse allegation is aided by the fact that children who indulge in fantasy lying tend to do so on a range of topics, not just abuse allegations, and typically, various aspects of their stories are readily identifiable as false. (p. 145)

Influences That Are Outside the Assessment Process

Everson lists four factors outside the assessment process that may work on children to distort memory.

The Impact of Mass Culture. Television, videos, the movies, books: All these can influence memory.

Cross-Contamination in Multiple-Victim Cases. When child abuse is suspected in a day care or other institutional setting, parents are immediately on the phone to each other. Multiple-victim cases involving young children raise special difficulties for investigators, not the least of which is that children's descriptions may be distorted as parents and children share information and concerns.

Is It a Dream or Reality? All children dream, and many children have nightmares. Sexually abused children often experience nightmares caused by their maltreatment. A few children have difficulty differentiating dreams from reality.

Psychosis. A small number of children are psychotic, and suffer from delusions.

Summary

Everson (1997) concluded his important contribution with these words:

> What is evident from this discussion of possible explanatory mechanisms for improbable and fantastic elements in children's accounts of abuse is that the presence of such material in a child's report should not lead to an automatic dismissal of the child's entire account. As we have seen, there are many reasonable explanations why such material may emerge in a otherwise credible and truthful account of abuse. (p. 147)

Everson's insights answer many questions. Yet there is still a nagging uncertainty. Are we confident that cases of real sexual abuse occur in the presence of exaggerated, fantastic, and impossible claims? (Dalenberg, Hyland, & Cuevas, in press). Clinical and investigative experience answer in the affirmative, and a study by Dalenberg (1996) adds support to the experience of police officers and therapists. Dalenberg studied a large data bank of videotaped investigative interviews in San Diego and cross-referenced the interviews to medical records and to criminal outcomes in San Diego County. In this way, Dalenberg identified

> a "gold standard" group of children . . . who met the highest criteria for certainty of abuse history. In these cases, perpetrators confessed to the crime, medical evidence was consistent with the alleged details of

> the crime, and, in more than 80% of the cases, at least one piece of persuasive external evidence was present (e.g., an eyewitness, a sibling telling a similar story). (p. 6)

Children in the "gold standard" group were compared to children with less certain evidence of abuse. Across all the children studied, abuse was categorized as "severe" or "nonsevere."

Dalenberg found that in both groups—"gold standard" and "less certain"—there were instances of implausible, exaggerated, or impossible acts. Although implausible, exaggerated, or impossible acts were uncommon, they were not rare. As might be expected, more severe abuse produced more implausible and fantastic allegations.

Contrary to the expectations of some critics of the interview process, "Fantastic elements were not related to leading questions by interviewers" in this sample of videotaped interviews (p. 7). If anything, interviewers appeared dismayed when children made implausible or impossible statements. Moreover, interviewers were not accepting of incredible statements:

> Fantastic statements were less likely to be met in a neutral way (e.g., Tell me more about that) or an accepting way (e.g., That must have been scary), and more likely to be challenged (e.g., That didn't happen, did it?), ignored (e.g., What else happened?), or skeptically addressed (e.g., But how could he touch your pee-pee or your skin when you had your clothes on?). (p. 7)

Dalenberg concluded:

> The most compelling result of this investigation is that fantastic elements occurred most frequently in the accounts of children known to have been abused, and indeed were most common among children *known* to have suffered severe abuse. These findings directly counter the hypothesis that fantastic elements in children's accounts of abuse give reason to discredit the entire account.
>
> Rather than state that this research shows unequivocally that the presence of fantasy elements increases the likelihood that the overall allegation is true, however, it is more correct to state that this research fails to support the common assumption that the presence of fantasy elements should lead evaluators to suspect the entire allegation. (pp. 8-9)

❏ Investigating Multiple-Victim Cases

During the 1980s and, to a lesser extent, the 1990s, a relatively small number of cases involving multiple young victims arose across the United States (Finkelhor & Williams, 1988). Some multiple-victim cases involved allegations of sexual abuse in preschool or day care settings. Several of these cases garnered extensive media attention. The most highly visible cases, such as the McMartin preschool case in Southern California and the prosecution of Margaret Michaels in New Jersey, fell apart due in large measure to improper investigative interviewing (*State v. Michaels*, 1994). Failed multivictim prosecutions fuel skepticism of children's credibility and investigative competence.

The National Center for Prosecution of Child Abuse (1993) described the numerous problems raised by multiple-victim cases involving young children: "Common problems include insufficient resources to investigate the allegations in an expedient manner, inadequate training, confusion about leadership for the investigation, contamination of evidence, failure to assure confidentiality of the investigation and the overwhelming magnitude of the investigation" (p. 133).

Lanning (1992a) of the FBI has provided excellent guidance on investigating child sex rings. See also Dalenberg (in press).

6

Balancing the Need for Confidentiality and the Requirements of Disclosure

This chapter discusses the broad ethical duty of professionals to protect confidential information about clients. In addition, the chapter addresses the narrower issue of privileged communications between clients and certain professionals, discusses informed consent, and analyzes circumstances in which confidentiality is limited.

Abused and neglected children and their families interact with many professionals. In one case, for example, 7-year-old Melanie disclosed to her teacher that she was being sexually abused by her father. The teacher reported to child protective services. A social worker interviewed Melanie. Next, Melanie visited a hospital for an examination and another set of questions. Melanie began seeing a therapist. So did her father. Lawyers became involved, and legal proceedings were commenced in juvenile court. The juvenile court judge ordered Melanie's father to undergo a psychological evaluation.

Each professional who interacts with an abused or neglected child or the child's family documents the interaction. It is not unusual for information about a family to be scattered through several agencies and offices. In Melanie's case, for example, the teacher to whom Melanie disclosed made an entry in Melanie's school record. The CPS social worker opened a file. The doctor at the hospital wrote a report that found its way into the hospital's medical records department. Each mental health professional serving the family had a file. Each lawyer had a file too. Finally, a file was growing at juvenile court. Needless to say, the records in Melanie's case contained highly sensitive, private, and embarrassing information. How would ethics codes and law protect Melanie's privacy?

❏ Defining Confidentiality

Confidential means "spoken or written as a secret" and "trusted with secret matters" (*World Book Dictionary*, 1993, p. 435). The essence of confidentiality is privacy, coupled with an expectation of nondisclosure. In practice, "A precise definition of confidentiality is elusive" (Green, 1995, p. 80). Keith-Spiegel and Koocher (1985) define confidentiality as "the general standard of professional conduct that obliges a professional not to discuss information about a client with anyone" (p. 57).

> *The essence of confidentiality is privacy, coupled with an expectation of nondisclosure.*

Confidentiality can be defined broadly or narrowly. Conceptualized narrowly, confidentiality is limited to what a client says (see Committee on Professional Practice, 1995, p. 378). More broadly, confidentiality includes *any* information about a client, no matter what the source is. In this book, confidentiality is viewed broadly to include information obtained in consultation, diagnosis, testing, examination, or therapy. In the absence of a waiver of confidentiality by the client, all information provided *by* a client is confidential. Thus, confidentiality includes everything the client says that is intended to be private, and the presumption is that everything is so intended. In addition, under a broad definition, confidentiality extends to the client's name, address, and physical and mental condition. Confidentiality reaches beyond information supplied *by* a client to include information *about* a client that is obtained from sources other than the client. Finally, confidentiality includes everything a professional says *to* a client. Thus, confidentiality is a two-way street. Everything the client says *and* everything a professional says is confidential.

❑ **The Importance of Confidentiality**

Confidentiality is important to every professional working with victims of maltreatment. Thus, confidentiality is vital to a physician examining for physical injury. Confidentiality is important in the work of CPS and, to a lesser degree, in the efforts of police. Few would disagree, however, that the greatest need for confidentiality is in psychotherapy. The court in *Taylor v. United States* (1955) described the central role of confidentiality in the psychotherapist-client relationship:

> The psychiatric patient confides more utterly than anyone else in the world. He exposes to the therapist not only what his words directly express, he lays bare his entire self, his dreams, his fantasies, his sins, and his shame. Most patients who undergo psychotherapy know that this is what will be expected of them, and they cannot get help except on that condition. . . . It would be too much to expect them to do so if they knew that all they say—and all that the psychiatrist learns from what they say—may be revealed to the whole world from a witness stand. (p. 401)

❑ **Three Sources of Confidentiality**

There are three primary sources of confidentiality: (a) the ethical duty to protect confidential client information, (b) laws making certain records confidential, and (c) privileges that apply in legal proceedings.

THE ETHICAL DUTY TO PROTECT
CONFIDENTIAL CLIENT INFORMATION

The ethics codes of all professional organizations place a premium on confidentiality. For example, the *Code of Ethics* of the American Professional Society on the Abuse of Children (APSAC, 1997) states:

> The right to privacy is central to a free society. It encompasses the freedom to determine the degree to which information about one's behavior, beliefs, history, and experience is shared with others; the conditions under which it is shared; and what specific information is shared. The right of clients to confidentiality, which is the assurance that nothing about an individual is revealed except under agreed-upon conditions, is fundamental to professional relationships with clients. Laws in all states define the rights of confidentiality and privacy. The rights of clients to privacy and confidentiality, except where limited by state and federal laws, are recognized and honored by APSAC members at all times.

The "Ethical Principles of Psychologists and Code of Conduct" of the American Psychological Association (1992) states that "psychologists have a primary obligation to take reasonable precautions to respect the confidentiality rights of those with whom they work or consult" (Standard 5.02). The *Code of Ethics* of the National Association of Social Workers (1997) provides that "social workers should protect the confidentiality of all information obtained in the course of professional services, except for compelling professional reasons" (Standard 1.07(c)). The ethics code of the American Nurses Association (1985) requires nurses to protect privacy. The *Principles of Medical Ethics* of the American Medical Association (1989) require physicians to "safeguard patient confidences within the constraints of the law" (Principle IV). The Hippocratic oath states that "whatsoever I shall see or hear in the course of my profession . . . if it be what should not be published abroad, I will never divulge, holding such things to be holy secrets." The importance of confidentiality was recognized well before Hippocrates practiced medicine on the Greek island of Cos some three centuries before Christ.

> Hindu physicians practicing long before Hippocrates understood their situation well and were admonished that "once with the patient [the physician] must in work and thought attend to nothing but his patient's case and what concerns it. . . . What happens in the house must not be mentioned outside." (Linderthal & Thomas, 1992, p. 119)

Violation of the ethical duty of confidentiality can lead to three types of proceedings against a professional. First, a member of a professional organization who violates the organization's ethical principles may be, so to speak, kicked out. Second, state licensing authorities may institute disciplinary proceedings to limit, suspend, or revoke the professional's license (e.g., *In re Schroeder*, 1988; *Rost v. State Board of Psychology*, 1995). Third, a client whose confidentiality is breached may sue the professional "for invasion of privacy, negligence, or breach of contract" (Smith, 1996, p. 82).

LAWS MAKING CLIENT RECORDS CONFIDENTIAL

Every state has a dizzying array of laws that make records confidential. These laws define the circumstances in which confidential information may be disclosed. Some of the laws pertain to records compiled by government agencies such as CPS, schools, and the juvenile court. Other laws govern records generated by professionals and institutions in the private sector, including psychotherapists, physicians, and private hospitals. Confidentiality laws vary so much from state to state that I can write only four things with confidence. First, your state has numerous laws making client records confidential. Second, the laws are complex, difficult to find, and, at times, conflicting. Third, confidentiality laws are a sure cure for insomnia. Fourth, confidentiality laws further the important policy of protecting privacy.

Confidentiality laws serve important functions. Nevertheless, they sometimes create problems. Hechler (1993) described what happens when child protection agencies hide behind the mask of confidentiality:

In theory, confidentiality laws are supposed to protect innocent adults and child victims. Sometimes, however, they protect no one but caseworkers and supervisors from unflattering publicity. When a family waives confidentiality, or when a child is killed and the parent is arrested and charged with the crime, why should the local social services department not be permitted—even required—to respond to questions about their prior involvement with the family? Why should they not be accountable? (p. 705)

Hechler argued that although confidentiality rules serve legitimate purposes—encouraging sources to speak who might otherwise remain silent, shielding child victims from stigma, and granting accused adults some protection—confidentiality rules "should not be invoked by a public agency for the sole purpose of shielding itself from scrutiny" (p. 707):

Too often confidentiality rules are used by agencies to prevent undesired news coverage. Lost in bureaucratic legerdemain are questions that demand responses. Does not true damage control require that agencies discipline incompetence—and let everyone know it?
  The real damage is not embarrassing publicity. The real damage is what results from a system accountable only to itself. It is a system that sometimes seems as self-contained as a mathematical equation, and one that is bent on proving this theorem: closed minds + closed ranks = closed case. (p. 707)

PRIVILEGES IN LEGAL PROCEEDINGS

The ethical duty to protect confidential client information applies to *all* professionals in *all* settings. Thus, the National Association of Social Workers' *Code of Ethics* (1997) states that "social workers should not discuss confidential information in any setting unless privacy can be ensured" (Standard 1.07(I)). The ethical duty to protect confidentiality is just as binding at the beach, the bowling alley, and the bistro as it is in the clinic and the courtroom. In the courtroom, however, and in ancillary legal proceedings, some

> *The ethical duty to protect confidentiality is just as binding at the beach, the bowling alley, and the bistro as it is in the clinic and the courtroom.*

professionals have an obligation to protect confidentiality that is *in addition* to the ethical obligation. In legal proceedings, the law reinforces the ethical duty with special rules, called *privileges*. Privileges such as the psychotherapist-client privilege and the physician-patient privilege add a second layer of protection to the protection provided by the ethical duty to protect confidential information.

Whether communication between a client and a professional is privileged has nothing to do with the professional's ethical duty to protect confidential information. With that in mind, it is reasonable to ask, "In legal proceedings, what difference does it make whether a privilege applies? The professional is ethically bound to protect confidential information. Isn't the ethical duty sufficient to prevent disclosure in court?" The answer is no. In legal proceedings, the existence of a privilege such as the psychotherapist-client privilege can make all the difference in the world. The reason is that in court, professionals generally have to answer questions that necessitate disclosure of information that they are ethically obligated to protect. In other words, when a professional is a witness in court, the duty to answer attorneys' questions generally overrides the professional's ethical duty to protect confidential information. However, a professional generally does *not* have to answer questions that require disclosure of privileged information. Thus, in legal proceedings, a privilege affords protection that is not available under the ethical duty to protect confidentiality.

Every state has a privilege for confidential communication between clients and attorneys. Most states also have some version of the following privileges:

- Physician-patient privilege
- Psychotherapist-client privilege
- Clergy member-penitent privilege

The psychotherapist-client privilege generally applies to psychologists and psychiatrists. In many states, the privilege also includes clinical social workers, counselors, nurses, and other professionals providing psychotherapy. Moreover, the privilege may apply to students and others practicing under the supervision of a professional who is covered by the privilege.

In addition to the foregoing privileges, a smaller number of states have versions of the following privileges:

- Sexual assault counselor-victim privilege
- Social worker-client privilege

To find out whether you are covered by a privilege, contact an attorney or get in touch with your state professional organization.

What Types of Communication Are Covered by Privileges?

Clearly, a client's confidential verbal statements are covered, as are a professional's notes documenting a client's words. In addition, a professional's verbal statements *to* a client are privileged. Communicative gestures can be privileged. Confidential written communication between client and professional can be privileged. Finally, in many states, especially with the physician-patient privilege, the professional's observations of the patient can be privileged.

How Long Does a Privilege Last?

Generally, privileged communications remain privileged after the termination of the professional relationship. In most situations, the death of the client does not end the privilege.

Whose Privilege Is It?

Privileges generally belong to the client, *not* the professional. In legal parlance, the client is the *holder* of the privilege. As the privilege holder, the client can prevent the professional from disclosing privileged communications in legal proceedings. For example, suppose that a psychotherapist is subpoenaed to testify about a client. While the therapist is on the witness stand, the attorney who subpoenaed the therapist asks questions that call for disclosure of privileged information. At that point, the client's attorney should object. The client's attorney asserts the privilege on behalf of the privilege holder, the client. The judge then decides whether a privilege applies.

Should a Professional Assert a Client's Privilege?

If a client's attorney fails to object to a question calling for privileged information, or if a client is not represented by an attorney, a professional may assert a privilege on behalf of a client. Indeed, a professional is probably ethically obligated to assert a privilege if no one else does. The professional might turn to the judge and say, "Your honor, I would prefer not to answer that question. Answering would require me to disclose information that I believe is privileged." When the judge is alerted that a privilege may exist, the judge decides whether this is so and whether the professional must answer. In the process, the judge and the attorneys may question the professional to see whether the requirements for a privilege are satisfied.

If the judge determines that a privilege applies, the professional will not have to answer the attorney's question. On the other hand, if the judge decides that no privilege applies or that the privilege is waived, the judge instructs the professional to answer. At that point, the professional has to make a decision: Answer the question as instructed by the judge, or continue to assert the client's privilege and decline to answer. In most cases, the professional obeys the judge and answers the question. The professional can hardly be criticized for following the judge's instruction. After all, a professional is in no position to second-guess a judge's decision. In one last effort to avoid disclosing privileged information, a professional might inform the judge of the professional's dilemma and ask the judge's permission to consult an attorney before deciding whether to answer. Some judges will grant such a request; others will not. In the end, if the professional refuses to answer after being ordered by the judge to do so, the judge has several options. The judge may simply let the matter drop. More likely, the judge will order the professional's testimony up to that point stricken from the record and dismiss the professional as a witness. In rare cases, a judge holds a professional in contempt of court for refusing to answer.

When Is Communication Between
a Client and a Professional Privileged?

Three requirements must be met for communication between clients and professionals to be privileged. First, the communication must be between a client and a professional with whom privileged communication is possible. Not all professionals are covered by privileges. For example, all states have some version of the psychotherapist-client privilege, but not all psychotherapists are covered by the privilege. If a client talks to a psychotherapist who is not covered, no privilege applies. Of course, the fact that no privilege applies does *not* undermine the therapist's ethical duty to protect confidential information.

The second requirement for privileged communication is that the client must seek professional services. With a psychotherapist, for example, the client must consult the therapist to obtain professional advice or therapy. If the client formally enters treatment, the privilege applies to confidential communications during therapy. Even when the client does not formally enter therapy, the privilege may apply to confidential communications between the client and the professional. For example, a client may consult a psychotherapist who refers the client to a second professional. In most states, communication between the client and the referring psychotherapist is privileged, even though the client does not enter treatment with the referring therapist.

The third requirement for privileged communication is that the communication must be in confidence. Privileges cover only communications that clients intend to be confidential. Privileges do not attach to communications that clients intend to be heard by other people.

What if some third person is present when a client communicates with a professional? Does the presence of the third person destroy the confidentiality required for privileged communication? The fact that a third person is present when a client discloses information may or may not eliminate privilege. The deciding factor is whether the third person is needed to assist the professional. For example, suppose that a physician is conducting a physical examination and interview of a child. The presence of an assisting nurse during the examination does not undermine the applicability of the physician-patient privilege. Furthermore, the presence of a child's parents need not defeat privilege. Again, the deciding factor is whether the third person is needed to help the professional.

A privilege is not eliminated when colleagues consult about cases. According to Nye (1980),

> A patient's confidential data may be shared without his/her consent within the clinic/agency or institution for purposes of the patient's treatment. It is generally accepted that supervisors and consultants are considered part of the patient's "treatment team." Any such professional with whom information is shared will have the same duty to maintain confidentiality as the patient's own therapist. (pp. 281-282)

Proper disclosure of client information to insurance companies and other third-party payers does not destroy privileges or the ethical duty to protect confidential client information.

Privileges Apply Only in Legal Proceedings

Unlike the across-the-board ethical duty to protect confidential client information, privileges apply *only* in legal proceedings. Privileges clearly apply when professionals testify in court and are asked to reveal privileged information. Privileges also apply during legal proceedings outside the courtroom. For example, in most civil cases, and in some criminal cases as well, attorneys take pretrial depositions of potential witnesses. Depositions often take place at an attorney's office. The professional being deposed takes the oath that is administered to witnesses in court. The attorneys ask questions similar to the questions asked during trial. The deposition is recorded and transcribed by a court reporter. Following the deposition, the professional reads the transcript and certifies that it is accurate. If questions are asked during a deposition that call for privileged information, the professional or one of the attorneys should raise the privilege issue. More is said earlier in this chapter about the professional's role in asserting a client's privilege.

Before You Talk to an Attorney, Think
About Privilege and Confidentiality

Professionals should be sensitive to issues of confidentiality and privilege whenever they communicate with attorneys. It is good practice to decline communication regarding confidential information—whether in writing, over the phone, or in person—until you obtain consent from the client or, in the case of a child, the child's parent or caretaker.

❏ Confidentiality When the Client Is a Child

Difficult issues can arise when the client is a child. The ethical obligation to protect confidentiality applies regardless of age, and confidential information cannot be revealed to outsiders unless consent is obtained or disclosure is required by law. But are parents "outsiders"? May professionals discuss confidential information with parents and caretakers without a child client's permission? An example illustrates why there is no across-the-board answer to this question. Suppose a professional's clients are 3 and 15 years of age. In the preschooler's case, it seems clear that the parents will be consulted regularly. The child may be informed that the therapist talks to mommy and daddy, but it would be developmentally inappropriate and legally unnecessary to seek the child's "consent" to disclose information to the parents. By contrast, it is developmentally appropriate, and perhaps legally necessary, to safeguard the teenager's confidential revelations from parents.

The 3- and 15-year-olds are easy. But what about a 9- or 10-year-old client? Where does such a child fit along the continuum of confidentiality? There is no simple, one-size-fits-all answer. Much depends on the maturity and mental stability of the child, the reasons for treatment, and the nature of the relationship between the parents and the child.

Regardless of age, a professional's first duty is to the child. This is so regardless of who pays for treatment. Thus, the fact that a child's parents pay for therapy does not entitle the parents to confidential information. A useful way to deal with potential conflicts over confidential information is to set ground rules *before* therapy begins. When the child is developmentally capable of participating in this process, the child's input should be obtained.

If a parent has abused or neglected a child, disclosure of the child's confidential information to the maltreating parent may be contraindicated regardless of the child's age.

❏ Confidentiality and Privilege in Group Therapy

The ethical duty to protect confidential information applies to professionals conducting group therapy. Members of the group, however, are not ethically bound to protect confidentiality (Roback, Moore, Waterhouse, & Martin, 1996). The District of Columbia may be the only jurisdiction to place legal limits on disclosure by group members. District of Columbia law provides that "no client in a group session shall disclose or permit the disclosure of mental health information relating to another client in the group session to any person" (§ 6-2002(b)).

Because group members generally have no duty to maintain confidentiality, it is advisable to engage the group in discussion of the importance of confidentiality. Appelbaum and Greer (1993) state that "it seems clear that group leaders should alert their patients that the sanctity of their communications depends on the goodwill of their fellow patients" (p. 312). The *Code of Ethics* of the National Association of Social Workers (1997) suggests that

> when social workers provide counseling services to families, couples, or groups, social workers should seek agreement among the parties involved concerning each individual's right to confidentiality and obligation to preserve the confidentiality of information shared by others. Social workers should inform participants in family, couples, or group counseling that social workers cannot guarantee that all participants will honor such agreements. (Principle 1.07(f))

Despite such good advice, Roback, Ochoa, Bloch, and Purdon (1992) found that many experienced group therapists do not discuss confidentiality with the group.

A group therapist's ethical duty to protect confidentiality is clear. Less clear is whether the psychotherapist-client and similar privileges apply in group therapy. The most frequently mentioned roadblock to privileged communication in group therapy is the rule that privileges do not apply when third parties are present. Thus, the question is: Are members of the group "third parties" for purposes of privilege law? The answer should be no, and the small number of court decisions on this point generally conclude that privileges apply to group treatment. In *State v. Andring* (1984), for example, the Minnesota Supreme Court wrote:

> We conclude that the medical privilege must be construed to encompass statements made in group psychotherapy. The participants in group psychotherapy sessions are not casual third persons who are strangers to the psychiatrist/psychologist/nurse-patient relationship. Rather every participant has such a relationship with the attending professional, and, in the group therapy setting, the participants actually become part of the diagnostic and therapeutic process for co-participants. (p. 133)

The California Court of Appeals employed similar reasoning in *Lovett v. Superior Court* (1988):

> The question here is whether communications made by a patient to other persons participating in a group therapy session come within the psychotherapist-patient privilege.
>
> "Group therapy" is designed to provide comfort and revelation to the patient who shared similar experiences and/or difficulties with other like persons within the group. The presence of each person is for the benefit of the others . . . and is designed to facilitate the patient's treatment. Communications such as these, when made in confidence, should not operate to destroy the privilege.
>
> Thus, we conclude that the communication with other participants in group therapy is reasonably necessary for the accomplishment of the purpose for which the psychotherapist was consulted and, therefore, comes within the privilege. (pp. 28-29)

In the case of *Sims v. State* (1984), the Georgia Supreme Court ruled that couples therapy is covered by the Georgia psychotherapist-client privilege.

❏ Informed Consent

Informed consent is a legal requirement for most treatment (American Psychological Association, 1992). The requirement for informed consent grows out of respect for autonomy (Faden & Beauchamp, 1986). Clients should decide for themselves whether to enter therapy, and to make that decision intelligently, they need information about the nature, benefits, and risks of therapy, as well as alternatives to therapy (Smith, 1986). The information required for informed consent is well described in the *Code of Ethics* of the National Association of Social Workers (1997):

> Social workers should provide services to clients only in the context of a professional relationship based, when appropriate, on valid informed consent. Social workers should use clear and under-standable language to inform clients of the purpose of the services, risks related to the services, limits to services because of the require-ments of a third-party payer, relevant costs, reasonable alternatives, clients' right to refuse or withdraw consent, and the time frame covered by the consent. Social workers should provide clients with an opportunity to ask questions. (Standard 1.03(a))

Harris (1995) discussed informed consent to mental health treatment:

> All practitioners should develop an informed consent policy that either is given to the patient in written form or is delivered orally and noted in one's records. . . . On first hearing this suggestion, many mental health providers express a fear that providing this information will damage the therapeutic relationship. . . . For the most part, these adverse consequences do not occur. Most patients are grateful to receive the information, and many consider it an aid, rather than a detriment to the therapeutic process. (p. 252)

Harris notes that informed consent is not always a one-time event at the beginning of therapy. With some clients, the consent process extends over time:

> Certain aspects of informed consent cannot be standardized nor can they be meaningfully communicated at the outset of treatment. Both the substance and the timing of certain information has to be tailored to the particular dynamics of the patient and the dynamics of the therapy. Even when the therapist knows the particular risks and benefits of treatment of a specific client, the client may not be able to tolerate their explication until there is a firmer alliance. With trauma victims in particular, informed consent is not a one-shot event, but rather an ongoing process of mutual information sharing and evaluation of risk. (pp. 252-253)

Failure to obtain informed consent can be malpractice. According to Smith (1986),

> Informed consent is a legal theory in medical malpractice which provides a patient a [right to sue] for not being adequately informed as to the nature and consequences of a particular medical procedure, process, or treatment prior to giving consent to the initiation of that treatment. (p. 160)

CHILDREN AND INFORMED CONSENT

Children are legally incapable of consenting to most forms of medical and mental health treatment. Thus, informed consent is obtained from parents or caretakers (American Psychological Association, 1992). It should be noted, however, that children above specified ages (e.g., 14) are allowed to consent to certain types of treatment, including, in many states, testing for venereal disease or pregnancy, abortion, and some kinds of mental health care.

EXPLAINING THE LIMITS OF CONFIDENTIALITY
IS PART OF INFORMED CONSENT

An important component of the consent process is informing clients of the limits of confidentiality (Deed, 1993). "Unless it is not feasible or is contraindicated, the discussion of confidentiality occurs at the outset of the relationship and thereafter as new circumstances may warrant" (American Psychological Association, 1992, Standard 5.01(b)).

The duty to report suspected child abuse limits confidentiality, and "It is advisable at the outset of treatment to inform your clients that the usual rule concerning confidentiality does not apply when the duty to report child abuse arises" (Committee on Professional Practice, 1995, p. 378). The child abuse reporting duty is discussed in Chapter 3.

RAW PSYCHOLOGICAL TEST DATA

Psychologists who administer psychological tests are aware of their ethical responsibility regarding release of raw test data. According to the "Ethical Principles of Psychologists and Code of Conduct" of the American Psychological Association (1992),

> Psychologists refrain from misuse of assessment techniques, interventions, results, and interpretations and take reasonable steps to prevent others from misusing the information these techniques provide. This includes refraining from releasing raw test results or raw data to persons, other than to patients or clients as appropriate, who are not qualified to use such information. (Standard 2.02(b))

Raw psychological data include "standardized scores, including IQs and percentiles," as well as "test scores, stimuli, and responses" (Tranel, 1994, pp. 34, 37). In some cases, the psychologist's ethical duty to protect raw data collides with a legal duty to disclose client information. Tranel (1994) analyzed such conflicts and offered practical advice:

> The APA Ethical Principles prohibit the release of raw data to unqualified individuals, and with rare exceptions, attorneys are not qualified individuals. A viable course of action if an attorney should request raw data from a psychologist (A), would be to advise the attorney to engage the consultation of another psychologist (B), who is qualified, by virtue of licensure, training, and experience, to receive the data. Psychologist A then could send the raw data to Psychologist B (provided the client or patient has given appropriate consent). Psychologist B could then interpret the data to the attorney. Needless to say,

Psychologist B must operate under the same rules and standards of ethics and confidentiality as Psychologist A. (p. 35)

MANAGED CARE, INFORMED CONSENT, AND CONFIDENTIALITY

Managed care, with its incentives to limit treatment, complicates informed consent. To be fully informed, clients should understand the limits of treatment. Yet, as Miller (1996) observed, "Oftentimes professionals who work in managed care are required to withhold information about" limits of care (p. 583). Indeed, "Managed care practices result in powerful incentives to withhold information about rationing from consumers" (p. 583).

Managed care complicates confidentiality. Davidson and Davidson (1996) observe that "with the use of managed care information systems that include telephone reviews, voice mail, faxes, cellular telephones, and highly unregulated computerized databases, there are few guarantees, if any, that sensitive information is stored securely" (p. 209).

❏ Disclosure of Confidential and Privileged Information

The remainder of this chapter discusses disclosure of confidential information. Also addressed is potential liability when confidential data are improperly released.

CLIENT CONSENT

Client consent plays the central role in release of confidential information (American Psychological Association, 1992). As Gutheil and Appelbaum (1982) observe, "With rare exceptions, identifiable information [about patients] can be transmitted to third parties only with the patient's explicit consent" (p. 5). A competent adult client may consent to release of information to attorneys, courts, and anyone else selected by the client. The client's consent must be informed and voluntary. The professional should explain any disadvantages of disclosing confidential information. For example, the client should be told that release to third persons may waive any privilege that would apply.

A professional who discloses confidential information without client consent can be sued. With an eye toward such lawsuits, Gutheil and Appelbaum (1982) offer good advice:

A professional who discloses confidential information without client consent can be sued.

It is probably wise for therapists always to require the written consent of the patient before releasing information to third parties. Written consent is advisable for at least two reasons: (1) it makes clear to both parties that consent has, in fact, been given; (2) if the fact, nature or timing of the consent should ever be challenged, a documentary record exists. The consent should be made a part of the patient's permanent chart. (p. 6)

When the client is a child, parents have authority to make decisions about confidential and privileged information regarding the child. When a parent is suspected of abusing a child, however, it may be inappropriate for the parent to make decisions regarding the child's confidential information. For example, a parent may attempt to hide pertinent information from a judge by asserting his or her child's psychotherapist-client privilege. Needless to say, judges are cool to such tactics. The South Dakota Supreme Court wrote in *In re D.K.* (1976) that

the parents are the proper parties to assert the privilege for the [child] under normal circumstances, but when it is the conduct of those same parents that is in issue, it would be an anomalous result to allow them to exercise the privilege. (p. 648)

In another case, *Ellison v. Ellison* (1996), the Oklahoma Supreme Court wrote that "a custodial parent may not invoke the [child's psychotherapist-client] privilege in a modification of custody proceeding to prevent testimony by a physician or psychotherapist as to the child-patient's communication relevant to abuse and neglect" (p. 3). When there is a conflict between the interests of a child and the interests of the parents, the judge may allow someone else, such as a guardian *ad litem,* to make decisions about release of confidential and privileged information (see *State v. Evans,* 1991; *State v. Hunt,* 1965).

SUBPOENAS

When a person is accused of child abuse, criminal prosecution may be commenced. Juvenile court proceedings may be instituted if the alleged perpetrator is the child's parent. If the accused denies the abuse, the defense attorney prepares for trial. Naturally, defense counsel seeks all information that might assist the defense. In particular, the defense attorney may seek confidential records about the child. To gain access, the attorney may subpoena the records. In addition to issuing a subpoena for the child's records, the attorney may issue a subpoena requiring the professional to testify.

A subpoena is a formidable-looking official document. A typical subpoena begins with these words:

> The People of the State of California, to [your name here]:
>   GREETINGS: YOU ARE ORDERED TO APPEAR AS A WITNESS
> at the date, time, and place set forth below. . . .

A subpoena is issued by a court at the request of an attorney. The subpoena bears the official seal of the court and is signed by a judge or court clerk. A subpoena may arrive by mail or in the hand of a process server, who gets your day off to a pleasant start by handing you the subpoena and saying, "You are hereby served with this subpoena. Please sign here to acknowledge receipt."

A subpoena is a command from a court and cannot be ignored or dropped in the circular file. Disobedience of a subpoena is disobedience of a court order and can be punished as contempt of court.

There are two types of subpoenas: (a) a subpoena that requires an individual to appear at a designated time and place to provide testimony, often called a subpoena *ad testificandum;* and (b) a subpoena that requires a person to appear at a designated time and place and to bring records or documents designated in the subpoena, often called a subpoena *duces tecum.*

It is critical to know that a subpoena does *not* override privileges such as the psychotherapist-client privilege. A subpoena requires a professional to go to court, but once in court, a subpoena does not eliminate privilege. As mentioned earlier in this chapter, an attorney may assert a privilege on behalf of a client. Alternatively, a professional may assert a client's privilege. The judge decides whether a privilege exists and whether privileged information must be disclosed.

Although professionals cannot ignore subpoenas, neither should they blindly obey them. Tranel (1994) states that "psychologists need not automatically translate the serving of a subpoena into prompt acquiescence to legal demands without regard for the ethics of the situation" (p. 36). In *Rost v. State Board of Psychology* (1995), a psychologist was reprimanded for *complying* with a subpoena. The psychologist supervised an unlicensed therapist who provided treatment to a child suffering chronic headaches that had allegedly been caused by a fall at a community center. The child's mother sued the community center. Some time later, the attorney for the community center mailed a subpoena to the supervising psychologist requesting the child's treatment records. Without contacting the child, her mother, or the child's attorney, the psychologist gave the child's records to the community center's attorney. Although the mother had previously given permission to disclose the child's records to the *child's* attorney, no permission had been given to disclose the records to anyone else. The state board of psychology disciplined the psychologist, and the court reviewing the board's decision agreed, writing that the psychologist

> had a duty to either obtain written permission to release the records from [the child] or challenge the propriety of the subpoena before a judge. [The psychologist] did neither. Instead, she unilaterally gave [the child's] records to [the attorney for the community center] without consulting with [the child] or her attorney. (p. 629)

Before responding to a subpoena, a professional should contact the client or, if the client is a child, the child's parent or guardian. The client may wish to release confidential or privileged information. If the client's decision is informed and voluntary, the professional may comply.

It is often useful—with the client's permission, of course—for the professional to communicate with the attorney who issued the subpoena. Unless the client consents, the professional should not disclose confidential or privileged information during such a conversation. In some cases, the conversation lets the attorney know that the professional has nothing to assist the attorney, and the subpoena is withdrawn. Even if the attorney insists on compliance with the subpoena, the telephone conversation may clarify the limits of relevant information in the professional's possession. Furthermore, if the subpoena requires production of records, the professional may use the conversation to clarify exactly what the attorney wants.

If questions arise about the validity of a subpoena or how to respond to it, consult an attorney. For example, if you receive a subpoena *duces tecum* directing you to send client files to an attorney's office, get legal advice *before* you comply. Professionals in government agencies can consult a government attorney who represents the agency. Hospitals and some clinics have an attorney on retainer. Professionals in private practice can contact attorneys they know in the community. Professional organizations may have useful information about responding to subpoenas, although professional organizations generally do not provide legal advice. The one attorney who is *not* in a position to give objective advice is the attorney who issued the subpoena. The Committee on Legal Issues of the American Psychological Association (1996) has published excellent guidelines on responding to subpoenas, and I recommend getting a copy.

In some cases, it is possible for an attorney to convince a judge to quash a subpoena (*quash*, not *squash*)—that is, declare the subpoena invalid. A subpoena may be quashed if it seeks information that is privileged from disclosure, if the subpoena is unduly burdensome, if it is not in proper form, and for other reasons.

A CRIMINAL DEFENDANT'S CONSTITUTIONAL
RIGHT TO CONFIDENTIAL RECORDS

In criminal cases, the defendant has a limited constitutional right to inspect confidential records on the victim (*Pennsylvania v. Ritchie,* 1987; *People v. Hammon,* 1997). This right extends in some cases to files of the CPS agency and records maintained by professionals in private practice. The rules governing the constitutional right of access are beyond the scope of this book (see Myers, 1997a). If your records are subpoenaed or requested in other ways, get legal advice.

REVIEWING CLIENT RECORDS BEFORE TESTIFYING

When a professional prepares to testify, it is often useful to review the client's file. Such review refreshes the professional's memory about pertinent details. Some professionals take files to court. Although reviewing files is usually necessary and proper, a word of caution is in order. Information in a client's file is confidential, and some of the information may be privileged. If a professional refers to a file *while* testifying in court, the cross-examining attorney may have a right to inspect the file, including privileged information! Thus, by referring to a client's file while testifying, a professional may unwittingly allow an attorney to gain access to sensitive information that would otherwise be privileged from disclosure.

When a professional reviews a client file *before* going to court, there is less likelihood the opposing attorney will seek the file. File review before testifying is not entirely without risk, however. Once a professional is in court on the witness stand, the cross-examining attorney may ask whether the professional reviewed files before coming to court. If the answer is yes, the attorney may ask questions about the files or may ask the judge to order the files produced in court.

Because reviewing client files before testifying could lead to disclosure of privileged information, professionals should consult an attorney to determine the best practice regarding file review.

EDUCATION RECORDS

Records maintained by schools contain confidential information about students (Code of Federal Regulations, Title 34, Part 99, 1997). Generally, educators must obtain parental consent to release such information to individuals outside the school system. Educators are allowed to release confidential information about students in response to a court order or a subpoena. Before school administrators comply with a court order or subpoena, however, they take reasonable steps to notify parents.

Sometimes, schools must release student information on short notice in an emergency. The law allows such release without advance parental permission.

CHILD ABUSE REPORTING LAWS

Child abuse reporting laws require professionals to report suspected maltreatment to designated authorities (see Chapter 3). The reporting requirement overrides the ethical duty to protect confidential client information. Furthermore, the reporting requirement overrides privileges for confidential communications between professionals and clients.

To illustrate the effect of the reporting obligation on confidentiality, consider a case in which a mental health professional is treating an adolescent for depression. The professional is ethically obligated to protect confidential information about the client. Furthermore, the psychotherapist-client privilege may apply. During the fifth session, the adolescent unexpectedly discloses that he sexually abused a young child. The professional must report the disclosure. In filing a report, however, the professional need not disclose *everything* about the client. Disclosure may be limited to information required to comply with the reporting law. In other words, the reporting law does not completely abrogate the obligation to protect confidential information.

THE DANGEROUS-CLIENT EXCEPTION TO CONFIDENTIALITY

In 1976, the California Supreme Court ruled in the famous *Tarasoff* case that a psychotherapist has a legal duty to take steps to protect the potential victim of a client who threatens the victim (*Tarasoff v. Regents of the University of California*, 1976). In *Tarasoff*, a disturbed young man murdered the woman he professed to love. The parents of the murdered woman sued the murderer's therapist, alleging that the therapist knew that his client posed a danger to their daughter but did not warn the victim or her parents. The California Supreme Court ruled that when a therapist determines, or pursuant to the standards of his profession should determine, that his patient presents a serious danger of violence to another, he incurs an obligation to use reasonable care to protect the intended victim against such danger. (p. 334)

Following *Tarasoff*, it was unclear how far a psychotherapist's duty to warn extended (Kaufman, 1991; Leong, Eth, & Silva, 1992, 1994b). Whom does a psychotherapist have to warn? Must a psychotherapist warn the public at large if a patient seems dangerous even though the patient has not made specific threats? Or is the duty to warn limited to individuals specifically threatened by the patient? In *Thompson v. County of Alameda* (1980), the California Supreme Court ruled that the duty to warn does not extend to the general public. The duty to warn arises only when a patient threatens a readily identifiable and foreseeable victim.

In the years since *Tarasoff*, the courts that have considered the dangerous-patient scenario have, for the most part, agreed with the California Supreme Court (Lake, 1994). Courts generally state that "the relationship between the psychotherapist and the outpatient constitutes a special relation that imposes upon the psychotherapist an affirmative duty to protect against or control the patient's violent propensities" (*Estate of Morgan*, 1997). In 1997, the Ohio Supreme Court summarized the law:

Recognizing that the duty is imposed by virtue of the relationship, these courts acknowledge that the duty can be imposed not only upon psychiatrists, but also on psychologists, social workers, mental health clinics and other mental health professionals who know, or should have known, of their patient's violent propensities. The courts do not impose any single formulation as to what steps must be taken to alleviate the danger. Depending upon the facts and the allegations of the case, the particular psychotherapist-defendant may or may not be required to perform any number of acts, including prescribing medication, fashioning a program for treatment, using whatever ability he or she has to control access to weapons or to persuade the patient to voluntarily enter a hospital, issuing warnings or notifying the authorities and, if appropriate, initiating involuntary commitment proceedings. (*Estate of Morgan*, 1997, pp. 1320-1321)

Some states have statutes on the duty to protect potential victims. In California, for example, a statute provides:

> There shall be no monetary liability on the part of, and no cause of action shall arise against, any person who is a psychotherapist . . . in failing to warn of and protect from a patient's threatened violent behavior or failing to predict and warn of and protect from a patient's violent behavior except where the patient has communicated to the psychotherapist a serious threat of physical violence against a reasonably identifiable victim or victims.
>
> If there is a duty to warn and protect under the limited circumstances specified above, the duty shall be discharged by the psychotherapist making reasonable efforts to communicate the threat to the victim or victims and to a law enforcement agency. (Cal. Civil Code § 43.92)

A *Tarasoff*-style duty to warn can arise if a psychotherapist learns that a client plans to sexually abuse a particular child (*Bradley v. Ray*, 1995). Although it would be less certain, a judge might extend the duty to warn to a case in which no particular child was targeted but in which a sexually dangerous client had access to readily identifiable children (see *Barry v. Turek*, 1990).

The *Tarasoff* duty to warn overrides the ethical duty to protect confidential information *and* the psychotherapist-client privilege. The *Tarasoff* court ruled that "the public policy favoring protection of the confidential character of patient-psychotherapist communications must yield to the extent to which disclosure is essential to avert danger to others. The protective privilege ends where the public peril begins" (p. 334). If a therapist fails to take reasonable steps to warn an identifiable victim, and if the dangerous client carries out whatever threats were made, the victim can sue the therapist for malpractice.

Occasionally, a client threatens a therapist (*Menendez v. Superior Court*, 1992). Perhaps the client reveals criminal activity during therapy and threatens the therapist to maintain secrecy. Leong, Eth, and Silva (1994a) wrote that "if a patient offers a deadly secret and then threatens the psychotherapist to ensure silence, the patient has sacrificed any claim to confidentiality (privacy) in the psychotherapist-patient (and physician-patient) relationship" (p. 241).

In a very useful article entitled "Limiting Therapist Exposure to *Tarasoff* Liability," Monahan (1993) provides guidance to therapists who work with clients who pose a danger to others. Monahan suggests that therapists do the following:

A. Risk Assessment

> 1. Become educated in risk assessment, stay current with developments in the field, and be conversant with the law of the jurisdiction.
> 2. Obtain reasonably available records of recent prior treatment and carefully review current treatment records.
> 3. Directly question the patient and relevant others about violent acts and ideation.
> 4. Communicate information and concerns about violence to the person responsible for making decisions about the patient, and make important items salient.

B. Risk Management

> 5. For cases that raise particular concerns about violence, consider intensified treatment, incapacitation, or target hardening.
> 6. For especially difficult cases, seek consultation from an experienced colleague.
> 7. Follow up on lack of compliance with treatment.

C. Documentation

> 8. Record the source, content, and date of significant information on risk and the content, rationale, and date of all actions to prevent violence.

D. Policy

> 9. Develop feasible guidelines for handling risk, and subject these guidelines to clinical and legal review.
> 10. Educate staff in the use of the guidelines, and audit compliance.
> 11. Revise forms to promote and document the information and activities contemplated in the guidelines.

E. Damage Control

> 12. Discourage public statements of responsibility and tampering with the record. (p. 250)

EMERGENCIES

In emergencies, professionals may release confidential information without client consent. For example, there may be no time to contact the client, or contacting the client may be contraindicated because the client is self-dangerous. According to Gutheil and Appelbaum (1982),

> When, in an emergency situation, a patient refuses to give consent or cannot be located for consent, a therapist may sometimes disclose appropriate data in the patient's interest. The situations in which this might be thought to be the case are so numerous . . . that if the exception is not to swallow the rule, such action should be limited to situations in which the patient's immediate welfare is clearly at stake. (p. 8)

COURT-ORDERED PSYCHOLOGICAL EVALUATION

A judge may order an individual to submit to a psychological evaluation for use in legal proceedings. The evaluation will be shared with the judge, the attorneys, and perhaps others. The ethical obligation to protect confidentiality is correspondingly limited. Yet, the evaluator should protect confidentiality within the constraints imposed by the judge. As for privileges such as the psychotherapist-client privilege, the effect of most court-ordered psychological evaluations is that privileges do not apply.

THE PATIENT-LITIGANT EXCEPTION TO PRIVILEGE

Privileges do not apply when a client deliberately makes the client's mental or physical condition an issue in a lawsuit. To use a simple illustration, suppose that an individual consults a physician to treat a broken leg suffered in an auto accident. Later, the patient sues the other driver, seeking money for the leg injury. The patient has made the injury an issue in the case. The other driver has a right to subpoena the doctor and ask not only about the broken leg but also about what the patient said to the doctor about the injury. Ordinarily, the physician-patient privilege would protect the patient's words. In this case, however, the patient made a legal issue of the injury, and the privilege is waived. This is the so-called patient-litigant exception to privileges.

The patient-litigant exception to privileges sometimes arises in child custody litigation in family court. In custody battles, parents accuse each other of all sorts of things, from mild malfeasance to raging psychosis. A parent who claims that the other parent is mentally ill may subpoena privileged mental health records to prove the illness. Should the patient-litigant exception apply in this situation? To put the question differently: Does contesting custody place both parents' mental health in issue, waiving privileges? On the one hand, the judge who will decide the child's future needs to know as much as possible about the parents, and mental health records may shed valuable light. On the other hand, stripping away privilege could undermine therapy. There is no easy answer to this dilemma, and judges reach different decisions depending on the facts of each case. The New Jersey Supreme Court wrote:

> Most courts do not pierce the psychotherapist-patient privilege automatically in disputes over the best interests of the child, but may require disclosure only after careful balancing of the policies in favor of the privilege with the need for disclosure in the specific case before the court. (*Kinsella v. Kinsella*, 1997, p. 581)

7

Expert Testimony

Child abuse is often very difficult to prove in court. Abuse occurs in secret, and the child is usually the only eyewitness. Although many children are excellent witnesses, some are too young to testify, and others are ineffective on the witness stand. Because evidence of abuse is difficult to come by, expert testimony plays an important role in some child abuse litigation. This chapter describes the scope and limits of expert testimony.

Experts testify in criminal court, juvenile court, family court, and other legal arenas. In many criminal cases, there is a jury. Juries are not universal in criminal court, however, and when there is no jury, the judge fulfills the fact-finding responsibility normally entrusted to jurors. In juvenile and family court cases, there usually is no jury. In this chapter, the word *jury* is used for convenience to describe the fact-finder, whether that is a jury or a judge.

❏ Lay and Expert Witnesses

Two types of witnesses testify in court: lay witnesses and experts. A *lay witness* is someone with personal knowledge of relevant facts. An example of a lay witness is an eyewitness to a bank robbery. The lay witness tells the jury what the witness saw or heard.

An *expert witness* is someone with special knowledge who helps the jury understand technical, clinical, or scientific issues. Depending on the type of case, an expert may or may not need personal knowledge of the facts of the case being litigated. An example of an expert witness is a mental health professional who helps the jury understand that some sexually abused children recant following disclosure.

In child abuse and neglect litigation, professionals provide both lay and expert testimony. For example, suppose that a child discloses sexual abuse to a psychotherapist. The child's disclosure is relevant evidence, and the therapist is an eyewitness to the disclosure. In court, the therapist testifies as a lay witness to repeat the child's disclosure. In another case, the same therapist might testify as an expert. Indeed, in some cases, a professional testifies as both a lay witness *and* an expert. Suppose, for example, that a child discloses sexual abuse to a nurse practitioner who is examining the child for possible sexual abuse. In court, the nurse practitioner testifies as a lay witness when she repeats the child's disclosure. She provides expert testimony when she interprets the results of the physical examination.

❏ Therapy vs. Forensic Evaluation: Avoiding Avoidable Dual Relationships

Should mental health professionals providing psychotherapy agree to perform forensic evaluations of their therapy clients? Or are the therapeutic and forensic roles incompatible? For example, should the psychotherapist for a woman who is divorcing her husband agree to perform a court-ordered child custody evaluation of the entire family? Should a psychotherapist who is treating a child for the effects of sexual abuse agree to conduct a formal forensic assessment of abuse and testify in court regarding the findings of the assessment?

Before attempting to answer these questions, it is useful to define forensic psychology. The *Specialty Guidelines for Forensic Psychologists* produced by the Committee on Ethical Guidelines for Forensic Psychologists (1991) provide the following definition:

> Forensic psychology means all forms of professional psychological conduct when acting, with definable foreknowledge, as a psychological expert on explicitly psycholegal issues, in direct assistance to courts, parties to legal proceedings, correctional and forensic mental health facilities, and administrative, judicial, and legislative agencies acting in an adjudicative capacity. (p. 657)

Examples of forensic psychology include a court-ordered evaluation by a mental health professional to determine whether a person charged with crime is competent to stand trial; expert testimony in criminal cases regarding the insanity defense; expert testimony in various types of civil proceedings, including involuntary civil commitment for psychiatric treatment, capacity to make a will, and guardianship. Finally, a mental health professional who conducts a child custody evaluation for use in family court acts as a forensic evaluator. (For useful guidance on when to accept forensic referrals see Hess, 1998.)

In an article that should be studied by every professional who practices at the interface of law and treatment, Greenberg and Shuman (1997) write that "a role conflict arises when a treating therapist also attempts to testify as a forensic expert addressing the psycholegal issues in the case" (p. 50). Melton and his colleagues (1997) add that "forensic assessment differs from a therapeutic assessment on a number of dimensions" (p. 42). The American Professional Society on the Abuse of Children notes that "forensic evaluations are different from clinical evaluations in generally requiring a different professional stance and additional components" (1996a, Guidelines for Psychosocial Evaluation of Suspected Sexual Abuse in Young Children, Statement of Purpose).

Ethics codes of professional organizations emphasize the potential conflict between therapeutic and forensic roles. The Ethical Principles of the American Psychological Association (1992) state that "[i]n most circumstances, psychologists avoid performing multiple and potentially conflicting roles in forensic matters" (Principle 7.03). The Specialty Guidelines for Forensic Psychologists (1991, Committee on Ethical Guidelines for Forensic Psychologists) state:

> Forensic psychologists recognize potential conflicts of interest in dual relationships with parties to legal proceedings, and they seek to minimize their effects. Forensic psychologists avoid providing professional services to parties in a legal proceeding with whom they have personal or professional relationships that are inconsistent with the anticipated relationship. When it is necessary to provide both evaluation and treatment services to a party in a legal proceeding (as may be the case in small forensic hospital settings or small communities), the forensic psychologist takes reasonable steps to minimize the potential negative effects of these circumstances on the rights of the party, confidentiality, and the process of treatment and evaluation. (p. 659)

The ethical guidelines of the American Academy of Psychiatry and the Law (1995) provide that "[t]reating psychiatrists should generally avoid agreeing to be an expert witness or to perform evaluations of their patients for legal purposes because a forensic evaluation usually requires that other people be interviewed and testimony may adversely affect the therapeutic relationship" (p. xiv). The Committee on Psychiatry and Law of the Group for the Advancement of Psychiatry (1991) states that "While, in some areas of the country with limited numbers of mental health practitioners, the therapist may have the role of forensic expert thrust upon him, ordinarily, it is wise to avoid mixing the therapeutic and forensic roles" (p. 44). The *Code of Ethics* of the American Professional Society on the Abuse of Children (1997) provides:

> Clear definitions of professional roles, responsibilities, duties, and tasks and the limits of professional conduct provide clients with maximal information upon which to base their own decisions and actions. The nature of child maltreatment, in which boundaries are blurred or broken, relationships are disturbed, and social positions such as parent, caregiver, and helper are perverted, makes the maintenance of clear professional relationships all the more critical for client protection and in creating the optimal conditions for growth and

development. . . . When a professional is called upon to engage in
more than one professional role, such as therapist and advocate,
investigator and therapist, assessor and healer, investigator and concerned citizen, the professional must be clear about the different
responsibilities and tasks required for each role; take appropriate steps
to guard against role conflict; and make sure that the client understands the nature and different responsibilities of each role. Assuming
more than one professional role in a given case at a given time does
not necessarily represent an unethical multiple-role relationship. (p. 3)

Ethical guidelines for mental health professionals performing
child custody evaluations in family court are quite specific regarding
the potential conflict between forensic and treatment roles. The *Model
Standards of Practice* of the Association of Family and Conciliation
Courts (1994) provide that "a person who has been a mediator or a
therapist for any or all members of the family should not perform a
custody evaluation because the previous knowledge and relationships may render him or her incapable of being completely neutral
and incapable of having unbiased objectivity" (Principle VI.B). The
Guidelines for Child Custody Evaluations in Divorce Proceedings of the
American Psychological Association (1994) provide that "[p]sycholo-
gists generally avoid conducting a child custody evaluation in a case
in which the psychologist served in a therapeutic role for the child or
his or her immediate family or has had other involvement that may
compromise the psychologist's objectivity" (Guideline 7). Glassman
(1998) writes that "[c]hanging roles from therapist to custody evaluator will most likely be interpreted as an ethics violation" (p. 123).
Glassman provides useful information for custody evaluators on
preventing complaints to ethics boards, and, when complaints are
filed, on coping strategies for professionals.

Treating professionals do not transgress ethical boundaries when
they testify as lay witnesses. For example, a child's psychotherapist
may testify as a lay witness in order to repeat the child's abuse
statements uttered during therapy. Before testifying, the therapist
discusses the impending testimony with the attorney requesting the
testimony and, assuming the child is old enough to understand, with
the child and the child's caretakers. The therapist may wish to request
that the attorney issue a subpoena for the therapist's lay testimony.
(For discussion of subpoenas see pp. 211-213.)

When it comes to expert testimony from treating professionals, Greenberg and Shuman (1997) describe two types of testimony: (1) *treating* expert testimony and (2) *forensic* expert testimony. Greenberg and Shuman write:

> [P]sychologists and psychiatrists may appropriately testify as treating experts (subject to privilege, confidentiality, and qualifications) without risk of conflict on matters of the reported history as provided by the patient; mental status; the clinical diagnosis; the care provided to the patient and the patient's response to it; the patient's prognosis; the mood, cognitions, or behavior of the patient; and any other relevant statements that the patient made in treatment. These matters, presented in the manner of descriptive "occurrences" and not psycholegal opinions, do not raise issues of judgment, foundation, or historical truth. Therapists do not ordinarily have the requisite database to testify appropriately about psycholegal issues of causation (i.e., the relationship of a specific act to claimant's current condition) or capacity (i.e., the relationship of diagnosis or mental status to legally defined or functional capacity). These matters raise problems of judgment, foundation, and historical truth that are problematic for treating experts.
>
> When faced with issues that seem to fall between these guideposts, it is useful to ask whether each opinion is one that could or should have been reached in therapy. Thus, if the legal system did not exist, would therapists be expected to reach these sorts of conclusions on their own? Would doing so ordinarily be considered an aspect of the therapy process? In doing so, would the opinion be considered exploratory, tentative, and speculative, or instead as providing an adequate basis for guiding legal action outside of therapy? Is the therapist generating hypotheses to facilitate treatment or is he or she reasonably scientifically certain that this opinion is accurate? Is it based on something substantially more than, "My patient said so," "My patient would have no reason to lie," or "My patient would not lie to me"? (p. 56)

To conclude this subsection, consider the following case: Dr. Jones is providing psychotherapy for 7-year-old Julie. Dr. Jones is treating Julie for the sequelae of incest. Julie's father is facing criminal charges of child sexual abuse. Additionally, Julie's mother is getting a divorce, and seeks sole custody in family court based on the alleged sexual abuse.

Suppose the prosecutor in the criminal case asks Dr. Jones to conduct a comprehensive forensic assessment of Julie to determine whether Julie was sexually abused by her father. The prosecutor wants Dr. Jones to testify in court about the results of the assessment. From the materials described above, it appears that Dr. Jones should decline the prosecutor's request to conduct a comprehensive forensic assessment. Assuming that Dr. Jones does not perform the forensic assessment, may Dr. Jones testify in any capacity at the criminal trial? Clearly, Dr. Jones could testify as a lay witness to repeat anything Julie said during therapy about abuse. Additionally, Dr. Jones could provide what Greenberg and Shuman (1997) call treating expert testimony. Suppose, however, that the prosecutor asks Dr. Jones to testify that, in the doctor's opinion, Julie was sexually abused? Does such an opinion fall within the category of treating expert testimony? Or is such an opinion more properly viewed as forensic expert testimony? Reasonable minds differ on this issue. Some mental health professionals, judges, and attorneys believe an opinion that abuse probably occurred is proper, whereas others believe professionals should not offer such testimony.

As you recall, Julie's mother is divorcing Julie's father—the alleged abuser—and mother seeks sole custody. Since Dr. Jones is Julie's therapist, the doctor should not perform a child custody evaluation for use by the judge in family court. Suppose, however, that Dr. Jones is on the witness stand in family court discussing her treatment of Julie when the judge asks, "Dr. Jones, let me ask you this. Do you believe Julie was sexually abused by her father? And do you think Julie was telling you the truth when she described the abuse to you in your office"? The judge has put Dr. Jones in an awkward position. The judge is really asking three questions: (1) Was Julie sexually abused? (2) If so, is the father the abuser? and (3) Was Julie telling the truth? As to the first question—was Julie abused?—we saw in the preceding paragraph that this question divides professionals. The issue of expert testimony on abuse is discussed in detail later in this chapter.

As for the judge's second and third questions, you may already know, or you will learn later in this chapter that expert witnesses are not supposed to testify that a particular person abused a child. Nor are experts generally allowed to testify that a child told the truth about abuse. Nevertheless, judges and attorneys sometimes ask questions that go beyond proper limits, and that is exactly what the judge did to Dr. Jones. What should the doctor do? My advice is for Dr. Jones to respond with, "Your honor, I appreciate why you ask me those questions, and I'll tell you everything I can. First, I have been treating Julie for sexual abuse. Julie has many of the signs and symptoms we observe in sexually abused children. Moreover, Julie has clearly and consistently described sexual abuse by her father. In my professional judgment, sexual abuse is the most likely explanation for Julie's symptoms and her statements. As for my opinion on whether Julie's father is the abuser? Well, on that score I am not comfortable offering an opinion. I can tell you that Julie has consistently named her father as the one who abused her. Finally, do I think Julie was telling the truth when she told me about the abuse? In my capacity as a therapist, I don't conduct an investigation to determine the factual truth of what my clients tell me. I can't offer an opinion on whether Julie told me the truth. I can tell you Julie has been consistent in what she has said, and that her affect and demeanor are consistent with the idea that she is trying to describe reality. I'm sorry that I'm unable to be more specific, but I'm sure you understand that because my role is limited to providing therapy rather than conducting a forensic evaluation, my knowledge is somewhat limited."

In some cases it is neither feasible nor desirable to rigidly separate forensic from treatment issues. In other cases, rigid separation is necessary. Much depends on the issue under consideration and the facts of the particular case. In the final analysis, sound professional judgment, based on common sense, experience, and knowledge of relevant legal principles, leads to the proper solution.

❑ **Evidence Defined**

Cases are won with evidence. But what is evidence? When my son Eric was 6, he defined evidence as "the stuff bad guys drop." Pretty good for a 6-year-old. Basically, evidence is anything that helps prove a point. Lilly (1996) defined evidence as "any matter, verbal or physical, that can be used to support the existence of a factual proposition" (p. 2). Thus, evidence includes testimony from lay and expert witnesses, written documents, photographs, and objects such as the gun used to hold up a bank. The admissibility of evidence is governed by complex rules administered by the judge.

❑ Substantive Evidence and Credibility Evidence

It is useful to distinguish two types of evidence: (a) substantive evidence and (b) credibility evidence. Although these two categories sometimes overlap, understanding the difference will be helpful later in this chapter when we discuss expert testimony in child sexual abuse cases.

SUBSTANTIVE EVIDENCE

Substantive evidence is evidence offered to prove a point that is legally relevant in a case. In a rape prosecution, for example, testimony identifying the defendant as the rapist is substantive evidence. In child abuse litigation, evidence offered to prove that abuse occurred or to identify the perpetrator is substantive evidence. In a physical abuse case, the substantive evidence might consist of the child's hospital record plus expert testimony on battered-child syndrome. In a sexual abuse case, the substantive evidence might be the findings of a physical examination, the child's disclosure statement to a social worker (hearsay), testimony from the child's mother, testimony from the child, and expert testimony from a mental health professional. All this evidence tends to prove the ultimate issue: abuse.

CREDIBILITY EVIDENCE

Any time a person gets on the witness stand, whether the person is a lay witness or an expert, and whether the person is a child or an adult, the jury must decide whether to believe the person. Thus, a witness's credibility is in issue. The attorney opposing a witness's testimony has a right to cross-examine the witness, and the purpose of cross-examination is often to diminish the witness's credibility in the eyes of the jury. The process of attacking credibility is called *impeachment* (see Chapter 8). Once a witness's credibility is impeached, the attorney presenting the witness's testimony is allowed to rehabilitate the witness's damaged credibility.

A simple example illustrates the impeachment/rehabilitation process. In a bank robbery case, the prosecutor offers the testimony of the teller who was robbed at gunpoint. The teller identifies the defendant as the robber. During cross-examination, the defense attorney impeaches the teller by getting the teller to admit that he was terrified of the gun and that he spent much of the time staring at the barrel. The defense attorney's goal is to convince the jury that the teller did not make an accurate identification because he was fixated on the gun. Now that the teller has been impeached, the prosecutor is allowed to rehabilitate. The prosecutor might bring out the fact that the teller got a good look at the robber.

Most of the time, impeachment and rehabilitation are accomplished without expert testimony. In sex offense prosecutions, however, expert testimony sometimes plays a role in rehabilitating the victim's credibility. In a child sexual abuse case, for example, defense counsel may focus the jury's attention on the fact that the child delayed reporting and recanted. The defense argues that delay and recantation prove that there was no abuse. Following such impeachment, most courts allow the prosecutor to rehabilitate the child's credibility by offering expert testimony that delayed disclosure and recantation are relatively common in children who have been abused. Notice that the expert's testimony is *not* offered as substantive evidence of sexual abuse. The expert does not say that the child was abused. Rather, the expert's testimony has the limited but important goal of explaining delay and recantation, thus rehabilitating the child's credibility.

In sexual abuse litigation, it is important to understand the difference between substantive evidence and credibility evidence. Some courts permit the latter but not the former. More is said later about both types of evidence.

❑ Expert Testimony in Criminal and Noncriminal Proceedings

On paper, similar rules govern expert testimony in criminal and noncriminal proceedings. In practice, however, judges often allow experts greater latitude in noncriminal cases, such as juvenile court proceedings and family court litigation regarding child custody or visitation.

Thus, in a juvenile court proceeding, a judge might allow an expert to give an opinion that the judge would not allow in a criminal case. Judges are most likely to limit or disallow expert testimony when there is a jury. Judges worry that some jurors defer too quickly to experts, thus abdicating their own responsibility to decide the case.

> *On paper, similar rules govern expert testimony in criminal and noncriminal proceedings. In practice, however, judges often allow experts greater latitude in noncriminal cases.*

❑ Metaprinciples of Expert Testimony

Expert testimony is allowed when members of the jury need help to understand technical, clinical, or scientific issues (Chadwick, 1990; Myers, 1997a). For example, in many physical abuse cases, the accused claims that the child's injuries were accidental. The jury lacks the knowledge required to differentiate accidental from inflicted injuries. To help the jury, therefore, a physician testifies as an expert. In some child sexual abuse cases, the child recants. Many jurors do not understand that recantation is relatively common among abused children (Morison & Greene, 1992). The defense attorney may focus on recantation in an effort to convince the jury that the *only* explanation for recantation is that abuse did not occur. In that case, an expert offered by the prosecution helps the jury understand that recantation is not uncommon.

Thus, experts are used to help jurors understand technical, clinical, and scientific issues. The acronym *HELP* is useful to organize the metaprinciples underlying expert testimony:

H—honesty
E—evenhandedness
L—limits of expertise
P—preparation

HONESTY

Expert witnesses must be honest with the jury, with the judge, with the attorneys, and, in the final analysis, with themselves (Committee on Ethical Guidelines for Forensic Psychologists, 1991). The duty to provide honest testimony derives in part from the witness oath in which the expert swears to "tell the truth, the whole truth, and nothing but the truth." Honesty has deeper roots, however. Honesty lies at the core of professionalism and personal integrity. Experts who allow half-truths to go unchecked or who shade the truth to favor one side in the litigation undermine the very purpose of the law. Half-honest experts seldom help the jury.

> *Experts who allow half-truths to go unchecked or who shade the truth to favor one side in the litigation undermine the very purpose of the law.*

EVENHANDEDNESS

In our legal system, experts are supposed to play a different role than attorneys. The attorney's job is to win. To be sure, the ultimate goal of the legal system is truth, but the theory of the adversary system of justice is that the truth emerges through the courtroom confrontation of adversaries (see Chapter 2). Thus, attorneys are advocates for their clients and are not supposed to be objective.

Unlike attorneys, experts are not—or, at least, should not be—partisan advocates (Chadwick & Krous, 1997). The expert's responsibility is not to win but to help the jury understand clinical, technical, or scientific issues. The expert's responsibility is to educate, not to claim victory. Experts who view litigation through advocates' eyes lose their bearings and sink to the level of "hired guns."

To avoid being an advocate, must an expert aspire to complete objectivity? Is an expert irreparably sullied if his or her sympathies lean toward one side or the other? Although it may be theoretically possible to attain unqualified objectivity, such purity is rare in the "real world" (Saks, 1990). Moreover, in a system in which each side retains its own expert, it is unrealistic to expect professionals to be completely dispassionate about the outcome. What is important is not unconditional evenhandedness but a degree of objectivity that is compatible with honesty and professionalism.

Just as important as reasonable objectivity is a willingness to acknowledge one's biases and recognize the shaping influence that bias can exert on testimony. Finally, experts should not represent themselves as objective when they are not. The latter requirement relates, of course, to the metaprinciple of honesty.

LIMITS OF EXPERTISE

During the past 30 years, much has been learned about child abuse, yet many questions remain. With sexual abuse in particular, our knowledge is in the formative stage. For example, controversy continues about the meaning of various genital and anal findings. Uncertainty, and no small degree of confusion, surrounds the meaning of psychological symptoms such as nightmares, regression, and acting out (as discussed later in this chapter).

Expert witnesses should be familiar with relevant literature and appreciate the limits of current knowledge. While on the witness stand, experts should acknowledge these limits and refuse to exceed them, even in the face of pressure from attorneys or the judge (Melton, Petrila, Poythress, & Slobogin, 1987). See Appendix D.

In addition to understanding the limits of knowledge in the field, experts should have a clear fix on the limits of their own knowledge (Saks, 1990).

PREPARATION

Preparation is the key to effective expert testimony. The expert should evaluate all relevant information. Before testifying, the expert should meet with the attorney who solicited the testimony. Chadwick (1990) emphasized that such meetings "are always desirable, and rarely impossible" (p. 963).

Before going to court, it is often necessary to review records. Reviewing records before trial, or using records while testifying, raises complex issues regarding the right of attorneys to inspect confidential records, and experts should be familiar with the rules on this topic in the locality where they testify (see Chapter 6, the section "Disclosure of Confidential and Privileged Information").

Although expert witnesses are not expected to know the legal rules governing expert testimony, they should know enough about the rules to avoid unnecessary and potentially costly mistakes. For example, professionals should understand that courts, especially criminal courts, do not allow experts to testify that children told the truth when disclosing abuse.

❏ Qualifying to Testify as an Expert

Before a person may testify as an expert, the judge must be convinced that the person possesses sufficient "knowledge, skill, experience, training, or education" to qualify as an expert (Fed. R. Evid. 702). Normally, the attorney offering expert testimony puts the professional on the witness stand and asks about educational accomplishments, specialized training, and relevant experience. A professional does not have to be a well-known authority to testify as an expert. For example, publication of books or articles is normally not required. The important question is whether the jury will be helped by the professional's testimony (Wigmore, 1904/1974). The type and degree of expertise required depends on the testimony.

The attorney opposing proposed expert testimony has the right to inquire into the professional's qualifications. Such questioning is called *voir dire*. If the professional is clearly qualified to testify, the opposing attorney may ask nothing.

When the judge has listened to the pros and cons of the professional's qualifications, the judge decides whether the professional will be allowed to testify as an expert and, if so, the parameters of the expert's testimony.

❑ The Form of Expert Testimony

Expert testimony usually takes one of the following forms: (a) an opinion, (b) an answer to a hypothetical question, (c) a lecture providing background information on a pertinent subject, or (d) some combination of the above.

OPINION TESTIMONY

An important difference between expert and lay witnesses is that lay witnesses are supposed to avoid opinions, whereas experts routinely give opinions. The job of a lay witness is to provide *factual* information: to tell the jury what the witness saw or heard. The jury uses the lay witness's factual testimony to reach its own opinions. Of course, it is not always feasible for lay witnesses to avoid opinions. For example, a lay witness is allowed to testify that someone looked intoxicated. Clearly, this is an opinion. Yet the opinion is permitted because it is rationally based on the witness's perception and helpful to the jury. Lay witnesses are permitted to give opinions on quite a few routine matters, including speed, distance, mood ("she seemed happy"), and physical appearance.

Although lay witnesses are allowed to offer opinions on some issues, the general principle remains that they should confine their testimony as much as possible to factual material. Experts, by contrast, routinely offer opinions. In a physical abuse case, for example, the physician could testify that, in the doctor's opinion, a child had battered-child syndrome. The doctor could go on to opine that the child's injuries were not accidental.

Experts must be reasonably confident of their opinions. Lawyers and judges use the term *reasonable certainty* to describe the necessary degree of confidence. Thus, the question to a medical expert might be, "Do you have an opinion, based on a reasonable degree of medical certainty, as to whether the child's injuries were accidental?"

Unfortunately, the reasonable certainty standard is not self-defining. It is clear that experts may not speculate or guess. It is equally clear that experts do not have to be completely certain. In the case of *Oxendine v. State* (1987), the Delaware Supreme Court discussed reasonable certainty in the context of expert testimony regarding the cause of death of a 6-year-old child:

> A finding of medical causation may not be based on speculation or conjecture. A doctor's testimony that a certain thing is possible is no evidence at all. His opinion as to what is possible is no more valid than the jury's own speculation as to what is or is not possible. Almost anything is possible, and it is improper to allow a jury to consider and base a verdict upon a "possible" cause of death. Therefore, a doctor's testimony can only be considered evidence when his conclusions are based on reasonable medical certainty that a fact is true or untrue. (p. 873)

Thus, the degree of certainty required for "reasonable certainty" lies somewhere between guesswork and complete certainty. Yet locating reasonable certainty somewhere between these extremes adds little to the concept, and, in the end, the reasonable certainty standard fails to provide a meaningful tool to evaluate the helpfulness of expert testimony.

A more productive approach to assessing expert testimony looks beyond the rubric of reasonable certainty and asks questions such as:

- In formulating an opinion, did the expert consider all relevant facts?
- How much confidence can be placed in the facts underlying the expert's opinion?
- Does the expert have an adequate understanding of pertinent clinical and scientific principles?
- To the extent that the expert's opinion rests on scientific principles, have the principles been tested?

- Have the principles or theories relied on by the expert been published in peer-reviewed journals?
- Are the principles or theories relied on by the expert generally accepted as reliable by experts in the field?
- Did the expert employ appropriate methods of assessment?
- Are the inferences and conclusions drawn by the expert defensible?
- Is the expert reasonably objective?

In the final analysis, the issue is whether the expert's opinion is logical, consistent, explainable, objective, and defensible. The value of the expert's opinion depends on answers to these questions (Black, 1988). For a useful analysis of expert testimony by mental health professionals, see Rogers and Barrett (1996).

THE HYPOTHETICAL QUESTION

In bygone days, many states required experts to testify in response to a hypothetical question asked by an attorney. With a hypothetical question, the attorney describes the facts of a "hypothetical" case. The facts in the hypothetical case are supposed to mirror the facts in the case on trial. Consider a physical abuse case, for example, in which a physician is the expert. The attorney presenting the doctor's testimony asks about a hypothetical child's injuries. Following this, the attorney asks, "Now, doctor, on the basis of these hypothetical facts, do you have an opinion, based on a reasonable degree of medical certainty, as to whether the hypothetical child's injuries were the result of an accident?" The doctor then offers an opinion about the hypothetical child's injuries. The jury takes the doctor's opinion about the hypothetical child and applies it to the "real" child.

As you can see, the hypothetical question is a rather cumbersome way to elicit expert testimony. Most states no longer require experts to testify in response to hypothetical questions. Today, most experts testify in their own words. Moreover, experts can discuss the facts of the case on trial rather than some hypothetical case. In the physical abuse case described above, an attorney in a modern courtroom would simply ask, "Doctor, do you have an opinion, based on reasonable medical certainty, about the cause of the child's injuries?"

The doctor would proceed directly to the opinion and the supporting data.

The attorney most likely to ask hypothetical questions is the cross-examining attorney. The cross-examiner may ask about hypothetical facts in an effort to get the expert to agree that if the facts were different, the expert's opinion would change.

EXPERT TESTIMONY PROVIDING BACKGROUND INFORMATION

Rather than offering an opinion, an expert may give testimony in the form of "a dissertation or exposition of scientific or other principles relevant to the case, leaving to the [jury] to apply them to the facts" (Fed. R. Evid. 702, Advisory Committee Note). An example of this form of expert testimony is a child sexual abuse case in which the child recanted before trial. The defense attorney focuses the jury's attention on the recantation and argues that recantation means that the jury should not believe the child's testimony at trial. In light of this attack on the child's credibility, the prosecutor may offer expert testimony to help the jury understand that recantation is relatively common among sexually abused children. The expert gives the jury information that it can use to evaluate the child's credibility. Note that in this scenario, the expert does not offer an opinion that the child was sexually abused. The expert's job is limited to equipping the jury with information that it can use to decide whether to believe the child.

COMBINING FORMS OF EXPERT TESTIMONY

The three forms of expert testimony described above are not mutually exclusive, and experts sometimes provide more than one form of testimony during the same stint on the witness stand. In a child sexual abuse case, for example, a mental health professional might testify that delayed disclosure is relatively common in sexually abused children (form—lecture; purpose—credibility) and offer an opinion that the preschool-aged child demonstrates developmentally unusual sexual knowledge (form—opinion; purpose—substantive evidence).

❏ Information on Which Experts May Rely for Testimony

Professionals draw from many sources of information to reach conclusions about child abuse. When it comes to expert testimony, the law generally allows professionals to base their testimony in court on the same sources of information that they rely on in their normal, day-to-day practice. Thus, in a sexual abuse case, a professional may base expert testimony on the child's disclosure, the results of a CPS investigation, and consultation with colleagues. In a physical abuse case, a physician may form an opinion based on physical examination of the child, statements of the child and parents, results of laboratory tests and X-rays, and reading in the literature (*State v. Hutto*, 1997).

❏ Expert Testimony Based on Novel Scientific Principles

A special rule governs the admissibility in court of expert testimony based on scientific principles or techniques that are novel or of dubious reliability. The purpose of the special rule is to exclude unreliable expert testimony. The rule takes two forms in the United States: (a) the general acceptance rule, commonly known as the *Frye* rule, and (b) relevance analysis, commonly known as the *Daubert* rule. The *Frye* and *Daubert* rules are described briefly below.

GENERAL ACCEPTANCE—*FRYE*

The general acceptance rule takes its name from a 1923 case called *Frye v. United States*. In *Frye*, the court ruled that expert testimony based on a novel scientific principle is admissible only when the principle gains "general acceptance in the field in which it belongs" (p. 1014). An attorney offering expert testimony based on a novel scientific principle must convince the judge that the principle is generally accepted as reliable in the relevant professional community.

The general acceptance rule was once the dominant rule in the United States. In recent years, however, an increasing number of courts have rejected general acceptance because the rule excludes some scientific and clinical information that helps the jury. Courts that reject *Frye* typically adopt some version of relevance analysis.

RELEVANCE ANALYSIS—*DAUBERT*

In 1993, the U.S. Supreme Court decided a case called *Daubert v. Merrell Dow Pharmaceuticals, Inc.* In *Daubert,* the Supreme Court rejected the general acceptance test (*Frye*) for the federal courts in favor of a more flexible approach to novel scientific evidence called *relevance analysis* (Black, Francisco, & Saffran-Brinks, 1994). With relevance analysis, the judge looks at more than general acceptance in the scientific community. The judge conducts a searching inquiry into the reliability of novel scientific evidence. To assess reliability, the judge considers the following:

- Whether the principle can be and has been tested to determine its reliability and validity
- How often the principle yields accurate results
- Existence of standards governing use of the technique to ensure accurate results (e.g., clear diagnostic criteria)
- Degree to which expert testimony is based on subjective analysis, as opposed to objective analysis. Expert testimony based on subjective analysis may be of questionable reliability because it is difficult to evaluate an expert's subjective decision-making process.
- Publication in peer-reviewed literature. In *Daubert,* the Supreme Court wrote:

    Another pertinent consideration is whether the theory or technique has been subjected to peer review and publication. Publication (which is but one element of peer review) is not a *sine qua non* of admissibility; it does not necessarily correlate with reliability, . . . and in some instances well-grounded but innovative theories will not have been published. . . . Some propositions, moreover, are too particular, too new, or of too limited interest to be published. But submission to the scrutiny of the scientific community is a component of "good science," in part because it increases the likelihood that substantive flaws in methodology will be detected. . . . The fact of publication (or lack thereof) in a

peer-reviewed journal thus will be a relevant, though not dispositive, consideration in assessing the scientific validity of a particular technique or methodology on which an opinion is premised.
(pp. 593-594)

- Whether the scientific or clinical principle is generally accepted by
  experts in the field (the *Frye* rule). The *Daubert* Court wrote that "widespread acceptance can be an important factor in ruling particular evidence admissible" (p. 594).

- Whether the principle or technique is consistent with established and
  proven modes of analysis

The U.S. Supreme Court's *Daubert* ruling applies only to federal
courts. State judges are free to accept *Daubert* or to retain the venerable *Frye* test. Although the general trend in state courts is toward
Daubert, the supreme courts of California, Florida, Nebraska, New
York, and Washington have retained *Frye*.

DOES *FRYE* OR *DAUBERT* APPLY TO
MENTAL HEALTH TESTIMONY?

There is some uncertainty about when testimony from mental
health professionals should be treated as scientific evidence subject
to *Frye* or *Daubert* (Rogers & Barrett, 1996). According to Faigman
(1995), "*Daubert*'s application to social science is not obvious. The
[*Daubert*] opinion itself is silent on the matter of social science.
Moreover, much psychology based expert testimony that today is
routinely admitted bears little resemblance to 'science'" (p. 961).
Despite uncertainty, courts apply *Frye* or *Daubert* to some mental
health testimony. The California Supreme Court wrote "that given
[*Frye*'s] prophylactic purpose, nothing precludes its application to 'a
new scientific process operating on purely psychological evidence' "
(*People v. Stoll*, 1989, p. 710). Courts have applied *Frye* or *Daubert* to
rape trauma syndrome (*People v. Bledsoe*, 1984), some forms of expert
testimony regarding child sexual abuse (*State v. Hadden*, 1997; *State
v. Rimmasch*, 1989), and other types of psychological expertise.

The special rule governing scientific evidence does not apply every
time an expert's testimony is based in whole or in part on scientific
principles. Many scientific principles are so well established that the
judge takes what is called *judicial notice* of the reliability of the

principles. When a judge takes judicial notice, there is no need to prove the reliability of the scientific principle. Battered-child syndrome, for example, is an accepted medical diagnosis. Judges take judicial notice of the reliability of the syndrome, eliminating the need for scrutiny under *Frye* or *Daubert*.

Several state supreme courts (e.g., California and Florida) have an odd rule regarding expert testimony. These courts apply *Frye* or *Daubert* to novel scientific evidence but *not* to personal opinions of expert witnesses. Unfortunately, the distinction (if there is one) between scientific evidence and "mere expert opinion" is not clear. The purported distinction seems to do little more than confuse analysis of when *Frye* or *Daubert* should apply. Carter (1989) pointed out that "the distinction between personal opinion and scientific evidence ignores the fact that all expert opinion is based on some underlying theory or process. To be consistent, expert testimony must be subjected to [*Frye* or *Daubert*] if the principle it is based on is novel" (pp. 1112-1113). One result of the "mere expert opinion" rule is that it is often difficult to tell when a judge will apply *Frye* or *Daubert* to psychological testimony.

❑ **Physical Abuse**

Expert testimony regarding physical abuse is a complex subject. Limitations of space preclude extended discussion of this important topic, and the reader is referred to other sources (see Helfer & Kempe, 1987; Ludwig & Kornberg, 1992; Lyon, Gilles, & Cory, 1996; Reece, 1994).

Briefly, in physical abuse litigation, accused individuals who deny responsibility usually raise one of two defenses. The most common defense is that the child's injuries were accidental. Alternatively, the accused may acknowledge that the child was abused but claim that someone else did it.

Expert testimony from medical professionals plays a key role in proving nonaccidental injury (Chadwick, 1990; Myers, 1997a). Physicians provide expert testimony about bruises, bites, head injuries, abdominal injuries, burns, and fractures (Johnson, 1996; Lyon et al., 1996; Reece, 1994; Schmitt, 1987).

EXPERT MEDICAL TESTIMONY ON CAUSE OF INJURY

A properly qualified medical professional may testify that a child's injuries were probably not accidental (see Willman, Bank, Senac, & Chadwick, 1997). In general, medical experts are allowed to describe the means used to inflict injury. In *People v. Jackson* (1971), for example, the court wrote that "an expert medical witness may give his opinion as to the means used to inflict a particular injury, based on his deduction from the appearance of the injury itself" (p. 921). Thus, an expert could state that a skull fracture was probably caused by a blow from a blunt instrument or that an injury probably was caused by a person of mature strength. An expert may offer an opinion on "whether the explanation given for the injuries is reasonable" (*Gideon v. State*, 1986, p. 1336). Finally, an expert may offer an opinion on the cause of death or on the potential harm of injuries.

BATTERED-CHILD SYNDROME

In their landmark article, Kempe et al. (1962) coined the term *battered-child syndrome* and described it as follows:

> The battered-child syndrome may occur at any age, but, in general the affected children are younger than 3 years. In some instances the clinical manifestations are limited to those resulting from a single episode of trauma, but more often the child's general health is below par, and he shows evidence of neglect, including poor skin hygiene, multiple soft tissue injuries, and malnutrition. One often obtains a history of previous episodes suggestive of parental neglect or trauma. A marked discrepancy between clinical findings and historical data as supplied by the parents is a major diagnostic feature of the battered-child syndrome. . . . Subdural hematoma, with or without fracture of the skull . . . is an extremely frequent finding even in the absence of fractures of the long bones. . . . The characteristic distribution of these multiple fractures and the observation that the lesions are in different stages of healing are of additional value in making the diagnosis. (p. 17)

Not all victims of physical abuse have injuries in various stages of healing. Kempe noted that abusive injury sometimes results from "a single episode of trauma" (p. 17). Many child abuse fatalities lack a pattern of repeated injury. According to Zumwalt and Hirsch (1987), "Fatalities from an isolated or single beating are as common as fatalities from repeated physical assault" (p. 258).

Expert testimony on battered-child syndrome is routinely allowed. Physicians are permitted to state that a child has the syndrome and probably suffered nonaccidental injury.

SHAKEN BABY SYNDROME

Frustrated caretakers sometimes grasp young children by the shoulders or under the arms and shake them. Neurological damage caused by violent shaking is called *shaken baby syndrome* (Duhaime, Christian, Moss, & Seidl, 1996; Johnson, 1996; Lazoritz et al., 1997; Lyon et al., 1996). The syndrome is an accepted medical diagnosis, and expert testimony on shaken baby syndrome is admissible (Myers, 1997a).

MUNCHAUSEN SYNDROME BY PROXY

Munchausen syndrome in adults is "a condition characterized by habitual presentation for hospital treatment of an apparent acute illness, the patient giving a plausible and dramatic history, all of which is false" (*Dorland's Illustrated Medical Dictionary*, 1994, p. 1635). Munchausen syndrome by proxy occurs when an adult uses a child as the vehicle for fabricated illness. Parnell and Day (1998) define Munchausen syndrome by proxy as "a form of child abuse in which a caretaker fabricates and/or induces illness in a child" (p. 5). According to Zumwalt and Hirsch (1987),

> Munchausen syndrome by proxy occurs when a parent or guardian falsifies a child's medical history or alters a child's laboratory test or actually causes an illness or injury in a child in order to gain medical attention for the child which may result in innumerable harmful hospital procedures. (p. 276)

There is no psychological test that detects adults with Munchausen syndrome by proxy (Rosenberg, 1994). Nor is there a "classic profile for a perpetrator, meaning that possessing certain characteristics does not entirely implicate a suspect and lacking certain characteristics does not entirely exclude a suspect" (Rosenberg, 1994, p. 270).

Rosenberg (1994) observed that in many cases the best way to diagnose the syndrome is to separate the child from the suspected adult. When children are hospitalized for evaluation of possible Munchausen syndrome by proxy, covert video surveillance (CVS) of the child's hospital room is useful to catch abusive parents "in the act." In a fascinating article, Southall, Plunkett, Banks, Falkov, and Samuels (1997) reported on 10 years' experience using CVS in England. The authors described numerous cases of apparently normal, loving parents who smother, poison, and otherwise cruelly abuse their young children as soon as medical personnel leave the room. "Professionals and members of the judiciary, who have not seen abuse in action as shown by CVS, may be almost unable to acknowledge that such acts can be and are committed by apparently caring mothers, fathers, and stepparents" (p. 740).

Munchausen syndrome by proxy appears to be uncommon (Rosenberg, 1994). When it occurs, however, "Children are at some risk of death" (Rosenberg, 1994, p. 268). Courts allow expert testimony on the syndrome (Myers, 1997a). In *People v. Phillips* (1981), for example, the court approved expert psychiatric testimony on the syndrome to establish the defendant's motive to poison her baby by putting large quantities of salt in the baby's food. The court ruled that the syndrome was not novel scientific evidence subject to *Frye*.

❏ Neglect

Neglect is a broad concept, covering many types of maltreatment (Erickson & Egeland, 1996). Although limitations of space foreclose detailed discussion of neglect, brief discussion of 10 types of neglect is presented below.

MEDICAL NEGLECT

Parents have a legal duty to provide necessary medical care for their children, and failure to do so is neglect (*Commonwealth v. Twitchell*, 1993). Dubowitz and Black (1996) conceptualize medical neglect

> as a situation in which a child's clear medical need is not met. . . . A "clear" medical need is one that a lay person could reasonably be expected to recognize as requiring professional health care *and* to act on by seeking such care. Many minor health problems (e.g., colds, diaper rash) are treated reasonably by parents and do not meet the standard of clear medical need. (p. 228)

When parents fail or refuse to provide essential medical care, the state, operating through CPS and the juvenile court, may intervene. Religious belief is often at the heart of parental refusal of medical care for children (see Bottoms, Shaver, Goodman, & Qin, 1995). For example, Jehovah's Witnesses do not believe in blood transfusions, and parents of this faith sometimes refuse to permit blood transfusions for their children. Members of the First Church of Christ, Scientist, believe in spiritual healing rather than conventional medicine (First Church of Christ, Scientist, 1989). Parents with these and similar religious convictions argue that state-enforced medical care violates their constitutionally protected freedom of religion. When parental religious belief stands as a barrier to essential medical care for children, however, judges often overrule parents and order treatment. This result can be traced to the distinction between freedom to *believe* in a particular religion and freedom to *act* according to religious belief. In *Reynolds v. United States* (1878), the U.S. Supreme Court stated that religious *belief* is completely beyond government control but that *conduct* "in violation of social duties or subversive of good order" may be prohibited (p. 164). The distinction between belief and con-

When parents fail or refuse to provide essential medical care, the state, operating through CPS and the juvenile court, may intervene.

duct has direct implications for medical neglect. In *Prince v. Massachusetts* (1944), the U.S. Supreme Court wrote:

> The family itself is not beyond regulation in the public interest, as against a claim of religious liberty. . . . And neither rights of religion nor rights of parenthood are beyond limitation. Acting to guard the general interest in youth's well being, the state as parens patriae may restrict the parent's control by requiring school attendance, regulating or prohibiting the child's labor, and in many other ways. Its authority is not nullified merely because the parent grounds his claim to control the child's course on religion or conscience. Thus, he cannot claim freedom from compulsory vaccination for the child more than for himself on religious grounds. The right to practice religion freely does not include liberty to expose the community or the child to communicable disease or the latter to ill health or death. . . . The catalogue need not be lengthened. It is sufficient to show . . . that the state has a wide range of power for limiting parental freedom and authority in things affecting the child's welfare; and that this includes, to some extent, matters of conscience and religious conviction. . . .
>
> Parents may be free to become martyrs themselves. But it does not follow they are free, in identical circumstances, to make martyrs of their children before they have reached the age of full and legal discretion when they can make that choice for themselves. (pp. 166-167, 170)

Judges exhibit great deference to the right of parents to inculcate religious beliefs in their children. When religion leads to refusal of essential medical care, however, judges often intervene. As the Arizona Supreme Court stated, "If there is a direct collision of a child's right to good health and a parent's religious beliefs, the parent's rights must give way" (*In re Appeal in Cochise County*, 1982, p. 465).

In medical neglect cases, expert testimony is usually indispensable. The testifying physician provides the judge with information on the following:

- The degree of harm that the child is suffering and will suffer without medical care
- The medical condition involved and whether the condition is progressive or stable

- The treatment required to alleviate the condition, and whether the treatment is well accepted or experimental
- The likelihood of successful treatment and the risks and side effects of treatment. Generally, as the degree of risk inherent in proposed treatment increases, judges demonstrate correspondingly greater deference to parental decision making. The same is true as the likelihood of successful treatment decreases. The less likely the success of treatment, the more likely the judge is to deny state-requested medical care.
- The probability that treatment will provide the child a normal and meaningful life, or as normal and meaningful a life as possible considering the child's condition

PSYCHOLOGICAL NEGLECT

Psychological maltreatment is extremely harmful to children (Brassard, Germain, & Hart, 1987; Garbarino, 1986; Hart, Brassard, & Karlson, 1996). Guidelines published by the American Professional Society on the Abuse of Children (APSAC, 1996b) describe psychological maltreatment as "a repeated pattern of caregiver behavior or extreme incident(s) that conveys to children that they are worthless, flawed, unloved, unwanted, endangered, or only of value in meeting another's needs."

NONORGANIC FAILURE TO THRIVE

Failure to thrive (FTT) describes several conditions in infants and children (Frank & Drotar, 1994). In some children, FTT is caused by medical problems. In a few children, however, FTT is attributable to extreme neglect. The *Diagnostic and Statistical Manual of Mental Disorders* (*DSM-IV*; American Psychiatric Association, 1994) uses the term *reactive attachment disorder of infancy or early childhood* to describe the psychological damage caused by extreme emotional neglect. The manual states: "The essential feature of Reactive Attachment Disorder is markedly disturbed and developmentally inappropriate social relatedness in most contexts that begins before age 5 years and is associated with grossly pathological care" (p. 116). Nonorganic FTT often causes cognitive deficits in children and is a legitimate reason to intervene in the family or terminate parental rights (Mackner, Starr, & Black, 1997).

MENTALLY RETARDED PARENTS

Parental mental retardation is not a legally sufficient basis to intervene in the family. In some cases, however, a parent's mental retardation causes serious harm or risk of harm to a child, and intervention is warranted.

PSYCHIATRICALLY DISABLED PARENTS

Parental mental illness is not a sufficient reason to disrupt the parent-child relationship. When mental illness impairs a parent's ability to provide for a child's basic needs, or otherwise endangers a child, however, intervention is appropriate.

PHYSICALLY DISABLED PARENTS

Physically handicapped parents are generally fully capable of providing for their children. In rare cases, however, the state must step in against the parent's will to assist a seriously disabled parent. In *In re Jacobs* (1989), for example, the mother of two young children suffered a stroke that made it impossible for her to care for the children without assistance. The children's father was unable to provide for them. A juvenile court judge ruled that the children were dependent, and the Michigan Supreme Court agreed. The primary issue before the supreme court was whether a juvenile court judge may assume authority over children whose needs are not met through no fault of the parents. The supreme court ruled that a finding of parental culpability or fault is not required to find that children are dependent.

DRUG ABUSE AS NEGLECT

Drug abuse by parents often contributes to abuse and neglect (Bays, 1990, 1994). Moreover, substance-abusing parents are often highly resistant to changing their behavior (Butler, Radia, & Magnatta, 1994). Famularo and his colleagues studied 136 juvenile court cases in which children were removed from parental custody due to serious maltreatment (Famularo, Kinscherff, Bunshaft, Spivak, & Fenton, 1989). The research disclosed that

> cases involving parental substance abuse and/or the more severe forms of child maltreatment are most resistant to treatment interventions ordered by the courts. . . . Courts and social service agencies cannot rely upon the mere fact of court involvement to yield effective interventions or compliance with service plans. (p. 512)

Murphy et al. (1991) examined 206 juvenile court cases involving serious child abuse or neglect and found a high rate of substance abuse. Substance-abusing parents were significantly less likely to comply with court-ordered services than parents who did not abuse drugs or alcohol. According to the authors, "Parents who fail to stop abusing substances are unlikely to change their behaviors or to provide safer environments for their children" (pp. 208-209).

GENERAL NEGLECT—"FILTHY HOME" CASES

One of the most troublesome cases for social workers and juvenile court judges is the child who lives in a chaotic and filthy home where the child's physical and psychological needs are not met but where it is difficult to find a clear legal "handle" on which to intervene. Professionals do not want to intervene through the courts when poverty is the reason that a child's needs are not met. Yet, it is often difficult to determine whether a child's problems result from poverty or neglect. About the best we can say is that juvenile court intervention is warranted when a child's physical or psychological well-being is significantly harmed, or when the risk of harm is high, and when the totality of circumstances indicate neglect. The Utah Supreme Court remarked in *In re K.S.* (1987) that

> children are entitled to the care of an adult who cares enough to provide the child with the opportunity to form psychological bonds, in addition to the physical necessities of life. . . . An unfit or incompetent parent is one who "substantially and repeatedly refuse[s] or fail[s] to render proper parental care and protection." (p. 173)

ABANDONMENT

Abandonment is often used as a reason to terminate parental rights. Abandonment is equally viable for initial juvenile court intervention. Although states vary slightly in their definitions of abandonment, the concept boils down to disregard of parental obligations.

EDUCATIONAL NEGLECT

Parents have an obligation to send their children to school or to comply with requirements for home schooling. Failure to obey compulsory attendance laws is neglect.

❑ Sexual Abuse

Expert testimony plays an important role in some child sexual abuse cases (Bulkley, 1992). It is useful to divide such testimony into four categories: (a) testimony describing medical evidence, (b) testimony based largely on psychological effects of abuse, (c) testimony describing developmental differences between children and adults, and (d) testimony about the alleged perpetrator.

MEDICAL EVIDENCE OF CHILD SEXUAL ABUSE

Medical evidence of sexual abuse is found only in a fraction of cases (Adams & Wells, 1993; American Medical Association, 1985; Bays & Chadwick, 1993; Finkel & De Jong, 1994). When such evidence exists, however, judges allow physicians and other qualified medical professionals to describe it (Myers, 1997a).

EXPERT TESTIMONY BASED LARGELY ON THE PSYCHOLOGICAL EFFECTS OF SEXUAL ABUSE

Expert testimony regarding the psychological effects of sexual abuse falls into two subcategories: (a) substantive evidence and (b) credibility evidence (defined earlier in this chapter).

Substantive Evidence

Substantive expert testimony from mental health professionals takes several forms. An expert may offer an opinion that a child has a diagnosis of sexual abuse. The expert may avoid diagnostic terminology and offer an opinion that a child was abused. The expert may state that a child's symptoms are consistent with sexual abuse. Alternatively, an expert may say that a child demonstrates sexual knowledge that is unusual for children of that age. Finally, the expert may avoid any mention of the child in the case at hand and confine testimony to a description of symptoms seen in sexually abused children as a group. Whatever form the testimony takes, it is offered for one purpose: to prove abuse. Thus, each form of testimony is substantive evidence.

Do Mental Health Professionals Know Enough About Sexual Abuse to Offer Substantive Evidence? There is controversy over whether mental health professionals know enough about sexual abuse to offer substantive evidence. In 1989, Melton and Limber argued against such testimony, writing that "under no circumstances should a court admit the opinion of [a mental health professional] about whether a particular child has been abused" (p. 1230). Six years later, Melton et al. (1995) asserted that mental health testimony is unnecessary because jurors can evaluate children's symptoms without assistance from professionals. Melton argued that "determination of whether particular behavior (e.g., a young child's graphic description of a sexual act) is indicative of a history of abuse is a matter of common sense, not specialized knowledge" (p. 67).

Melton et al.'s views are entitled to respect, but Melton does not speak for the entire field. Other professionals support limited use of mental health testimony as substantive evidence of sexual abuse (see Corwin, 1988; Faller, 1990; Myers et al., 1989). Faller (1990) observed that "there appears to be a fair amount of consensus among mental health professionals about both the strategy and the criteria for deciding whether a child has been sexually victimized" (p. 115). Oberlander (1995) surveyed 31 Massachusetts mental health professionals who evaluate children for sexual abuse.

Evaluators were asked whether it was possible to determine whether a child's behavior and symptoms were consistent with typical responses to sexual abuse. . . . In this sample, 67.7% said they believed it was possible to make such a determination, 9.7% said they were unsure or that it depends on the case, and 22.5% said they believed it was not possible to make such a determination.

Evaluators were asked to indicate their opinions about whether evaluation results could establish that a child was sexually abused. . . . In this sample, 58.1% said they believed evaluation results could establish abuse, 12.9% said they were unsure or that it depends on the case, and 29.0% said they believed evaluation results could not establish abuse. (Most evaluators drew a distinction between "establish" and "prove," suggesting that their opinions are probabilistic.) (pp. 482-483)

In 1996, APSAC (1996a) published guidelines for the psychosocial evaluation of suspected sexual abuse in young children. The guidelines recognize that an "evaluator may state an opinion that abuse did or did not occur, an opinion about the likelihood of the occurrence of abuse, or simply provide a description and analysis of the gathered information." (The APSAC guidelines are reproduced in Appendix C of this book.)

Controversy will continue over expert testimony offered as substantive evidence of sexual abuse. Neither side of the debate has such a clear lock on truth that it can foreclose reasoned counterargument.

Putting aside the controversy over substantive expert testimony *in court*, it is important to keep in mind that *outside the courtroom*, mental health professionals have long evaluated children for sexual abuse and will continue to do so. Whether or not judges allow professionals to provide substantive evidence in court, psychosocial assessment of sexual abuse serves vital clinical and child protection purposes.

Significance of Symptoms Observed in Sexually Abused Children. Before discussing the significance of symptoms observed in sexually abused children, allow me to stake out some territory. First, there is no single symptom or set of symptoms observed in all or even a majority of sexually abused children. Indeed, "Approximately one third of sexually abused children demonstrate no apparent symptomatology"

(Deblinger et al., 1996, p. 310). Thus, there is no symptom or symptom cluster that is pathognomonic of sexual abuse (Goodman, Emery, & Haugaard, 1998; Poole & Lindsay, 1998).

Second, there is no "sexually abused child syndrome" that detects or diagnoses child sexual abuse (Lamb, 1994). Kendall-Tackett et al. (1993) reviewed the literature on the impact of sexual abuse and concluded:

> The first and perhaps most important implication is the apparent lack of evidence for a conspicuous syndrome in children who have been sexually abused. The evidence against such a syndrome includes the variety of symptoms children manifest and the absence of one particular symptom in a large majority of children. (p. 173)

The third important point is that there is no psychological test that determines whether a child was sexually abused. Certain psychological instruments, particularly the Child Sexual Behavior Inventory (discussed later in this chapter), play a role in evaluating possible abuse, but there is no "sex abuse test."

Although there is no test or syndrome that detects sexual abuse, certain psychological symptoms can provide evidence of abuse, and professionals pay close attention to such symptoms. Many psychological symptoms are observed in sexually abused children. Symptoms of anxiety are particularly common, including fear, sleep disturbance and nightmares, flashbacks, startle reactions, hypervigilance, regression, phobic behavior, withdrawal from usual activities, nervousness, and clinginess (Berliner & Saunders, 1996; Browne & Finkelhor, 1986; Kendall-Tackett et al., 1993; Mannarino & Cohen, 1986). Some sexually abused children are depressed (Lanktree, Briere, & Zaidi, 1991; Lipovsky, Saunders, & Murphy, 1989; Wozencraft, Wagner, & Pellegrin, 1991).

However, the fact that a child has anxiety-related symptoms such as nightmares and regression says little about sexual abuse. Other circumstances cause such symptoms. In fact, if all you know about a child is that the child has nightmares and regression, you are probably looking at a nonabused child. To emphasize this important point, consider 4-year-old Sally, who, until a month ago, appeared to be a perfectly normal, happy-go-lucky little preschooler living with mom and dad. Sally's mother and father work full time, and Sally attends day care while her parents are at the office. A month ago, Sally began having terrifying nightmares in which she is chased by monsters. The nightmares happen three or four times a week and wake Sally and her parents in the middle of the night. Sally also started wetting her bed at night, something she had not done in years.

Has something happened to Sally? Are her nightmares and regression evidence that she was sexually abused, perhaps at day care? The literature tells us that sexual abuse causes nightmares and regression, including bed wetting, in some children. It is tempting to assume that Sally's nightmares and regression are evidence of sexual abuse. In fact, however, if all we know about Sally is that a month ago she starting having nightmares and wetting her bed, the probability is that Sally is not abused. This conclusion flows from the base rate at which nightmares and regression occur in the population of *non*abused children (Melton & Limber, 1989).

The base rate of a symptom is essentially the prevalence of the symptom: How often does it occur? To continue with Sally's nightmares and regression, assume for purposes of illustration that there are 30 million *non*abused children in the United States, and that 5% of these nonabused children experience serious nightmares and regression. At that rate, in the total population of nonabused children, 1.5 million have nightmares and regression. Figure 7.1 illustrates the number of nonabused children with nightmares and regression.

Now shift your attention away from nonabused children and concentrate on sexually abused children. Assume that there are 300,000 sexually abused children in the United States and that 25% of them have nightmares and regression. Why the higher percentage for sexually abused children? Because sexual abuse may cause nightmares and regression in quite a few children. Thus, among sexually abused children, 75,000 experience nightmares and regression. Figure 7.2 illustrates the number of sexually abused children with nightmares and regression.

When the abused and the nonabused children with nightmares and regression are combined, the total number of children with these symptoms is 1,575,000. Figure 7.3 illustrates the important point that in the *total* population of children with nightmares and regression, the great majority are nonabused.

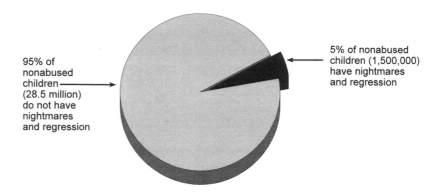

95% of
nonabused
children
(28.5 million)
do not have
nightmares
and regression

5% of nonabused
children (1,500,000)
have nightmares
and regression

Figure 7.1. 30 Million Nonabused Children, 5% of Whom Have Nightmares and Regression.
SOURCE: Created by Gail S. Goodman.

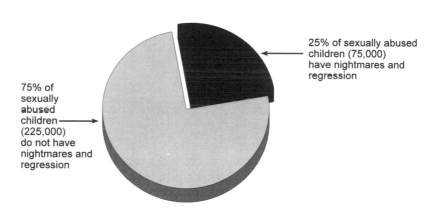

25% of sexually abused
children (75,000)
have nightmares and
regression

75% of
sexually
abused
children
(225,000)
do not have
nightmares and
regression

Figure 7.2. 300,000 Sexually Abused Children With Nightmares and Regression.
SOURCE: Created by Gail S. Goodman.

Figure 7.3, however, is a little misleading because the sexually abused children clearly stand out from the nonabused children. To bring home the base rate effect, we need one more figure, one in which we intermingle the 1.5 million nonabused children and the 75,000 abused children to form one large, undifferentiated gaggle (see Figure 7.4).

Now that we have created this huge mass of children with nightmares and bed wetting, we put them on buses and transport all 1,575,000 of them to your home town, where we turn them loose. With children swarming everywhere, your assignment is to open your door (carefully, of course), reach out, and—completely at random—grab the first kid who scampers by. Got one? Good. Now, did you pick an abused child or a nonabused child? It doesn't take a math whiz to realize that you probably picked a nonabused child. The nonabused children vastly outnumber the abused ones, so the odds are that you nabbed a nonabused child with nightmares and regression. If you happened to pick Sally, you can see why she is probably among the 1.5 million nonabused children.

To reiterate, if all you know about Sally is that she has nightmares and bed wetting (or any other anxiety-related symptom), Sally is probably not sexually abused. Why? Because of the base rate at which nightmares and bed wetting occur in nonabused children. The base rate phenomenon is complex (Melton & Limber, 1989). Indeed, the illustration with Sally's nightmares and bed wetting is an oversimplification. In some cases, nightmares provide stronger evidence of abuse. Suppose, for example, that in Sally's nightmares she is anally raped by her day care provider!

We cannot plumb the depths of base rates and mathematical probability in this short volume. Indeed, like some of you, I avoided math courses in college, and my eyes glaze over with too many numbers. Fortunately, you do not have to master Bayes' theorem or other esoteric mathematical formulas to appreciate the importance of base rates. Once you understand the essential effect of base rates, it is easy to understand why decisions about sexual abuse should not be predicated largely on symptoms that are seen routinely in nonabused as well as abused children. By the way, for those of you who actually like math, four articles provide excellent instruction on the

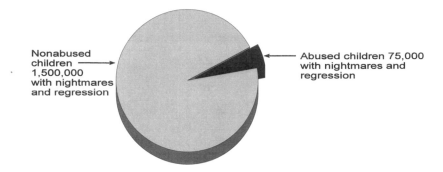

Figure 7.3. 1,575,000 Children—Abused and Nonabused—With Nightmares and Regression.
SOURCE: Created by Gail S. Goodman.

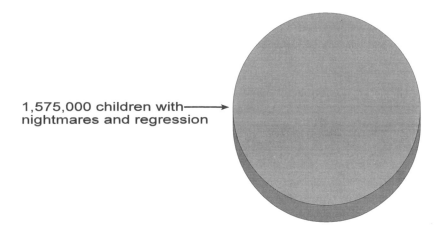

Figure 7.4. All the Children—Abused and Nonabused—With Nightmares and Regression, in One Large, Undifferentiated Group. The nonabused children vastly outnumber the abused children.
SOURCE: Created by Gail S. Goodman.

effect of base rates on decision making (Koehler, 1993; Ruscio, 1998; Wood, 1996; Wood & Wright, 1995).

Symptoms That Can Provide Relatively Strong Evidence of Sexual Abuse. Many symptoms observed in sexually abused children provide weak evidence of abuse (e.g., nightmares). Other symptoms, however, provide stronger evidence of personal or vicarious sexual experience, especially in young children. Symptoms that appear to have a closer connection to sexual abuse include developmentally unusual knowledge of sex and sexualized play in young children (Beitchman et al., 1991; Friedrich, 1993; Kolko & Moser, 1988; Mannarino & Cohen, 1986; Wells, McCann, Adams, Voris, & Dahl, 1997).

Of course, before one can say that a child's sexual knowledge or behavior is developmentally abnormal, one has to know what sexual knowledge and behavior is normal (see AACAP, 1997; Brilleslijper-kater & Baartman, in press; Gordon, Schroeder, & Abrams, 1990a, 1990b). Only when a child's sexual knowledge or behavior departs from the norm is there anything to worry about. Friedrich et al. (1991) studied normative sexual behavior and found "that 2- through 12-year-old children exhibit a wide variety of sexual behaviors at relatively high frequencies, e.g., self-stimulatory behavior and exhibitionism" (p. 462).

Although certain sexual behaviors are relatively common in non-abused children, other sexual behaviors are seldom observed in nonabused children. Friedrich et al. reported that nonabused children seldom demonstrate sexual behaviors that "are either more aggressive or more imitative of adult sexual behavior" (p. 462). In Friedrich et al.'s research, the sexual behaviors observed *least* often in nonabused children were

- Placing the child's mouth on a sex part
- Asking to engage in sex acts
- Masturbating with an object
- Inserting objects in the vagina or anus
- Imitating intercourse
- Making sexual sounds
- French kissing

- Undressing other people
- Asking to watch sexually explicit television
- Imitating sexual behavior with dolls

The fact that a child demonstrates one or more of these uncommon sexual behaviors is not conclusive evidence of sexual abuse, although "a child who is exhibiting several of the least frequent [behaviors] appears to be unusual" (Friedrich et al., 1991, p. 463). Friedrich et al. remind us that "sexual behavior in children is related to the child's family context, most specifically the sexual behavior in the family" (p. 462). Before one can conclude that developmentally unusual sexual behavior points to abuse, one has to rule out alternative explanations for the child's knowledge. For example, did the child view pornography? Did the child observe adults engaging in sexual activity? If nonabusive explanations are excluded, developmentally unusual sexual behavior in young children can be a good marker of sexual abuse (Friedrich, 1993).

Lindblad, Gustafsson, Larsson, and Lundin (1995) examined the frequency of sexual behaviors in 251 Swedish children attending preschool day care centers. In this study, 99.6% of the children were not observed trying to make an adult at day care touch the child's genitals; 91.2% of the children did not attempt to touch a female staff member's breasts; 99.6% of the children were not observed attempting to touch an adult's genitals; 91.6% of the children did not expose their genitals; 92.0% did not play sexually explorative games; and 96.8% did not initiate games simulating adult sexual activity. According to Lindblad et al., "The low frequency of the behaviors mentioned above corresponds with the results from the Friedrich study" (p. 575).

Phipps-Yonas, Yonas, Turner, and Kauper (1993) surveyed 564 licensed family day care providers in Minnesota regarding the providers' "observations of children's behavior and apparent sexual knowledge" (p. 2). Phipps-Yonas reports that

> we are all sexual creatures and sexual learning begins in early infancy. ... Among preschoolers there is often considerable freedom regarding their bodies as well as touching of themselves, their peers, and family members. Children at this stage engage in games such as playing

doctor or house which involve explorations through touch and sight of each other's so-called private parts. (p. 1)

When asked how children aged 1 to 3 and aged 4 to 6 behave, day care providers reported that

older children were . . . much more curious than the younger ones regarding the mechanics of sexual activities and reproduction. They were also much more likely to engage in exploratory "sexual" games such as "I'll show you mine, if you show me yours" or doctor or house. (p. 3)

In Phipps-Yonas et al.'s study, the following behaviors were observed very infrequently by day care providers:

- Efforts by a child to engage in pretend sexual intercourse
- French kissing
- Requests by a child to have someone suck, lick, or kiss the child's genitals
- Attempts by a child to insert objects into their own or someone else's anus or vagina

Conte, Sorenson, Fogarty, and Dalla Rosa (1991) surveyed 212 professionals who regularly evaluate children for sexual abuse. The professionals were asked to rank the importance of 41 indicators of sexual abuse. The following indicators were thought important by more than 90% of the evaluators:

- Medical evidence of abuse
- Age-inappropriate sexual knowledge
- Sexualized play during the interview
- Precocious or seductive behavior
- Excessive masturbation
- Child's description remains consistent over time
- Child's description reveals pressure or coercion

As Conte et al. summarized, "There are essentially many areas of agreement among the professionals in this sample" (p. 433). Like all good empiricists, however, Conte et al. acknowledged the weakness of their research. In particular, they cautioned against placing too much confidence in consensus among professionals. Although the experts may agree on what is important to evaluate sexual abuse, the experts may be wrong! Maybe the experts are looking north when they should be looking south. To put it in more sophisticated language, consensus "does not ensure that professional practice or professional beliefs are knowledge-based, and agreement among these respondents should not be assumed to validate various practices as reliable and effective" (Conte et al., 1991, p. 433). To place confidence in Conte et al.'s findings, one has to take a leap of faith. One has to be willing to assume that the experts probably get it right most of the time.

Hibbard and Hartman (1992) compared a broad range of symptoms observed in 81 children who were alleged to be sexually abused and 90 children who were not abused. The children ranged from 4 to 8 years of age. Consistent with other research, the children who were thought to be sexually abused were more symptomatic than non-abused children. Hibbard and Hartman reported a statistically significant difference between the two groups on sexual behavior problems, with 19% of the allegedly abused children demonstrating sexual behavior problems but only 1% of the nonabused children demonstrating such problems.

Wells, McCann, Adams, Voris, and Ensign (1995) studied symptoms in three groups of prepubescent girls: no abuse, confirmed abuse, and suspected but unconfirmed abuse. Children with confirmed or suspected sexual abuse were more likely than nonabused children to demonstrate sudden behavioral changes. The abused children were more frightened than nonabused children of being left alone with particular people. Children with confirmed or suspected abuse tended to "know more about sex and to be more interested and curious about sex matters or private parts" than nonabused children (p. 159). Wells et al. found no differences between the groups on bed-wetting, headaches, constipation, or vaginal bleeding.

> These symptoms do not appear to be necessarily reflective of abuse. In contrast, specific fears of a particular person, self-consciousness about her body and fearfulness of males appear to be questions that

discriminate amongst abused and nonabused samples. . . . Sudden changes in children's behaviors and particularly increased and specific fears and heightened interest and curiosity regarding sexual matters appears to happen relatively infrequently in the nonabused sample, but are present in 30 to 66% of children who are suspected victims of abuse. (pp. 159-161)

Before we leave the subject of developmentally unusual sexual knowledge, it is important to revisit base rates, discussed in conjunction with generic symptoms such as nightmares and regression. Base rate issues arise not only with generic symptoms, but also with developmentally unusual sexual knowledge. With respect to developmentally unusual sexual knowledge, Melton and his colleagues (1997) point out that "[b]ecause a large proportion of a small population still may be smaller than a small population and because sexualized behavior is exhibited by only a minority of the sexually abused population, the base-rate problem still applies" (p. 758, note 211). Thus, as pointed out earlier, the fact that a child demonstrates developmentally unusual sexual knowledge is not definitive evidence of sexual abuse. Nevertheless, giving base rates their full measure of respect, developmentally unusual sexual knowledge remains important because such knowledge is acquired through learning, and sexual abuse is a likely source of such learning.

Current research has limitations, and much remains to be learned. Nevertheless, I am struck by the overlapping findings of Hibbard and Hartman (1992), Wells et al. (1995), Conte et al. (1991), Phipps-Yonas et al. (1993), Lindblad et al. (1995), and Friedrich et al. (1991). The research described above lays an empirical foundation for the conclusion that sexual behaviors that are seldom observed in nonabused children provide evidence of sexual abuse.

The Child Sexual Behavior Inventory. Although there is no psychological test to detect child sexual abuse, the Child Sexual Behavior Inventory (CSBI), developed by Friedrich (1995), is a valid and reliable instrument that assists in the assessment of possible abuse in children aged 2 through 12 (Friedrich et al., 1992). According to Friedrich (1995),

The CSBI was developed to better assess sexual behavior in children. Empirical findings with sexually abused children indicate that sexual behavior is one of the more reliable and valid markers of sexual abuse. . . .

The child's primary female caretaker is asked to complete a 36-item measure that rates the numerical frequency of each behavior over the previous six-month period. The behaviors included in the [various versions of the CSBI] measure such aspects of sexual behavior as self-stimulation, sexually intrusive behavior with other children or adults, sexual interest, boundary permeability, and gender-based behaviors. . . .

The CSBI must be used with interviews and other forms of assessment in order to understand the child, particularly the sexually abused child. It must never be used by itself, and it should never be the sole basis for a determination of sexual abuse. There is no item, or combination of items, that without fail, are solely indicative of sexual abuse. (pp. 1, 17)

When Is Evidence of Sexual Abuse Strong or Weak? When is it reasonable to place confidence in evidence of sexual abuse? Confidence may be warranted when there is a coalescence of five types of data:

1. Developmentally unusual sexual behavior, knowledge, or symptoms providing relatively strong evidence of sexual experience (e.g., 4-year-old with detailed knowledge of fellatio, including ejaculation)
2. Nonsexual behavior or symptoms observed in sexually abused children (e.g., symptoms such as nightmares and regression)
3. Medical evidence of sexual abuse
4. Convincing disclosure by the child (see Chapter 4)
5. Evidence that corroborates the abuse (e.g., incriminating statements by the alleged perpetrator)

Confidence in the evidence of abuse often (although not invariably) grows as the amount and quality of evidence increases. For example, confidence may grow as the persuasiveness of developmentally unusual sexual behavior increases, as the persuasiveness of nonsexual symptoms increases, as the strength of medical evidence grows, as corroborating evidence becomes more convincing, and as confidence grows in the way professionals interviewed the child. A case with all this going for it is very strong.

Confidence in the evidence often (although not invariably) declines as the amount and quality of evidence decreases. Declining confidence is particularly precipitous when evidence providing relatively strong proof is lacking. Consider, for example, a case in which there is no medical evidence, no developmentally unusual sexual behavior, and no evidence to corroborate the child's story. In this scenario, the evidence consists entirely of *non*sexual symptoms and the child's disclosure. Although you may be convinced by the evidence— depending largely on the child's disclosure—it seems pretty clear that the case is weaker than the one in the preceding paragraph.

Now, take the process of eliminating evidence one step further. Imagine a case in which the only evidence of sexual abuse is nonsexual symptoms observed in sexually abused children (e.g., nightmares). No longer is there any medical evidence, developmentally unusual sexual behavior, corroboration, or convincing disclosure. In this state of affairs, can you place any confidence in the evidence? No. Why? Because of the base rate effect.

It would be a mistake to conclude that the *quantity* of evidence is a satisfactory basis for decision making. In one case, two or three items of evidence may provide convincing proof of abuse, whereas in another case, a plethora of evidence may fail to persuade. Decisions rest on careful assessment of the quantity, quality, and context of the evidence.

In the final analysis, there are no easy answers. Gathering and evaluating evidence of sexual abuse is a complex endeavor requiring thorough knowledge of the literature combined with long experience. There is no profit in shortcuts. Remember Mencken's (1949) insight: "There is always an easy solution to every human problem— Neat, plausible, and *wrong*" (p. 442).

What Do Courts Say About Expert Mental Health Testimony Offered as Substantive Evidence? Before discussing the response of courts to expert mental health testimony offered as substantive evidence of sexual abuse, it is important to note that a judge sitting in family or juvenile court might allow expert testimony that the same judge would not allow in a criminal case. Judges tend to be more restrictive of expert testimony in criminal cases, especially when there is a jury.

So if you testify as an expert, what you are allowed to say may depend on the type of case.

The response of criminal courts to expert mental health testimony offered as substantive evidence is complex and evolving. In this book, it would not be worth the pages it would take to unravel the complexity (see Myers, 1993, 1997a). It will suffice to say that courts generally take one of three positions on expert mental health testimony offered as substantive evidence: yes, no, or maybe.

Courts in the "yes" camp allow qualified mental health professional to provide some forms of substantive evidence in some cases.

Courts in the "no" camp reject some or all forms of substantive evidence from mental health professionals.

Now for the "maybe" camp. It is not that judges in the "maybe" camp cannot make up their minds. In fact, the "maybe" judges have given the issue a lot of thought. Basically, they reason as follows:

> Child sexual abuse is difficult to prove. If mental health professionals can provide reliable information about abuse, they should testify. But there's the rub! Is mental health testimony about sexual abuse *reliable*? Only if the answer is yes should mental health professionals offer substantive evidence.

The "maybe" judges are on to something. They must be reading the psychological literature. As you recall from our review of the literature, there is controversy over whether mental health professionals know enough about sexual abuse to make their testimony reliable. With this controversy in mind, "maybe" judges take the sensible position that before substantive mental health testimony is permitted, the attorney offering the testimony should convince the judge that the testimony is reliable. The best way to assess reliability is under the well-established rules governing novel scientific evidence, that is, *Frye* or *Daubert* (discussed earlier in this chapter). This makes sense. Judges in the "maybe" category do not want to close the door completely to mental health testimony as substantive evidence. Yet, they are worried about reliability. By subjecting mental health testimony to scrutiny under *Frye* or *Daubert*, "maybe" judges essentially say, "Mental health professionals will be allowed to offer substantive evidence of sexual abuse if, but only if, the evidence is reliable." Works for me.

Expert Testimony Identifying the Perpetrator. In several criminal cases, expert witnesses testified that a particular person abused a child. Nothing in the professional literature suggests that experts on child abuse possess knowledge that allows them to identify the perpetrator. Judges in criminal cases uniformly reject expert testimony indicating that a particular person abused a child.

Credibility Evidence

You will recall that earlier in this chapter we discussed the distinction between substantive evidence and credibility evidence. Mental health testimony offered as substantive evidence of sexual abuse is complicated, and judges and mental health professionals are divided on whether such testimony should be allowed. When attention turns from substantive evidence to credibility evidence, however, things get simpler, and judges generally allow credibility evidence.

Attacking a Child's Credibility Due to Delayed Reporting, Inconsistency, or Recantation. In many child sexual abuse cases, the child delayed reporting, was inconsistent, or recanted. (See Chapter 4, the section "Interviewing," subsection "The Interviewer's Dilemma," sub-subsection "The Disclosure Process in Child Sexual Abuse.") When the child testifies in court, the defense attorney may impeach the child's credibility by asking questions about delay, inconsistency, and recantation. Such impeachment is entirely legitimate, and defense attorneys act responsibly when they focus on such matters. When the defense attacks the child's credibility in this way, however, the question becomes: Should the prosecutor be allowed to rehabilitate the child's damaged credibility with expert testimony that helps the jury understand that delayed reporting, inconsistency, and recantation are relatively common in children who *have* been sexually abused? With the apparent exceptions of Pennsylvania, Kentucky, and Tennessee, judges allow expert testimony to explain why sexually abused children delay reporting, recant, and are inconsistent.

Expert testimony to rehabilitate a child's credibility is simple and straightforward. The expert does not offer substantive evidence. The expert does not express an opinion on whether abuse happened or whether the child has symptoms of abuse. Indeed, in most cases, the expert does not need to mention the child in this case at all! The expert can talk about sexually abused children *as a group*. The expert simply helps the jury understand that delay, inconsistency, and recantation are relatively common among abused children. The simple task of educating the jury should take no more than 5 to 10 minutes. It is then up to the jury to apply the information provided by the expert to the evidence in the case. Because expert testimony offered to rehabilitate credibility is so straightforward, it is not subject to the rule governing novel scientific evidence (*Frye* or *Daubert*).

As I said above, expert testimony on delay, inconsistency, and recantation should be simple. Unfortunately, sometimes it is not. Once in a while, an expert whose testimony is supposed to be limited to explaining delay, inconsistency, or recantation ends up giving a long-winded lecture on everything we have ever learned about sexual abuse, from dysfunctional families, to dynamics of abuse, to personality profiles, to nightmares, to who knows what else. Do you see what is wrong with this testimony? One obvious problem is that such testimony may confuse the jury. More important, however, the expert's far-flung lecture went far beyond what the expert was supposed to do. The expert was in court for the limited purpose of rehabilitating a child's credibility by explaining delay, inconsistency, and recantation. When the expert ventured beyond these matters, the expert left the domain of credibility evidence and entered the realm of *substantive evidence*, something the expert was not supposed to do. Crossing the boundary of permissible expert testimony leads to confusion and sometimes injustice.

The following guidelines help avoid the boundary confusion described above:

1. Before a prosecutor offers expert testimony to rehabilitate a child's impeached credibility, the prosecutor tells the judge and the defense attorney what the expert will say. For example, if a defense attorney attacks a child's credibility by focusing on delayed reporting, the prosecutor informs the judge and defense counsel that the expert's

testimony will be limited to explaining delay. The judge or the defense attorney can intervene if the expert gets off course.

2. In most cases of expert testimony to rehabilitate credibility, the expert does not need to refer to a specific child. The expert can describe the behavior of sexually abused children *as a group*.

3. If it is necessary to refer to the child in the present case, the expert should avoid using the word *victim*. Referring to the child as a "victim" sends a message to the jury that the expert believes the child was abused (i.e., substantive evidence). Remember, however, that when expert testimony is offered to rehabilitate credibility, the expert is *not* supposed to give substantive evidence.

4. Avoid reference to syndromes, including child sexual abuse accommodation syndrome. An expert does not need to use the loaded word *syndrome* to help the jury understand delay in reporting, recantation, or inconsistency. Indeed, in my experience, the mere mention of the word *syndrome* muddles clear thinking.

Nonabusive parents sometimes delay reporting the abuse of their children. In *People v. McAlpin* (1991), the defendant was charged with molesting his girlfriend's daughter. The mother did not break off the relationship the moment she learned of the molestation. Moreover, the mother had sexual intercourse with the defendant a week following the molestation of the child. At the defendant's trial, the defense counsel impeached the *mother's* "credibility by strongly implying that her behavior after the alleged incident was inconsistent with that of a mother who believed her daughter had been molested" (p. 570). The California Supreme Court approved expert "testimony that it is not unusual for a parent to refrain from reporting a known molestation of his or her child" (p. 569).

Expert Testimony That a Child Told the Truth About Abuse. Expert testimony about delayed reporting, inconsistency, and recantation has the indirect effect of rehabilitating a child's credibility. Equipped with this information, jurors can decide for themselves whether to believe the child. Should experts be allowed to venture beyond *indirect* bolstering of credibility to a *direct* opinion on truthfulness? Should experts be permitted to offer their *own* assessment of a child's credibility? The answer from the courts is a resounding *no*. Judges agree, especially in criminal cases, that experts should not comment directly on the credibility of individual children or on the credibility of sexually abused children as a group. The Oregon Supreme Court did not mince words when it said, "We have said before, and we will say it again, but this time with emphasis—we really mean it—*no psychotherapist may render an opinion on whether a witness is credible in any trial conducted in this state.* The assessment of credibility is for the trier of fact and not for psychotherapists" (*State v. Milbradt*, 1988, p. 624). Judges firmly believe that assessment of credibility is the *exclusive* province of the jury. As one court put it, "The jury is the lie detector in the courtroom" (*United States v. Barnard*, 1973, p. 912).

The Degree of Expertise Required to Testify Depends on Whether the Expert Offers Substantive Evidence or Credibility Evidence

Professionals with relatively little training and experience can provide expert testimony to rehabilitate a child's credibility. Credibility testimony is typically limited to explaining delayed reporting, inconsistency, and recantation. The expert does not venture an opinion that the child in the case at hand was abused. Credibility testimony is straightforward and simple. The only requirement for such testimony is knowledge of relevant literature.

Compare the relatively limited expertise needed to provide credibility testimony with the extraordinary expertise required for substantive evidence of sexual abuse. Only a fraction of professionals working with sexually abused children are qualified to provide substantive evidence.

EXPERT TESTIMONY REGARDING DEVELOPMENTAL DIFFERENCES BETWEEN CHILDREN AND ADULTS

Defense attorneys sometimes undermine children's credibility by arguing that developmental differences between adults and children render children *as a group* less credible than adults. The defense may assert that children are highly suggestible and have poor memory capacity (*Idaho v. Wright*, 1990; *State v. Michaels*, 1994). In some cases, the defense offers its own expert to discuss suggestibility or to challenge the way children were interviewed. In response to this strategy, the judge may allow the prosecutor to offer expert testimony to inform jurors that children have adequate memory capacity and are not invariably suggestible. In some cases, the prosecutor offers expert testimony about the complex task of interviewing young children (see Chapter 4).

EXPERT TESTIMONY REGARDING THE ALLEGED PERPETRATOR

In the effort to prove that a person sexually abused a child, may a prosecutor offer expert testimony that the accused fits the psychological profile of a sex offender or pedophile? For psychological as well as legal reasons, the answer should be no.

From the psychological perspective, the clinical and scientific literature indicates that people who sexually abuse children are a heterogeneous group with few shared characteristics apart from a predilection for deviant sexual behavior with children.

Several methods of psychological assessment are used to evaluate sex offenders. It is important to emphasize at the outset, however, that there is no psychological test or combination of tests that reliably determines whether a person has engaged or will engage in deviant sexual behavior. Hall and Crowther (1991) note that "there appears to be no psychological method of identifying sexual aggressors and predicting recurrence of sexually abusive behavior that has unequivocal empirical support" (p. 80). Nichols and Molinder (1984) state that "no test, no device, has the power to pick out a sexually deviant person from any other person in a crowd" (1984, p. 3). Finally, Salter (1995) observes that "research confirms the fact that many sex offenders have no pathology discernible by generic psychological tests or clinical interview" (p. 30).

Assessment techniques used with sex offenders include the clinical interview; personality tests such as the Minnesota Multiphasic Personality Inventory (MMPI); projective tests, including the Rorschach ink blot test; and penile plethysmography.

The clinical interview is a common method for evaluating sex offenders. Although the interview is useful for clinical purposes, the rampant denial and minimization among sex offenders render the interview an unreliable marker of offending (Nugent & Kroner, 1996). According to Becker and Quinsey (1993),

Interviews of the offender are similar to other clinical interviews except the validity of the information provided by the offender is more likely to be suspect. Frequently, alleged child molesters distort information, falsely deny that the alleged offense occurred, and report difficulty in recalling events surrounding the offense. (p. 170)

The MMPI is a well-accepted psychological test, but it does not determine whether a person sexually abused a child (Hall & Crowther, 1991; Levin & Stava, 1987). According to Becker and Quinsey (1993), the MMPI "has been used extensively in assessment of sexual offenders. While the MMPI can be useful in clinical assessment for the purposes for which it was designed, its discriminant validity in the assessment of child molesters is poor" (p. 172). Marshall and Hall (1995), in reviewing the literature on the MMPI, concluded that responses on the MMPI do not differentiate any type of sex offender from any other sex offender and that the MMPI should not be used as evidence of whether a person sexually abused a child. Murphy, Rau, and Worley (1994) add that

what the MMPI literature actually suggests is that individual offenders against children vary tremendously in their psychological functioning, as measured by the MMPI. No particular profile predicts a propensity for sexual offending. A significant proportion of offenders may exhibit no measurable psychopathology. (p. 4)

Penile plethysmography is not considered sufficiently reliable for forensic decision making (Simon & Schouten, 1993). A penile plethysmograph is a mechanical device that fits around the base of a man's flaccid penis. With the device in place, the man is presented deviant and nondeviant sexual stimuli, and his erectile response is measured. Although the plethysmograph is useful for purposes of treatment, experts on sex offenders warn against relying on the device in legal decision making (Abel & Blanchard, 1976). Penile response is subject to voluntary control—that is, faking (Hall & Crowther, 1991; Nugent & Kroner, 1996; Prentky et al., 1997). Lanyon, Dannenbaum, and Brown (1991) state that "in cases of child sexual abuse, the use of the penile plethysmograph is gaining favor. This procedure, however, is even more controversial [than the polygraph], and is not considered appropriate in adversarial situations" (p. 301). Becker and Quinsey (1993) add that phallometric assessment cannot "detect whether someone has committed a specific sexual offense" (p. 172).

Psychological tests are useful tools in the clinical assessment of individuals who acknowledge their behavior and seek treatment. In work with individuals who deny deviant behavior, however, all available psychological tests are subject to faking and concealment. There is no psychological litmus test to detect sexual deviancy. Nor can psychological tests determine whether an act occurred. Becker and Quinsey (1993) captured the thinking of many experts when they wrote that "there are no psychological tests or techniques that indicate whether someone has engaged in sexual behaviors with children; such questions are best left to detectives and the courts" (p. 169). Thus, under the current state of scientific knowledge, there is no profile of a "typical" child molester.

From the legal perspective, the inappropriateness of profile testimony derives from the rule that prosecutors generally are not allowed to establish guilt through evidence that a person has a particular character trait or propensity. Thus, evidence of a person's character is not admissible in court to prove that the person acted in conformity with character on a particular occasion. The rule against character evidence to convict is applicable in sexual abuse litigation. The prosecutor cannot establish guilt through expert testimony that the accused person has a character trait or propensity for sexual abuse. Expert testimony that the accused fits the profile of a "typical" sex offender is character evidence and inadmissible for that reason.

In 1994, Congress changed the rules in sex offense cases in federal court (Fed. R. Evid. 413-415). Under the new rules, a prosecutor in a sexual abuse case in federal court *is* allowed to prove that the defendant molested other children (Fed. R. Evid. 414). This evidence is admitted to convince the jury that because the defendant molested other children in the past, he probably molested the child in the case at hand. In 1997, California adopted a similar rule (Cal. Evid. Code § 1108).

The fact that a prosecutor in federal court or in a California state court is allowed to offer *lay* testimony describing an accused's earlier acts of abuse does not necessarily mean that prosecutors in these jurisdictions will be allowed to offer *expert* testimony about perpetrator profiles. If scientific and clinical knowledge is any guide, the answer should be no.

In states that continue to adhere to the rule that prosecutors may not offer evidence of an accused person's character to prove guilt— and this is likely to remain the majority view—a related question arises: May a prosecutor offer expert testimony that there is *no* profile of a "typical" child molester? The California Supreme Court addressed this issue a few years before the California Legislature changed the rule against character evidence in sex offense cases. In *People v. McAlpin* (1991), the California Supreme Court said that at least in some cases, a prosecutor may offer expert testimony that there is *no* profile of a typical child molester. Such testimony helps the jury understand that child molesters come from all walks of life and backgrounds.

Unlike a prosecutor, the defendant in a criminal case *is* allowed to offer evidence of good character to prove innocence (Fed. R. Evid. 404(a)(1)). With this rule in mind, should an accused person be allowed to offer expert testimony that the person does *not* fit the profile or share the character traits of child molesters? From the scientific perspective, the accused has the same problem encountered by the prosecutor. There is no profile of a typical pedophile or sex offender. Despite this fact, some mental health professionals are willing to testify that a profile exists. Most courts reject such testimony as scientifically unsound. On the other hand, a few courts allow experts to describe profiles or to testify that a person does not have characteristics seen in individuals who abuse children (*People v. Stoll*, 1989).

Once a defendant offers expert testimony that the defendant does not share the characteristics of child molesters, the prosecutor is allowed to fight fire with fire and offer expert testimony to contradict the defendant's expert witness.

EXPERT TESTIMONY ABOUT PSYCHOLOGICAL SYNDROMES

This section briefly discusses four psychological syndromes that play a role in child sexual abuse litigation. For detailed discussion of syndromes, see Myers (1997a).

Child Sexual Abuse Accommodation Syndrome

In 1983, Summit described child sexual abuse accommodation syndrome (CSAAS). Summit noted five characteristics in sexually abused children: (a) secrecy; (b) helplessness; (c) entrapment and accommodation; (d) delayed, conflicted, and unconvincing disclosure; and (e) retraction. Summit's purpose in describing the accommodation syndrome was to provide a "common language" for professionals working to protect sexually abused children. Summit did not intend the accommodation syndrome as a diagnostic device. The syndrome is not an illness or a diagnosis. Nor can it be used to tell whether a child has been sexually abused (Meinig, 1991). The accommodation syndrome does not detect sexual abuse. Rather, it assumes that abuse occurred and explains a child's reaction to it. Thus, the accommodation syndrome does not prove abuse and should not be offered as substantive evidence.

Although the accommodation syndrome should not be used as *substantive evidence*, the elements of the syndrome can be used as *credibility evidence* to rehabilitate a child's impeached credibility. Thus, the syndrome helps explain why some sexually abused children delay reporting and why some abused children recant. When the accommodation syndrome is confined to this rehabilitative purpose, it serves a useful forensic function.

Rape Trauma Syndrome

Rape trauma syndrome (RTS) was originally described by Burgess and Holmstrom (1974) as "the acute phase and long-term reorganization process that occurs as a result of forcible rape or attempted forcible rape. This syndrome of behavioral, somatic, and psychological reaction is an acute stress reaction to a life-threatening situation" (p. 982).

Although expert testimony on RTS is used most often in litigation involving adult victims, RTS is useful in child sexual abuse litigation involving children and adolescents. Expert testimony on RTS has been offered by prosecutors for two purposes: (a) as substantive evidence to prove lack of consent to sexual relations and (b) as credibility evidence to explain behavior such as delayed reporting of rape.

Courts are divided on admissibility of RTS to prove lack of consent. Several courts reject RTS to prove lack of consent (*Commonwealth v. Gallagher*, 1988; *People v. Bledsoe*, 1984; *People v. Taylor*, 1990; *State v. Black*, 1987). Other courts allow expert testimony describing RTS when the defendant asserts that the victim consented (*State v. Alberico*, 1993; *State v. Allewalt*, 1986; *State v. Brodniak*, 1986; *State v. Huey*, 1985; *State v. Marks*, 1982; *State v. McCoy*, 1988; *United States v. Carter*, 1988). Courts that allow RTS to prove lack of consent place limits on the evidence. Thus, courts do not permit experts to testify that the alleged victim was, in fact, raped.

Most courts allow expert testimony on RTS to rehabilitate a victim's credibility (*People v. Hampton*, 1987; *State v. Graham*, 1990). In *People v. Bledsoe* (1984), for example, the California Supreme Court wrote that "expert testimony on rape trauma syndrome may play a particularly useful role by disabusing the jury of some widely held misconceptions about rape and rape victims, so that it may evaluate the evidence free of the constraints of popular myths" (p. 457). In *People v. Taylor* (1990), the New York Court of Appeals approved expert testimony explaining why a rape victim might not appear upset following the assault.

Courts place limits on RTS offered to explain behaviors observed in rape victims. For example, several courts state that experts should describe behaviors observed in rape victims *as a group* and should not refer to the victim in the case at hand (*People v. Coleman*, 1989).

Post-Traumatic Stress Disorder

Evidence of PTSD is sometimes admissible as substantive evidence of abuse. In addition, evidence of PTSD is sometimes admissible to rehabilitate the victim's credibility. (For more on PTSD, see Chapter 1, the section "Sexual Abuse," subsection "Short-Term Effects of Child Sexual Abuse," sub-subsection "Post-Traumatic Stress Disorder.")

Parental Alienation Syndrome

Gardner (1987) describes what he called parental alienation syndrome, which he states occurs in child custody cases in family court:

One outgrowth of this warfare [over child custody] was the development in children of what I refer to as the parental alienation syndrome.
Typically, the child viciously vilifies one of the parents and idealizes
the other. This is not caused simply by parental brainwashing of the
child. Rather the children themselves contribute their own scenarios
in support of the favored parent. My experience has been that in about
80 to 90 percent of cases the mother is the favored parent and the father
the vilified one. (p. 2)

Parental alienation syndrome has not, to my knowledge, been
subjected to empirical study. Nor, to my knowledge, is the syndrome
published in the peer-reviewed literature. Rather, the syndrome represents Gardner's personal views. Of course, judges have known for
a long time that custody battles sometimes bring out the worst in
people. In some cases, one parent tries to turn the child against the
other parent. We really do not need a scientific-sounding label—
parental alienation syndrome—to help us understand what goes on
in family court. Parental alienation syndrome is cogently criticized
by Faller (1998), Ricketson (1991), Russ (1996), and Wood (1994). In
State ex rel. George B.W. v. Kaufman (1997), the West Virginia Supreme
Court noted that "the philosophies espoused by Dr. Gardner have
apparently been the subject of some debate" (p. 856).

Another innovation of Gardner's is the Sex Abuse Legitimacy
Scale. Of this scale, Berliner and Conte (1993) wrote:

A specific and disturbing example of using [behavioral] indicators as
determinative of true versus false cases is that of the Sexual Abuse
Legitimacy (SAL) Scale. This "scale" claims to be able to discriminate
between "bona fide" and "fabricated" cases by indicating the presence
or absence of a series of characteristics of cases. There are 26 criteria
dealing with the alleged victim, 11 dealing with the accuser (usually
the mother), and 13 dealing with the accused (usually the father).
Criteria are divided into those which are very valuable (worth 3 points
if present), moderately valuable (2 points), and low but potentially
valuable (1 point). Separate scores are generated for the child, the
accused, and the accuser. Scores in the range of 50% of the maximum
or more are highly suggestive of bona fide sexual abuse and those
quite low (below 10%) are fabricated. Sample criteria are: for the child,
very hesitant to divulge the abuse or if no quality of a litany; for the
accuser, appreciates importance of relationship between child and

father or initially denies abuse; for the accused, allegation not in the context of divorce or career choice involving children.

The SAL scale suffers many of the problems that all indicator approaches suffer and a number which are unique. It is based entirely on the author's personal observations of an unknown number of cases seen in a specialized forensic practice. Although reference is made to studies carried out "between 1982 and 1987" these are unpublished, not described, and are of unknown value. There are no studies which have determined if the scale can be coded reliably. Many of the criteria are poorly defined. There have been no scientific tests of the ability of the SAL scale to discriminate among cases. There is no evidence that the numerical scores have any real meaning. Indeed, to our knowledge, the entire scale and parental alienation syndrome upon which it is based have never been subjected to any kind of peer review or empirical test. In sum, there is no demonstrated ability of this scale to make valid predictions based on the identified criteria. (p. 114)

In 1988, Conte remarked that the Sex Abuse Legitimacy Scale is "probably the most unscientific piece of garbage I've seen in the field in all my time. To base social policy on something as flimsy as this is exceedingly dangerous" (quoted in Moss, 1988, p. 26).

❏ Conclusion

Expert testimony plays an important role in child abuse litigation. As long as experts realize the limits of their knowledge and keep their testimony within those limits, they will continue to help juries decide these difficult cases.

❏ Two Cases of Expert Testimony for Your Consideration

Now that we have examined the rules on expert testimony and the psychological literature on symptoms observed in sexually abused children, put yourself in the position of a judge and make rulings in two cases. In each case, decide whether you will allow the expert testimony that is offered by the prosecutor.

COMMONWEALTH V. SPRING

Charles Spring is charged in criminal court with sexually abusing his 7-year-old daughter, Sue. The defense is that the charged act of oral copulation did not occur. At trial, the prosecutor offers the testimony of Kathleen Turner, PhD, who is a professor of social work at State University and an expert on child sexual abuse. The prosecutor informs the judge that Dr. Turner will offer an opinion that Sue was sexually abused and that the child has PTSD. The defense attorney objects to any testimony from Dr. Turner, arguing that mental health professionals cannot reliably diagnose sexual abuse. The defense also argues that an opinion that a child was sexually abused is nothing more than a thinly veiled opinion that the child told the truth. In deciding whether to allow Dr. Turner to testify, the judge asks the prosecutor to describe the basis of Dr. Turner's opinion. The prosecutor summarizes the data on which the doctor's opinion rests: Sue's mother and father (defendant) are divorced. The mother has custody of Sue. Until the allegations of sexual abuse arose, the defendant exercised visitation twice a month, taking Sue to his home for the weekend. On her return from a weekend visit, Sue was unusually quiet. The mother asked, "Is everything okay?" Sue replied, "Yes." A week later, mother noticed Sue drawing in her room. The mother approached and quietly looked over Sue's shoulder. The mother was shocked by what she saw. Sue had drawn a picture of a man with an erect penis. The mother said, "What on earth are you drawing? Who taught you such things?" Sue cried and blurted out, "Daddy said not to tell." The mother said, "What has your father done?" Sue replied, "Oh, mommy, daddy plays nasties with me. He puts his pee-pee in my mouth. White stuff comes out that tastes yucky."

On the advice of the family pediatrician, the mother took Sue to Dr. Turner's clinic for evaluation. During the first session at the clinic, Dr. Turner said, "Sue, your mother brought you here because she is concerned about you. I'm concerned too. Can you tell me about what your dad did to you?" In response, Sue revealed more than she had disclosed to her mother. Sue said that on weekend visits, her father had been "touching" her for about 4 months. Touching had started with fondling of Sue's breasts and genitals. As the "touching" had progressed on succeeding weekends, the defendant had undressed Sue and himself and had fondled and digitally penetrated Sue's vagina. Oral copulation occurred two or three times.

Sue has symptoms of depression. In the months before disclosure, she had recurrent nightmares in which she was attacked by monsters. Sue was also fearful and withdrawn.

You are the judge. Will you allow Dr. Fuller's testimony? Do the facts in this case support the doctor's opinion that Sue was sexually abused and has PTSD? My own thoughts on *Commonwealth v. Spring* appear in the "Analysis of Problems" section at the end of this book (p. 335).

Now try your hand at a second case.

COMMONWEALTH V. MILTON

Commonwealth v. Milton is based on a hypothetical case created by Horner, Guyer, and Kalter (1993). Jim Milton is charged in criminal court with sexually abusing his 3-year-old daughter, Melissa. Milton pleaded not guilty, and the defense is that the charged act of genital fondling did not occur. At trial, the prosecutor offers the testimony of Roger Friedrich, MD, a child psychiatrist. The prosecutor informs the judge and the defense attorney that Dr. Friedrich will offer an opinion that Melissa has two diagnoses: child sexual abuse accommodation syndrome (CSAAS) and sexual abuse syndrome. Defense counsel agrees that Dr. Friedrich is an expert on sexual abuse, but the defense objects to the doctor's testimony, arguing that the doctor's opinion is not sufficiently reliable.

The prosecutor informs the judge that Dr. Friedrich will testify to a reasonable degree of medical certainty that because Melissa has CSAAS and sexual abuse syndrome, she was sexually abused. Dr. Friedrich's opinion is based on the following facts: The defendant and Melissa's mother never married. Melissa is their only child. Since Melissa's birth, the defendant and Melissa's mother spent substantial amounts of time together, although they maintained separate residences. Both parents work outside the home in stable employment. The mother originally suspected sexual abuse when Melissa was barely 3. According to the mother, Melissa began to exhibit behaviors that the mother learned might be associated with sexual abuse. The behaviors included Melissa's nightmares, her interest in sex (e.g., "Where's my dick?" "That's my tits"), her occasional resistance to having her diapers changed, her emergent negativism, and her protests against separation from her mother. On one occasion, when the mother was changing Melissa's diaper, the child said, "Daddy hurt 'gina." On another diapering occasion, the mother discovered a hair in the diaper. According to the mother, the hair was the color of the defendant's hair, and the mother believed it was a pubic hair. The mother did not save the hair. On discovering the hair, the mother took Melissa to her pediatrician. The doctor conducted a physical examination but discovered no physical evidence of sexual abuse. On the advice of the pediatrician, the mother took Melissa to Dr. Friedrich for evaluation. Dr. Friedrich spent three 1-hour sessions with Melissa. Although Melissa repeated on several occasions that "Daddy hurt 'gina," the child would say nothing else about the alleged abuse.

You are the judge. Will you allow Dr. Friedrich to testify? See the "Analysis of Problems" section at the end of this book for my thoughts (p. 336).

8

Cross-Examination and Impeachment: Special Accommodations When Children Testify

Two types of witnesses testify in court: lay witnesses and expert witnesses. A lay witness is an individual with personal knowledge of relevant facts. An expert witness is someone with special knowledge, experience, or education, who helps the jury understand technical, clinical, or scientific issues. In child abuse litigation, professionals provide both lay and expert testimony (see Chapter 7).

Testifying begins with direct examination. During direct examination, the witness answers questions from the attorney who asked to the witness to testify. The purpose of direct examination is to elicit information favorable to the party on whose behalf the witness testifies. Following direct examination, the opposing attorney has the right to cross-examine. Cross-examination is sometimes followed by redirect examination. Redirect examination affords the attorney who asked the witness to testify an opportunity to clarify issues that were discussed during cross-examination. Finally, in rare cases, redirect examination is followed by re-cross-examination.

Attorneys view cross-examination as essential to the search for truth. A leading legal commentator stated that "for two centuries, common law judges and lawyers have regarded the opportunity of cross-examination as an essential safeguard of the accuracy and completeness of testimony, and they have insisted that the opportunity is a right and not a mere privilege" (*McCormick on Evidence*, 1984, p. 47). Another leading authority asserted that cross-examination "is beyond any doubt the greatest legal engine ever invented for the discovery of truth" (Wigmore, 1904/1974, § 1367).

Cross-examination causes anxiety. It is disturbing because it is adversarial and a bit mysterious. Nonlawyers generally are not privy to the secrets of the cross-examiner's art. The following discussion is intended to demystify cross-examination by explaining the techniques and strategies of the cross-examiner. Understanding the art of cross-examination—going behind enemy lines, if you will—reduces anxiety and allows professionals to deal on more equal terms with the cross-examiner. See Appendix D for the ABCs of coping with cross-examination.

Basically, there are two types of cross-examination: positive and negative. The purpose of negative cross-examination is to attack the witness's credibility or impartiality and to undermine the witness's testimony. Negative cross-examination is risky for the cross-examining attorney. When a witness is attacked, the witness resists providing information favorable to the attacker. Furthermore, the witness tends to find opportunities to refute points that the cross-examiner is trying to make. Positive cross-examination avoids many of these risks. With positive cross-examination, the attorney avoids attacking the witness and uses a positive, matter-of-fact, even friendly approach in the hope of eliciting information favorable to the client. For example, the attorney might limit cross-examination to reiterating parts of the witness's direct testimony that could be viewed as favorable to the cross-examiner's client.

When an attorney uses negative cross-examination, the attorney hopes to impeach the witness's credibility. Impeachment is the primary goal of negative cross-examination. No two cross-examiners are alike, of course, and each attorney's style is influenced by the attorney's personality and experience. Nevertheless, attorneys usually select from a small arsenal of established impeachment techniques. The techniques described in the next section are used primarily with lay witnesses, although the techniques can be used with experts. Impeachment techniques reserved primarily for experts are discussed later in this chapter.

❑ Impeachment of Lay Witnesses

This section briefly describes six impeachment techniques available to the cross-examiner.

IMPEACHMENT WITH THE WITNESS'S PRIOR INCONSISTENT STATEMENTS

A witness's testimony may be impeached with evidence that, before testifying, the witness told a different story.

> The theory of attack by prior inconsistent statements is not based on the assumption that the present testimony is false and the former statement true but rather upon the notion that talking one way on the stand and another way previously is blowing hot and cold, and raises a doubt as to the truthfulness of both statements. (*McCormick on Evidence*, 1984, p. 74)

When the cross-examiner confronts a witness with a prior inconsistent statement, the witness is usually allowed to explain the inconsistency.

BIAS

Testimony from biased witnesses is subject to doubt, and the cross-examiner is allowed to ask questions designed to bring out bias or favoritism. *McCormick on Evidence* (1984) noted that the law recognizes the slanting effect upon human testimony of the emotions or feelings of the witness toward the parties or the self-interest of the witness in the outcome of the case. . . . Partiality, or any acts, relationships or motives reasonably likely to produce it, may be proved to impeach credibility. (p. 85)

EVIDENCE THAT THE WITNESS HAS A CHARACTER TRAIT FOR UNTRUTHFULNESS

A witness may be impeached with evidence that the witness is an untruthful person. The theory of such impeachment is that an untruthful person may be willing to lie under oath. The cross-examiner is allowed to confront the witness with specific instances of the witness's behavior that tend to prove untruthfulness.

CONVICTION OF CERTAIN CRIMES

It is human nature to question the testimony of people who have been convicted of serious crimes, particularly crimes involving deceit or fraud. Within limits that vary from state to state, the cross-examining attorney is permitted to impeach a witness by proving that the witness was convicted of a crime.

DEFECTS IN CAPACITY

A witness may be impeached with evidence that the witness's ability to perceive, remember, or communicate is impaired.

INADEQUATE OPPORTUNITY TO OBSERVE EVENTS

A common method of impeachment is to prove that the witness did not have a good opportunity to observe an event. For example, if a witness testifies that a car was weaving from side to side as it sped down the road, the cross-examiner may bring out the fact that it was dark at the time and that the witness had only a brief glimpse of the car.

❏ Impeachment of Expert Witnesses

When cross-examining experts, attorneys use the impeachment techniques described above. In addition, attorneys draw on the following principles:

- In most cases, avoid a frontal attack.
- In appropriate cases, conduct only positive cross-examination, and avoid, or at least postpone, negative cross-examination.
- Raise doubts about the expert's testimony that can be used during closing argument to the jury.
- Impeach the expert with a "learned treatise."
- Raise the possibility of bias.

These common cross-examination techniques are described below.

AVOID THE FRONTAL ATTACK

When people think of cross-examination, they think of Perry Mason or some other TV attorney ruthlessly boring in on a perspiring witness until the beleaguered fellow finally blurts out, "All right, you win, I did it." That may be the way it is on television, but such dramatic cross-examination is seldom seen in real courtrooms, especially with expert witnesses. The skilled cross-examiner seldom uses a sledgehammer, preferring instead more subtle techniques.

CONDUCT A POSITIVE CROSS-EXAMINATION

As discussed earlier, cross-examination can be positive or negative. In some cases, with some experts, the attorney avoids the risks of negative cross-examination and limits cross-examination to the positive approach. If the cross-examiner's questions are fair and accurate, the professional should agree with them. There is nothing wrong with agreeing with a cross-examiner. In fact, an expert who stubbornly refuses to give an inch in the face of reasonable questions undermines his or her credibility in the eyes of the jury.

When the cross-examiner intends to conduct a negative cross-examination, the attorney may begin with a positive approach, hoping to elicit favorable information before the witness is alerted—and alienated—by the onset of negative questions. Expert witnesses should remember that even though a cross-examiner uses a positive approach at the beginning, the negative segment of cross-examination may be just around the corner.

RAISE DOUBTS ABOUT THE EXPERT'S TESTIMONY, AND SAVE THOSE DOUBTS FOR CLOSING ARGUMENT TO THE JURY

At the end of the case, the attorneys present closing arguments. One goal of closing argument is to persuade the jury that certain witnesses should not be believed. With this goal in mind, a cross-examining attorney may try to raise questions and doubts about an expert's testimony. During the closing argument, the attorney reminds the jury of those questions and doubts.

Attorneys know that they are unlikely to hit the jackpot during cross-examination. An expert is not likely to do a complete about-face and change the opinion given during direct examination. Therefore, cross-examiners use indirect methods to undermine the testimony of experts. The cross-examiner abandons the idea of a direct hit and hopes instead to poke a few little holes in the expert's testimony, to raise a few questions. These questions are *deliberately left unanswered* until the cross-examiner's closing argument to the jury, when the expert is safely off the witness stand and unable to explain or clarify as the cross-examiner painstakingly reminds the jury of the little holes in the expert's testimony and then answers those unanswered questions. Needless to say, the cross-examiner's answers are quite different from those the expert would give. But the attorney, not the expert, has the last word with the jury.

How does a cross-examiner accomplish the goal of raising questions and doubts about an expert's testimony that can be used against the expert during the attorney's closing argument? The answer lies in the attorney's ability to control the witness during cross-examination. Witness control is accomplished three ways: (a) by asking leading questions, (b) by limiting the witness's opportunity to explain, and (c) by using a technique called "hiding the ball."

Leading Questions

The attorney conducting direct examination is not supposed to ask leading questions. By contrast, the cross-examiner is allowed to use leading questions, and some cross-examiners ask *only* leading questions. A leading question suggests the answer to the question. (See Chapter 4 for discussion of leading questions.) For example, suppose that a cross-examiner wants an expert witness to acknowledge that a child recanted. The cross-examiner controls the expert by using leading questions that require short, specific answers—answers that the attorney wants the jury to hear. The attorney might say, "It's true, isn't it, that Sally recanted her allegations?" Or, "The child recanted more than once, didn't she?" The questions permit only short, specific answers, preferably limited to yes or no.

> *The cross-examiner is allowed to use leading questions, and some cross-examiners ask only leading questions.*

The cross-examiner keeps the expert hemmed in with leading questions and seldom asks why or how something happened. How and why questions permit the witness to explain, and explanation is precisely what the cross-examiner does not want. Naturally, when a question calls for a simple yes or no, it is often necessary to expand on the answer. With Sally's recantation, for example, the jury should know that she recanted because her life was threatened. But the cross-examiner tries to limit the witness's ability to explain, and this is where the second aspect of witness control comes in.

Limiting the Witness's Ability to Explain

When the witness tries to explain, the attorney may interrupt and say, "Please just answer yes or no." If the witness persists, the attorney may ask the judge to admonish the witness to limit answers to the questions asked. Experts are understandably frustrated when the cross-examiner thwarts their efforts to clarify. An expert may wonder, "How can this process possibly lead to the truth? The cross-examiner's questions paint a completely one-sided picture, and the attorney refuses to let me give balanced and complete answers to the questions!" This frustration is understandable. Before giving up on the adversary system of justice, however, remember three things.

First, the cross-examiner has *one* overriding responsibility: to represent the cross-examiner's client zealously. The cross-examiner's job is to present the client's view of the facts, not to give the expert *another* opportunity to repeat unfavorable testimony. To represent the client's interests adequately, the cross-examiner must have fairly wide latitude to control the course of cross-examination and to control what the expert—who is an adverse witness—is permitted to say.

> *The cross-examiner's job is to present the client's view of the facts, not to give the expert another opportunity to repeat unfavorable testimony.*

Second, sometimes it is proper to say, "Counsel, it is not possible for me to answer with a simple yes or no. May I explain myself?" Chadwick (1990) advises, "When a question is posed in a strictly 'yes or no' fashion, but the correct answer is 'maybe,' the witness should find a way to express the true answer. A direct appeal to the judge may be helpful in some cases" (p. 967). Many judges permit witnesses to explain themselves during cross-examination if the jury needs more information to make sense of the witness's testimony.

When "Maybe" or "It depends" is the correct answer, the expert may say so. Interestingly, "Maybe" and "It depends" put the cross-examiner in a bind. The next words out of the cross-examiner's mouth should be "What do you mean, 'Maybe'?" or " 'Depends' on what?" Do you see the bind? The cross-examiner's follow-up question permits the expert to explain, and as soon as that happens, the cross-examiner loses control.

Third, remember that after cross-examination comes redirect examination, during which the attorney who asked the expert to testify is allowed to ask further questions. During redirect examination, the expert can clarify matters that were left unclear during cross-examination.

Hiding the Ball

The third witness control technique, "hiding the ball," is used when the cross-examiner wants the expert to concede a point that the expert will probably deny if the cross-examiner comes right out and asks. So the cross-examiner conceals the real purpose of cross-examination and hopes to lead the expert into a trap. By the time the expert figures out what the cross-examiner has in mind, it is too late, and the expert has to concede the cross-examiner's point.

How does a cross-examiner hide the ball? The attorney may ask a lengthy series of apparently innocuous questions that do not seem closely related to sensitive topics. The attorney hopes that the expert will not perceive the need to answer carefully. The cross-examiner uses leading questions so that the expert has to answer as the examiner desires. But because the questions seem harmless, the expert goes along. To keep the expert off balance, and to keep the ultimate objective hidden, the cross-examiner may bounce from topic to topic, always returning, however, to questions that lead to the ultimate objective. Gradually, through a series of carefully structured questions, the cross-examiner locks the expert into a predetermined position. Only then, when the expert is painted into a corner, does the cross-examiner raise the subject that the examiner had in mind all along.

With this subtle cat-and-mouse game in mind, it is easy to see why it is important for experts to keep their guard up. The skilled cross-examiner is like a good chess player, always thinking several moves ahead. This is not to say, however, that experts should try to out-lawyer the lawyer or guess where the lawyer is going with questions. Experts get in trouble when they stop concentrating on the questions and try to play the lawyer's game. The best course for the expert is to listen carefully to each question and answer accordingly. In nearly all cases, the expert sees what is developing and has little difficulty coping with the attorney's questions. Moreover, most lawyers are not very good at hiding the ball.

UNDERMINE THE EXPERT'S ASSUMPTIONS

One of the most effective cross-examination techniques is to commit the expert to the facts and assumptions that support the expert's testimony and then to dispute one or more of those facts or assumptions. Consider, for example, a case in which a physician testifies on direct examination that a child experienced vaginal penetration. The cross-examiner begins by committing the doctor to the facts and assumptions underlying the doctor's opinion. The attorney says, "So, doctor, your opinion is based exclusively on the history, the physical examination, and on what the child told you. Is that correct?" Then the attorney asks, "And there is nothing else you relied on to form your opinion. Is that correct?" The attorney commits the doctor to a specific set of facts and assumptions so that when the attorney disputes those facts and assumptions, the doctor's opinion cannot be justified on some other basis.

Once the cross-examiner pins down the basis of the doctor's opinion, the examiner attacks the opinion by disputing one or more of the facts or assumptions supporting it. The attorney might ask whether the doctor's opinion would change if certain facts were different. The attorney might press the doctor to acknowledge alternative explanations. The attorney might ask the doctor whether other experts might come to a different conclusion. Finally, the cross-examiner might confront the doctor with a hypothetical question that favors the examiner's client. According to Chadwick (1990), it is "common to encounter hypothetical questions based on hypotheses that are extremely unlikely, and the [expert] witness may need to point out the unlikelihood" (p. 967).

Rather than attacking the doctor's assumptions during cross-examination itself, the attorney may limit cross-examination to pinning the doctor down to a limited set of facts and assumptions and then, when the doctor has left the witness stand, offering other witnesses to dispute those facts and assumptions.

It is useful to think of expert testimony as a stool with three legs, like the old milking stool. The legs of the stool are the facts and assumptions supporting the expert's testimony. The cross-examiner tries to knock one of those legs away so that the testimony comes tumbling down. With this technique of cross-examination in mind, the importance of preparation is clear. The expert should possess a thorough knowledge of the facts of the case and should be confident of the inferences, assumptions, and conclusions that flow from those facts.

IMPEACH AN EXPERT WITH A "LEARNED TREATISE"

The judge may allow a cross-examining attorney to undermine an expert's credibility by confronting the expert with authoritative books or articles that contradict the expert's opinion. The rules on impeachment with "learned treatises" vary from state to state, and professionals should discuss the learned-treatise rule with the attorney who asks them to testify. The professional can prepare in advance for this type of impeachment by keeping up with the literature.

When an expert is questioned from a book or article, the expert has a right to read relevant passages to make sure that the attorney is not taking things out of context. See Appendix D.

RAISE THE POSSIBILITY OF BIAS

As explained earlier, testimony from biased witnesses is open to question, and the cross-examiner is permitted to inquire about bias. With an expert medical witness, for example, questioning might proceed as follows:

Attorney: You met with the district attorney prior to testifying today, didn't you, doctor?

Witness: Yes.

Attorney: And during that meeting you discussed the testimony you gave on direct examination today, didn't you?

Witness: Yes.

Attorney: Now, doctor, you work at Children's Hospital, don't you?

Witness: Yes.

Attorney: You work in the child abuse unit of the pediatrics department, don't you?

Witness: Yes.

Attorney: And you regularly perform evaluations at the request of the district attorney, don't you, doctor?

Witness: Yes, some of my work is for the district attorney's office.

Attorney: You often testify for the prosecution in child abuse cases, don't you, doctor?

Witness: Yes.
Attorney: Thank you, doctor. I have no further questions.

Notice that the cross-examiner did not ask the final question. The attorney did not say, "So, doctor, because of your close working relationship with the district attorney's office, you are biased in favor of the prosecution, aren't you?" The attorney knows the doctor will say no to such a question, so the attorney simply raises the possibility of bias and waits until closing argument to remind the jury of the doctor's relationship with the district attorney's office—"A relationship, ladies and gentlemen of the jury, that is just a bit too cozy."

In the foregoing cross-examination, the attorney intimated that the expert did something wrong by meeting with the prosecutor to discuss the expert's testimony. Quite the reverse is true. There is nothing improper in meeting with the attorney who asks a professional to testify, and there is nothing wrong with discussing what will be said in court.

In an effort to raise questions about an expert's objectivity, is the cross-examiner allowed to ask whether the *expert* was a victim of child abuse? It is not illogical to suggest that victimization clouds the objectivity of some individuals. Nevertheless, this question should almost never be permitted. Such cross-examination entails a massive invasion of the expert's privacy. The psychological literature does not support the conclusion that victimization leads to impaired objectivity. Permitting such cross-examination would discourage professionals from providing expert testimony. Finally, the nexus—if there is one—between victimization and bias is simply too tenuous to merit such a significant intrusion into private matters (Myers, 1997a).

SUMMARY

Cross-examination is usually not pleasant, but in our system of justice, it is vitally important. Thus, although cross-examination is not easy, it is necessary. Armed with greater understanding of the techniques and goals of cross-examination, professionals become less anxious and more effective witnesses.

❏ Limits on Cross-Examination

The right to cross-examine is important, but it is not unlimited. Judges have authority to control cross-examination. For example, the judge may prohibit questions that are unduly embarrassing. In the context of child abuse, the nature of the litigation often makes embarrassing questions necessary. Nevertheless, the judge may instruct an attorney to refrain from questions that are designed merely to harass or annoy.

❏ Reviewing Client Records in Preparation for Testifying

When a professional prepares to testify, it is often necessary to review a client's file. Reviewing files in preparation for testimony raises confidentiality issues that are discussed in Chapter 6.

❏ Special Accommodations for Children Who Testify

Ask a young child to define *court*, and the child is likely to say, "It's a place to play basketball" (Saywitz, 1989). Many children are confused about the goings-on in court and about the people who work there (Saywitz, Jaenicke, & Camparo, 1990). One bewildered 5-year-old remarked as he was ushered into court that "he thought he was in a police station and that the robed judge was a karate expert" (*State v. Phelps*, 1985, p. 453). Fortunately, steps are being taken to make testifying less frightening and confusing for children (Myers, 1996, 1997a). For example, judges generally permit young witnesses to have a supportive adult nearby while the child testifies. Judges and

attorneys are increasingly sensitive to the developmental and linguistic differences between adults and children and to the need to
provide special accommodations for children.

For many children, the most traumatic aspect of testifying is facing
the adult accused of abusing them (Flin, Bull, Boon, & Knox, 1993;
Goodman et al., 1992; Murray, 1995; Myers, 1997a; Whitcomb,
De Vos, et al., 1994). Some children simply cannot do it. Others are
able to sit in the witness chair but have difficulty talking. For a few
children, the best way to elicit their testimony is to allow them to
testify away from the defendant. For example, most states have laws
that allow selected children to testify from a separate room. The
child's voice and image appear on a television monitor in the courtroom. In criminal cases, however, witnesses generally must testify in
the physical presence of the defendant. The Sixth Amendment of the
U.S. Constitution guarantees defendants in criminal cases the right
to face-to-face confrontation with witnesses against them. The Constitution does not require that witnesses actually look at the defendant, but the opportunity for face-to-face confrontation is an important constitutional right (*Coy v. Iowa*, 1988).

In 1990, the U.S. Supreme Court ruled that the Sixth Amendment
right to confront accusatory witnesses in criminal cases is not absolute (*Maryland v. Craig*, 1990). At times, children may be spared the
trauma of face-to-face confrontation with the defendant. The Supreme Court made clear, however, that there can be no across-the-
board presumption that all, most, or even very many children can be
spared face-to-face confrontation. For example, there can be no presumption that children below a specified age should be protected in
this way. Face-to-face confrontation in criminal cases remains the
norm, and exceptions must be rare and must be made on a case-by-
case basis. Fortunately, research and experience indicate that with
preparation and emotional support, most children are able to testify
in court in the traditional manner, and that such testimony does not
cause lasting psychological harm (Myers et al., 1996).

When a prosecutor asks a judge to allow a child to testify away
from the defendant, the prosecutor must convince the judge that
dispensing with face-to-face confrontation is needed to protect the
child from serious emotional stress. The distress experienced by the

child must be more than the nervousness and reluctance exhibited by most witnesses. Face-to-face confrontation with the defendant must pose a risk of serious psychological harm. Furthermore, the judge must find that the source of the harm is the defendant, not the courtroom.

In some cases, professionals familiar with a child provide expert testimony on whether the child will be harmed by face-to-face confrontation. For example, the child's therapist may have useful information for the judge. In a few cases, however, a therapist's testimony appears to reflect more about the therapist's *own* anxiety about testifying than it does about the child. Indeed, in a few cases, a therapist's testimony seems to rest on the unspoken assumption that face-to-face confrontation is *always* seriously harmful for children. Yet, this kind of assumption is exactly what the U.S. Supreme Court said violates the constitutional rights of defendants.

As an example of the kind of vague expert testimony that is not very helpful, consider the following testimony from a child's therapist: "I believe that it would be very difficult for the child to sit in the same room with the defendant and discuss the abuse. The child would probably stop talking and would withdraw and curl up." This testimony is too conclusory. The expert's opinion may help a little, but the judge needs more than conclusions. What the judge needs are specific facts that support the conclusion that testifying will be harmful.

The most useful testimony about the difficulty of face-to-face confrontation provides specific information that the judge can use to reach a conclusion about the effect of face-to-face confrontation on a specific child. The following types of information may help:

1. *Predicting future behavior from past behavior.* One way to predict how a child will react to face-to-face confrontation is to find out whether the child has faced the defendant in other settings. If so, and if the child fared poorly, the professional has concrete data on which to base an opinion about the likelihood of trauma. For example, if a child was abused by a stranger, the child may have gone to the police station to pick the defendant out of a lineup. Did the child freeze at the sight of the defendant? Did the child show signs of serious emotional distress? In an intrafamilial abuse case, the professional can find out whether the child visited with the alleged perpetrator, and, if so, how the visits went. If the child testified in the defendant's presence at a preliminary

hearing or some other proceeding, the professional can find out how the child reacted to face-to-face confrontation.

2. *Child's reaction when the subject of testifying comes up at home or in therapy.* If the subject of testifying comes up in therapy, at home, or in other settings, how does the child react? In one case, every time testifying was mentioned, the child cried.

3. *Signs of psychological distress as the date for testifying approaches.* Some children regress and experience other symptoms of psychological distress as the day for testifying approaches. Parents observe the child's worsening condition and can provide this information to the judge. In some cases, the best evidence of the need to dispense with face-to-face confrontation is a combination of expert testimony from a child's therapist and lay testimony from the child's parents.

4. *The child's mental health status.* If a child has serious mental health problems that could be exacerbated by face-to-face confrontation, the professional can inform the judge.

5. *Sources and severity of the child's fear of the defendant.* A professional can describe the impact of any threats against the child. A professional can help the judge understand that because of the child's immaturity, threats that an adult would not take seriously may paralyze a child. For example, suppose the defendant threatened a child that if she said anything, a terrible monster would slither out of her closet at night and devour her and her parents. An adult would dismiss such a threat, but to a young child this threat may be frighteningly real. The professional can help the judge put threats in developmental perspective.

6. *Impact of face-to-face confrontation on the child's ability to communicate effectively.* If a professional has concrete evidence that face-to-face confrontation would impair a child's ability to communicate fully and accurately, the judge should be informed.

7. *Lack of any psychological test to determine trauma.* Professionals can help the judge understand that there is no psychological test that predicts whether face-to-face confrontation will harm a child.

Liability of Professionals

Liability is an increasing concern for professionals working with abused and neglected children and with adult survivors of childhood abuse. Twenty years ago, lawsuits against mental health, medical, and social work professionals in this field were uncommon. Today, however, the threat of litigation is all too real. Recent years have witnessed a steady rise in lawsuits and ethics complaints against professionals (Peterson, 1996). This chapter analyzes the underpinnings of liability, outlines the three settings for legal action against professionals, discusses malpractice and negligence, and discusses liability based on principles of constitutional law.

Liability arises from several sources. For organizational reasons, some liability issues are discussed in this chapter, whereas other issues are addressed in other chapters. The following "road map" will help locate discussion of specific sources of potential liability:

- Negligence—Chapter 9
- Malpractice—Chapter 9

- Constitutional rights—Chapter 9
- Reporting laws—Chapter 3
- Dangerous clients—Chapter 6
- Confidentiality—Chapter 6
- Informed consent—Chapter 6
- Repressed-memory litigation—Chapters 4 and 9

❏ Settings for Legal Action Against Professionals

Legal action against professionals working with abused and neglected children and adult survivors occurs in three settings: (a) civil actions, (b) administrative law proceedings, and (c) criminal prosecutions.

CIVIL ACTIONS AGAINST PROFESSIONALS

A civil action is a lawsuit brought by one person or organization against another. Among the many types of civil actions, three are particularly relevant here: (a) negligence/malpractice lawsuits seeking monetary compensation for harm allegedly caused by a professional, (b) civil rights actions under federal and state laws, and (c) lawsuits seeking injunctions.

Lawsuits Seeking Money Damages

Civil actions against professionals may assert negligence or malpractice. In the typical negligence/malpractice action, the plaintiff seeks monetary compensation (called *damages*) from a professional or the professional's employer. Civil damages actions are brought against professionals in private practice and in government service.

Most civil actions seeking damages are dismissed or settled without a trial. If there is a trial, a jury or judge decides whether the professional was negligent or committed malpractice and, if so, how much money is needed to compensate the plaintiff.

Civil Rights Actions

In the field of child abuse and neglect, parents sometimes sue professionals, claiming interference with constitutionally protected rights. Parents usually sue under a federal law known as Section 1983, discussed in the section "Constitutional Rights" later in this chapter. Generally, civil rights cases are brought against professionals employed by the government, including child protective services and the police.

Lawsuits Seeking Injunctive Relief

An injunction is a court order requiring a person or organization to stop some activity. There are two types of injunctions: (a) a temporary injunction, often called a *temporary restraining order* (TRO for short), and (b) a permanent injunction. A TRO is issued for a short duration, typically 10 to 15 days. A permanent or long-term injunction may last months or years.

In the field of child protection, parents occasionally seek an injunction against CPS to stop what the parents claim is illegal conduct by social workers.

ADMINISTRATIVE LAW PROCEEDINGS

Administrative law is a complex branch of civil (i.e., noncriminal) law. "Administrative law is the law concerning the powers and procedures of administrative agencies" (Davis, 1972, p. 2). Administrative law affects two critical aspects of child abuse and neglect: (a) licensure of day care, foster care, and other institutional child care and (b) licensure of professionals.

Principles of administrative law govern the granting, suspension, and revocation of licenses to foster parents, day care facilities, and other providers of child care. When abuse or neglect occurs in a licensed home or facility, government attorneys invoke the machinery of administrative law to suspend or revoke the license.

Licensed professionals must abide by the requirements of licensure. A professional who engages in serious misconduct or who is unable, due to illness or incapacity, to practice competently may be subjected to administrative law proceedings to limit, suspend, or revoke the professional's license. Such proceedings are commenced by government attorneys.

CRIMINAL PROSECUTION

In rare cases, professionals commit acts that violate criminal law. For example, child abuse reporting statutes generally provide that it is a crime to fail to report suspected abuse. In *State v. Hurd* (1986), a school administrator was convicted of willfully failing to report suspected child abuse.[1]

❑ Malpractice and Negligence

This section discusses malpractice and negligence. The fountainhead of malpractice and negligence is breach of professional responsibility.

BREACH OF PROFESSIONAL RESPONSIBILITY

Playwright George Bernard Shaw (1906) wrote in *The Doctor's Dilemma* (Act 1) that "all professions are conspiracies against the laity." Be that as it may, even Shaw would have to agree that professionals play an important role in society. But what exactly is a "professional"? In the broadest sense of the word, everyone is a professional something or other: Thus, "He's a professional plumber," "She's a professional athlete," and even "He's a professional thief." When it comes to malpractice and related liability, however, *professional* has a narrower, more technical meaning. In the liability arena, a "professional" typically is a person "engaged in one of the learned professions" (*Random House Unabridged Dictionary*, 1993, p. 1544). What, then, is a "learned profession"? Historically, the learned professions were theology, medicine, and law. Today, the list includes psychology, social work, and similar callings.

Practitioners of the learned professions share the characteristic of "special, usually advanced, education and skill" (*Black's Law Diction-*

ary, 1979, p. 1089). A by-product of this specialized knowledge and skill is enormous *responsibility* for the well-being of others. Indeed, responsibility for others is a hallmark of the helping professions. But responsibility has two aspects. On the one hand, assuming responsibility for others—particularly victims of maltreatment—is a source of unparalleled personal and professional fulfillment. At the same time, however, the very responsibility that is so rewarding is the source of professional liability. *It is the violation of professional responsibility that creates liability.*

NEGLIGENCE

Before discussing malpractice, which applies only to individuals in the learned professions, it is important to describe negligence, which applies to everyone, professional and nonprofessional alike. Everyone has a legal duty to exercise reasonable care to avoid foreseeable harm to others. Thus, if you fail to exercise reasonable care and if, as a result, someone is hurt, the injured person can sue you for *negligence*. Consider a common example: Drivers have a legal duty to exercise reasonable care in the operation of motor vehicles. Suppose you drive your car at such an excessive speed that you fail to negotiate a curve, cross the center line, and collide with Ruth. Ruth is injured. You were negligent. You failed to conform your conduct to the standard of reasonable care required of drivers. In legal parlance, you breached your duty to exercise reasonable care under the circumstances. Your breach of duty constitutes negligence, rendering you financially liable for Ruth's injuries.

Negligence Is Part of the Law of Torts

Negligence is part of the law of torts. A tort is a civil (as opposed to criminal) wrong for which the law provides a remedy. As explained by Keeton (1984), the law of torts covers a wide range of subjects:

> Included under the head of torts are miscellaneous civil wrongs, ranging from simple, direct interferences with the person, such as assault, battery and false imprisonment, or with property, as in the

case of trespass or conversion, up through various forms of negligence, to disturbances of intangible interests, such as those in good reputation, or commercial or social advantage. (p. 3)

Lawsuits against professionals often are based on the tort of negligence. Indeed, most forms of malpractice fall under the heading of negligence.

The Three Requirements of Negligence

Negligence has three requirements, and a person claiming negligence must prove all three to hold the alleged wrongdoer (called the *defendant* or *tortfeasor*) accountable. The elements of negligence are: (a) duty, (b) breach of duty, and (c) causation.

Duty. In negligence law, a duty is "an obligation, to which the law will give recognition and effect, to conform to a particular standard of conduct toward another" (Keeton, 1984, p. 356). People do not owe a duty of care to the entire world. A duty of care exists only between certain persons in certain circumstances. Suppose, for example, that A was careless and injured B. It does not automatically follow that A is liable to B. In law, A is liable to B *only* if A had a legal duty to act carefully toward B. If A had no duty of care toward B, then B cannot sue A, no matter how careless A's behavior.

In most cases, the existence of a legal duty is obvious. Thus, automobile drivers owe a duty of care to other drivers and pedestrians. A surgeon owes a duty of care to the patient under the knife. A psychotherapist owes a duty of care to the client, and if the psychotherapist breaches that duty, the client can sue for negligence.

In some situations, the existence of a duty of care is disputed. For example, does a psychotherapist owe a duty of care to *nonclients*? (Slovenko, 1996). This question is being litigated in lawsuits brought by nonclient family members of adult survivors of child sexual abuse (see this chapter's section "Nonclient Lawsuits Against Mental Health Professionals"). In a recurring scenario, an adult enters psychotherapy for treatment of anxiety, depression, or other problems. During therapy, the client recovers memories of child sexual abuse by a family member, often the father. The client then confronts the father, who denies the allegation and sues the therapist for "manufacturing false memories." In such lawsuits, a critical first question is whether the psychotherapist owed a duty of care to the nonclient father. If the answer is no, then the father's lawsuit dies without reaching the issue of the therapist's alleged negligence. If, however, the therapist owed a duty of care to the nonclient father, then the father's lawsuit proceeds. This is not to say that the father will win his suit. The point is that if the therapist owed a duty of care to the father, then the father will be allowed to press the lawsuit in the hope of proving that the therapist breached the duty of care owed to him.

When the existence of a duty of care is disputed, or when a novel kind of lawsuit is filed, raising new duty questions, the judge in charge of the case decides whether a duty of care should be imposed on the person being sued. Judges "will find a duty where, in general, reasonable persons would recognize it and agree that it exists" (Keeton, 1984, p. 359). In *Vu v. Singer Co.* (1981), a federal court described the factors that judges consider in determining whether to extend a duty of care to new situations:

> The court must balance the following factors when determining the existence of duty in each particular case: (1) foreseeability of harm to plaintiff; (2) degree of certainty that plaintiff suffered injury; (3) closeness of connection between defendant's conduct and injury suffered; (4) moral blame attached to defendant's conduct; (5) policy of preventing future harm; (6) extent of burden to defendant and the consequences to the community of imposing a duty to exercise care with resulting liability for breach; and (7) availability, cost, and prevalence of insurance for the risk involved. (p. 29)

How might a judge apply these factors in a case involving a psychotherapist? Consider the case described above, in which the nonclient father sued the psychotherapist for allegedly "manufacturing false memories" of child sexual abuse in the adult client. The father's attorney argues that the therapist owed a duty of care not only to the client but also to the nonclient father. The therapist's attorney, by contrast, argues that the only duty of care was the duty owed to the client.

The judge decides whether a duty of care was owed to the nonclient father. In deciding this issue, one factor that looms large in the judge's analysis is the likelihood that subjecting psychotherapists to lawsuits by nonclients will drive therapists away from providing therapy to adult survivors of child sexual abuse (Appelbaum & Zoltek-Jick, 1996). If imposing a duty of care in favor of nonclients could have this undesirable consequence, the decision-making scale tips away from imposing a duty.

The judge also considers whether harm to the father was foreseeable to someone in the therapist's position. For example, would a reasonable therapist realize that an adult survivor might confront a suspected perpetrator and that such a confrontation could cause psychological pain and humiliation to the suspect?

The judge evaluates whether the therapist's action and advice caused harm to the father. For example, did the therapist encourage the client to confront the father or file a lawsuit against him? (See *Montoya v. Bebensee*, 1988.)

The judge considers the social utility of the therapist's behavior. Of course, there is high social utility to providing psychotherapy for adult survivors (Bowman & Mertz, 1996).

As far as preventing future harm is concerned, the judge considers at least two kinds of harm. First, the judge considers the harm that befalls people who are wrongly accused of sexual abuse. Second, as mentioned earlier, the judge considers the harm to victims and to society if therapists shy away from treating adult survivors because of fear that they—the therapists—will be sued by angry nonclients.

What will the judge decide? Reasonable minds can differ on this issue. Moreover, the facts of individual cases push judges in different directions. If the judge finds that a duty of care exists toward the nonclient father, the next question is: Did the therapist breach the duty of care owed the father?

Breach of Duty. The second requirement for negligence is breach of duty. The question is whether the person with the duty of care failed to conform to the required standard of conduct.

Causation. In legal texts on negligence, the subject of causation fills many pages with arcane discussion of "cause in fact," "proximate cause," "foreseeable intervening causes," "superseding intervening causes," and further legal exotica. For our purposes, it will suffice to say that the law requires a reasonably close causal connection between act and injury.

Nonclient Lawsuits Against Mental Health Professionals: Where Are the Courts Headed?

Before we analyze the "reasonable person" standard in negligence cases, we digress briefly to discuss an increasing concern among mental health professionals who treat victims of sexual abuse: lawsuits by nonclients. Beginning in the 1990s, a small number of lawsuits were filed by nonclients against professionals who treated adult survivors or children (Bowman & Mertz, 1996). The courts are still sorting through this litigation. In 1997, the Connecticut Supreme Court ruled in *Zamstein v. Marvasti* that a psychiatrist owed no duty to the nonclient father of two children. The psychiatrist was hired by the children's mother to evaluate the children regarding possible sexual abuse by the father. Thus, the psychiatrist's clients were the children. The father sued the psychiatrist, claiming that mental health professionals who evaluate children for sexual abuse owe a duty of care to the individual suspected of abuse. The Connecticut Supreme Court rejected the father's claim, writing:

> We conclude that imposing upon mental health professionals, who have been engaged to evaluate whether there has been sexual abuse, a duty of care running to the benefit of the alleged sexual abuser would be contrary to the public policy of this state. . . .
> We conclude that imposing a duty on mental health professionals pursuant to the [father's] theory of liability in the present case would carry with it the impermissible risk of discouraging such professionals in the future from performing sexual abuse evaluations of children altogether, out of a fear of liability to the very persons whose conduct they may implicate. Such a result would necessarily run contrary to the state's policy of encouraging the reporting and investigation of suspected child abuse. . . . In addition, imposing such a duty creates too high a risk that, in close cases, mental health professionals would conclude that no sexual abuse had occurred because they feared potential liability to the suspected abusers, rather than because of their professional judgment that, in all likelihood, no abuse had occurred.

Because "rules of law have an impact on the manner in which society conducts its affairs," we conclude that the sounder judicial ruling is to hold that no such duty exists. (pp. 786-787)

The Texas Supreme Court reached a similar "no duty" conclusion in *Bird v. W.C.W.* (1994). An occasional court, however, reaches the opposite conclusion and imposes a duty (see *Althaus v. Cohen*, 1998; Appelbaum & Zoltek-Jick, 1996; *Montoya v. Bebensee*, 1988).

Knapp and VandeCreek (1996) provide useful guidance to professionals treating adults who recover memories of child sexual abuse. Much of Knapp and VandeCreek's discussion is pertinent for professionals who treat children. They state that

> psychologists can reduce their legal risk to acceptable levels by maintaining appropriate therapeutic boundaries, diagnosing patients carefully, using sound clinical techniques that are based on scientific knowledge, obtaining informed consent for experimental procedures, and showing concern for the patients' future relationships with their families. (p. 452)

Knapp and VandeCreek (1996) caution psychotherapists about "aligning too closely with the patients. Psychotherapists who become strong advocates for the rights of victims risk losing their objectivity and critical judgment" (p. 455). The authors pay particular attention to intervention methods used by some psychotherapists, citing "questionable techniques used to retrieve lost memories" such as "age regression, body memory interpretation, suggestive questioning, guided visualization, sexualized dream interpretation, high-pressure survivor groups, aggressive sodium amytal interviews, and misleading bibliotherapy" (p. 456). Knapp and VandeCreek note that

> many experienced clinicians believe that it is therapeutically indicated, under certain circumstances, to seek to retrieve (or "de-repress") memories of abuse through hypnotherapy or sodium amytal interviews. According to Gold, Hughs, and Hohnecker (1994); Terr (1994); and Herman (1992), these techniques may be justified when hidden trauma is strongly suspected on the basis of objective criteria and the patient's suffering is severe. We would add that they are justified only when more prosaic techniques of memory recovery (e.g., talking) have

failed and the patient has been informed of the limitations of these techniques and the potential for creating false memories.

To minimize the possibility that therapist bias could influence the content of the memory, contextual cues should be kept as neutral as possible. Psychologists should record in detail the patient's statements about possible past abuse ahead of time and should video- or audio-tape the sessions to protect against possible allegations that they, the psychologists, implanted false memories. (p. 456)

Hypnosis has important legal implications (Myers, 1997a). In some states, individuals who have been hypnotized are not allowed to testify about events remembered during hypnosis. "Many courts have held or recognized that testimony concerning matters consciously recalled for the first time through pretrial hypnosis is inadmissible" (Fleming, 1990, p. 934). A professional whose client may someday serve as a witness should seek legal advice *before* inducing hypnosis or using sodium amytal.

Hopefully, as additional courts tackle the nonclient duty issue, they will agree with the supreme courts of Connecticut and Texas, and will decline to impose such a duty. Now, with this digression disposed of, let us move on to the "reasonable person" standard in negligence law.

"Reasonable Person" Standard

When a duty of care is owed from one person to another, the law requires the duty-bound person to exercise reasonable care to avoid harm or injury. But what is "reasonable care"? How is our conduct evaluated to see if we measure up? First, reasonable care is not the highest possible degree of care. The law does not require us to be perfect. Mistakes do not necessarily equal negligence. Nor are we required to be hypervigilant to the slightest trace of risk. Rather, the law measures our conduct against the imagined performance of a hypothetical "reasonable person." If we act as a "reasonable person" would act under similar circumstances, we cannot be faulted, even if somebody gets hurt. Life, after all, is filled with risk, and unavoid-

> *Mistakes do not necessarily equal negligence.*

able accidents for which no one is to blame happen every day. On the other hand, if we fail to conform to the standard of a "reasonable person," we may be liable for resulting harm.

Keeton (1984) described the "reasonable person":

> The whole theory of negligence presupposes some uniform standard of behavior. Yet the infinite variety of situations which may arise makes it impossible to fix definite rules in advance for all conceivable human conduct. . . . The standard of conduct which the community demands must be an external and objective one, rather than the individual judgment, good or bad, of the particular actor; and it must be, so far as possible, the same for all persons, since the law can have no favorites. At the same time, it must make proper allowance for the risk apparent to the actor, for his capacity to meet it, and for the circumstances under which he must act.
>
> The courts have dealt with this very difficult problem by creating a fictitious person, who never has existed on land or sea: the "reasonable [person] of ordinary prudence." . . . The actor is required to do what such an ideal individual would be supposed to do in his place. A model of all proper qualities, with only those human shortcomings and weaknesses which the community will tolerate on the occasion, "this excellent but odious character stands like a monument in our Courts of Justice, vainly appealing to his fellow-citizens to order their lives after his own example." (p. 174)

Thus, if bad luck strikes and you are involved in a harm-producing event, your liability for negligence turns in major part on whether your conduct comports with the standard set by the mythical "reasonable person." As we shall see in the discussion of malpractice to follow, the "reasonable person" standard is adjusted to take account of the greater knowledge and skill possessed by the "reasonable *professional* person."

MALPRACTICE

Malpractice is defined as "bad or unskillful practice on the part of a [professional] resulting in [physical or mental] injury to the patient, or a [professional's] breach of a duty imposed on [the professional] by law" (*Corpus Juris Secundum*, 1987, Vol. 70, p. 455). Many malpractice cases are based on negligence (Smith, 1996). The person claiming malpractice (the plaintiff) alleges that the professional (defendant/tortfeasor) breached a duty of care owed to the plaintiff and failed to live up to the standard of performance required of professionals. Malpractice covers more than negligence, however. "Thus, malpractice consists of any professional misconduct, unreasonable lack of skill or fidelity in professional or fiduciary duties, evil practice, or illegal or immoral conduct" (*Corpus Juris Secundum*, 1987, Vol. 70, p. 455). Malpractice includes criminal conduct by professionals, such as sexual assault of a client.

Malpractice Based on Negligence

As stated earlier, malpractice claims often are based on negligence. "Negligence on the part of a [professional] generally consists of the [professional] doing something a reasonable [professional] under the circumstances would not have done or omitting to do something a reasonable [professional] would have done" (Smith, 1986, pp. 5-6).

When a professional is sued for negligence, the requirements are similar to the requirements of ordinary negligence: That is, the plaintiff must prove (a) a duty of care to the injured person, (b) breach of duty, and (c) causation. As is true with laypersons, professionals are held to the standard of the "reasonable person." With professionals, however, the reasonable person is not the average "person on the street." Professionals are held to a higher standard. Because they have special skill and knowledge, professionals "are required not only to exercise reasonable care in what they do, but also to possess a standard minimum of special knowledge and ability" (Keeton, 1984, p. 185). Thus, they are judged according to the performance of competent practitioners in good standing. In his book on psychiatric malpractice, Smith (1986) discusses circumstances in which a psychiatrist's level of patient care falls below acceptable standards:

> A physician's level of care is judged by whether it was reasonable under the circumstances and pursuant to the practice of the physician's general field of specialty. Therefore, if the care provided by a psychiatrist for a particular illness would be considered unreasonable, as judged by the general knowledge and practices of the psychiatric

profession, then a psychiatrist is said to have breached the duty of care to a patient. (p. 78)

Smith's description of psychiatric malpractice is equally applicable to social workers, psychologists, and other clinicians.

Every major professional group has a code of ethics. These codes are promulgated by professional organizations such as the National Association of Social Workers, the American Psychological Association, the American Medical Association, and the American Bar Association. Ethics codes establish two types of standards: aspirational and mandatory. If a code contains mandatory standards of conduct, a professional who belongs to the promulgating organization must adhere to the standards. Aspirational standards set nonbinding goals of professional conduct.

Failure to abide by an ethics code can influence membership in the promulgating organization. For example, the American Psychological Association has procedures to discipline or expel members who violate its ethical standards.

When a professional is sued for negligence or malpractice, an ethics code may establish the standard of care against which the professional's conduct is measured. Falling below the standard set forth in an ethics code can be evidence of malpractice.

Professionals are not required to measure up to unrealistically high standards. Nor must a generalist possess the knowledge of a specialist, unless, of course, the generalist holds herself out as or practices as a specialist. Professionals "do not warrant, guarantee, or insure a good result or that they will effect a cure, or that their diagnosis will be correct or even that their treatment will be beneficial" (*Corpus Juris Secundum*, 1987, Vol. 70, p. 465). Again, however, professionals who expressly or impliedly promise a particular result or outcome commit themselves to that end, and failure to deliver can lead to liability for malpractice or breach of contract. With the foregoing in mind, it is a good idea to inform prospective clients, as part of the informed-consent process, about the risks, limitations, and uncertainties of diagnosis and treatment. (Informed consent is discussed in Chapter 6.)

Professionals are not liable for honest mistakes or errors in judgment. The fields of mental health and social work practice are inexact.

Errors are neither uncommon nor automatic evidence of negligence. The bottom line with regard to error in judgment, whether pertaining to a diagnosis or selection of treatment, is that liability will not be imposed if ordinary and reasonable skill, care, and judgment were applied. (Smith, 1986, p. 79)

Psychotherapeutic Malpractice

Just as a surgeon may commit malpractice in the operating room, so a psychotherapist may commit malpractice in "talk therapy." Both the surgeon and the psychotherapist must comply with the applicable standard of care, and if either one falls below the standard, liability may follow. In one respect, however, the "cutter" and the "shrink" are situated quite differently. Lawsuits for negligent surgery number in the thousands, whereas lawsuits for negligent psychotherapy are rare (Smith, 1986, p. 85). Gutheil and Appelbaum (1982) explain why lawsuits for psychotherapeutic malpractice are uncommon:

Among the reasons advanced to explain this are the good relationship most patients have with their psychotherapists (although negative transference reactions of significant severity are hardly unusual); the patient's low index of suspicion for negligent acts, given the patient's usual unfamiliarity with technical aspects of psychotherapy; the difficulty of proving that the act was negligent, both because of the absence of witnesses and other corroborative data and because the techniques of many forms of psychotherapy have diverged so greatly from the original analytical model that a professional consensus on what constitutes an adequate standard of care is almost impossible to obtain; the crucial role of the patient's own participation and, hence, responsibility; and the problems in establishing a causal link between a therapist's statements and subsequent harm that accrues to the patient. (p. 152)

Gutheil and Appelbaum (1982) suggest one aspect of psychotherapy that could lead to liability:

A divergence from the standard of care for psychotherapists usually implies an intrusion of countertransference feelings into the treatment process. Thus, a therapist who, in anger at a patient's provocative behavior, berates that patient or suggests that the patient undertake some action that is not in the patient's best interest would, problems of proof aside, be liable for whatever harm occurs. (p. 152)

Respondeat Superior

Professionals who employ other professionals, paraprofessionals, students, or unlicensed practitioners need to be aware that employers can be legally liable for negligence committed by persons in their employ. The Latin phrase *respondeat superior* describes this kind of vicarious liability. *Respondeat superior* means "Let the master answer": That is, let the master (i.e., employer) be liable for negligence committed by employees. So long as the employee was performing assigned responsibilities (e.g., treatment) when negligence or malpractice occurred, the general rule is that the employer is liable along with the employee. Moreover, the master is liable even though the master is *completely blameless*! Under *respondeat superior*, the negligence of the master is immaterial. As a matter of policy, the law holds the master accountable for the negligence or malpractice of the employee.

Section 1983 of Title 42 of the U.S. Code allows certain lawsuits against government employees and agencies. Although Section 1983 is not discussed until later in this chapter, this is the appropriate place to mention that there is no *respondeat superior* liability under Section 1983 (*Monnell v. Department of Social Services*, 1978).

Negligent Hiring or Supervision

As an alternative to liability based on *respondeat superior*, in which an employer's negligence is immaterial, a professional can be liable for negligent hiring, retention, or supervision of unqualified employees. With negligent hiring, retention, or supervision, the employer's *own* negligence is what counts. Consider, for example, a psychologist who owns a clinical practice. The owner hires a clinician to treat clients. The owner of the practice does not check the references of the prospective employee. Nor does the owner inquire about the employee's license. Six months later, during a therapy session, the employee sexually assaults a client. As it turns out, the employee has a history of similar offenses in other communities. Moreover, the employee's license was revoked in another state. A background check would have revealed the problem. There is no doubt that the victim can sue the perpetrator. In addition, the victim is likely to sue the employing psychologist for negligent hiring. It seems pretty clear that failure to conduct any form of background check was negligent. The victim will probably win *both* lawsuits.

On the issue of supervision, a professional can be liable for negligent supervision of unlicensed practitioners, students, and others. A supervising professional must exercise the degree of oversight that a competent supervisor would exercise in similar circumstances.

Negligent Failure to Refer

Malpractice occurs when a professional negligently fails to refer a client to a specialist or a practitioner in a more appropriate discipline (Smith, 1996). For example, a psychologist or social worker may be liable for failing to refer a client who needs medical treatment to a physician.

Abandoning a Client

Termination of therapy is a delicate and important part of treatment. Professionals may not simply abandon clients. Smith (1996) observes that "the therapist must not 'dump' or suddenly stop seeing a patient. After treatment has begun, the professional's failure to attend to the patient or to make reasonable provision for the patient to see another competent professional may constitute abandonment" (p. 82).

Educational Malpractice

Teachers are professionals. Can they be sued for malpractice? Are they liable to their students if they fail to exercise the skill and knowledge possessed by competent educators? Although a few so-called "educational malpractice" lawsuits have been filed, judges generally reject the idea of subjecting educators to malpractice liability (see *Gupta v. New Britain General Hospital*, 1996; *Moss Rehab v. White*, 1997).

Reducing Potential Malpractice Liability

Professionals can reduce the likelihood of being sued, although the risk cannot be eliminated. Professionals of the highest competence and ethical standards sometimes find themselves in court. The best way to avoid a lawsuit is to practice competently and compassionately. Smith (1996) urges professionals to "promote an atmosphere of concern for patients and respect for their legal rights" (p. 91). Knapp and Vande-Creek (1996) reinforced the importance of concern for clients and their families.

The best way to avoid a lawsuit is to practice competently and compassionately.

Regular consultation and peer review decrease the likelihood of liability. Harris (1995) advises:

> In my judgment, any mental health professional, no matter how senior or experienced, who accepts a case in one of the high-risk categories would be wise to be involved in a formal consultative-supervisory relationship where that case is regularly discussed and notes are taken of the discussion. If consultation is properly used, it will often prevent a complaint by avoiding or responding to the problem before it reaches crisis proportions. Even if a complaint is filed, it provides real corroborative support for the mental health professional's version of events, and professional support for the clinical interventions that the mental health professional undertook to resolve the problems which were developing in the therapeutic relationship. (p. 253)

Knapp and VandeCreek (1996) offer equally good advice:

> Psychologists should consult with other psychotherapists as part of the larger process of self-monitoring and self-improvement of their professional services. When challenged in court, psychologists will be evaluated on the extent to which they adhered to the standards of their profession. Seeking consultation helps to ensure that psychologists are providing good treatment to their patients. At times, it may be desirable to seek consultation with an expert who has a different perspective. . . . The consultation should be documented and include responses to specific questions, including, but not limited to, the diagnosis or presenting problem, specific treatment plans, and alternative treatment strategies. (p. 458)

Documentation is critical to risk management (Moline, Williams, & Austin, 1998). "An axiom among malpractice defense attorneys is 'If it isn't written down, it didn't occur' " (Knapp & VandeCreek, 1996, p. 458). Thorough, accurate, ongoing documentation is a powerful defense against charges of improper practice (Harris, 1995). Avoid "humorous" remarks in client records. What seemed funny at the time may appear callous and unprofessional when an attorney reads the professional's notes aloud in court. Finally, never alter records. "This is particularly true once litigation involving the records is anticipated" (Smith, 1996, p. 92). Of course, records can be corrected. Corrections, however, should be noted as such.

STATE LAW AS A BASIS OF CIVIL LIABILITY

In addition to negligence and malpractice liability, professionals can be sued, or, in extreme cases, prosecuted criminally, for violating specific state laws regulating practice. The most common sources of liability are described briefly in this section and are elaborated more fully elsewhere.

State Licensing Laws

Practicing social work, psychiatry, nursing, psychology, law, or other professions without the required state license is against the law. A practitioner who lacks proper licensure can be sued by a dissatisfied client and by state licensing authorities. In addition, unlicensed practice is a crime.

It should be mentioned that professionals employed by the federal government may or may not need a state license.

In the helping professions, nonlicensed practitioners (e.g., graduate students) are permitted to practice under the supervision of a licensed or otherwise qualified professional.

Reporting Laws

The child abuse reporting law raises three liability issues: (a) liability for *failure* to report suspected abuse, (b) liability *for* reporting suspected abuse, and (c) liability for unauthorized release of confidential information during the course of reporting. As long as professionals act reasonably and in good faith, reporting suspected abuse or neglect carries a low risk of liability. (Liability under reporting laws is discussed in Chapter 3.)

Confidential Client Information

Complex legal and ethical rules govern the release of confidential information on clients. These rules are discussed in Chapter 6. For present purposes, it will suffice to say that unauthorized release of confidential information can lead to liability (*Pettus v. Cole*, 1996; *Renzi v. Morrison*, 1993).

State Tort Claim Acts

In early English law, "The king could do no wrong." To put it another way, you could not sue the sovereign. The king was absolutely immune from liability. The doctrine of absolute sovereign immunity put to sea and found its way to America. In the United States, of course, there is no monarchy, and sovereign immunity attached itself instead to the federal, state, and local governments.

Sovereign immunity gradually fell into disfavor in the United States, and today most, if not all, states waive sovereign immunity and allow certain lawsuits against the government. State laws partially waiving immunity are commonly called tort claims acts. Like the states, the federal government waived absolute sovereign immunity. The Federal Tort Claims Act allows limited lawsuits against the United States.

❑ Constitutional Rights

When professionals working with abused and neglected children think of liability, they usually do not have the Constitution in mind. Yet the Constitution plays a central role in some litigation against professionals, especially professionals employed by government. Here is how. The Constitution bestows important rights on individuals, and when a government employee violates the constitutional rights of a citizen, the violator can be sued. Two examples illustrate the point. First, a police officer who uses excessive force to make an arrest violates the constitutional rights of the arrestee. Second, a social worker who unlawfully removes a child from home may violate the parents' constitutional right of family autonomy.

Constitutional rights emanate from two sources. First, amendments to the U.S. Constitution contain the Bill of Rights, which guarantees fundamentally important rights such as freedom of speech and religion, the right to equal protection of the law, and the right to due process of law. In addition to rights bestowed by the U.S. Constitution, every state has its own constitution and bill of rights. State bills of rights generally mirror the rights contained in the U.S. Constitution's Bill of Rights.

The rights guaranteed by the U.S. and state constitutions are, for the most part, rights vis-à-vis the government. Constitutional rights shield us from acts of government employees that violate our fundamental liberties. The U.S. Constitution provides, for example, that the *state* shall not deprive a person of equal protection of the law. Because constitutional rights generally apply against the government, most lawsuits based on the constitution target government agencies and employees. Professionals who are not government employees are less likely to face allegations that they violated someone's constitutional rights. It must be said, however, that professionals in private practice have been and will continue to be sued along with government employees.

Among government employees, it is useful to distinguish between law enforcement and non-law-enforcement professionals. Law enforcement officers investigating allegations of child abuse concern themselves with constitutional rights that have only a tangential impact on mental health, social work, and medical professionals. Thus, law enforcement officers deal with the constitutional implications of interrogating suspects, search and seizure, and arrest. (For more information on the criminal justice system, see Chapter 2.) Individuals who believe that the police violated their constitutional rights can sue. For example, you remember the case of Rodney King, whose brutal beating at the hands of Los Angeles police officers was caught on videotape. The police violated Mr. King's constitutional rights, and in his lawsuit against the city of Los Angeles, King was awarded more than $3 million.

One constitutional right plays a particularly important role in litigation against professionals engaged in child protection. The U.S. Constitution and state constitutions protect parental rights. The constitutional right of family autonomy is discussed below.

PARENTAL RIGHTS UNDER THE CONSTITUTION

In an unbroken line of decisions extending back to 1923, the U.S. Supreme Court ruled that the U.S. Constitution protects parental rights. In *Meyer v. Nebraska* (1923), the Supreme Court wrote that the Constitution protects "the right of the individual . . . to marry, establish a home and bring up children" (p. 399). In *Pierce v. Society of Sisters* (1925), the Court added that "the child is not the mere creature of the State; those who nurture him and direct his destiny have the right, coupled with the high duty, to recognize and prepare him for additional obligations" (p. 535). In *Prince v. Massachusetts* (1944), the Court stated that "it is cardinal with us that the custody, care and nurture of the child reside first in the parents, whose primary function and freedom include preparation for obligations the state can neither supply nor hinder" (p. 166). In *Ginsberg v. New York* (1968), the Court observed that the right of parents to make decisions for their children is "basic in the structure of our society" (p. 639). In *Hodgson v. Minnesota* (1990), the Court added that "the family has a privacy interest in the upbringing and education of children . . . which is protected by the Constitution against undue state interference" (p. 446). Finally, in *M.L.B. v. S.L.J.* (1996), the Court wrote that

> choices about marriage, family life, and the upbringing of children are among associational rights this Court has ranked as "of basic impor-

In an unbroken line of decisions extending back to 1923, the U.S. Supreme Court ruled that the U.S. Constitution protects parental rights.

tance in our society," . . . rights sheltered by the Fourteenth Amendment [of the U.S. Constitution] against the State's unwarranted usur-
pation, disregard, or disrespect. (p. 564)

Thus, the U.S. Constitution creates a "private realm of family life
which the state cannot enter" (*Prince v. Massachusetts*, 1944, p. 166).

The constitutional right to family autonomy both mirrors and
contributes to the most lasting debate in child protection: When
should the state—through social workers and the juvenile court—
intervene in the family? At what point should society draw the line
between family privacy and child protection? Champions of parental
rights and family privacy draw considerable strength from the U.S.
Supreme Court decisions quoted above.

Although the decisions of the U.S. Supreme Court provide strong
support for parental rights, the Court has made clear that parental
rights are not absolute. The Court wrote in *Prince v. Massachusetts*
(1944) that the state has a "wide range of power for limiting parental
freedom and authority in things affecting the child's welfare"
(p. 167). The Court added in *Wisconsin v. Yoder* (1972) that the state
may intervene "if it appears that parental decisions will jeopardize
the health or safety of the child" (p. 234). In *Watterson v. Page* (1993),
the U.S. Court of Appeals for the First Circuit wrote that "the right
to family integrity clearly does not include a constitutional right to
be free from child abuse investigations" (p. 8). The First Circuit
added in *Wojcik v. Town of North Smithfield* (1996) that "there is no way
for the government to protect children without making inquiries that
in many cases do turn out to be baseless" (p. 3). Finally, a different
federal circuit court wisely observed that "the only way that a state
can ensure that parents have not exceeded the limits of their responsibility to discipline their children is to permit public officers to
investigate alleged incidents of child abuse" (*Sweaney v. Ada County,
Idaho*, 1997, p. 1392).

Decisions of the U.S. Supreme Court and lower courts do not
resolve the debate over parental rights and state intervention in the
family. Nevertheless, the pronouncements of judges establish the
constitutional parameters of the debate.

SOURCES OF GOVERNMENT AUTHORITY
TO INTERVENE IN THE FAMILY

Government authority to intervene in the family derives from two sources of government power: (a) the *parens patriae* authority and (b) the police power. *Parens patriae* authority is the inherent power of government to protect persons, including children, who are incapable of self-protection. The U.S. Supreme Court has written that "the state as *parens patriae* may restrict the parent's control by requiring school attendance, regulating or prohibiting the child's labor and in many other ways" (*Prince v. Massachusetts*, 1944, p. 166).

The police power is the authority of the state to protect the health, safety, morals, and general welfare of the public. Under the police power, the government has authority to protect children from abuse and exploitation, whether perpetrated by parents or by others. For example, in *New York v. Ferber* (1982), the U.S. Supreme Court ruled that the police power gives states authority to prohibit distribution of child pornography. The Court wrote that states have a compelling interest in protecting the physical and psychological well-being of children, and that criminalizing distribution of child pornography is a permissible exercise of police power. In *Osborne v. Ohio* (1990), the Court went a step beyond *distribution* of child pornography and held that the Constitution allows states to prohibit *possession* of child pornography.

Laws protecting children draw equally from the police power and *parens patriae* authority of the state. These basic sources of government authority underpin the juvenile court, CPS, child abuse reporting laws, and prosecution.

HOW U.S. CONSTITUTIONAL RIGHTS
ARE ENFORCED IN COURT: SECTION 1983

To ensure that rights guaranteed by the U.S. Constitution are vindicated, Congress passed laws specifically authorizing lawsuits against government employees who violate rights protected by the U.S. Constitution. The most notable of these federal laws is in Section 1983 of Title 42 of the U.S. Code, which reads in part:

> Every person who, under color of any statute, ordinance, regulation, custom, or usage, of any State or Territory or the District of Columbia, subjects, or causes to be subjected, any citizen of the United States or other person within the jurisdiction thereof to the deprivation of any rights, privileges, or immunities secured by the Constitution and laws, shall be liable to the party injured. (1998, § 1983).

At first glance, Section 1983 seems relatively straightforward. In fact, however, the intricacies of litigation under Section 1983 boggle the mind. The subject is so complex that it took Nahmod (1991) well over 1,000 pages to explain Section 1983 in his book entitled *Civil Rights and Civil Liberties Litigation: The Law of Section 1983*. Obviously, we can do little more here than scratch the surface of Section 1983.

In Section 1983, the words *every person* and *under color of any statute* require explanation. Under Section 1983, the word *person* includes individuals, cities, and counties (*Pitts v. County of Kern*, 1998). "In contrast, however, states and their agencies are not persons suable directly under § 1983" (Nahmod, 1991, p. 13). Thus, a California parent who claims that county CPS social workers violated the parents' constitutional rights can employ Section 1983 to sue the individual social workers and the county CPS agency for damages. The parent could not rely on Section 1983 to sue the state of California for damages. Here too, however, Section 1983 is complicated. Although employees of the state (as opposed to a county) cannot be sued in their official capacity, state employees can be sued in their individual capacity.

Section 1983 permits lawsuits only against persons acting "under color of law." Boiled down to its essentials, *color of law* means official government action or, as it is usually called, "state action." Nahmod (1991) explains:

> State action is obviously present where the individual official clearly acted in an official capacity in a manner authorized by state law. It is somewhat more difficult to find, although the Supreme Court has already done so, where the individual official acted in an official capacity but in a manner not authorized by state law. However, the hardest state action problems of all arise where private persons or entities act in a situation where government may also be involved. (pp. 57-58)

Most of the time, "state action" is clear. Thus, a CPS social worker engages in state action when the worker investigates reported child abuse. Sometimes, however, it is unclear whether conduct constitutes "state action." Judges look at the facts of each case to determine whether "state action" is present. Suppose, for example, that a psychotherapist in private practice is treating a child who may be sexually abused. The therapist provides information to the police. Does communicating with the police amount to "state action" by the psychotherapist? In *Lowe v. Aldridge* (1992), the court said no. The court observed that "only in rare circumstances can a private party be viewed as a 'state actor' for Section 1983 purposes" (p. 1572). In another case, *Robbing v. Hamburger Home for Girls* (1995), the court wrote that "private parties ordinarily are not subject to suit under section 1983, unless, sifting the circumstances of the particular case, the state has so significantly involved itself in the private conduct that the private parties may fairly be termed state actors" (p. 541).

Section 1983 "was designed both to prevent the states from violating the [U.S. Constitution] and certain federal statutes and to compensate injured plaintiffs for deprivations of their federal rights" (Nahmod, 1991, p. 5). Since its enactment in 1871, Section 1983 has been at the heart of thousands of lawsuits, ranging from allegations of police brutality to interference with religious freedom to a wide range of other issues.

Section 1983 figures prominently in lawsuits by angry parents against CPS agencies. Suits against CPS arise when social workers investigate reports of abuse, remove children from parental custody, refuse to return children, or terminate parental rights. Aggrieved parents allege that such activities violate the parents' constitutional right to family autonomy.

IMMUNITY FROM LIABILITY

When a professional is sued under Section 1983 or certain other statutes such as state tort claims acts, or when a professional is sued for malpractice, the professional may have absolute or qualified immunity from liability. "Immunity serves as a shield to protect officials from undue interference with their duties and from potentially disabling threats of liability" (*Austin v. Borel*, 1987). With specific reference to CPS social workers, the court in *Millspaugh v. County Department of Public Welfare of Wabash County* (1991) observed that

> social workers often act on limited information; those who tarry, or resolve all doubts in favor of the parents, chance enduring damage to the children. Immunity helps social workers put their private interests aside and concentrate on the welfare of children. Unfortunately, immunity also may embolden social workers to pursue their private agendas. . . . One effect is inseparable from the other. (pp. 1176-1177)

Before discussing immunity, it is important to understand what immunity does *not* do: Immunity does not prevent a lawsuit from being filed against a professional. For example, an angry parent may file suit against a CPS social worker even though a judge eventually determines that the social worker has immunity. Well, then, if immunity does not prevent a lawsuit from being filed, what good is it? The answer is that immunity is very good indeed. To continue the illustration of the CPS social worker, if the attorney representing the angry parent believes that the social worker has immunity, the attorney may convince the parent not to sue. If a lawsuit is filed, the social worker's attorney can ask the judge to declare that the worker has immunity and to dismiss the suit—that is, throw the suit out of court. Basically, immunity gives a professional an escape hatch from a lawsuit. Moreover, in many cases, escape comes quite early in the process, well before a trial.

A professional who lacks immunity—qualified or absolute—will not necessarily lose a lawsuit brought under Section 1983 or other laws. After all, the professional may have done nothing wrong (see *Renn v. Garrison*, 1996). If the professional lacks immunity, however, the professional's exposure to the possibility of money damages increases. The case may settle or go all the way to trial.

What is the difference between absolute and qualified immunity? With absolute immunity, the professional is nearly always entitled to early dismissal from the lawsuit. Moreover, "There can be no inquiry into the objective reasonableness of the absolutely immune defendant's conduct" (Nahmod, 1991, p. 3). So long as the alleged wrongdoing was within the scope of the immunity, there is no liability (*Hodorowski v. Ray*, 1988).

Qualified immunity provides less protection than absolute immunity. In *Renn v. Garrison* (1996), the court wrote that "qualified immunity shields public officials from personal liability for discretionary actions provided their conduct does not violate 'clearly established statutory or constitutional rights of which a reasonable person would have known' " (p. 349). Thus, a professional with qualified immunity is dismissed from a lawsuit only if the professional's conduct did not violate rights that a reasonable professional would have understood. Still, qualified immunity is a powerful defense. Government employees "are not liable for bad guesses in gray areas; they are liable for transgressing bright lines" (*Maciariello v. City of Lancaster*, 1992). Qualified immunity "provides ample protection to all but the plainly incompetent or those who knowingly violate the law" (*Malley v. Briggs*, 1986, p. 341). In most cases, professionals escape lawsuits on the basis of either qualified or absolute immunity.

Qualified immunity applies to most government employees and to some professionals in private practice. Absolute immunity is more limited and applies only in the circumstances described below.

Absolute Immunity for Prosecutors and, by Analogy, CPS Social Workers

Prosecutors engaged in normal prosecutorial activities such as courtroom advocacy, preparing cases for trial, and filing criminal charges enjoy absolute immunity for such acts. "It is clear that prosecutorial immunity from liability for damages attaches to those acts of the prosecutor performed in the role of advocate" (Nahmod, 1991, p. 67). Absolute immunity does not extend to everything prosecutors do, however. For example, a prosecutor conducting a criminal investigation has much in common with a police officer, and, like the police officer, the investigating prosecutor enjoys only qualified immunity (*Kalina v. Fletcher*, 1997). So too, a prosecutor engaged in purely administrative activities has qualified immunity. It is sometimes difficult to tell when a prosecutor crosses the line separating advocacy (absolute immunity) from investigation or administration (qualified immunity).

In some circumstances, CPS social workers have absolute prosecutorial immunity (*Ernst v. Child and Youth Services of Chester County,*

1997). Absolute immunity is most likely when a CPS professional files or participates in filing dependency proceedings in juvenile court. In *Ernst v. Child and Youth Services of Chester County* (1997), the court wrote that "child welfare workers and attorneys who prosecute proceedings on behalf of the state are entitled to absolute immunity from suit for all of their actions in preparing for and prosecuting such dependency proceedings" (pp. 488-489). The court added that absolute immunity extends to "the formulation and presentation of recommendations to the court in the course of [dependency] proceedings" (p. 495).

It is sometimes difficult to tell whether a judge will grant absolute prosecutorial immunity to CPS social workers. Thus, in *Austin v. Borel* (1987), the court ruled that social workers were "not entitled to absolute immunity for their conduct in filing an allegedly false verified complaint seeking the removal of two children" (p. 1363). By contrast, in *Salyer v. Patrick* (1989), the court granted absolute immunity to social workers for filing a petition in juvenile court. The judge's decision depends on the facts of the specific case and relevant state law.

Absolute immunity does not extend to CPS social workers conducting investigations (*Gilliam v. Department of Social and Health Services*, 1998). Nor does absolute immunity protect purely administrative activities. Absolute immunity is restricted to conduct that is intimately associated with the judicial process (*Achterhof v. Selvaggio*, 1989). Thus, when a judge evaluates a social worker's claim of absolute immunity, the judge looks to "the distinction between prosecutorial . . . duties and duties which are administrative or investigatory" (*Achterhof v. Selvaggio*, 1989, p. 829).

Absolute Judicial Immunity and Its
Application to Court-Appointed Professionals

Judges enjoy absolute immunity for most judicial activities. A judge lacks absolute immunity only "where the challenged conduct is accompanied by a clear absence of jurisdiction or where the challenged conduct is not a judicial act but is, for example, administrative in nature. Otherwise, absolute judicial immunity applies" (Nahmod, 1991, p. 23).

A mental health professional who is appointed *by a judge* to conduct a psychological assessment *for the judge* is typically protected by absolute judicial immunity. In *Delcourt v. Silverman* (1996), for example, parents battled in family court over custody of their young child. The judge appointed Dr. Silverman to evaluate the child and the parents and to file a written report with the court. Eventually, the mother sued Dr. Silverman. In ruling that the doctor was absolutely immune from liability, the Texas Court of Appeals stated:

> A party is entitled to absolute immunity when the party is acting as an integral part of the judicial system or an "arm of the court."
>
> A psychologist who is appointed by the court is entitled to absolute immunity if he or she is appointed to fulfill quasijudicial functions intimately related to the judicial process.
>
> Numerous courts have extended absolute immunity to psychiatrists and other mental health experts assisting the court in criminal cases.
>
> We believe this reasoning also applies to mental health experts appointed to provide psychological expertise in child custody suits. Many courts recognize that psychiatrists and psychologists performing court-ordered custody evaluations perform a judicial function and enjoy absolute immunity. (pp. 782-783)

Thus, in child custody litigation, a professional who is appointed by the judge to perform a custody evaluation is normally protected by absolute judicial immunity (*Lythgoe v. Guinn*, 1994). Immunity extends to the evaluation, the resulting report, and testimony in court. Generally speaking, however, a professional who is retained by one or both parents to conduct a custody evaluation does not enjoy absolute judicial immunity. Judicial immunity attaches only when a judge formally appoints the professional to conduct an evaluation for the court. Some professionals require one or both parents to agree in advance that the professional will be court appointed. The parents' agreement is put in writing and submitted to the judge. The judge signs the agreement, converting the agreement into a court order appointing the professional. Absolute judicial immunity accompanies the appointment.

Absolute Witness Immunity

In most if not all states, witnesses, including expert witnesses, have absolute immunity for testimony that they provide in court (California Civil Code § 47; American Law Institute, Restatement of the Law of Torts, § 588, 1977). Thus, the court in *General Electric Co. v. Sargent and Lundy* (1990) wrote that "courts have long recognized that statements in judicial proceedings, if relevant to the issues involved, are absolutely privileged, even though it may be claimed that they are false and alleged with malice" (p. 1126). The California Supreme Court defined the public policy that supports absolute witness immunity, writing that "the principal purpose of [the privilege] is to afford litigants and witnesses the utmost freedom of access to the courts without fear of being harassed subsequently by derivative court actions" (*Silberg v. Anderson*, 1990, p. 642). The California Court of Appeals added, with particular emphasis on expert witnesses, that

> freedom of access to the courts and encouragement of witnesses to testify truthfully will be harmed if neutral experts must fear retaliatory lawsuits from litigants whose disagreement with an expert's opinions perforce convinces them the expert must have been negligent in forming such opinions. (*Gootee v. Lightner*, 1990, p. 700)

Absolute witness immunity applies to testimony at a trial or hearing in court. It also applies to testimony given at a deposition (*Darragh v. Superior Court*, 1995). Moreover, it extends to "preparatory activity leading to the witnesses' testimony" (*Gootee v. Lightner*, 1990, p. 701). Thus, a report prepared by an expert who is retained to testify falls within the absolute privilege so long as the report has some relation to the litigation (*Adams v. Peck*, 1979; *Bruce v. Byrne-Stevens & Associates*, 1989; *Durand Equipment Co. v. Superior Carbon Products, Inc.*, 1991; *Kahn v. Burman*, 1987; *Rainier's Dairies v. Raritan Valley Farms*, 1955; *Woodward v. Weiss*, 1996). In *Darragh v. Superior Court* (1995), the court wrote:

> Courts have agreed that reports, consultations, and advice, which are relevant to litigation as preliminary steps in the institution or defense of a case, are a part of the preparation for trial and are therefore within

the absolute privilege accorded communications in judicial proceedings. (p. 1218)

Even when litigation is not underway, absolute witness immunity may attach to experts who are retained to evaluate potential litigation or to work on issues that are likely to end up in court (*Mershon v. Beasley*, 1993).

Although absolute witness immunity protects expert witnesses from nearly all types of civil liability, an occasional allegation slips past the protective shield. For example, absolute witness immunity may not protect an expert against allegations of malicious prosecution (*Silberg v. Anderson*, 1990) or conspiracy (*Darragh v. Superior Court*, 1995). In *Deatherage v. Examining Board of Psychology* (1997), the Washington Supreme Court ruled that absolute witness immunity does not apply in disciplinary proceedings against professionals. Thus, the state board of psychology could maintain a disciplinary action against a psychologist for work that the psychologist did in a child custody case (see also *Moses v. McWilliams*, 1988; *Moses v. Parwatikar*, 1987; *Silberg v. Anderson*, 1990).

The case of *Gootee v. Lightner* (1990) is a useful example of absolute witness immunity. Irene and Michael Gootee were divorced and had three children. In 1985, Irene went to family court requesting a change in child custody. Irene and Michael agreed to undergo psychological testing and evaluation regarding custody. They further agreed to retain Marshall Lightner, a mental health professional, to perform the testing and to evaluate the family. Lightner prepared a report and testified in court, recommending that Irene have custody of the children, with visitation for Michael. Upset with Lightner's report and testimony, Michael sued Lightner, alleging professional negligence. The trial judge threw out Michael's lawsuit, ruling that Lightner's conduct, report, and testimony were protected by absolute witness immunity. On appeal, the California Court of Appeals endorsed the trial judge, writing:

It is undisputed that [Lightner's] role was a limited one: to evaluate the partisans in the custody matter for purposes of testifying concerning the custody dispute. Because the gravamen of [Michael's] claim relies on negligent or intentional tortious conduct committed by

[Lightner] in connection with the testimonial function, we conclude
the absolute privilege bars civil lawsuits (other than for malicious
prosecution) seeking to impose liability on [Lightner]. (p. 699)

The court further concluded that "the protective mantle of the privilege embraces not only the courtroom testimony of witnesses, but
also protects prior preparatory activity leading to the witnesses'
testimony" (p. 701).

Qualified Immunity

Qualified immunity applies to a broad range of government
employees, including police officers, educators, prison officials, mental health professionals, and social workers. In *Renn v. Garrison*
(1996), the court wrote, "We have held that social services officials
engaged in child abuse investigations 'may properly assert qualified
immunity in appropriate situations' " (p. 349). In *Manzano v. South
Dakota Department of Social Services* (1995), the court added that

> when a state official pursuing a child abuse investigation takes an
> action which would otherwise unconstitutionally disrupt familial
> integrity, he or she is entitled to qualified immunity, if such action is
> properly founded upon a reasonable suspicion of child abuse.
> (pp. 509-511)

As an example of qualified immunity, consider the case of *Garramone v. Romo* (1996). In *Romo*, CPS social workers filed a juvenile court
neglect petition against a parent. Although state law required CPS to
inform the parent of the right to an attorney in juvenile court, the
social workers failed to inform the parent. The parent sued, claiming
that the failure to inform her of the right to an attorney violated her
constitutional rights. The parent was right. The CPS social workers
violated the parent's constitutional rights. Nevertheless, the court
ruled that the social workers were not liable for the violation because
the workers had qualified immunity.

The *Romo* case makes an important point. Qualified immunity is
not limited to cases where there is no violation of the Constitution. A
professional who violates the Constitution may nevertheless be
shielded by qualified immunity. As the court put in *Millspaugh v.*

County Department of Public Welfare of Wabash County (1991), "Immunity that applies only when the defendant did no wrong is no immunity at all" (p. 1175).

A Case for Your Consideration

Test your grasp of the foregoing principles with the following case, which is based on *Thomason v. SCAN Volunteer Services, Inc.* (1996). How would you rule if you were the judge?

Smith v. Allred and Jones. Susan Allred is the director of CPS for the county. Fred Jones is a CPS social worker. At noon, Susan received a letter from a local pediatrician, Dr. Denodio. The letter stated that Dr. Denodio was concerned about one of her patients, 8-month-old Anthony Smith. Dr. Denodio's letter read:

> I have been treating 8-month-old Anthony since birth. For 2 months Anthony has experienced periods of tachycardia (rapid heart rate). Until 2 months ago, the baby was doing well and was completely healthy. Anthony's mother reports that the baby has had several periods of apnea and has experienced numerous episodes of paleness, grayness, and sweatiness. Two weeks ago, I admitted the child to the hospital for observation and tests. While in the hospital for 5 days, everything was normal, and our nursing staff noticed no apnea, paleness, grayness, or sweatiness. Following Anthony's discharge from the hospital, the mother has called my office eight times to report paleness, grayness, and sweatiness. Yesterday, mother reported to me that 1 week ago, Anthony had a severe apnea episode resulting in blueness. Mother did not seek medical attention for this episode. Although mother is clearly concerned about the baby, her affect seems strange. I am concerned that the mother may be suffering Munchausen syndrome by proxy and that there is a possibility that she is partially suffocating the child. I believe that this possibility needs to be explored.

After reading the letter, Susan Allred, the CPS director, filled out a child abuse report, writing, "Dr. Denodio reports that the mother is intermittently smothering the infant." Allred called Fred Jones to her office and handed him Dr. Denodio's letter and her child abuse report. Allred said, "I believe the baby should be removed from the home immediately. Take the baby into emergency protective custody and have him admitted to the hospital for a complete evaluation." Within an hour, Jones arrived at the Smith home. Mrs. Smith answered the door and Jones said, "Hello, I am with Child Protective Services. We have received a report that your baby is being smothered and that you are the one responsible." Mrs. Smith became extremely upset and said she had done "nothing of the sort." Jones took Anthony into custody and had him admitted to the hospital. The next day, Jones submitted a petition to the juvenile court recommending that Anthony be placed in the custody of the state. The petition was supported by an affidavit signed by Jones. When Jones signed the affidavit, he had reviewed no medical records, and he based the affidavit entirely on Dr. Denodio's letter quoted above. The affidavit stated that "medical records and physician concur that Anthony Smith showed evidence of intermittent smothering." The judge entered an order placing Anthony in state custody. Anthony remained in state custody for 2 months. Eventually, the petition in juvenile court was dismissed for lack of evidence of maltreatment, and Anthony was returned to his parents.

The Smiths sued Allred and Jones under Section 1983, alleging that (a) Allred and Jones' removal of Anthony from the family home violated the Smiths' parental rights guaranteed by the U.S. Constitution, (b) Jones violated the Smiths' rights by petitioning the juvenile court for custody, and (c) Jones violated the Smiths' rights by filing a false affidavit in juvenile court.

Questions:

1. Did Allred or Jones violate the Smiths' constitutionally protected parental rights?
2. Did Jones violate the Smiths' constitutional rights by filing the petition in juvenile court?
3. Did Jones violate the Smiths' rights by filing the affidavit in juvenile court?
4. If any rights were violated, do Allred and/or Jones have immunity from liability?

Answers and analysis from the court that decided the case are located in the "Analysis of Problems" section at the back of this book (p. 337).

❏ Note

1. On appeal, the administrator won a new trial because the trial judge made an error in instructing the jury on the proper law to apply.

Analysis of Problems

❑ **Sally's Case (Chapter 3)**

The question in Sally's case is, If you were Sally's teacher, would you file a report with CPS? I hope you aren't looking for "the answer" because I don't have it. It seems to me that reasonable minds can differ in Sally's case. But you say, "Wait a minute, John, you are the author! You owe me an answer." All right, all right, if you insist: If I were Sally's teacher, I would not report. For me, the evidence does not rise to the level of reasonable suspicion. I don't see reasonable suspicion of maltreatment. Sally's parents are locked in a bitter divorce, and Sally's sadness and withdrawal seem like a normal reaction to an acrimonious divorce. (See Chapter 7 for discussion of the meaning of various symptoms as evidence of sexual abuse.) As for the kissing episode with Eric, I don't know whether Sally initiated the kissing or whether it was Eric's idea. It seems clear that Sally is suffering, and I'm pretty sure she *and* her parents need help, but I don't think a report to child protective services is mandated.

What would I do? I would take the advice of Kalichman (1993):

> If an examination of the indicators leading to the suspicion is incon-
> clusive and the reportability of the situation remains ambiguous, the
> professional could seek consultation with a colleague, a fellow man-
> dated reporter who might not necessarily be of the same professional
> background. (p. 156)

In addition, I would consult with the school psychologist and my
principal to brainstorm ways to help this troubled little girl and her
parents. Finally, I would keep my antenna up.

❑ Bill's Confession (Chapter 3)

What about Bill? Bill made a clear confession of child sexual abuse.
Ordinarily, there would be no doubt about the duty to report. If the
victim were still a child, or if there were evidence that other children
are at risk, reporting would be obvious. But the abuse happened 8
years ago, and the victim is now an adult. Bill says it only happened
once. There is no indication that Bill is molesting other children. On
the other hand, Bill is fantasizing about the 8-year-old molestation.
He can't get it out of his mind. He's lonely and depressed. Psychologically, Bill may be vulnerable to relapse.

So what is the answer in Bill's case? Again, I'm not sure. The
reporting laws generally don't place a time limit on reporting. The
fact that the abuse happened 8 years ago does not necessarily eliminate the duty to report. Kalichman (1993) advises that "mandated
reporters facing difficult reporting decisions can always contact a
child protection worker and request feedback on a case before reporting to verify that particular indicators constitute a reportable situation" (p. 156).

❑ *Commonwealth v. Spring* (Chapter 7)

The facts in *Commonwealth v. Spring* make a fairly strong case for
admitting Dr. Turner's testimony as substantive evidence of sexual

abuse. The following factors support admissibility of Dr. Turner's testimony:

- Dr. Turner is well qualified.
- Post-traumatic stress disorder is a recognized syndrome seen in sexually abused children.
- The child's depression, nightmares, fear, and withdrawal support the diagnosis of sexual abuse, although such symptoms in isolation would not suffice for a diagnosis.
- The child's disclosure to her mother is typical of sexually abused children and demonstrates detailed knowledge of fellatio and ejaculation. Barring some other source of this knowledge, the child's statement supports the doctor's diagnosis.
- The child describes the progressive nature of her abuse. This pattern is common in incest cases.

As discussed in Chapter 7, courts in the United States differ on the admissibility of expert testimony offered as substantive evidence. Some courts allow such testimony, others reject it. A third group of courts subject such testimony to the special admissibility test for novel scientific evidence.

Expert testimony such as that of Dr. Turner is more likely to be allowed in civil than in criminal cases. Thus, a judge might allow Dr. Turner's testimony in juvenile or family court but not permit the testimony in a criminal trial.

❏ *Commonwealth v. Milton* (Chapter 7)

It seems clear that Dr. Friedrich's testimony should be rejected. First, child sexual abuse accommodation syndrome (CSAAS) is not a diagnosis, and CSAAS does not detect sexual abuse. Dr. Friedrich clearly does not understand CSAAS. Moreover, there is no child sexual abuse syndrome. Putting these rather serious shortcomings aside, the evidence in *Milton* is simply too weak to support a conclusion that sexual abuse occurred. Melissa's nightmares tell us little. The child's statements "Where's my dick?" and "That's my tits" seem innocuous. The other behaviors—resistance to diaper changes, emerging negativism, and separation anxiety—are unremarkable. The child's statement "Daddy hurt 'gina" is too ambiguous to have meaning. Finally, the hair in the diaper adds little. The total picture may raise concern, but the evidence does not support Dr. Friedrich's opinion.

❏ *Smith v. Allred and Jones* (Chapter 9)

This hypothetical case is based on the facts of a real case: *Thomason v. SCAN Volunteer Services* (1996). In *Thomason*, the court ruled in favor of the social workers. Although the court felt that the social workers should have conducted a more thorough investigation before removing Anthony, the court nevertheless ruled that the removal did not violate the Smiths' constitutional rights. Because the removal did not violate the Smiths' rights, there was no need for immunity.

The Smiths also charged that Jones violated their rights by filing a petition in juvenile court and supporting the petition with a false affidavit. On these matters, the Court ruled (a) that Jones had absolute witness immunity for filing the affidavit and (b) that Jones enjoyed absolute prosecutorial immunity for filing the petition in juvenile court.

The court's decision is instructive, and is quoted in part below:

> We have little difficulty in holding that defendants, upon receiving the [letter from Dr. Denodio], formed a reasonable suspicion of abuse which would justify some degree of interference with plaintiffs' rights as the parents of Anthony.
>
> The difficulty in the present case is not whether such a reasonable suspicion can be found, but rather, whether the actions taken by defendants and the resulting disruption to plaintiffs' familial relations with Anthony were so disproportionate under the circumstances as to rise to the level of a constitutional deprivation. . . . The evidence demonstrates that, upon receiving [Dr. Denodio's letter, Jones] proceeded to plaintiffs' residence with the intent to remove Anthony from the plaintiffs' home without so much as a telephone call [to the doctor] to verify the source of the [letter]. Moreover, without even reviewing the purported evidence of abuse in [CPS's] possession, [Jones]

appeared at plaintiffs' doorstep and inaccurately asserted to [the mother] that [CPS] had "received a report [that] her child was being smothered and that she was the perpetrator." Finally, in seeking and obtaining an ex parte protective custody order from the [juvenile] court, [Jones] submitted a signed affidavit that arguably mischaracterized [Dr. Denodio's letter] and exaggerated the strength of defendants' evidence of abuse.

Nevertheless, while we recognize that plaintiffs are justified in feeling that more background investigation could have been done and that [Jones] handled the initial encounter with [the mother] in an unprofessional manner, we hold that plaintiff's constitutional rights were not violated as a result of the removal of Anthony from their home.

In the child abuse context, the abstract substantive due process right to familial integrity must be continually subjected to "a balancing test which weighs the interest of the parent against the interests of the child." In the present case, the constitutional inquiry requires weighing the interest of plaintiffs not to have the state physically remove their eight-month-old child from their home against the state's interests in immediately removing the child from a potentially life-threatening abusive home setting for medical evaluation and protection. We recognize that the parents' private interest in this type of acutely sensitive case is "of the highest order." We also recognize the vital importance of curbing overzealous suspicion and intervention on the part of health care professionals and government officials, particularly where such overzealousness may have the effect of discouraging parents or caretakers from communicating with doctors or seeking appropriate medical attention for children with real or potentially life-threatening conditions. The consequences of such a chilling effect could be devastating. Our holding today is therefore limited to the facts of this case. Where a treating physician has clearly expressed his or her reasonable suspicion that life-threatening abuse is occurring in the home, the interest of the child (as shared by the state as parens patriae) in being removed from that home setting to a safe and neutral environment outweighs the parents' private interest in familial integrity as a matter of law. (pp. 1371-1373)

Appendix A

American Professional Society on the Abuse of Children, Practice Guidelines, Use of Anatomical Dolls in Child Sexual Abuse Assessments

❏ I. Uses and Limitations of Guidelines

These Guidelines have been developed to reflect current knowledge and generally accepted practice concerning the use of anatomical dolls in interviewing children during assessments of suspected child sexual abuse. The Guidelines are offered to encourage appropriate use of anatomical dolls and to provide direction in the development of training for professionals. The Guidelines are not intended to establish a legal standard of care or a rigid standard of practice to which professionals are expected to adhere. Interviewers must have the flexibility to exercise judgment in individual cases. Laws and local customs may influence accepted methods in a given community. Professionals should be knowledgeable about various constraints on practice and prepared to justify their decisions about particular practices in specific cases. As experience and scientific knowledge expand, further revision of these Guidelines is expected.

These Guidelines apply to the use of anatomical dolls in investigative and diagnostic interviews of children in cases of alleged or suspected child sexual abuse. Such interviews are designed to determine whether an allegation is likely true, and if so, the nature of the abuse. Investigative interviews are typically conducted by child protective services and law enforcement professionals and by child interview specialists in specialized child abuse programs. Diagnostic interviews are typically conducted by mental health or health care professionals as a part of psychological or medical evaluations (American Medical Association, 1985). Diagnostic interviews often go beyond the focus of investigative interviews in also assessing the child's psychological status and the possible need for psychological treatment.

These Guidelines are not designed to address the use of anatomical dolls in psychotherapy. Furthermore, these Guidelines do not address the broad issue of questioning techniques during investigative or diagnostic interviews. These Guidelines have the narrower purpose of providing direction on the use of dolls as an adjunct to the questioning process. It is also not the purpose of these Guidelines to provide a comprehensive discussion of the clinical and empirical rationale for the use of anatomical dolls in child sexual abuse assessments.

❏ II. Introduction

Anatomical dolls are widely used as interview aids by professionals involved in the investigation and evaluation of child sexual abuse (Boat & Everson, 1988a; Conte, Sorenson, Fogarty, & Dalla Rosa, 1991; Kendall-Tackett & Watson, 1992). Nevertheless, concern has been expressed about possible harm through the use of anatomical dolls in this context. One concern is that anatomical dolls may suggest sexual material, encouraging false reports from non-abused children. Another is that the dolls may be overstimulating or even traumatizing to non-abused children. Another is that the dolls may be overstimulating or even traumatizing to non-abused children by introducing them prematurely to sexual ideas and body parts. A final concern is that interviewers using the dolls may be poorly trained and overzealous in their search for sexual abuse, eliciting unreliable, if not erroneous, evidence of abuse.

Research does not support the concern that anatomical dolls are inherently too suggestive or sexually stimulating (Everson & Boat, 1994). Followup interviews of parents whose young children had previously been exposed to anatomical dolls do not support the concern that the dolls are traumatizing to non-abused children or may induce them to become preoccupied with sexual issues (Boat, Everson, & Holland, 1990; Bruck, Ceci,

Francoeur, & Renick, 1995; Dawson, Vaughn, & Wagner, 1992). Research suggests that the level of training among interviewers using the dolls has increased substantially over the last several years (Boat & Everson, 1988a; Kendall-Tackett & Watson, 1992). The actual skill level of interviewers, however, has only recently become the focus of systematic study and empirical findings on this topic are still limited (Boat & Everson, 1995).

When used by a knowledgeable and experienced professional, anatomical dolls can be an effective tool to aid in interviewing children to determine (1) whether an allegation of sexual abuse is likely true, and (2) if so, the nature of the abuse. Anatomical dolls are, however, only one of many useful interview tools (e.g., drawing materials, puppets, anatomical drawings) and cannot take the place of sound, child-sensitive interview skills and reasoned clinical judgment. Professionals should be able to describe how the dolls were used in the particular case and how this use conforms to accepted practice (Myers & White, 1989). Professionals should also be familiar with current research on the dolls.

❑ III. Summary of Research Findings

A. Suggestibility

1. The majority of available research does not support the position that the dolls are inherently too suggestive and overly stimulating to be useful in sexual abuse investigations and evaluations (see review by Dickson & Boat, 1991; Dickson & Boat, 1990). Specifically, there is little empirical evidence that exposure to the dolls induces non abused, sexually naive children to have sexual fantasies and to engage in sex play that is likely to be misinterpreted as evidence of sexual abuse.

2. Although analogue studies of children's memory and suggestibility find children four and younger more suggestible than older ones (see review by Ceci & Bruck, 1993), anatomical dolls have not generally been found to be a significant source of increased suggestibility and recall error. Three studies using anatomical dolls as interview aids with children in the 3- to 7-year old range have found that the dolls increased recall accuracy with little or no increase in false reports of genital touching (Katz, Schonfeld, Carter, Leventhal, & Cicchetti, 1995; Saywitz, Goodman, Nicholas, & Moan, 1991; Steward & Steward, in press). In contrast, one study reported high rates of false assertions and false denials of genital touching among children under age 3-1/2 years when the dolls were used as interview aids in conjunction with direct, leading and misleading questions (Bruck et al., 1995).

B. Interpreting Behavior With Dolls

Young children suspected or known to be sexually abused are statistically more likely than presumably non-abused children to engage in explicit sexualized interactions with dolls. However, many victims of sexual abuse do not display such behavior, and some non-abused children may display such behavior (White, Strom, Santilli, & Halpin, 1986; Jampole & Weber, 1987; August & Forman, 1989). Following are empirical findings that provide some guidance for interpreting sexual behavior with the dolls:

1. Explicit sexual positioning of dolls (e.g., penile insertion in vaginal, oral, and anal openings) is uncommon among non-referred, presumably non-abused young children (see review by Everson & Boat, 1990). When allowed to manipulate the dolls, especially in the absence of adults, a small percentage of presumably non-abused children demonstrate explicit sexual intercourse between dolls or, more rarely, attempt to enact apparent sexual acts between themselves and a doll. Such behavior with the dolls appears to be related to prior sexual exposure (Glaser & Collins, 1989; Everson & Boat, 1990) and to age, gender, socioeconomic status, and possibly race, with four- and five-year-old boys from lower socioeconomic status families somewhat more likely to enact explicit sexual acts with dolls than younger children, girls, or children from higher socioeconomic status families (Boat & Everson, 1994; Everson & Boat, 1990). Therefore, while explicit demonstrations of sexual intercourse with anatomical dolls always deserve further exploration, such activities among younger children and children without known prior sexual exposure are of particular concern.

2. Among non-referred, presumably non-abused children, mouthing or sucking a dolls' penis is very rare prior to about age four and infrequent after age four (Sivan, Schor, Koeppl, & Noble, 1988; Glaser & Collins, 1989; Everson & Boat, 1990). This finding suggests that penises on dolls do not encourage most young children to seek oral gratification by sucking them. Sucking a doll's penis therefore should raise serious concerns about possible prior sexual exposure.

3. When a young child's positioning of the dolls indicates detailed knowledge of the mechanics of sexual acts, the probability of sexual abuse is increased, and further investigation of the source of the child's sexual knowledge is warranted. This is especially true for children under approximately four years of age and for children displaying knowledge of oral and anal intercourse (Everson & Boat, 1990).

4. Manual exploration of a doll's genitalia, including inserting a finger into a doll's vaginal or anal openings, is fairly common behavior among young, presumably non-abused children (Boat & Everson,

1994; Glaser & Collins, 1989). Such behavior is likely to be more concerning if it is accompanied by distress reactions (e.g., anxiety, fear), behavioral regression, or displays of anger and aggression (Gordon, Schroeder, & Abrams, 1990a, 1990b), or by obsessive repetition (Terr, 1981).

C. The Efficacy of Anatomical Dolls

1. When compared to reliance solely on verbal communication, the use of anatomical dolls has been shown to enhance children's ability to recall and describe events (Katz et al., 1995; Leventhal, Hamilton, Rekedal, Tebano-Micci, & Eyster, 1989; Saywitz et al., 1991; Steward & Steward, 1995). However, the dolls may not necessarily be superior to other interview aids such as anatomical drawings or regular dolls (Britton & O'Keefe, 1991; Goodman & Aman, 1990; Steward & Steward, in press). Additional research is needed, especially examining the various functions anatomical dolls can serve in the assessment process among children of different developmental levels.

❏ IV. Appropriate Uses

A. No predetermined amount of time must expire before dolls are introduced, nor must a predetermined number or type of questions be asked before using dolls. Every child is unique and interviewers should use their judgement to determine when, and if, dolls may be useful.

B. If possible, the interviewer should be aware of the extent and nature of the child's possible prior exposure to anatomical dolls. This information is important for assessing the likely usefulness of the dolls in the current interview and for better understanding the child's reaction to and behavior with the dolls. Such information is especially important in cases in which children may have had multiple, prior doll interviews or may have been exposed to the dolls in a play therapy format in which fantasy play was encouraged.

C. The number of dolls presented (e.g., individual dolls vs. set of two, three, or four) depends upon their specific use in the interview.

D. When sexual abuse is suspected, dolls can be used as part of the assessment process in the following ways (Everson & Boat, 1994):

1. Anatomical Model: The dolls can function as anatomical models for assessing a child's labels for parts of the body, understanding of bodily functions, and possible precocious knowledge of the mechanics of

sexual acts. The interviewer may point to sexual and non-sexual body parts and ask questions like, "What do you call this part?," "What is it for?," and, "Is it for anything else?"

The dolls can also serve as visual aids for direct inquiries about the child's personal experiences with private parts. This may include questions such as, "Do you have one (vagina)?," "Has anything ever happened to yours?," and "Has it ever been hurt?"

If the child uses a non-standard term, such as "kitty cat," to refer to a body part, the dolls can be used to clarify the child's meaning. It is appropriate to use the child's terms for body parts.

2. Demonstration Aid: The dolls can serve as props to enable children to "show" rather than "tell" what happened, especially when limited verbal skills or emotional issues, such as fear of telling or embarrassment about discussing sexual activities, interfere with direct verbal description. This function of the dolls also includes their use to clarify a child's statement after a disclosure of abuse has been made. Whether or not a child experiences difficulty communicating about sexual abuse, dolls are sometimes useful to confirm an interviewer's understanding of a child's description of abuse and to reduce the likelihood of miscommunication between the child and the interviewer.

Interviewers should be cautious in using anatomical dolls as demonstration aids with children under approximately age $3\frac{1}{2}$ years. This caution is based on questions about the cognitive ability of young preschoolers to use dolls to represent themselves in behavioral reenactments (DeLoache, 1995) and on concerns about the potential of the dolls to distract very young children (e.g., Goodman & Aman, 1990). These concerns do not preclude other uses of the dolls with young children. Furthermore, young children may use an anatomical doll to represent someone other than themselves and may, for example, demonstrate with a doll on their own bodies what they experienced.

3. Memory Stimulus: Exposure to the dolls, and especially to such features as secondary sexual characteristics, genitalia, and articles of clothing, may be useful in stimulating or triggering a child's recall of specific events of a sexual nature. Supporting this use is research suggesting that props and concrete cues may be more effective in prompting memories in young children than are verbal cues or questions (e.g., Nelson & Ross, 1980). To encourage recall, it may be appropriate for the interviewer to ask questions such as, "Have you seen one

(penis)?," or "Do the dolls help you remember anything else that happened?"

4. Screening Tool: This function, which sometimes overlaps with the Memory Stimulus use, is based on the premise that exposure to the dolls in a non-threatening setting may provide an opportunity for the child to spontaneously reveal his/her sexual interests, concerns, or knowledge. Typically, the child is given the opportunity freely to examine and manipulate the dolls while the interviewer observes the child's play, reaction, and remarks. The interviewer can be either present or absent (observing through a one-way mirror) during this time, although children are likely to be less inhibited in their manipulations of the dolls without an adult present. After a period of uninterrupted manipulation and exploration of the dolls without an adult present, the interviewer asks follow-up questions about the child's behavior with, or reaction to, the dolls (e.g., behavior, unusual emotional responses, as well as spontaneous "suspicious" statements made by the child [e.g., "Daddy's pee-pee gets big sometimes"] should be the focus of follow-up questions to the child).

5. Icebreaker: The dolls can serve as a conversation starter on the topic of sexuality by focusing the child's attention in a non-threatening, non-leading manner on sexual issues and sexual body parts. This may be especially important in the case of younger children and children with less well developed language skills who may require very direct cuing to understand what, from the universe of possibilities, the interviewer wants the child to talk about (Steward & Steward, in press). Dolls can also be useful in helping a child feel comfortable about talking about body parts, sexuality, etc., and in conveying tacit permission for the child to describe or demonstrate sexual knowledge and experience.

Sexually abused children are not always able to give a coherent verbal account of sexual abuse for a variety of reasons, including developmental level, language limitations, fear, embarrassment, and guilt. When a child's characteristics allow it, however, interviewers should generally attempt to obtain a verbal description from the child before asking the child to demonstrate with the dolls.

E. Generally accepted practice is to present the dolls clothed, but exceptions exist. For example, it may be appropriate to present the dolls unclothed when they are being used as a demonstration aid with a child who has already indicated that the individuals in his/her account were naked.

F. Depending upon individual child characteristics, anatomical dolls can be appropriately used in interviews with children from a wide age range, including with some adolescents. Some uses, however, such as screening tool and icebreaker, are less common among older children (Boat & Everson, 1995; Kendall-Tackett & Watson, 1992).

❏ V. Inappropriate Uses

A. The use of anatomical dolls as a diagnostic test for child sexual abuse is not supported by the empirical evidence (Everson & Boat, 1994). Specifically, it is not appropriate to draw definitive conclusions about the likelihood of abuse based solely upon interpretations of a child's behavior with the dolls. There is no known behavior with the dolls that can be considered a definitive marker of sexual abuse in the absence of other factors, such as the child's verbal account or medical evidence (Everson & Boat, 1990; Realmuto, Jensen, & Wescoe, 1990; Boat & Everson, 1994).

B. Interviewers should refrain from making statements that might encourage the child to view the dolls as toys or objects for fantasy play. This includes the use of words such as "play," "pretend," or "make believe." Interviewers should also be cautious in the use of conjecture in questioning with dolls because of the possibility of encouraging fantasy (e.g., "If someone were to touch a girl in a way she didn't like, show me how they would do it."). The interviewer should consider giving the child the clear admonition that the dolls are used to help talk about and show "things that really happened."

C. The practice of the interviewer placing the dolls in sexually explicit positions and asking the child to relate the depiction to the child's experience (e.g., "Did this ever happen to you?") is leading and should be avoided.

D. Like any interview tool or technique, anatomical dolls can be misused. For example, dolls can be used in conjunction with inappropriately suggestive questions. Interviewers should monitor themselves to avoid improperly suggestive use of dolls (White & Quinn, 1988; Quinn, White, & Santilli, 1989).

❏ VI. Doll Specifications

A. The utility of dolls in the interview process depends in large measure on the presence of certain physical features of the dolls. The following are considered to be important features:

1. Genitalia and breasts that are proportional to body size and appropriate to the gender and age of the given doll.
2. Oral, vaginal, and anal openings that will accommodate the adult male doll's penis.

3. Facial expressions that are at least reasonably attractive and devoid of negative emotions, such as fear or anxiety.

4. A size that can reasonably be manipulated by young children.

5. Sturdy construction that can withstand rough handling.

6. Clothes that can be easily removed.

7. Clothes, including underwear, that are appropriate to the doll's represented age and gender.

B. The impact of the racial features and skin color of the dolls on the child's response has not been empirically examined. Preferred practice is to match the dolls with the race of the child. If it is likely that the alleged perpetrator is a different race from the child, the interviewer should consider presenting dolls of both races or a set of race non-specific dolls with neutral skin tones.

❑ VII. Training and Skill Level of Interviewers

A. Professionals using dolls should possess the training and/or knowledge and experience required to conduct forensic investigative or diagnostic interviews with children suspected of having been sexually abused. Refer to the APSAC Guidelines for Psychosocial Evaluation of Suspected Sexual Abuse in Young Children for general requirements regarding training, skill level, and supervision for interviewers.

B. Before using the dolls, the interviewer should acquire the requisite skills through familiarity with the research literature and applicable guidelines, consultation with colleagues, and/or clinical supervision. The interviewer should be familiar with developmental issues in the use of the dolls, appropriate and inappropriate uses of the dolls, and potential problems caused by using leading questions or other suggestive techniques with the dolls.

C. A formal, structured protocol detailing the use of dolls in interviews is not required and, given the state of our knowledge and the need for flexibility in individual cases, rigid protocols are probably not advisable. However, these guidelines and other general guidelines on the use of anatomical dolls in sexual abuse evaluations are available and may be helpful (e.g., Boat & Everson, 1986, 1988b; Levy, Kalinowski, Markovic, Pittman, & Ahart, 1991; Morgan, 1995; White, 1991).

❑ VIII. Documentation

A. Detailed documentation of the interview process should be provided. Because of the potential subtlety and richness of the child's behavior with anatomical dolls, videotape recording of the interview may offer advantages. If videotaping is impracticable or contraindicated, the interviewer's questions and the child's verbal, non-verbal, and affective responses regarding sexual abuse allegations or concerns should be documented. This can be done in writing or using a combination of audiotape and written notes.

B. It is desirable to prepare a verbatim record of all portions of the interview specifically relating to the issue of possible sexual abuse. This includes a description of the child's behavior with dolls, including the child's positioning of the dolls, critical verbal statements, and any verbal, non-verbal, or affective behavior with the dolls, such as avoidance, anxiety, fear, anger, or regression.

❑ IX. Conclusions

A. Anatomical dolls are a useful and accepted tool for investigative and diagnostic interviews of children in cases of possible abuse.

B. Professionals using anatomical dolls in child sexual abuse assessments should be knowledgeable and experienced in conducting forensically sound interviews with children and in the specific use of anatomical dolls.

C. Interviewers should be prepared to describe how they used anatomical dolls in each specific case and how this use conforms to accepted practice.

D. Interviewers should be aware of the limitations in the use of anatomical dolls. Specifically, anatomical dolls should not be considered to be a diagnostic test of sexual abuse, nor be over-emphasized in the assessment process to the exclusion of broader interview techniques.

❑ References

American Medical Association. (1985). AMA diagnostic and treatment guidelines concerning child abuse and neglect. *Journal of the American Medical Association, 254,* 796-803.

American Professional Society on the Abuse of Children. (1990). *Guidelines for psychosocial evaluation of suspected sexual abuse in young children.* Chicago: Author.

August, R. L., & Forman, B. D. (1989). A comparison of sexually and non-sexually abused children's behavioral responses to anatomically correct dolls. *Child Psychiatry and Human Development, 20,* 39-47.

Boat, B. W., & Everson, M. D. (1995, April). *Interview errors in the use of anatomical dolls in child protective services investigations.* Paper presented at the Biennial Conference of the Society for Research in Child Development.

Boat, B. W., & Everson, M. D. (1994). Anatomical doll exploration among non-referred children: Comparisons by age, gender, race, and socioeconomic status. *Child Abuse & Neglect, 18,* 139-153.

Boat, B. W., & Everson, M. D. (1988a). Use of anatomical dolls among professionals in sexual abuse evaluation. *Child Abuse & Neglect, 12,* 171-179.

Boat, B. W., & Everson, M. D. (1988b). Interviewing young children with anatomical dolls. *Child Welfare, 67,* 337-351.

Boat, B. W., & Everson, M. D. (1986). *Using anatomical dolls: Guidelines for interviewing young children in sexual abuse investigations.* Chapel Hill: University of North Carolina.

Britton, H., & O'Keefe, W. A. (1991). Use of anatomical dolls in the sexual abuse interview. *Child Abuse & Neglect, 15,* 567-573.

Bruck, M., Ceci, S., Francoeur, D., & Renick, A. (1995). Anatomical detailed dolls do not facilitate preschoolers' reports of a pediatric examination involving genital touching. *Journal of Experimental Psychology: Applied, 1,* 95-109.

Ceci, S. J., & Bruck, M. (1993). Suggestibility of the child witness: A historical review and synthesis. *Psychological Bulletin, 113,* 403-439.

Conte, J. R., Sorenson, E., Fogarty, L., & Dalla Rosa, J. (1991). Evaluating children's reports of sexual abuse: Results from a survey of professionals. *American Journal of Orthopsychiatry, 61,* 428-437.

DeLoache, J. (1995). The use of dolls in interviewing young children. In M. S. Zaragoza, J. R. Graham, G. H. Hall, R. Hirschman, & Y. S. Ben-Porath (Eds.), *Memory and testimony in the child witness.* Newbury Park, CA: Sage.

Everson, M. D., & Boat, B. W. (1990). Sexualized doll play among young children. Implications for the use of anatomical dolls in sexual abuse evaluations. *Journal of the American Academy of Child and Adolescent Psychiatry, 29,* 736-742.

Everson, M. D., & Boat, B. W. (1994). Putting the anatomical doll controversy in perspective: An examination of the major uses and criticisms of the dolls in child sexual abuse evaluations. *Child Abuse & Neglect, 18,* 113-129.

Glaser, D., & Collins, C. (1989). The response of young non-sexually abused children to anatomically correct dolls. *Journal of Child Psychology and Psychiatry, 30,* 547-560.

Goodman, G., & Aman, C. (1990). Children's use of anatomically correct dolls to report an event. *Child Development, 61,* 1859-1871.

Gordon, B. N., Schroeder, C., & Abrams, J. M. (1990a). Children's knowledge of sexuality: A comparison of sexually abused and nonabused children. *American Journal of Orthopsychiatry, 60,* 250-257.

Gordon, B. N., Schroeder, C., & Abrams, J. M. (1990b). Age and social class differences in children's knowledge of sexuality. *Journal of Clinical Child Physiology, 19,* 33-43.

Jampole, L., & Weber, M. K. (1987). An assessment of the behavior of sexually abused and non-sexually abused children with anatomically correct dolls. *Child Abuse & Neglect, 11,* 187-192.

Katz, S., Schonfeld, D. J., Carter, A. S., Leventhal, J. M., & Cicchetti, D. V. (1995). The accuracy of children's reports with anatomically correct dolls. *Developmental and Behavioral Pediatrics, 16*(2), 71-76.

Kendall-Tackett, K. A., & Watson, M. W. (1992). Use of anatomical dolls by Boston-area professionals. *Child Abuse & Neglect, 16,* 423-428.

Koocher, G. P., Goodman, G. S., White, S., Friedrich, W. N., Sivan, A. B., & Reynolds, C. R. (1995). Psychological science and the use of anatomically detailed dolls in child sexual abuse assessments: Final report of the American Psychological Association Anatomical Doll Task Force. *Psychological Bulletin, 118,* 2.

Leventhal, J. M., Hamilton, J., Rekedal, S., Tebano-Micci, A., & Eyster, C. (1989). Anatomically correct dolls used in interviews of young children suspected of having been sexually abused. *Pediatrics, 84,* 900-906.

Levy, J., Kalinowski, N., Markovic, J., Pittman, M., & Ahart, S. (1991). *Victim-sensitive interviewing in child sexual abuse.* Chicago: Mount Sinai Hospital Medical Center.

Morgan, M. (1995). *How to interview sexual abuse victims.* Newbury Park, CA: Sage.

Myers, J. E. B., & White, S. (1989). Dolls in court? *APSAC Advisor, 2*(3), 5-6.

Nelson, K., & Ross, G. (1980). The generalities and specifics of long-term memory in infants and young children. *New Directions for Child Development, 10,* 87-101.

Realmuto, G. M., Jensen, J. B., & Wescoe, S. (1990). Specificity and sensitivity of sexually anatomically correct dolls in substantiating abuse: A pilot study. *Journal of the American Academy of Child and Adolescent Psychiatry, 19,* 743-746.

Sivan, A., Schor, D., Koeppl, G. K., & Noble, L. D. (1988). Interactions of normal children with anatomically correct dolls. *Child Abuse & Neglect, 12,* 295-304.

Steward, M., & Steward, D. (In press). Interviewing young children about body touch and handling. *Monograph Series for the Society for Research in Child Development.*

Terr, L. (1981). Forbidden games: Post-traumatic child's play. *Journal of the American Academy of Child Psychiatry, 20,* 740-759.

White, S. (1991). Using anatomically detailed dolls in interviewing preschoolers. In C. Schaefer, K. Gitlund, & D. Sandgrund (Eds.), *Play diagnosis and assessment* (pp. 317-330). New York: John Wiley.

White, S., & Quinn, K. (1988). Investigatory independence in child sexual abuse evaluations: Conceptual considerations. *Bulletin of the American Academy of Psychiatry and Law, 16,* 269-278.

White, S., Strom, G., Santilli, G., & Halpin, B. (1986). Interviewing young children with anatomically correct dolls. *Child Abuse & Neglect, 19,* 519-529.

ADDITIONAL RESOURCES ON INTERVIEWING

American Professional Society on the Abuse of Children. (1990). *APSAC Advisor, 3*(2). (Special issue dedicated to child interviewing).

Faller, K. C. (1995). *APSAC study guide: Interviewing children suspected of having been sexually abused.* Newbury Park, CA: Sage.

Faller, K. C. (1990). *Understanding child sexual maltreatment.* Newbury Park, CA: Sage Publications.

Garbarino, J., & Stott, F. M. (1990). *What children can tell us.* San Francisco: Jossey-Bass.

Jones, D. P. H., & McQuiston, M. (1985). *Interviewing the sexually abused child.* Denver, CO: C. Henry Kempe National Center for the Prevention and Treatment of Child Abuse and Neglect.

MacFarlane, K., & Waterman, J. (1986). *Sexual abuse of young children*. New York: Guilford.

Myers, J. E. B. (1992). *Legal issues in child abuse and neglect practice*. Newbury Park, CA: Sage.

Perry, N. W., & Wrightsman, L. S. (1991). *The child witness*. Newbury Park, CA: Sage.

❏ Acknowledgments

These Guidelines are the product of APSAC's Task Force on the Use of Anatomical Dolls in Child Sexual Abuse Assessments chaired by Mark D. Everson, Ph.D., John E. B. Myers, J.D., and Sue White, Ph.D. The first draft was published for comment in *The APSAC Advisor* in Spring, 1993. In addition, four open Task Force meetings were held to request input on early drafts of the Guidelines: at the San Diego Conference on Responding to Child Maltreatment in January 1993; at the First National APSAC Colloquium in Chicago, June 1993; at the Second National APSAC Colloquium in Cambridge, Massachusetts, May 1994; and at the San Diego Conference on Responding to Child Maltreatment in January, 1995. The current version of the Guidelines reflects the experience and expertise of a large number of APSAC members as well as the APSAC Board of Directors. We gratefully acknowledge the many individuals who contributed their time and expertise to make these Guidelines possible and especially to Kathleen Coulborn Faller, Ph.D., A.C.S.W.

These Guidelines will be updated periodically. Any comments or suggestions should be directed to Mark E. Everson, Ph.D., through APSAC, 407 South Dearborn, Suite 1300, Chicago, IL 60605.

Appendix B

Sample Protective Order for Videotapes of
Investigative Interviews on Child Abuse

❏ **Protective Order**

(1) For purposes of this order, *tape(s)* means any videotape or audiotape of a child.

(2) Tapes may be viewed only by parties, their counsel and their counsel's employees, investigators, experts for the purpose of prosecuting or defending this action, and the child's guardian ad litem.

(3) No tape, or the substance of any portion thereof, shall be divulged by any person subject to this protective order to any other person, except as necessary for the trial or preparation for trial in this proceeding, and such information shall be used only for purposes of the trial and preparation for trial herein.

(4) No person shall be granted access to the tape, any transcription thereof, or the substance of any portion thereof unless that person has first signed an agreement in writing that the person has received and read a copy of this protective order, that the person submits to the Court's jurisdiction with

respect to the protective order, and that the person will be subject to the Court's contempt powers for any violation of the protective order.

(5) Each of the tape cassettes and transcripts thereof available to the parties, their attorneys and respective agents shall bear the following legend:

> THIS OBJECT OR DOCUMENT AND THE CONTENTS THEREOF IS SUBJECT TO A PROTECTIVE ORDER ENTERED BY THE COURT IN *STATE V.* _____. CASE NUMBER _____. THIS OBJECT OR DOCUMENT AND THE CONTENTS THEREOF MAY NOT BE EXAMINED, INSPECTED, READ, VIEWED, OR COPIED BY ANY PERSON, OR DISCLOSED TO ANY PERSON, EXCEPT AS PROVIDED IN THE PROTECTIVE ORDER. ANY PERSON VIOLATING SUCH PROTECTIVE ORDER IS SUBJECT TO THE FULL CONTEMPT POWER OF THE COURT AND MAY BE GUILTY OF A CRIME.

(6) Unless otherwise provided by order of this Court, no additional copies of the tape or any portion of the tape shall be made without prior court order.

(7) The tape shall not be given, loaned, sold, or shown to any person except as provided by this order or by subsequent order of this Court.

(8) Upon final disposition of this case any and all copies of the tape and any transcripts thereof shall be returned to the Court for safekeeping, except those tapes booked into and kept as evidence by the investigating law enforcement agencies. Those materials subject to this order so kept by any law enforcement agency shall remain subject to this order and those materials shall remain secured in evidence in accordance with the agency's policies and procedures.

(9) This protective order shall remain in full force and effect until further order of this Court.

Appendix C

American Professional Society on the Abuse of Children, Guidelines for Psychosocial Evaluation of Suspected Sexual Abuse in Young Children

STATEMENT OF PURPOSE

These Guidelines for mental health professionals reflect current knowledge and an emerging consensus about the psychosocial evaluation of suspected sexual abuse in children. They are not intended as a standard of practice to which practitioners are expected to adhere in all cases. Evaluators must have the flexibility to exercise clinical judgment in individual cases. Laws and local customs may also influence the accepted method in a given community. Practitioners must be prepared to justify their decisions about particular practices in specific cases. As experience and scientific knowledge expand, further refinement and revision of these Guidelines are expected.

These Guidelines are specific to psychosocial evaluations. Psychosocial evaluations are a systematic process of gathering information and forming professional opinions about the source and meaning of statements, behav-

354

ior, and other evidence that are the basis of concern about possible sexual abuse. The results of such evaluations may be used to direct treatment planning and to assist in legal decision making.

Psychosocial evaluators should first establish the purpose of the evaluation and their role in the evaluation process. Psychological evaluations may be conducted for purely clinical reasons or be forensic in nature. These Guidelines pertain to both situations.

Clinical evaluations may be requested by parents, guardians or other professionals to determine whether there is reason to be concerned about possible abuse. It is also customary for clinicians to precede treatment for the effects of sexual abuse with an assessment of the sexual abuse history.

Forensic evaluations have the explicit purpose of contributing to legal decision making or legal proceedings. Such evaluations may be requested by parents or guardians, public child protective services (CPS) agencies, attorneys, guardians ad litem (or court appointed special advocates), or other professionals. The results may be used in civil or criminal proceedings. As noted in these Guidelines, forensic evaluations are different from clinical evaluations in generally requiring a different professional stance and additional components.

In all cases, evaluators should be aware that any interview with a child regarding possible sexual abuse may be subject to scrutiny and have significant implications for legal decision making and the child's safety and well-being.

❏ Guidelines

I. THE EVALUATOR

A. Characteristics

1. The evaluator should possess a graduate level mental health degree in a recognized discipline (e.g., psychiatry, psychology, social work, nursing, child development) or be supervised by a professional with a graduate level degree.

2. The evaluator should have professional experience assessing and treating children and families, and professional experience with sexually abused children. A minimum of two years of professional experience with sexually abused children is expected; three to five years is preferred for forensic evaluators. If the evaluator does not possess such experience, supervision is essential.

3. The evaluator must have had specialized training in child development and child sexual abuse. This training should be documented in terms of formal course work, supervision, or attendance at conferences, seminars, and workshops.

4. The evaluator should be knowledgeable about the dynamics and the emotional and behavioral consequences of sexual abuse experiences. The evaluator should be familiar with the professional literature and with current issues relevant to understanding and evaluating sexual abuse experiences.

5. The evaluator should be familiar with different cultural values and practices that may affect definitions of sexual abuse, child and/or family comfort with the evaluation process, child and/or family willingness to provide complete and accurate information, and the evaluator's own interpretation of responses.

6. If the purpose of the evaluation is forensic, the evaluator should have experience in conducting forensic evaluations and providing expert testimony. If the evaluator does not possess such experience, supervision is essential.

7. The evaluator should approach the evaluation with an open mind to all possible responses from the child and all possible explanations for the concern about sexual abuse. The evaluator should recognize that all sources of information have limitations and may contain inaccuracies. In forming an opinion, the evaluator should consider plausible alternative hypotheses.

❑ II. Components of the Evaluation

A. PROTOCOL

1. A written protocol is not necessary; however, evaluations should ordinarily involve reviewing those materials considered relevant for the type of evaluation; conducting collateral interviews when necessary; establishing rapport; assessing the child's developmental status, cognitive capacity, level of functioning and level of distress; and specifically evaluating the possibility of abuse. The evaluator may use discretion in the order and method of assessment. Forensic evaluations differ from evaluations conducted for purely clinical reasons in that they generally involve reviewing relevant materials and conducting collateral interviews.

2. If information is available prior to the evaluation that meets the respective state's definition of reasonable suspicion for a CPS report, but no CPS report has yet been made, the evaluator should make the report and may choose to defer the evaluation until the CPS investigation has been conducted.

3. When possible, unsupervised contact between the child and the suspected offender should be strongly discouraged during the evaluation process.

B. EMPLOYER OF THE EVALUATOR

1. Evaluation of the child may be conducted at the request of a legal guardian prior to court involvement. When only one parent has requested the evaluation, evaluators should give careful consideration to informing the other parent about the evaluation whether or not that parent is the focus of concern. When the other parent is the focus of concern, that parent is likely to request another evaluation; evaluators should consider whether it would be in the child's best interest to have a mutually agreed upon or court appointed evaluator to avoid unnecessary evaluations.

2. If the evaluation is specifically requested or intended for use in a legal proceeding or a court is already involved, the preferred practice is a court-appointed or mutually agreed upon evaluator of the child. In some circumstances exceptions to this practice are acceptable or are customary practice (e.g., contractual arrangements with child protective services, civil damage suits, when one party refuses to cooperate).

3. Discretion should be used in agreeing to conduct an evaluation of a child when the child has already been evaluated. Additional evaluations should be conducted only if they clearly further the best interests of the child. When a second opinion is required, a review of the records may eliminate the need for re-interviewing the child.

C. NUMBER OF EVALUATORS

1. The evaluation may be conducted by a single evaluator or by a team of professionals.

D. COLLATERAL INFORMATION GATHERED
AS PART OF THE EVALUATION

1. Evaluators may seek and review background materials or conduct interviews as part of the evaluation process. The amount and nature of information reviewed depends on the purpose of the evaluation and the extent to which such information will be helpful in addressing the referral question and understanding the child's presenting problems or concerns. For clinical evaluations, clinical judgment should determine the necessity for additional records, materials, or interviews. Evaluators should request that background material be made available and collateral interviews be permitted for forensic evaluations.

2. The evaluation report should reflect an objective review of collateral information relied upon in the evaluation or opinion forming process.

E. INTERVIEWING THE ACCUSED OR SUSPECTED INDIVIDUAL

1. It is not necessary to interview the accused or suspected individual in order to form an opinion about possible sexual abuse of the child.

2. An interview with or review of the statements from a suspected or accused individual may provide additional relevant information (e.g., alternative explanations, admissions, insight into relationship between child and accused individual).

3. If the accused or suspected individual is a parent who seeks to participate in the evaluation and there are no contraindications (e.g., criminal investigation or charges pending, civil suit), interviewing of the accused or suspected parent should be given strong consideration.

F. RELEASING INFORMATION

1. Suspected abuse should always be reported to authorities as dictated by state law. Except as specified by law, clinical evaluators have no affirmative duty to disclose confidential clinical information.

2. Permission should be obtained from legal guardian(s) to request collateral materials and for release of information about the evaluation to relevant medical or mental health professionals, other professionals (e.g., schoolteachers), and involved legal systems (e.g., CPS, law enforcement, lawyers, courts). Discretion should be used in releasing sensitive individual and family history that does not directly relate to the purpose of the assessment.

3. Feedback about the results of the evaluation should usually be offered to parent(s) or legal guardian(s) and may be offered to the child, except where doing so would not be in the best interests of the child.

❏ III. Interviewing

A. RECORDING OF INTERVIEWS

1. Written documentation is the minimum requirement. Verbatim quotation of significant questions and answers is desirable. Forensic evaluations

should contain specific documentation of questions and responses (verbal and nonverbal) regarding possible sexual abuse.

2. Audio or video recording may be preferred practice in some communities. Professional preference, logistics, or clinical considerations may contraindicate recording of interviews. Professional discretion is permitted in recording policies and practices.

3. When audio and video recording are used, the child and legal guardian should be informed. It is desirable to obtain assent from the child (when age appropriate) and consent from legal guardian(s).

B. OBSERVATION OF THE INTERVIEW

1. Professional discretion is permitted in observation policies and practices. Observation of interviews by involved professionals (CPS, law enforcement, etc.) may be indicated if it reduces the need for additional interviews and will not compromise the evaluation process.

2. Observation by non-accused and non-suspected primary caregiver(s) may be indicated for particular clinical reasons; however, great care should be taken that the observation is clinically appropriate, does not unduly distress the child, and does not affect the validity of the evaluation process.

3. If interviews are observed, the child must be informed. It is desirable to obtain assent from the child (when age appropriate) and consent from legal guardian(s).

C. NUMBER OF INTERVIEWS

1. The evaluator determines the number of interviews necessary to address the referral question and assess the child's presenting problems or concerns. This does not imply that all sessions must include specific questioning about possible sexual abuse. The evaluator may decide, based on the individual case circumstances, to adopt a less direct approach and reserve questioning about possible sexual abuse for subsequent interviews. Repeated direct questioning of the child regarding sexual abuse when the child is not reporting or is denying abuse is usually contraindicated.

2. If the child does not report abuse and further direct questioning is judged to be counterproductive, but the evaluator has continuing concerns about the possibility of abuse, the child may be referred for an extended evaluation or therapy that is less directive, but diagnostically focused. Recommendations regarding conditions necessary to insure the child's protection from possible abuse should be made.

D. FORMAT OF INTERVIEW

1. When possible, interviewing the primary caregiver and reviewing other collateral data first to gather background information may facilitate the evaluation process.

2. The child should be seen individually, except when the child refuses to separate from a parent/guardian. Discussion of possible abuse with the child in the presence of the caregiver during evaluation interviews should be avoided except when necessary to elicit information from the child. In such cases, the interview setting should be structured to reduce the possibility of improper influence by the caregiver on the child's behavior or statements.

3. In some cases, joint sessions with the child and the non-accused caregiver or accused or suspected individual might be helpful to obtain information regarding the overall quality of the relationships. Such joint sessions should not be conducted for the purpose of determining whether abuse occurred based on the child's reactions to the participating adult. Joint sessions should not be conducted if they will cause significant distress for the child.

4. Joint sessions with a child and an accused or suspected individual should only be considered when the individual is a parent or primary caregiver. In making a decision about conducting a joint session with a child and the accused or suspected parent, the evaluator should carefully weigh the possibility of gaining valuable information against the significant potential for negative consequences for an abused child and for the evaluation process. A child should never be asked to discuss the possible abuse in front of an accused or suspected parent.

❏ IV. Child Interview

A. GENERAL PRINCIPLES

1. The evaluator should create an atmosphere that enables the child to talk freely, including providing physical surroundings and a climate that facilitates the child's comfort and communication.

2. The evaluator should convey to all parties that no assumptions have been made about whether abuse has occurred.

3. Language and interviewing approach should be developmentally and culturally appropriate.

4. The evaluator should take the time necessary to perform a complete evaluation and should avoid any coercive quality to the interview.

5. Interview procedures may be modified in cases involving very young, minimally verbal children or children with special problems (e.g., developmentally delayed, electively mute, non-native speakers).

6. The difference between the evaluation phase and a treatment phase should be articulated. Under certain circumstances (e.g., disputed custody cases), it may be preferable to obtain agreement from the parties before proceeding with treatment following evaluation.

B. QUESTIONING

1. It may be helpful to preface questioning with specific statements designed to reduce misunderstandings during the interview(s), and promote accuracy and completeness.

2. It may be helpful to begin the interview with open-ended questions about neutral topics (e.g., family, school, recent event) so that the child has an opportunity to practice providing free recall responses.

3. Initial substantive questioning should be open-ended and as non-directive as possible to elicit free recall responses. More focused or specific questioning should follow. Once information is provided in response to a specific question, open-ended prompts should again be used.

4. The child should be questioned directly about possible sexual abuse at some point in the evaluation if less directive approaches have not yielded adequate information to answer the referral question.

5. The evaluator may use the form of questions deemed necessary and justified to elicit information on which to base an opinion. Highly specific questioning should only be used when other methods of questioning have failed, when previous information warrants substantial concern, or when the child's developmental level precludes more non directive approaches However, responses to these questions should be carefully evaluated and weighed accordingly. Coercive or intimidating questioning is never justified.

C. USE OF DOLLS AND OTHER DEVICES

1. A variety of non-verbal tools may be used to assist young children in communication, including drawings, toys, dollhouses, dolls, puppets, etc. Since such materials have the potential to be distracting or misleading they should be used with care. They are discretionary for older children.

2. Anatomical dolls are accepted interview aids. Evaluators using anatomical dolls should be knowledgeable about the functions they may serve and should conform to accepted practice. (Refer to the APSAC Guidelines on the Use of Anatomical Dolls in Child Sexual Abuse Assessments.)

3. Anatomical dolls should not be used as a diagnostic test for sexual abuse. Definitive conclusions about a history of sexual abuse should not be based solely on interpretation of behavior with the dolls. Unusual behavior with the dolls may suggest further lines of inquiry that should be pursued. The unusual behavior and the responses to further questioning should be noted in the evaluation report.

4. Story books, coloring books or videos that contain explicit descriptions of abuse situations are potentially suggestive and are primarily teaching tools. They are typically not appropriate for evaluation purposes.

D. PSYCHOLOGICAL TESTING

1. Formal psychological testing of the child is not necessary for the purpose of proving or disproving a history of sexual abuse.

2. Psychological testing may be useful when the clinician has questions about the child's intellectual or developmental level. Psychological tests can also provide helpful information regarding a child's emotional status and general functioning.

3. Psychological testing of parents is not a routine component of child evaluations. An evaluation that includes assessment of parents may involve psychological tests.

❏ V. Conclusions/Report

A. GENERAL PRINCIPLES

1. The evaluation report should document the sources of information and/or data relied on in forming an opinion and making recommendations.

2. The evaluator may state an opinion that abuse did or did not occur, an opinion about the likelihood of the occurrence of abuse or simply provide a description and analysis of the gathered information.

3. Opinions should include supporting information (e.g., the child, parent(s)/guardian(s) and/or the accused individual's statements, behavior, psychological symptoms). Possible alternative explanations should have been considered. The evaluator should not suggest that mental health professionals have any special ability to detect whether an individual is telling the truth.

4. The evaluation may be inconclusive. If so, the evaluator should cite the information that causes continuing concern but does not enable confirmation or disconfirmation of abuse. If inconclusiveness is due to such problems

as missing information or an untimely or poorly-conducted investigation, these obstacles should be clearly noted in the report.

5. Recommendations should be made regarding therapeutic or environmental interventions to address the child's emotional and behavioral functioning and to ensure the child's safety.

❑ Acknowledgments

These Guidelines are the product of APSAC's Task Force on the Psychosocial Evaluation of Suspected Sexual Abuse in Children, chaired by Lucy Berliner, MSW. The initial version was the result of a lengthy, iterative process. These revisions are the result of a similar process conducted in 1996.

Appreciation goes to the many APSAC members who contributed their time and expertise to produce these Guidelines.

The Guidelines will be updated periodically. Any comments or suggestions about them should be directed to Lucy Berliner through APSAC, 332 South Michigan Avenue, Suite 1600, Chicago, Illinois, 60604.

Appendix D

ABCs of Coping with Cross-Examination

Adversary System

Understand the adversary system so you know what makes lawyers tick.

Be Calm

Be calm; breathe. Don't let the cross-examiner throw you off. If the attorney blusters and intimidates, lower your voice, speak calmly. Resist or restate unfair or ambiguous questions.

Control

Control is the name of the game. The cross-examiner seeks to **control** you. To avoid undue control:

- **Admit-Deny.** Brodsky describes the admit-deny technique. The cross-examiner focuses on what you could have done differently. E.g., "You could have done additional testing, couldn't you?" Go ahead and acknowledge whatever it is fair to acknowledge. However, stand by your testimony and deny you did anything wrong. E.g. "Although additional testing was possible, further testing was unnecessary in this case because . . ." (Brodsky, S.L. 1991. *Testifying in court: Guidelines for the expert witness*. Washington, D.C.: American Psychological Association).

- **Leading questions.** The cross-examiner controls you with leading questions that require short answers, preferably "yes" or "no." When "yes" or "no" is not the correct answer, try "Maybe" or "That depends" or "I can't answer that with a simple yes or no, may I explain myself?"

- **Communicate with confidence,** but don't be a know-it-all.

- **Don't retreat.** Do not change your opinion on cross-examination.

- **Level the linguistic playing field.** The cross-examiner refers to you by name. If you refer to the attorney as "Sir" or "Ma'am," your deference gives a measure of control to the attorney. Why not refer to the attorney by name? Doing so puts you on a linguistic par with the attorney.

Don't Get Defensive

Getting defensive undermines your credibility. Acknowledge your limits, and confidently reaffirm your expertise and testimony. When you are attacked, borrow from the martial arts; Redirect the attacker's energy to your advantage. E.g., the cross-examiner asks, "Don't you think your assessment would have been more complete if you had contacted additional people?" Your answer, "There are additional people I could have contacted. In this case, however, I contacted everyone necessary for a complete and thorough assessment."

Eye Contact

Look 'em in the eye. Maintain frequent--although not continuous--eye contact with the jury. The cross-examiner may try to divert your gaze away from the jury.

Fishing Expeditions

A cross-examiner who has little to work with may go on a fishing expedition; seeking a chink in your armor. The cross-examiner asks general questions to reveal weaknesses or lack of knowledge. Don't get hooked.

Goofs and Gaffes

When you make a mistake, correct it quickly during cross-examination, or let is slide, or fix it during redirect examination.

Holes in Your Testimony

One of the most effective cross-examination techniques is to poke a few little holes in your testimony--to raise a few doubts about you--and to leave those holes unfilled and those doubts unexplained until closing argument.

I don't know

"I don't know" is sometimes the correct answer. Remember, though, that a string of "I don't knows" looks bad.

Junk Science

The cross-examiner who can't think of anything better to do may attack the entire field as junk science. Acknowledge the limits of our knowledge, but confidently reassert what we do know.

Keep it Simple

Avoid jargon that will confuse the jury.

Learned Treatises

Don't let the lawyer take things out of context; insist on reading it: "I cannot comment on one sentence in a 20 page article. If you will give me an hour to read the entire article, I'll be happy to discuss it."

References

AACAP, American Academy of Child and Adolescent Psychology. (1997). Practice parameters for the forensic evaluation of children and adolescents who may have been physically or sexually abused. *Journal of the American Academy of Child and Adolescent Psychiatry, 36,* 423-442.

Abel, G. G., & Blanchard, E. B. (1976). The measurement and generation of sexual arousal in male sexual deviants. In M. Hersen, R. M. Eisler, & P. M. Miller (Eds.), *Progress in behavior modification* (Vol. 2). New York: Academic Press.

Abel, G., Mittleman, M., & Becker, J. (1985). Sexual offenders: Results of assessment and recommendations for treatment. In M. R. Ben-Aron, S. J. Hukle, & C. D. Webster (Eds.), *Clinical criminology: The assessment and treatment of criminal behavior* (pp. 191-205). Toronto. M. & M. Graphics.

Achterhof v. Selvaggio, 886 F.2d 826 (6th Cir. 1989).

Adams, J. A., & Wells, R. (1993). Normal versus abnormal genital findings in children: How well do examiners agree? *Child Abuse & Neglect, 17,* 663-675.

Adams v. Peck, 403 A.2d 840 (Md. Ct. App. 1979).

Adoption Assistance and Child Welfare Act of 1980, 42 U.S.C. §§ 620-628, 670-679a.

Adoption and Safe Families Act of 1997, Pub. L. No. 105-153.

Althaus v. Cohen, 1998 WL169490 (Pa. Super. 1998).

American Academy of Pediatrics. (1996). Consensus statements on the short- and long-term consequences of corporal punishment. *Pediatrics, 98,* 98.

American Academy of Psychiatry and the Law. (1995). Ethical guidelines for the practice of forensic psychiatry. In *Membership directory of American Academy of Psychiatry and the Law.* Bloomfield, CT: Author.

American Humane Association. (1914). *38th annual report.* Denver, CO: Author.

American Humane Association, Children's Division. (1963). *Guidelines for legislation to protect the battered child.* Denver, CO: Author.

American Law Institute. (1977). *Restatement of the law of torts.* St. Paul, MN: Author.

American Medical Association. (1965). *Physical abuse of children: Suggested legislation.* Chicago: Author.

American Medical Association. (1985). AMA diagnostic and treatment guidelines concerning child abuse and neglect. *Journal of the American Medical Association, 254,* 796-803.

American Medical Association. (1989). *Principles of medical ethics.* Chicago: Author.

American Nurses Association. (1985). *Code for nurses.* Washington, DC: Author.

American Professional Society on the Abuse of Children. (1995). *Use of anatomical dolls in child sexual abuse assessments.* Chicago: Author.

American Professional Society on the Abuse of Children. (1996a). *Guidelines for psychosocial evaluation of suspected sexual abuse in young children.* Chicago: Author.

American Professional Society on the Abuse of Children. (1996b). *Psychosocial evaluation of suspected psychological maltreatment in children and adolescents.* Chicago: Author.

American Professional Society on the Abuse of Children. (1997). *Code of ethics.* Chicago: Author.

American Psychiatric Association. (1994). *Diagnostic and statistical manual of mental disorders* (4th ed.). Washington, DC: Author.

American Psychological Association. (1992). Ethical principles of psychologists and code of conduct. *American Psychologist, 47,* 1597-1611.

American Psychological Association. (1994). Guidelines for child custody evaluations in divorce proceedings. *American Psychologist, 49,* 677-680.

Anderson, J., Martin, J., Mullen, P., Romans, S., & Herbison, P. (1993). Prevalence of childhood sexual abuse experiences in a community sample of women. *Journal of the American Academy of Child and Adolescent Psychiatry, 32,* 911-919.

Anson, D. A., Golding, S. J., & Gully, K. J. (1993). Child sexual abuse allegations: Reliability of criteria-based content analysis. *Law and Human Behavior, 17,* 331-341.

Appelbaum, P. S., & Greer, A. (1993). Confidentiality in group therapy. *Law and Psychiatry, 44,* 311-312.

Appelbaum, P. S., & Zoltek-Jick, R. (1996). Psychotherapists' duties to third parties: *Ramona* and beyond. *American Journal of Psychiatry, 153,* 457-465.

Arata, C. M. (1998). To tell or not to tell: Current functioning of child sexual abuse survivors who disclosed their victimization. *Child Maltreatment, 3,* 63-71.

Association of Family and Conciliation Courts. (1994). Model standards of practice. *Family and Conciliation Courts Review, 32,* 504-513.

Austin v. Borel, 830 F.2d 1356 (5th Cir. 1987).

Baker-Ward, L., Gordon, B. N., Ornstein, P. A., Larus, D. M., & Clubb, P. A. (1993). Young children's long-term retention of a pediatric examination. *Child Development, 64,* 1519-1533.

Banyard, V. L. (1997). The impact of childhood sexual abuse and family functioning on four dimensions of women's later parenting. *Child Abuse & Neglect, 21,* 1095-1107.

Barry v. Turek, 267 Cal. Rptr. 553 (Ct. App. 1990).

Batterman-Faunce, J. M., & Goodman, G. S. (1993). Effects of context on the accuracy and suggestibility of child witnesses. In G. S. Goodman & B. L. Bottoms (Eds.), *Child victims, child witnesses: Understanding and improving testimony.* New York: Guilford.

Bauer, P. J. (1994). What do infants recall of their lives? *American Psychologist, 51,* 29-41.

Bauer, P. J., & Mandler, J. M. (1990). Remembering what happened next: Very young children's recall of event sequences. In R. Fivush & J. Hudson (Eds.), *Knowing and remembering in young children* (pp. 9-29). New York: Cambridge University Press.

Bays, J. (1990). Substance abuse and child abuse: The impact of addiction on the child. *Pediatric Clinics of North America, 37*, 881-904.

Bays, J. (1994). Child abuse by poisoning. In R. M. Reece (Ed.), *Child abuse: Medical diagnosis and treatment* (pp. 92-96). Philadelphia: Lea & Febiger.

Bays, J., & Chadwick, D. L. (1993). Medical diagnosis of the sexually abused child. *Child Abuse & Neglect, 17*, 91-110.

Becker, J. V. (1994). Offenders: Characteristics and treatment. *Future of Children, 4*, 176-180.

Becker, J. V., & Quinsey, V. L. (1993). Assessing suspected child molesters. *Child Abuse & Neglect, 17*, 169-174.

Beckett, K. (1996). Culture and the politics of signification: The case of child sexual abuse. *Social Problems, 43*, 57-76.

Beitchman, J. H., Zucker, K. J., Hood, J. E., daCosta, G. A., & Akman, D. (1991). A review of the short-term effects of child sexual abuse. *Child Abuse & Neglect, 15*, 537-556.

Bender, L., & Blau, A. (1937). The reaction of children to sexual relation with adults. *American Journal of Orthopsychiatry, 7*, 500-518.

Bender, L., & Grugett, A. E. (1952). A follow-up report on children who had atypical sexual experience. *American Journal of Orthopsychiatry, 22*, 825-837.

Benedek, E. P., & Schetky, D. H. (1985). Allegations of sexual abuse in child custody and visitation disputes. In D. H. Schetky & E. P. Benedek (Eds.), *Emerging issues in child psychiatry and law* (pp. 145-146). New York: Brunner/Mazel.

Berger, V. (1977). Man's trial, woman's tribulation: Rape cases in the courtroom. *Columbia Law Review, 77*, 1-100.

Berlin, F. S., Malin, M., & Dean, S. (1991). Effects of statutes requiring psychiatrists to report suspected sexual abuse of children. *American Journal of Psychiatry, 148*, 449-453.

Berliner, L. (1988). Deciding whether a child has been sexually abused. In E. B. Nicholson & J. Buckley (Eds.), *Sexual abuse allegations in custody and visitation cases* (pp. 48-69). Washington, DC: American Bar Association, National Legal Resource Center for Child Advocacy and Protection.

Berliner, L. (1997). Research findings on child sexual abuse investigations. In R. Lieb, L. Berliner, & P. Toth (Eds.), *Protocols, and training standards: Investigating allegations of child sexual abuse* (pp. 5-23). Olympia: Evergreen State College, Washington State Institute for Public Policy.

Berliner, L., & Briere, J. (1998). Trauma, memory, and clinical practice. In L. Williams (Ed.), *Trauma and memory*. Thousand Oaks, CA: Sage.

Berliner, L., & Conte, J. R. (1993). Sexual abuse evaluations: Conceptual and empirical obstacles. *Child Abuse & Neglect, 17*, 111-125.

Berliner, L., & Elliott, D. M. (1996). Sexual abuse of children. In J. Briere, L. Berliner, J. A. Bulkley, C. Jenny, & T. Reid (Eds.), *The APSAC handbook on child maltreatment* (pp. 51-71). Thousand Oaks, CA: Sage.

Berliner, L., & Saunders, B. E. (1996). Treating fear and anxiety in sexually abused children: Results of a controlled 2-year follow-up study. *Child Maltreatment, 1*, 294-309.

Bird v. W.C.W., 868 S.W.2d 767 (Tex. 1994).

Bjorklund, D. F. (1995). *Children's thinking: Developmental functions and individual differences.* Pacific Grove, CA: Brooks/Cole.

Black, B. (1988). A unified theory of scientific evidence. *Fordham Law Review, 56,* 595-695.

Black, B., Francisco, J., & Saffran-Brinks, C. (1994). Science and the law in the wake of *Daubert*: A new search for scientific knowledge. *Texas Law Review, 72,* 715-802.

Black's law dictionary. (1979). St. Paul, MN: West.

Blackstone, W. (1769). *Commentaries on the law of England* (Vol. 4). P. 214.

Blackstone, W. (1915). *Commentaries on the laws of England* (W. C. Jones, Ed.). San Francisco: Bancroft-Whitney. (Original work published 1765)

Boat, B.W., & Everson, M.D. (1986). *Using anatomical dolls: Guidelines for interviewing young children in sexual abuse investigations.* Chapel Hill: University of North Carolina, Department of Psychiatry.

Boat, B. W., & Everson, M. D. (1988a). Use of anatomical dolls among professionals in sexual abuse evaluation. *Child Abuse & Neglect, 12,* 171-179.

Boat, B. W., & Everson, M. D. (1988b). Interviewing young children with anatomical dolls. *Child Welfare, 67,* 337-351.

Boat, B. W., & Everson, M. D. (1993). The use of anatomical dolls in sexual abuse evaluations: Current research and practice. In G. S. Goodman & B. L. Bottoms (Eds.), *Child victims, child witnesses: Understanding and improving testimony* (pp. 47-69). New York: Guilford.

Boat, B. W., & Everson, M. D. (1994). Anatomical doll exploration among non-referred children: Comparisons by age, gender, race, and socioeconomic status. *Child Abuse & Neglect, 18,* 139-153.

Boat, B. W., & Everson, M. D. (1996). Concerning practices of interviewing when using anatomical dolls in child protective services investigations. *Child Maltreatment, 1,* 96-104.

Boat, B. W., Everson, M. D., & Holland, J. (1990). Maternal perceptions of nonabused young children's behaviors after the children's exposure to anatomical dolls. *Child Welfare, 69,* 389-400.

Boswell, J. (1988). *The kindness of strangers: The abandonment of children in western Europe from late antiquity to the Renaissance.* New York: Pantheon.

Bottoms, B. L., & Davis, S. L. (1997). The creation of satanic ritual abuse. *Journal of Social and Clinical Psychology, 16,* 112-132.

Bottoms, B. L., Shaver, P. R., & Goodman, G. S. (1996). An analysis of ritualistic and religion-related child abuse allegations. *Law and Human Behavior, 20,* 1-34.

Bottoms, B. L., Shaver, P. R., Goodman, G. S., & Qin, J. (1995). In the name of God: A profile of religion-related child abuse. *Journal of Social Issues, 51,* 85-111.

Bower, M. E., & Knutson, J. F. (1996). Attitudes toward physical discipline as a function of disciplinary history and self-labeling as physically abused. *Child Abuse & Neglect, 20,* 689-699.

Bowman, C. G., & Mertz, E. (1996). A dangerous direction: Legal intervention in sexual abuse survivor therapy. *Harvard Law Review, 109,* 549-639.

Bradley, A. B., & Wood, J. M. (1996). How do children tell? The disclosure process in child sexual abuse. *Child Abuse & Neglect, 20,* 881-891.

Bradley v. Ray, 904 S.W.2d 302 (Missouri Ct. App. 1995).

Brainerd, C., & Ornstein, P. A. (1991). Children's memory for witnesses events: The developmental backdrop. In J. Doris (Ed.), *The suggestibility of children's recollec-*

tions: Implications for eyewitness testimony (pp. 10-20). Washington, DC: American Psychological Association.

Brainerd, C. J., & Poole, D. A. (1997). Long-term survival of children's false memories: A review. *Learning and Individual Differences, 9,* 125-151.

Brannigan, A., & Van Brunschot, E. G. (1997). Youthful prostitution and child sexual trauma. *International Journal of Law and Psychiatry, 20,* 337-354.

Brassard, M. R., Germain, R., & Hart, S. N. (Eds.). (1987). *Psychological maltreatment of children and youth.* New York: Pergamon.

Bremner, R. H. (Ed.). (1970). *Children and youth in America: A documentary history.* Cambridge, MA: Harvard University Press.

Brewer, K. D., Rowe, D. M., & Brewer, D. D. (1997). Factors related to prosecution of child sexual abuse cases. *Journal of Child Sexual Abuse, 6,* 91-111.

Brewster, A. L., Nelson, J. P., Hymel, K. P., Colby, D. R., Lucas, D. R., McCanne, T. R., & Milner, J. S. (1998). Victim, perpetrator, family, and incident characteristics of 32 infant maltreatment deaths in the United States Air Force. *Child Abuse & Neglect, 22,* 91-101.

Briere, J. N. (1992). *Child abuse trauma: Theory and treatment of the lasting effects.* Newbury Park, CA: Sage.

Briere, J. N., & Elliott, D. M. (1994). Immediate and long-term impacts of child sexual abuse. *Future of Children, 4,* 54-69.

Briere, J., & Zaidi, L. Y. (1989). Sexual abuse histories and sequelae in female psychiatric emergency room patients. *American Journal of Psychiatry, 146,* 1602-1206.

Brilleslijper-kater, S. N., & Baartman, H. E. M. (in press). What do young children know about sexuality? Research of the knowledge of sexuality of children between the ages of 2 and 7 years. *Child Abuse Review.*

Brown, M. (1926). *Legal psychology.* New York: Bobbs-Merrill.

Browne, A., & Finkelhor, D. (1986). Impact of child sexual abuse: A review of the research. *Psychological Bulletin, 99,* 66-77.

Brownmiller, S. (1975). *Against our will: Men, women, and rape.* New York: Simon & Shuster.

Bruce v. Byrne-Stevens & Associates, 776 P.2d 666 (Wash. 1989).

Bruck, M., Ceci, S. J., Francoeur, E., & Barr, R. (1995). "I hardly cried when I got my shot!" Influencing children's reports about a visit to their pediatrician. *Child Development, 66,* 193-208.

Bruck, M., Ceci, S. J., Francoeur, E., & Renick, A. (1995). Anatomically detailed dolls do not facilitate preschoolers' reports of a pediatric examination involving genital touching. *Journal of Experimental Psychology, 1,* 95-109.

Brunhold, H. (1964). Observations after sexual trauma suffered in childhood. *Excerpta Criminologica, 11,* 5-8.

Bryant, S. L., & Range, L. M. (1997). Type and severity of child abuse and college students' lifetime sexuality. *Child Abuse & Neglect, 21,* 1169-1176.

Bugental, D. B., Blue, J., Cortez, V., Fleck, K., & Rodriguez, A. (1992). Influences of witnessed affect on information processing in children. *Child Development, 63,* 774-786.

Bulkley, J. A. (1992). The prosecution's use of social science expert testimony in child sexual abuse cases: National trends and recommendations. *Journal of Child Sexual Abuse, 1,* 73-93.

Bull, R. (1995). Innovative techniques for the questioning of child witnesses, especially those who are young and those with learning disability. In M. S. Zaragoza,

J. R. Graham, G. C. N. Hall, R. Hirschman, & Y. S. Ben-Porath (Eds.), *Memory and testimony in the child witness* (pp. 179-194). Thousand Oaks, CA: Sage.

Burgess, A., & Holmstron, L. (1974). Rape trauma syndrome. *American Journal of Psychiatry, 131,* 981-986.

Butler, S. M., Radia, N., & Magnatta, M. (1994). Maternal compliance to court-ordered assessment in cases of child maltreatment. *Child Abuse & Neglect, 18,* 203-211.

California Attorney General's Office. (1994). *Child victim witness investigative projects: Research and evaluation final report.* Sacramento: California Attorney General's Office.

Cantlon, J., Payne, G., & Erbaugh, C. (1996). Outcome based practice: Disclosure rates of child sexual abuse comparing allegation blind and allegation informed structured interviews. *Child Abuse & Neglect, 20,* 1113-1120.

Carter, C. A., Bottoms, B. L., & Levine, M. (1996). Linguistic and socioemotional influences on the accuracy of children's reports. *Law and Human Behavior, 20,* 335-358.

Carter, L. E. (1989). Admissibility of expert testimony in child sexual abuse cases in California: Retire Kelly-Frye and return to a traditional analysis. *Loyola of Los Angeles Law Review, 22,* 1103-1160.

Cassel, W. S., & Bjorklund, D. F. (1995). Developmental patterns of eyewitness memory and suggestibility: An ecologically based short term longitudinal study. *Law and Human Behavior, 19,* 507-532.

Cassel, W. S., Roebers, C. E. M., & Bjorklund, D. F. (1996). Developmental patterns of eyewitness responses to repeated and increasingly suggestive questions. *Journal of Experimental Child Psychology, 61,* 116-133.

Ceci, S. J., & Bruck, M. (1993). Suggestibility of the child witness: A historical review and synthesis. *Psychological Bulletin, 113,* 403-439.

Ceci, S. J., & Bruck, M. (1995). *Jeopardy in the courtroom: A scientific analysis of children's testimony.* Washington, DC: American Psychological Association.

Ceci, S. J., & Huffman, M. L. C. (1997). How suggestible are preschool children? *Journal of the American Academy of Child and Adolescent Psychiatry, 36,* 948-957.

Ceci, S. J., Huffman, M. L. C., Smith, E., & Loftus, E. F. (1994). Repeatedly thinking about a non-event: Source misattributions among preschoolers. *Consciousness and Condition, 3,* 388-407.

Ceci, S. J., Ross, D. F., & Toglia, M. P. (1987). Age differences in suggestibility: Narrowing the uncertainties. In S. J. Ceci, M. P. Toglia, & D. F. Ross (Eds.), *Children's eyewitness memory* (pp. 79-91). New York: Springer-Verlag.

Cerezo, M. A. (1997). Abusive family interaction: A review. *Aggression and Violent Behavior, 2,* 215-240.

Chadwick, D. L. (1990). Preparation for court testimony in child abuse cases. *Pediatric Clinics of North America, 37,* 955-970.

Chadwick, D. L., & Krous, H. F. (1997). Irresponsible testimony by medical experts in cases involving the physical abuse and neglect of children. *Child Maltreatment, 2,* 313-321.

Chaffey, J. (1946). Multiple fractures in the long bones of infants suffering from chronic subdural hematoma. *American Journal of Roentgenology, 56,* 163-173.

Chaffey, J. (1972). On the theory and practice of shaking infants. *American Journal of Diseases of Children, 124,* 161-169.

Chaffey, J. (1974). The whiplash shaken infant syndrome: Manual shaking by the extremities with whiplash-induced intracranial and introcular bleedings, linked with residual permanent brain damage and mental retardation. *Pediatrics, 54,* 396-403.

Chaffin, M., Lawson, L., Selby, A., & Wherry, J. N. (1997). False negatives in sexual abuse interviews: Preliminary investigation of a relationship to dissociation. *Journal of Child Sexual Abuse, 6,* 15-29.

Chandy, J. M., Blum, R. W., & Resnick, M. D. (1996). Female adolescents with a history of sexual abuse: Risk outcome and protective factors. *Journal of Interpersonal Violence, 11,* 503-518.

Child Abuse Prevention and Treatment Act of 1974, 42 U.S.C. §5101.

Children's Bureau, U.S. Department of Health, Education, and Welfare. (1963). *The abused child: Principles and suggested language for legislation on reporting the physically abused child.* Washington, DC: Government Printing Office.

Choquet, M., Darves-Bornoz, J., Ledoux, S., Manfredi, R., & Hassler, C. (1997). Self-reported health and behavioral problems among adolescent victims of rape in France: Results of a cross-sectional survey. *Child Abuse & Neglect, 21,* 823-832.

Coffey, P., Leitenberg, H., Henning, K., Turner, T., & Bennett, R. T. (1996). Mediators of the long-term impact of child sexual abuse: Perceived stigma, betrayal, powerlessness, and self-blame. *Child Abuse & Neglect, 20,* 447-455.

Cohen, J. A., & Mannarino, A. P. (1998). Interventions for sexually abused children: Initial treatment outcome findings. *Child Maltreatment, 3,* 17-26.

Cole, C. B., & Loftus, E. F. (1987). The memory of children. In S. J. Ceci, M. P. Toglia, & D. F. Ross (Eds.), *Children's eyewitness memory* (pp. 178-208). New York: Springer-Verlag.

Committee on Ethical Guidelines for Forensic Psychologists. (1991). Specialty guidelines for forensic psychologists. *Law and Human Behavior, 15,* 655-665.

Committee on Legal Issues of the American Psychological Association. (1996). Strategies for private practitioners coping with subpoenas or compelled testimony for client records or test data. *Professional Psychology: Research and Practice, 27,* 245-251.

Committee on Professional Practice and Standards, A Committee of the Board of Professional Affairs of the American Psychological Association. (1995). Twenty-four questions (and answers) about professional practice in the area of child abuse. *Professional Psychology: Research and Practice, 26,* 377-385.

Committee on Psychiatry and Law. Group for the Advancement of Psychiatry. (1991). *The mental health professional and the legal system* (Rep. No. 131). New York: Brunner/Mazel.

Committee on Psychosocial Aspects of Child and Family Health, American Academy of Pediatrics. (1998). Guidance for effective discipline. *Pediatrics, 101,* 723-728.

Commonwealth v. Berrio, 551 N.E.2d 496 (Mass. 1990).

Commonwealth v. Gallagher, 547 A.2d 355 (Pa. 1988).

Commonwealth v. Twitchell, 617 N.E.2d 609 (Mass. 1993).

Conte, J., & Berliner, L. (1988). The impact of sexual abuse on children: Empirical findings. In J. Walker (Ed.), *Handbook on sexual abuse of children.* New York: Springer.

Conte, J. R., Sorenson, E., Fogarty, L., & Dalla Rosa, J. (1991). Evaluating children's reports of sexual abuse: Results from a survey of professionals. *American Journal of Orthopsychiatry, 61,* 428-437.

Corpus Juris Secundum. (1987). St. Paul, MN: West.

Corwin, D. L. (1988). Early diagnosis of child sexual abuse: Diminishing the lasting effects. In G. E. Wyatt & G. J. Powell (Eds.), *Lasting effects of child sexual abuse* (pp. 251-269). Newbury Park, CA: Sage.

Corwin, D. L., Berliner, L., Goodman, G. S., Goodwin, J., & White, S. (1987). Child sexual abuse and custody disputes. *Journal of Interpersonal Violence, 2*, 91-105.

Corwin, D., & Olafson, E. (1997). Videotaped discovery of a reportedly unrecallable memory of child sexual abuse: Comparison with a childhood interview videotaped 11 years before. *Child Maltreatment, 2*, 91-112.

Council of Juvenile Court Judges. (1949). 15 recommendations made by national council in reviewing juvenile court and children's problems. *Juvenile Court Judges Journal, 1*, 19-24.

Coy v. Iowa, 487 U.S. 1012 (1988).

Crenshaw, W. B., & Lichtenberg, J. W. (1993). Child abuse and the limits of confidentiality: Forewarning practices. *Behavioral Sciences and the Law, 11*, 181-192.

Dalenberg, C. J. (1996). Fantastic elements in child disclosure of abuse. *APSAC Advisor, 9*, 1, 5-10.

Dalenberg, C. J. (in press). Overcoming obstacles to just evaluation and successful prosecution of multivictim cases. In K. Faller & R. Vanderlaan (Eds.), *Interviewing the victim of trauma: Science, research and practice.* Haworth Press.

Dalenberg, C. J., Hyland, K. J., & Cuevas, C. A. (in press). Sources of fantastic elements in allegations of abuse by adults and children. In M. Eisen, G. S. Goodman, & J. A. Quas (Eds.), *Memory and suggestibility in the forensic interview.* Mahwah, NJ: Erlbaum.

Daro, D., & Lung, C. T. (1996). *Current trends in child abuse reporting and fatalities: NCPCA's 1995 annual fifty state survey.* Chicago: National Committee to Prevent Child Abuse.

Daro, D., & Wang, C. (1997). *1997 current trends in child abuse reporting and fatalities: The results of the 1996 annual fifty state survey.* Chicago: National Committee for the Prevention of Child Abuse.

Darragh v. Superior Court, 900 P.2d 1215 (Ariz. Ct. App. 1995).

Daubert v. Merrell Dow Pharmaceuticals, Inc., 509 U.S. 579 (1993).

Davidson, J. R., & Davidson, T. (1996). Confidentiality and managed care: Ethical and legal concerns. *Health and Social Work, 21*, 208-215.

Davies, D., Cole, J., Albertella, G., McCulloch, L., Allen, K., & Kekevian, H. (1996). A model for conducting forensic interviews with child victims of abuse. *Child Maltreatment, 1*, 189-199.

Davies, G. M. (1996). Children's identification evidence. In S. L. Sporer, R. S. Malpass, & G. Koehnken (Eds.), *Psychological issues in eyewitness identification* (pp. 233-258). Mahwah, NJ: Lawrence Erlbaum.

Davis, K. C. (1972). *Administrative Law.* Boston: Little, Brown.

Davis, S. L. (1998). Social and scientific influences on the study of children's suggestibility: A historical perspective. *Child Maltreatment, 3*, 186-194.

Davis, S. L., & Bottoms, B. L. (in press). The effects of social support on the accuracy of children's reports: Implications for the forensic interview. In M. L. Eisen, G. S. Goodman, & J. A. Quas (Eds.), *Memory and suggestibility in the forensic interview.* Mahwah, NJ: Erlbam.

Davis v. State, 47 N.W. 854 (Neb. 1891).

Dawson, B., Geddie, L., & Wagner, W. (1996). Low-income preschoolers' behavior with anatomically detailed dolls. *Journal of Family Violence, 11*, 363-378.

Deatherage v. State Examining Board of Psychology, 948 P.2d 828 (Wash. 1997).

Deblinger, E., Lippmann, J., & Steer, R. (1996). Sexually abused children suffering posttraumatic stress symptoms: Initial treatment outcome findings. *Child Maltreatment*, 1, 310-321.

Deed, M. L. (1993). Mandated reporting revisited: *Roe v. Superior Court. Law and Policy*, 14, 219-239.

DeFrancis, V. (1968). Child protective services—1967. *Juvenile Court Judges Journal*, 19, 24-30.

Delcourt v. Silverman, 919 S.W.2d 777 (Tex. Ct. App. 1996).

DeLoache, J. S. (1995). The use of dolls in interviewing young children. In M. S. Zaragoza, J. R. Graham, G. C. N. Hall, R. Hirschman, & Y. Ben-Porath (Eds.), *Memory and testimony in the child witness* (pp. 160-178). Thousand Oaks, CA: Sage.

deMause, L. (1974). *The history of childhood*. New York: Psychohistory.

DeMott, B. (1980). The pro-incest lobby. *Psychology Today*, 13(10), 11-12, 15-16.

Dent, H. (1991). Experimental studies of interviewing child witnesses. In J. Dorris (Ed.), *The suggestibility of children's recollections: Implications for eyewitness testimony* (pp. 138-146). Washington, DC: American Psychological Association.

Dent, H. (1992). The effects of age and intelligence on eyewitnessing ability. In H. Dent & R. Flin (Eds.), *Children as witnesses* (pp. 1-13). New York: John Wiley.

DeShaney v. Winnebago County, 489 U.S. 189 (1989).

Doe v. Pataki, 120 F.3d 1263 (2nd Cir. 1997).

Doe v. Poritz, 662 A.2d 367 (N.J. 1995).

Dorland's illustrated medical dictionary (28th ed.). (1994). Philadelphia: W. B. Saunders.

Dubowitz, H., & Black, M. (1996). Medical neglect. In J. Briere, L. Berliner, J. A. Bulkley, C. Jenny, & T. Reid (Eds.), *The APSAC handbook on child maltreatment* (pp. 227-241). Thousand Oaks, CA: Sage.

Dubowitz, H., Black, M., & Harrington, D. (1992). The diagnosis of child sexual abuse. *American Journal of Diseases of Children*, 146, 688-693.

Duhaime, A., Christian, C., Moss, E., & Seidl, T. (1996). Long-term outcome in infants with shaken-impact syndrome. *Pediatric Neurosurgery*, 24, 292-298.

Durand Equipment Co. v. Superior Carbon Products Inc., 591 A.2d 987 (N.J. Super. A.D. 1991).

E.B. v. Verniero, 119 F.3d 1077 (3rd Cir. 1997).

Edwards, L. P. (1987). The relationship of juvenile and family courts in child sexual abuse cases. *Santa Clara Law Review*, 27, 201-278.

Edwards, L. P. (1996). Corporal punishment and the legal system. *Santa Clara Law Review*, 36, 983-1023.

Elliott, D. M., & Briere, J. (1994). Forensic sexual abuse evaluations of older children: Disclosures and symptomatology. *Behavioral Sciences and the Law*, 12, 261-277.

Elliott, D. M., & Briere, J. (1995). Posttraumatic stress associated with delayed recall of sexual abuse: A general population study. *Journal of Traumatic Stress*, 8, 629-647.

Ellison v. Ellison, 919 P.2d 1 (Okla. 1996).

Erickson, M. F., & Egeland, B. (1996). Child neglect. In J. Briere, L. Berliner, J. A. Bulkley, C. Jenny, & T. Reid (Eds.), *The APSAC handbook on child maltreatment* (pp. 4-20). Thousand Oaks, CA: Sage.

Ernst v. Child and Youth Services of Chester County, 108 F.3d 486 (3rd Cir. 1997).

Estate of Morgan, 673 N.E.2d 1131 (Ohio 1997).

Everson, M. D. (1997). Understanding bizarre, improbable, and fantastic elements in children's accounts of abuse. *Child Maltreatment*, 2, 134-149.

Everson, M. D., & Boat, B. W. (1989). False allegations of sexual abuse by children and adolescents. *Journal of the American Academy of Child and Adolescent Psychiatry, 28,* 230-235.

Everson, M. D., & Boat, B. W. (1990). Sexualized doll play among young children: Implications for the use of anatomical dolls in sexual abuse evaluations. *Journal of the American Academy of Child and Adolescent Psychiatry, 29,* 736-742.

Everson, M. D., & Boat, B. W. (1994). Putting the anatomical doll controversy in perspective: An examination of the major uses and criticisms of the dolls in child sexual abuse evaluations. *Child Abuse & Neglect, 18,* 113-129.

Everson, M. D., Boat, B. W., Bourg, S., & Robertson, K. R. (1996). Beliefs among professionals about rates of false allegations of child sexual abuse. *Journal of Interpersonal Violence, 11,* 541-553.

Ewigman, B., Kivlahan, C., & Land, G. (1993). The Missouri child fatality study: Underreporting of maltreatment fatalities among children younger than five years of age, 1983 through 1986. *Pediatrics, 91,* 330-337.

Faden, R. R., & Beauchamp, T. L. (1986). *A history and theory of informed consent.* New York: Oxford University Press.

Faigman, D. L. (1995). The evidentiary status of social science under *Daubert:* Is it "scientific," "technical," or "other" knowledge? *Psychology, Public Policy, and Law, 1,* 960-979.

Fain v. State, 462 So.2d 1054 (Ala. Crim. App. 1985).

Faller, K. C. (1988). *Child sexual abuse: An interdisciplinary manual for diagnosis, case management and treatment.* New York: Columbia University Press.

Faller, K. C. (1990). *Understanding child sexual maltreatment.* Newbury Park, CA: Sage.

Faller, K. C. (1995). *APSAC study guide: Interviewing children suspected of having been sexually abused.* Thousand Oaks, CA: Sage.

Faller, K. C. (1998). The parental alienation syndrome: What is it and what data support it? *Child Maltreatment, 3,* 100-115.

Famularo, R., Fenton, T., Augustyn, M., & Zuckerman, B. (1996). Persistence of pediatric post traumatic stress disorder after 2 years. *Child Abuse & Neglect, 20,* 1245-1248.

Famularo, R., Fenton, T., Kinscherff, R., & Augustyn, M. (1996). Psychiatric comorbidity in childhood post traumatic stress disorder. *Child Abuse & Neglect, 20,* 953-961.

Famularo, R., Kinscherff, R., Bunshaft, D., Spivak, G., & Fenton, T. (1989). Parental compliance to court-ordered treatment interventions in cases of child maltreatment. *Child Abuse & Neglect, 13,* 507-514.

Ferenczi, S. (1932). Confusion of tongues between adults and the child: The language of tenderness and of passion [Originally titled "The passions of adults and their influence on the sexual and character development of children"]. In M. Balint (Ed.) & E. Mosbacher (Trans.), *Final contributions to the problems and methods of psychoanalysis.* New York: Basic Books.

Fergusson, D. M., Horwood, L. J., & Lynskey, M. T. (1997). Childhood sexual abuse, adolescent sexual behaviors and sexual revictimization. *Child Abuse & Neglect, 21,* 789-803.

Fergusson, D. M., & Lynskey, M. T. (1997). Physical punishment/maltreatment during childhood and adjustment in young adulthood. *Child Abuse & Neglect, 21,* 617-630.

Finkel, M. A., & De Jong, A. R. (1994). Medical findings in child sexual abuse. In R. M. Reece (Ed.), *Child abuse: Medical diagnosis and management* (pp. 185-247). Philadelphia: Lea & Febiger.

Finkelhor, D. (1979). *Sexually victimized children*. New York: Free Press.

Finkelhor, D. (1986). *A sourcebook on child sexual abuse*. Newbury Park, CA: Sage.

Finkelhor, D. (1987). The trauma of child sexual abuse. *Journal of Interpersonal Violence, 2*, 348-366.

Finkelhor, D. (1994). Current information on the scope and nature of child sexual abuse. *Future of Children, 4*, 31-53.

Finkelhor, D., & Berliner, L. (1995). Research on the treatment of sexually abused children: A review and recommendations. *Journal of the American Academy of Child and Adolescent Psychiatry, 34*, 1408-1423.

Finkelhor, D., & Browne, A. (1985). The traumatic impact of child sexual abuse: A conceptualization. *American Journal of Orthopsychiatry, 55*, 530-541.

Finkelhor, D., Hotaling, G. T., Lewis, I. A., & Smith, C. (1989). Sexual abuse and its relationship to later sexual satisfaction, marital status, religion, and attitudes. *Journal of Interpersonal Violence, 4*, 379-399.

Finkelhor, D., Hotaling, G., Lewis, I. A., & Smith, C. (1990). Sexual abuse in a national survey of adult men and women. *Child Abuse & Neglect, 14*, 19-28.

Finkelhor, D., & Williams, L. M. (1988). *Nursery crimes*. Newbury Park, CA: Sage.

Finkelhor, D., & Zellman, G. L. (1991). Flexible reporting options for skilled child abuse professionals. *Child Abuse & Neglect, 15*, 335-341.

First Church of Christ, Scientist. (1989). *Freedom and responsibility: Christian Science healing for children*. Boston: Author.

Fisher, R. P., & McCauley, M. R. (1995). Improving eyewitness testimony with the cognitive interview. In M. S. Zaragoza, J. R. Graham, G. C. N. Hall, R. Hirschman, & Y. S. Ben-Porath (Eds.), *Memory and testimony in the child witness* (pp. 141-159). Thousand Oaks, CA: Sage.

Fivush, R. (1993). Developmental perspectives on autobiographical recall. In G. S. Goodman & B. L. Bottoms (Eds.), *Child victims, child witnesses: Understanding and improving testimony* (pp. 1-24). New York: Guilford.

Fivush, R., & Hudson, J. A. (Eds.). (1990). *Knowing and remembering in young children*. New York: Cambridge University Press.

Fivush, R., & Schwarzmueller, A. (1995). Say it once again: Effects of repeated questions on children's event recall. *Journal of Traumatic Stress, 8*, 555-580.

Fivush, R., & Shukat, J.R. (1995). Content, consistency, and coherence of early autobiographical recall. In M. S. Zaragoza, J. R. Graham, G. C. N. Hall, R. Hirschman, & Y. S. Ben-Porath (Eds.), *Memory and testimony in the child witness* (pp. 1-23). Thousand Oaks, CA: Sage.

Fleming, T. J. (1990). Admissibility of hypnotically refreshed or enhanced testimony. *American Law Reports 4th, 77*, 927-983.

Flemming, J. (1997). Prevalence of childhood sexual abuse in a community sample of Australian women. *Medical Journal of Australia, 166*, 65-68.

Flin, S., Bull, R., Boon, J., & Knox, A. (1993). Child witnesses in Scottish criminal trials. *International Review of Victimology, 2*, 309-329.

Flisher, A. J., Kramer, R. A., Hoven, C. W., Greenwald, S., Alegria, M., Bird, H. R., Canino, G., Connell, R., & Moore, R. E. (1997). Psychosocial characteristics of physically abused children and adolescents. *Journal of the American Academy of Child and Adolescent Psychiatry, 36*, 123-131.

Flynn, C. P. (1996). Regional differences in spanking experiences and attitudes: A comparison of northeastern and southern college students. *Journal of Family Violence, 11*, 59-80.

Fox, S. J. (1996). The early history of the court. *Future of Children, 6*, 29-39.

Frank, D. A., & Drotar, D. (1994). Failure to thrive. In R. M. Reece (Ed.), *Child abuse: Medical diagnosis and management* (pp. 298-324). Philadelphia: Lea & Febiger.

Freeman-Longo, R. E. (1996). Feel good legislation: Prevention or calamity. *Child Abuse & Neglect, 20*, 95-101.

Freud, S. (1966). *Introductory lectures on psychoanalysis* (J. Strachey, Ed. & Trans.). New York: Norton. (Original work published 1916-1917)

Freyd, J. J. (1996). *Betrayal trauma: The logic of forgetting childhood abuse.* Cambridge, MA: Harvard University Press.

Friedrich, W. N. (1993). Sexual victimization and sexual behavior in children: A review of recent literature. *Child Abuse & Neglect, 17*, 59-66.

Friedrich, W. N. (1995). The clinical use of the Child Sexual Behavior Inventory. *APSAC Advisor, 1*, 8, 17-20.

Friedrich, W. N., Brambsch, P., Broughton, K., & Beilke, R. L. (1991). Normative sexual behavior in children. *Pediatrics, 88*, 456-464.

Friedrich, W. M., Brambsch, P., Damon, L., Hewitt, S., Koverola, C., Lang, R., Wolfe, V., & Broughton, D. (1992). The Child Sexual Behavior Inventory: Normative and clinical findings. *Psychological Assessment, 4*, 303-311.

Frye v. United States, 293 F. 1013 (D.C. Cir. 1923).

Furby, L., Weinrott, M. R., & Blackshaw, L. (1989). Sex offender recidivism: A review. *Psychological Bulletin, 105*, 3-30.

Garbarino, J. (1986). *The psychologically battered child.* San Francisco: Jossey-Bass.

Garbarino, J., & Scott, F. M. (1990). *What children tell us.* San Francisco: Jossey-Bass.

Gardner, R. A. (1987). *The parental alienation syndrome and the differentiation between fabricated and genuine child sex abuse.* Cresskil, NJ: Creative Therapeutics.

Garramone v. Romo, 94 F.3d 1446 (10th Cir. 1996).

Geddie, L., Dawson, B., & Weunsch, K. (1998). Socioeconomic status and ethnic differences in preschoolers' interactions with anatomically detailed dolls. *Child Maltreatment, 3*, 43-52.

Geiselman, R. E., Fisher, R. P., MacKinnon, D. P., & Holland, H. L. (1985). Eyewitness memory enhancement in the police interview: Cognitive retrieval mnemonics versus hypnosis. *Journal of Applied Psychology, 70*, 401-412.

Geiselman, R. E., Saywitz, K. J., & Bornstein, G. K. (1993). Effects of cognitive questioning techniques on children's recall performance. In G. S. Goodman & B. L. Bottoms (Eds.), *Child victims, child witnesses: Understanding and improving testimony* (pp. 71-93). New York: Guilford.

General Electric Co. v. Sargent and Lundy, 916 F.2d 1119 (6th Cir. 1990).

Gideon v. State, 721 P.2d 1336 (Okla. Crim. App. 1986).

Giles, L. E. (1976). The admissibility of a rape-complainant's previous sexual conduct: The need for legislative reform. *New England Law Review, 11*, 497-507.

Gilliam v. Department of Social and Health Services, 1998 WL 34649 (Wash. Ct. App. 1998).

Ginsberg v. New York, 390 U.S. 629 (1968).

Glassman, J.B. (1998). Preventing and managing board complaints: The downside risk of custody evaluation. *Professional Psychology: Research and Practice, 29* 121-124.

Gold, S. N., Hughes, D. M., & Swingle, J. M. (1996). Characteristics of childhood sexual abuse among female survivors in therapy. *Child Abuse & Neglect, 20*, 323-335.

Goldman, J. D. G., & Padayachi, U. K. (1997). The prevalence and nature of child sexual abuse in Queensland, Australia. *Child Abuse & Neglect, 21*, 489-498.

Goodman, G. S. (1984a). The child witness: An introduction. *Journal of Social Issues, 40*, 1-7.

Goodman, G. S. (1984b). Children's testimony in historical perspective. *Journal of Social Issues, 40*, 9-31.

Goodman, G., & Aman, C. (1990). Children's use of anatomically correct dolls to report an event. *Child Development, 61*, 1859-1871.

Goodman, G. S., & Bottoms, B. L. (Eds.). (1993). *Child victims, child witnesses: Understanding and improving testimony.* New York: Guilford.

Goodman, G. S., Bottoms, B. L., Schwartz-Kenney, B. M., & Rudy, L. (1991). Children's testimony about a stressful event: Improving children's reports. *Journal of Narrative and Life History, 1*, 69-99.

Goodman, G. S., & Clark-Stewart, A. (1991). Suggestibility in children's testimony: Implications for sexual abuse investigations. In J. Dorris (Ed.), *The suggestibility of children's recollections: Implications for eyewitness testimony* (pp. 92-105). Washington, DC: American Psychological Association.

Goodman, G. S., Emery, R. E., & Haugaard, J. J. (1998). Developmental psychology and law: The cases of divorce, child maltreatment, foster care, and adoption. In I. E. Sigel & K. A. Renninger (Eds.), *Handbook of child psychology: Vol. 4. Child psychology in practice* (5th ed., pp. 775-874). New York: John Wiley.

Goodman, G. S., Hirschman, J., Hepps, D., & Rudy, L. (1991). Children's memory for stressful events. *Merrill-Palmer Quarterly, 37*, 109-158.

Goodman, G. S., Quas, J. A., Batterman-Faunce, J. M., Riddlesberger, M. M., & Kuhn, J. (1994). Predictors of accurate and inaccurate memories of traumatic events experienced in childhood. *Consciousness and Cognition, 3*, 269-294.

Goodman, G. S., Quas, J. A., Bottoms, B. L., Qin, J., Shaver, P. R., Orcutt, H., & Shapiro, C. (1997). Children's religious knowledge: Implications for understanding satanic ritual abuse allegations. *Child Abuse & Neglect, 21*, 1111-1130.

Goodman, G. S., Rudy, L., Bottoms, B. L., & Aman, C. (1990). Children's concerns and memory: Issues of ecological validity in the study of children's eyewitness testimony. In R. Fivush & J. A. Hudson (Eds.), *Knowing and remembering in young children* (pp. 249-284). New York: Cambridge University Press.

Goodman, G. S., & Saywitz, K. J. (1994). Memories of abuse: Interviewing children when sexual victimization is suspected. *Child and Adolescent Psychiatric Clinics of North America, 3*, 645.

Goodman, G. S., & Schwartz-Kenney, B. M. (1992). Why knowing a child's age is not enough: Influences of cognitive, social, and emotional factors on children's testimony. In H. Dent & R. Flin (Eds.), *Children as witnesses* (pp. 15-32). New York: John Wiley.

Goodman, G. S., Taub, E. P., Jones, D. P. H., England, P., Port, L. K., Rudy, L., & Prady, L. (1992). Testifying in criminal court. *Monographs of the Society for Research in Child Development, 57*, 1-163.

Goodpaster, G. S., & Angel, K. (1975). Child abuse and the law: The California system. *Hastings Law Journal, 26*, 1081-1125.

Goodwin, J. M. (1994). Credibility problems in sadistic abuse. *Journal of Psychohistory, 21*, 479-496.

Goodwin, J., Sahd, D., & Rada, R. T. (1982). False accusations and false denials of incest: Clinical myths and clinical realities. In J. Goodwin (Ed.), *Sexual abuse: Incest victims and their families.* Boston: John Wright.

Gootee v. Lightner, 274 Cal. Rptr. 697 (Ct. App. 1990).

Gordon, B. N., & Follmer, A. (1994). Developmental issues in judging the credibility of children's testimony. *Journal of Clinical Child Psychology, 23,* 283-294.

Gordon, B. N., Schroeder, C., & Abrams, J. M. (1990a). Age and social class differences in children's knowledge of sexuality. *Journal of Clinical Child Physiology, 19,* 33-43.

Gordon, B. N., Schroeder, C., & Abrams, J. M. (1990b). Children's knowledge of sexuality: A comparison of sexually abused and nonabused children. *American Journal of Orthopsychiatry, 60,* 250-257.

Gordon, L. (1988). *Heroes of their own lives: The politics and history of family violence: Boston 1880-1960.* New York: Penguin.

Gorey, K. M., & Leslie, D. R. (1997). The prevalence of child sexual abuse: Integrative review adjustment for potential response and measurement biases. *Child Abuse & Neglect, 21,* 391-398.

Graziano, A. M., Lindquist, C. M., Kunce, L. J., & Munjal, K. (1992). Physical punishment in childhood and current attitudes: An exploratory comparison of college students in the United States and India. *Journal of Interpersonal Violence, 7,* 147-155.

Graziano, A. M., & Namaste, K. A. (1990). Parental use of physical force in child discipline: A survey of 679 college students. *Journal of Interpersonal Violence, 5,* 449-463.

Green, A. H. (1986). True and false allegations of sexual abuse in custody disputes. *Journal of the American Academy of Child Psychiatry, 25,* 449-456.

Green, S. A. (1995). The ethical limits of confidentiality in the therapeutic relationship. *General Hospital Psychiatry, 17,* 80-84.

Greenberg, S. A., & Shuman, D. W. (1997). Irreconcilable conflict between therapeutic and forensic roles. *Professional Psychology: Research and Practice, 28,* 50-57.

Gresh v. State, 560 So.2d 1266 (Fla. Ct. App. 1990).

Grimes v. State, 17 So. 184 (Ala. 1895).

Groth, A., Longo, R., & McFadin, J. (1982). Undetected recidivism among rapists and child molesters. *Crime and Delinquency, 28,* 450-458.

Gupta v. New Britain General Hospital, 687 A.2d 111 (Conn. 1996).

Gutheil, T. G., & Appelbaum, P. S. (1982). *Clinical handbook of psychiatry and the law.* New York: McGraw-Hill.

Gutierres, S.E., & Todd, M. (1997). The impact of childhood abuse on treatment outcomes of substance abusers. *Professional Psychology: Research and Practice, 28,* 348-354.

Hall, G. C. N. (1995). Sexual offender recidivism revisited: A meta-analysis of recent treatment studies. *Journal of Clinical and Consulting Psychology, 63,* 802-809.

Hall, G. C. N., & Crowther, J. H. (1991). Psychologists' involvement in cases of child maltreatment: Additional limits on assessments methods. *American Psychologist, 46,* 79-80.

Hardin, M. (1996). Responsibilities and effectiveness of the juvenile court in handling dependency cases. *Future of Children, 6,* 111-125.

Harper, G., & Irvin, E. (1985). Alliance formation with parents: Limit setting and the effect of mandated reporting. *American Journal of Orthopsychiatry, 55,* 550-560.

Harris, E. A. (1995). The importance of risk management in a managed care environment. In M. B. Sussman (Ed.), *A perilous calling: The hazards of psychotherapy practice*. New York: John Wiley.

Hart, H. M., & McNaughton, J. (1958). *Evidence and inference in the law*. Washington, DC: American Academy of Arts and Sciences.

Hart, S. N., Brassard, M. R., & Karlson, H. C. (1996). Psychological maltreatment. In J. Briere, L. Berliner, J. A. Bulkley, C. Jenny, & T. Reid (Eds.), *The APSAC handbook on child maltreatment* (pp. 72-89). Thousand Oaks, CA: Sage.

Hechler, D. (1993). Commentary: Damage control. *Child Abuse & Neglect, 17*, 703-708.

Heinemann's Appeal, 96 Pa. 112 (1880).

Helfer, R. E., & Kempe, R. S. (Eds.). (1987). *The battered child* (4th ed.). Chicago: University of Chicago Press.

Henderson, D. J. (1975). Incest. In A. M. Freedman, H. I. Kaplan, & B. J. Sadock (Eds.), *Comprehensive textbook of psychiatry*. Baltimore: Williams & Wilkins.

Hennington v. State, 702 So.2d. 403 (Miss. 1997).

Herman, J. L. (1981). *Father-daughter incest*. Cambridge, MA: Harvard University Press

Heoo, A.K. (1998). Accepting forensic case referrals: Ethical and professional considerations. *Professional Psychology: Research and Practice, 29*, 109-114.

Hewitt, S. K. (1998). *Small voices: Assessing allegations of sexual abuse in preschool children*. Thousand Oaks, CA: Sage.

Hibbard, R. A., & Hartman, G. (1992). Behavioral problems in alleged sexual abuse victims. *Child Abuse & Neglect, 16*, 755-762.

Hildreth v. Iowa Department of Human Services, 550 N.W.2d 157 (Iowa 1996).

Hodgson v. Minnesota, 497 U.S. 417 (1990).

Hodorowski v. Ray, 844 F.2d 1210 (5th Cir. 1988).

Horner, T. M., Guyer, M. J., & Kalter, N. M. (1993). Clinical expertise and the assessment of child sexual abuse. *Journal of the Academy of Child and Adolescent Psychiatry, 32*, 925-931.

Hubbard, R. S. (1933). Child protection. In F. S. Hall (Ed.), *Social work yearbook 1933*. New York: Russell Sage.

Hudson, J. A. (1990). The emergence of autobiographical memory in mother-child conversation. In R. Fivush & J. A. Hudson (Eds.), *Knowing and remembering in young children* (pp. 166-196). New York: Cambridge University Press.

Hurley, T. (1907). *Origin of the Illinois juvenile court law* (3rd ed.). Chicago: Visitation and Aid Society.

Idaho v. Wright, 110 S. Ct. 3139 (1990).

In re Appeal in Cochise County, 650 P.2d 459 (1982).

In re B.G., 674 A.2d 178 (N.J. Sup. Ct. App. Div. 1996).

In re D.K., 245 N.W.2d 644 (S.D. 1976).

In re Jacobs, 444 N.W.2d 789 (Mich. 1989).

In re K.S., 737 P.2d 170 (Utah 1987).

In re Schroeder, 415 N.W.2d 436 (Minn. Ct. App. 1988).

Index to Legal Periodicals. (1888). Boston: Boston Book.

Index to Legal Periodicals and Books. (1997). Bronx, NY: H. W. Wilson.

Individuals With Disabilities Education Act of 1975, 20 U.S.C. \sec 1400.

Jampole, L., & Weber, M. K. (1987). An assessment of the behavior of sexually abused and non-sexually abused children with anatomically correct dolls. *Child Abuse & Neglect, 11*, 187-192.

Jaudes, P. K., & Martone, M. (1992). Interdisciplinary evaluations of alleged sexual abuse cases. *Pediatrics, 89*, 1164-1168.

Johnson, C. F. (1996). Physical abuse: Accidental versus intentional trauma in children. In J. Briere, L. Berliner, J. A. Bulkley, C. Jenny, & T. Reid (Eds.), *The APSAC handbook on child maltreatment* (pp. 206-226). Thousand Oaks, CA: Sage Publications.

Jones, D. P. H. (1991). Ritualism and child sexual abuse. *Child Abuse & Neglect, 15*, 163-170.

Jones, D. P. H. (1992). *Interviewing the sexually abused child: Investigation of suspected abuse*. London: Royal College of Psychiatrists, Gaskell.

Jones, D. P. H., & Krugman, R. D. (1986). Can a three-year-old child bear witness to her sexual assault and attempted murder? *Child Abuse & Neglect, 10*, 253-258.

Jones, D. P. H., & McGraw, C. M. (1986). Reliable and fictitious accounts of sexual abuse to children. *Journal of Interpersonal Violence, 2*, 27-45.

Jones, D. P. H., & Seig, A. (1988). Child sexual abuse allegations in custody and visitation disputes. In E. B. Nicholson & J. Buckley (Eds.), *Sexual abuse allegations in custody and visitation cases* (pp. 22-36). Washington, DC: American Bar Association, National Legal Resource Center for Child Advocacy and Protection.

Kahn v. Burman, 673 F.Supp. 210 (E.D. Mich. 1987).

Kalichman, S.C. (1993). *Mandated reporting of suspected child abuse: Ethics, law, and policy.* Washington, DC: American Psychological Association.

Kalina v. Fletcher, 118 S. Ct. 502 (1997).

Kansas v. Kendricks, 117 S. Ct. 2072 (1997).

Kaufman, M. (1991). Post-*Tarasoff* legal developments and the mental health literature. *Bulletin of the Menninger Clinic, 55*, 308-322.

Kaufman, K. L., Hilliker, D. R., & Daleiden, E. L. (1996). Subgroup differences in the modus operandi of adolescent sexual offenders. *Child Maltreatment, 1*, 17-24.

Keeton, W. P. (1984). *Prosser and Keeton on torts* (5th ed.). St. Paul, MN: West.

Keith-Spiegel, P., & Koocher, G. P. (1985). *Ethics in psychology: Professional standards and cases.* New York: Random House.

Kelly, S. J. (1996). Ritualistic abuse of children. In J. Briere, L. Berliner, J. A. Bulkley, C. Jenny, & T. Reid (Eds.), *The APSAC handbook on child maltreatment.* (pp. 90-99). Thousand Oaks, CA: Sage.

Kempe, C. H., Silverman, F. N., Steele, B. F., Droegmuller, W., & Silver, H. K. (1962). The battered-child syndrome. *Journal of the American Medical Association, 181*, 17-24.

Kempe, H. (1978). Sexual abuse, another hidden pediatric problem (the 1977 C. Anderson Aldrich Lecture). *Pediatrics, 62*, 382-389.

Kendall-Tackett, K. A., Williams, L. M., & Finkelhor, D. (1993). Impact of sexual abuse on children: A review and synthesis of recent empirical studies. *Psychological Bulletin, 113*, 164-180.

Kenney, L. M., & Vigil, D. (1996). A lawyer's guide to therapeutic interventions in domestic relations court. *Arizona State Law Journal, 28*, 629-672.

Kinsella v. Kinsella, 696 A.2d 556 (N.J. 1997).

Kinsey, A. C. (1953). *Sexual behavior in the human female.* Philadelphia: W. B. Saunders.

Kirkpatrick, H. D. (1997). Commentary: A response to Everson's "Understanding bizarre, improbable, and fantastic elements in children's accounts of abuse." *Child Maltreatment, 2*, 307-310.

Kirshner, R. H., & Wilson, H. L. (1994). Fatal child abuse: The pathologist's perspective. In R. M. Reece (Ed.), *Child abuse: Medical diagnosis and management* (pp. 325-357). Philadelphia: Lea & Febiger.

Knapp, S., & VandeCreek, L. (1996). Risk management for psychologists: Treating patients who recover lost memories of childhood abuse. *Professional Psychology: Research and Practice, 27,* 452-459.

Koehler, J. J. (1993). The normative status of base rates at trial. In N. J. Castellan (Ed.), *Individual and group decision making: Current issues* (pp. 137-149). Hillsdale, NJ: Erlbaum.

Kolko, D. J., & Moser, J. T. (1988). Behavioral/emotional indicators of sexual abuse in child psychiatric inpatients: A controlled comparison with physical abuse. *Child Abuse & Neglect, 12,* 529-541.

Koocher, G. P., Goodman, G. S., White, C. S., Friedrich, W. N., Sivan, A. B., & Reynolds, C. R. (1995). Psychological science and the use of anatomically detailed dolls in child sexual-abuse assessments. *Psychological Bulletin, 118,* 199-222.

Koop, C. E. (n.d.). U.S. Department of Health and Human Services. *The Surgeon General's letter on child sexual abuse.* Washington, DC: Government Printing Office.

Kuhn, P. (1997). Sigmund Freud's discovery of the etiological significance of childhood sexual traumas. *Journal of Child Sexual Abuse, 6,* 107-122.

LaFave, W. R., & Israel, J. H. (1991). *Criminal procedure* (2nd ed.). St. Paul, MN: West

Lake, P. F. (1994). Revisiting *Tarasoff. Albany Law Review, 58,* 97-173.

Lamb, M. E. (1994). The investigation of child sexual abuse: An interdisciplinary consensus statement. *Child Abuse & Neglect, 18,* 1021-1028.

Lamb, M. E., Hershkowitz, I., Sternberg, K. J., Esplin, P. W., Hovav, M., Manor, T., & Yudilevitch, L. (1996). Effects of investigative utterance types on Israeli children's responses. *International Journal on Behavioral Development, 19,* 627-637.

Lamb, M. E., Sternberg, K. J., & Esplin, P. W. (1994). Factors influencing the reliability and validity of statements made by young victims of sexual maltreatment. *Journal of Applied Developmental Psychology, 15,* 255-280.

Lamb, M. E., Sternberg, K. J., & Esplin, P. W. (1995). Making children into competent witnesses: Reactions to the amicus brief *In re Michaels. Psychology, Public Policy and Law, 1,* 438-449.

Lamb, M. E., Sternberg, K. J., Esplin, P. W., Hershkowitz, I., Orbach, Y., & Hovav, M. (1997). Criterion-based content analysis: A field validation study. *Child Abuse and Maltreatment, 21,* 255-264.

Landeros v. Flood, 551 P.2d 389 (Cal. 1976).

Lanktree, C., Briere, J., & Zaidi, L. (1991). Incidence and impact of sexual abuse in a child outpatient sample: The role of direct inquiry. *Child Abuse & Neglect, 15,* 447-453.

Lanning, K. V. (1992a). *Child sex rings: A behavioral analysis.* Quantico, VA: Federal Bureau of Investigation, National Center for Missing and Exploited Children.

Lanning, K.V. (1992b). *Investigator's guide to allegations of "ritual" child abuse.* Quantico, VA: Federal Bureau of Investigation, National Center for the Analysis of Violent Crime.

Lanyon, R. I., Dannenbaum, S. E., & Brown, A. R. (1991). Detection of deliberate denial in child abusers. *Journal of Interpersonal Violence, 6,* 301-309.

Lawson, L., & Chaffin, M. (1992). False negatives in sexual abuse disclosure interviews: Incidence and influence of caretaker's belief in abuse cases of accidental abuse discovery by diagnosis of STD. *Journal of Interpersonal Violence, 7,* 532-542.

Lazoritz, S. (1990). Whatever happened to Mary Ellen? *Child Abuse & Neglect, 14,* 143-149.

Lazoritz, S. (1992). Child abuse: An historical perspective. In S. Ludwig & A. E. Kornberg (Eds.), *Child abuse: A medical reference* (2nd ed., pp. 85-90). New York: Churchill Livingstone.

Lazoritz, S., Baldwin, S., & Kini, N. (1997). The whiplash shaken infant syndrome: Has Chaffey's syndrome changed or have we changed his syndrome? *Child Abuse & Neglect, 21,* 1009-1014.

LeGrand, C. E. (1973). Rape and rape laws: Sexism in society and law. *California Law Review, 61,* 919-941.

Leiby, J. (1978). *A history of social welfare and social work in the United States.* New York: Columbia University Press.

Leichtman, M. D., & Ceci, S. J. (1995). The effects of stereotypes and suggestions on preschoolers' reports. *Developmental Psychology, 31,* 568-578.

Leong, G. B., Eth, S., & Silva, J. A. (1992). The psychotherapist as witness for the prosecution: The criminalization of *Tarasoff. American Journal of Psychiatry, 149,* 1011-1015.

Leong, G. B., Eth, S., & Silva, J. A. (1994a). Silence or death: The limits of confidentiality when a psychotherapist is threatened by the patient. *Journal of Psychiatry and Law, 22,* 235-244.

Leong, G. B., Eth, S., & Silva, J. A. (1994b). "Tarasoff" defendants: Social justice or ethical decay? *Journal of Forensic Sciences, 39,* 86-93.

Lepore, S. J., & Sesco, B. (1994). Distorting children's reports and interpretations of events through suggestion. *Journal of Applied Psychology, 79,* 108-120.

Letourneau, E. J., & Lewis, T. C. (in press). *Backlash in the classroom: The portrayal and betrayal of child sexual assault victims in introductory psychology textbooks.*

Levin, S. M., & Stava, L. (1987). Personality characteristics of sex offenders: A review. *Archives of Sexual Behavior, 16,* 57-79.

Levitt, C. J., Smith, W. L., & Alexander, R. C. (1994). Abusive head trauma. In R. M. Reece (Ed.), *Child abuse: Medical diagnosis and management* (pp. 1-??). Philadelphia: Lea & Febiger.

Lilly, G. C. (1996). *An introduction to the law of evidence* (3rd ed.). St. Paul, MN: West.

Lindblad, F., Gustafsson, P. A., Larsson, I., & Lundin, B. (1995). Preschoolers' sexual behavior at daycare centers: An epidemiological study. *Child Abuse & Neglect, 19,* 569-577.

Lindenthal, J. J., & Thomas, C. S. (1992). Confidentiality in clinical psychiatry. *Medicine and Law, 11,* 119-125.

Lindsay, D. S. (1994). Memory source monitoring and eyewitness testimony. In D. F. Ross, J. D. Read, & M. P. Toglia (Eds.), *Adult eyewitness testimony: Current trends and developments* (pp. 27-55). New York: Cambridge University Press.

Lindsay, D. S., & Read, J. D. (1994). Psychotherapy and memories of childhood sexual abuse: A cognitive perspective. *Applied Cognitive Psychology, 8,* 281-338.

Lipovsky, J. A., Saunders, B. E., & Murphy, S. M. (1989). Depression, anxiety, and behavior problems among victims of father-child sexual assault and nonabused siblings. *Journal of Interpersonal Violence, 4,* 452-468.

Loftus, E. F. (1997, September). Creating false memories. *Scientific American,* pp. 70-75.

Lovett v. Superior Court, 250 Cal. Rptr. 25 (Ct. App. 1988).

Lowe v. Aldridge, 958 F.2d 1565 (11th Cir. 1992).

Ludwig, S., & Kornberg, A. E. (Eds.). (1992). *Child abuse: A medical reference* (2nd ed.). New York: Churchill Livingstone.

Lyon, T. D., Gilles, E. E., & Cory, L. (1996). Medical evidence of physical abuse in infants and young children. *Pacific Law Journal, 28*, 93-167.

Lythgoe v. Guinn, 884 P.2d 1085 (Alaska 1994).

M.L.B. v. S.L.J., 117 S. Ct. 555 (1996).

MacFarlane, K., & Waterman, J. (1986). *Sexual abuse of young children.* New York: Guilford.

Maciariello v. City of Lancaster, 973 F.2d 295 (4th Cir. 1992).

Mack, J. W. (1909). The juvenile court. *Harvard Law Review, 23*, 104-122.

Mackner, L. M., Starr, R. H., & Black, M. M. (1997). The cumulative effect of neglect and failure to thrive on cognitive functioning. *Child Abuse & Neglect, 21*, 691-700.

Malinosky-Rummell, R., & Hansen, D. J. (1993). Long-term consequences of childhood physical abuse. *Psychological Bulletin, 114*, 68-79.

Malley v. Briggs, 475 U.S. 335 (1986).

Mannarino, A. P., & Cohen, J. A. (1986). A clinical-demographic study of sexually abused children. *Child Abuse & Neglect, 10*, 17-23.

Manzano v. South Dakota Department of Social Services, 60 F.3d 505 (8th Cir. 1995).

Marneffe, C. (1996). Child abuse treatment: A fallow land. *Child Abuse & Neglect, 20*, 379-384.

Marshall, W. L., & Hall, G. C. N. (1995). The value of the MMPI in deciding forensic issues in accused sex offenders. *Sexual Abuse: A Journal of Research and Treatment, 7*, 205-217.

Martone, M., Jaudes, P. K., & Cavins, M. K. (1996). Criminal prosecution of child sexual abuse cases. *Child Abuse & Neglect, 20*, 457-464.

Marxsen, D., Yuille, J. C., & Nisbet, M. (1995). The complexities of eliciting and assessing children's statements. *Psychology, Public Policy and Law, 1*, 450-460.

Maryland v. Craig, 497 U.S. 836 (1990).

Masson, J. M. (1984). *The assault on truth: Freud's suppression of the seduction theory.* New York: Farrar, Straus & Giroux.

Matter of Schroeder, 415 N.W.2d 436 (Minn. Ct. App. 1988).

May v. Southeast Wyoming Mental Health Center, 866 P.2d 732 (Wyo. 1993).

McCauley, J., Kern, D. E., Kolodner, K., Dill, L., Schroeder, A. F., De Chant, H. K., Ryden, J., Derogatis, L. R., & Bass, E. B. (1997). Clinical characteristics of women with a history of childhood sexual abuse: Unhealed wounds. *Journal of the American Medical Association, 277*, 1362-1368.

McClain, P. W., Sacks, J. J., Froehlke, R. G., & Ewigman, B. G. (1993). Estimates of fatal child abuse and neglect, United States. *Pediatrics, 91*, 338-343.

McCormick on evidence (3rd ed., E. W. Cleary, Ed.). (1984). St. Paul, MN: West.

McDermott, T. E. (1975). California rape evidence reform: An analysis of Senate Bill 1678. *Hastings Law Journal, 26*, 1551-1573.

McGough, L. S. (1994). *Child witnesses: Fragile voices in the American legal system.* New Haven, CT: Yale University Press.

Mencken, H. L. (1949). *A Mencken chrestomathy.* New York: Knopf.

Meinig, M. B. (1991). Profile of Roland Summit. *Violence Update, 1*, 6-7.

Melton, G. B., Goodman, G. S., Kalichman, S. C., Levine, M., Saywitz, K. J., & Koocher, G. P. (1995). Empirical research on child maltreatment and the law. *Journal of Clinical Child Psychology, 24*, 47-77.

Melton, G. B., & Limber, S. (1989). Psychologists' involvement in cases of child maltreatment. *American Psychologist, 44*, 1225-1233.

Melton, G. B., Petrila, J., Poythress, N., & Slobogin, C. (1987). *Psychological evaluations for the courts.* New York: Guilford.

Melton, G. B., Petrila, J., Poythress, N., & Slobogin, C. (1997). *Psychological evaluations for the courts* (2nd ed.). New York: Guilford.

Memon, A., & Vartoukian, R. (1996). The effects of repeated questioning on young children's eyewitness testimony. *British Journal of Psychology, 87,* 403-415.

Menendez v. Superior Court, 834 P.2d 786 (Cal. 1992).

Meriwhether, M. H. (1986). Child abuse reporting laws: Time for a change. *Family Law Quarterly, 20,* 141-171.

Merritt, K. A., Ornstein, P. A., & Spiker, B. (1994). Children's memory for a salient medical procedure: Implications for testimony. *Pediatrics, 94,* 17-30.

Mershon v. Beasley, 994 F.2d 449 (8th Cir. 1993).

Meyer v. Nebraska, 262 U.S. 390 (1923).

Mian, M., Marton, P., & LeBaron, D. (1996). The effects of sexual abuse on 3- to 5-year-old girls. *Child Abuse & Neglect, 20,* 731-745.

Miller, I. J. (1996). Ethical and liability issues concerning invisible rationing. *Professional Psychology: Research and Practice, 27,* 583-587.

Millspaugh v. County Department of Public Welfare of Wabash County, 937 F.2d 1172 (7th Cir. 1991).

Miranda v. Arizona, 384 U.S. 436 (1966).

Moline, M. E., Williams, G. T., & Austin, K. M. (1998). *Documenting psychotherapy: Essentials for mental health practitioners.* Thousand Oaks, CA: Sage.

Monahan, J. (1993). Limiting therapist exposure to *Tarasoff* liability: Guidelines for risk containment. *American Psychologist, 48,* 242-250.

Monck, E. (1997). Evaluating therapeutic intervention with sexually abused children. *Child Abuse Review, 6,* 163-177.

Monnell v. Department of Social Services, 436 U.S. 658 (1978).

Montoya v. Bebensee, 761 P.2d 285 (Colo. Ct. App. 1988).

Morgan, M. (1995). *How to interview sexual abuse victims.* Newbury Park, CA: Sage.

Morgan v. Foretich, 846 F.2d 941 (4th Cir. 1988).

Morison, S., & Greene, E. (1992). Juror and expert knowledge of child sexual abuse. *Child Abuse & Neglect, 16,* 595-613.

Morrow, J., Yeager, C. A., & Lewis, D. O. (1997). Encopresis and sexual abuse in a sample of boys in residental treatment. *Child Abuse & Neglect, 21,* 11-18.

Moses v. McWilliams, 549 A.2d 950 (Pa. Super. 1988).

Moses v. Parwatikar, 813 F.2d 891 (8th Cir. 1987).

Moss, D. C. (1988). Abuse scale: Point system for abuse claims. *American Bar Association Journal, 74,* 26.

Moss Rehab v. White, 692 A.2d 902 (Del. 1997).

Mosteller, R. P. (1989). Child sexual abuse and statements for the purpose of medical diagnosis or treatment. *North Carolina Law Review, 67,* 257-294.

Murphy, J. M., Jellinek, M., Quinn, D., Smith, G., Poitrast, F. G., & Goshko, M. (1991). Substance abuse and serious child mistreatment: Prevalence, risk, and outcome in a court sample. *Child Abuse & Neglect, 15,* 197-211.

Murphy, W., Rau, T., & Worley, P. (1994). The perils and pitfalls of profiling child sex abusers. *APSAC Advisor, 7,* 3-4, 28-29.

Murphy, W. D., & Smith, T. A. (1996). Sex offenders against children: Empirical and clinical issues. In J. Briere, L. Berliner, J.A. Bulkley, C. Jenny, & T. Reid (Eds.), *The APSAC handbook on child maltreatment* (pp. 175-191). Thousand Oaks, CA: Sage.

Murray, K. (1995). *Live television link: An evaluation of its use by child witnesses in Scottish criminal trials.* Edinburgh: Scottish Office, Central Research Unit.

Myers, J. E. B. (1992). *Legal issues in child abuse and neglect practice.* Newbury Park, CA: Sage.

Myers, J. E. B. (1993). Expert testimony regarding psychological syndromes. *Pacific Law Journal, 24,* 1449-1464.

Myers, J. E. B. (1994). The literature of the backlash. In J. E. B. Myers (Ed.), *The backlash: Child protection under fire* (pp. 86-103). Thousand Oaks, CA: Sage.

Myers, J. E. B. (1995). The new era of skepticism regarding children's credibility. *Psychology, Public Policy, and Law, 1,* 387-398.

Myers, J. E. B. (1996). A decade of international legal reform regarding child abuse investigation and litigation: Steps toward a child witness code. *Pacific Law Journal, 28,* 169-241.

Myers, J. E. B. (1997a). *Evidence in child abuse and neglect cases* (3rd ed.). New York: John Wiley.

Myers, J. E. B. (1997b). *A mother's nightmare: Incest: A practical legal guide for parents and professionals.* Thousand Oaks, CA: Sage.

Myers J. E. B., Bays, J., Becker, J., Berliner, L., Corwin, D., & Saywitz, K. (1989) Expert testimony in child sexual abuse litigation. *Nebraska Law Review, 68,* 1-145.

Myers, J. E. B., Diedrich, S., Lee, D., & McClanahan-Fincher, K. M. (1998). Prosecution of child sexual abuse in the United States. In J. Conte (Ed.), *Child sexual abuse: Knowns and unknowns. A volume in the tradition of Roland Summit.* Thousand Oaks, CA: Sage.

Myers, J. E. B., Goodman, G. S., & Saywitz, K. J. (1996). Psychological research on children as witnesses: Practical implications for forensic interviews and courtroom testimony. *Pacific Law Journal, 28,* 3-92.

Nahmod, S. H. (1991). *Civil rights and civil liberties litigation: The law of Section 1983.* Colorado Springs, CO: Shepards/McGraw-Hill.

National Association of Social Workers. (1997). *Code of ethics.* Washington, DC: Author.

National Center for Prosecution of Child Abuse. (1993). *Investigation and prosecution of child abuse* (2nd ed.). Alexandria, VA: National District Attorneys Association.

Nelson, K., & Ross, G. (1980). The generalities and specifics of long-term memory in infants and young children. *New Directions for Child Development, 10,* 87-101.

New York v. Ferber, 458 U.S. 747 (1982).

Nichols, H. R., & Molinder, I. (1984). *Multiphasic Sex Inventory manual.* Tacoma, WA: Authors.

Note. (1938). Statutory rape: Desirability of evidence that female was previously unchaste or married in mitigation of punishment. *Virginia Law Review, 24,* 335-341.

Note. (1952). Forcible and statutory rape: An exploration of the operation and objective of the consent standard. *Yale Law Journal, 62,* 55-83.

Note. (1954). Rape and battery between husband and wife. *Stanford Law Review, 6,* 719-728.

Note. (1960). Statutory rape: Previous chaste character in Florida. *University of Florida Law Review, 13,* 201-214.

Note. (1966). The resistance standard in rape legislation. *Stanford Law Review, 18,* 680-689.

Note. (1970). The corroboration rule and crimes accompanying a rape. *University of Pennsylvania Law Review, 118,* 458-472.

Note. (1972). The rape corroboration requirement: Repeal not reform. *Yale Law Journal,* *81,* 1365-1391.

Nugent, P., & Kroner, D. G. (1996). Denial, response styles, and admittance of offenses among child molesters and rapists. *Journal of Interpersonal Violence, 11,* 475-486.

Nye, S. G. (1980). Legal issues in the practice of child psychiatry. In D. H. Schetky & E. P. Benedek (Eds.), *Child psychiatry and the law* (pp. 266-286). New York: Brunner/Mazel.

Oates, K., Lunch, D. L., & Stearn, A. E. (1995). The criminal justice system and the sexually abused child: Help or hindrance? *Medical Journal of Australia, 70,* 435-441.

Oates, R. K., Jones, D. P. H., Denson, S., Sirotnak, A., & Krugman, R. D. (in press). Erroneous accounts of child sexual abuse. *Child Abuse & Neglect.*

Oberlander, L. B. (1995). Psycholegal issues in child sexual abuse evaluations: A survey of forensic mental health professionals. *Child Abuse & Neglect, 19,* 475-490.

Olafson, E., Corwin, D. L., & Summit, R. C. (1993). Modern history of child sexual abuse awareness: Cycles of discovery and suppression. *Child Abuse & Neglect, 17,* 7-24.

Opinion of the Justices to the Senate, 668 N.E.2d 738 (Mass. 1996).

Osborne v. Ohio, 495 U.S. 103 (1990).

Oxendine v. State, 528 A.2d 870 (Del. 1987).

Parnell, T. F., & Day, D. O. (Eds.). (1998). *Munchausen by proxy syndrome: Misunderstood child abuse.* Thousand Oaks, CA: Sage.

Paulsen, M. G. (1967). Child abuse reporting laws: The shape of the legislation. *Columbia Law Review, 67,* 1-49.

Pelton, L. H. (1985). Child abuse and neglect: The myth of classlessness. In L. H. Pelton (Ed.), *The social context of child abuse and neglect.* New York: Human Sciences Press.

Pence, D., & Wilson, C. (1994). *Team investigation of child sexual abuse.* Thousand Oaks, CA: Sage.

Pennsylvania v. Ritchie, 480 U.S. 39 (1987).

People v. Battaglia, 203 Cal. Rptr. 370 (Cal. Ct. App. 1984).

People v. Bernal, 10 Cal. 66 (Cal. 1858).

People v. Bledsoe, 681 P.2d 291 (Cal. 1984).

People v. Cavaiani, 432 N.W.2d 409 (Mich. Ct. App. 1988).

People v. Coleman, 768 P.2d 32 (Cal. 1989).

People v. Hammon, 938 P.2d 986 (Cal. 1997).

People v. Hampton, 746 P.2d 947 (Colo. 1987).

People v. Jackson, 95 Cal. Rptr. 919 (Ct. App. 1971).

People v. McAlpin, 812 P.2d 563 (Cal. 1991).

People v. Phillips, 175 Cal. Rptr. 703 (Ct. App. 1981).

People v. Stoll, 783 P.2d 698 (Cal. 1989).

People v. Taylor, 552 N.E.2d 131, 552 N.Y.S.2d 883 (1990).

People v. Whitehurst, 12 Cal. Rptr.2d 33 (Ct. App. 1992).

Perry, N. (1987). Child and adolescent development: A psychological perspective. In J. E. B. Meyers (Ed.), *Child witness law and practice* (pp. 459-525). New York: John Wiley.

Perry, N. W., & Wrightsman, L. S. (1991). *The child witness.* Newbury Park, CA: Sage.

Peters, D. (1991). The influence of stress and arousal on the child witness. In J. Dorris (Ed.), *The suggestibility of children's recollections* (pp. 60-76). Washington, DC: American Psychological Association.

Peters, J. J. (1976). Children who are victims of sexual assault and the psychology of offenders. *American Journal of Psychotherapy, 30,* 399-421.

Peterson, C. (1996). The preschool child witness: Errors in accounts of traumatic injury. *Canadian Journal of Behavioral Science, 28,* 36-42.

Peterson, C., & Bell, M. (1996). Children's memory for traumatic injury. *Child Development, 67,* 3045-3070.

Pettus v. Cole, 57 Cal. Rptr. 2d 46 (Ct. App. 1996).

Pezdek, K., Finger, K., & Hodge, D. (1997). Planting false childhood memories: The role of event plausibility. *Psychological Science, 8,* 437-441.

Pezdek, K., & Greene, J. (1993). Testing eyewitness memory: Developing a measure that is more resistant to suggestibility. *Law and Human Behavior, 17,* 361-369.

Pezdek, K., & Roe, C. (1997). The suggestibility of children's memory for being touched: Planting, erasing and changing memories. *Law and Human Behavior, 21,* 95-106.

Phipps-Yonas, S., Yonas, A., Turner, M., & Kauper, M. (1993). Sexuality in early childhood: The observations and opinions of family day care providers. *University of Minnesota CURA Reporter, 23,* 1-5.

Pierce v. Society of Sisters, 268 U.S. 510 (1925).

Pipe, M., Gee, S., & Wilson, C. (1993). Cues, props, and context: Do they facilitate children's event reports? In G. S. Goodman & B. L. Bottoms (Eds.), *Child victims, child witnesses: Understanding and improving testimony* (pp. 25-45). New York: Guilford.

Pitts v. County of Kern, 949 P.2d 920 (Cal. 1998).

Ploscowe, M. (1960). Sex offenses: The American legal context. *Law and Contemporary Problems, 25,* 217-224.

Pomeroy, W. B. (1976, November). A new look at incest. *Forum,* pp. 9-13.

Poole, D. A., & Lamb, M. E. (1998). *Investigative interviews of children.* Washington, DC: American Psychological Association.

Poole, D. A., & Lindsay, D. S. (1998). Assessing the accuracy of young children's reports: Lessons from the investigation of child sexual abuse. *Applied and Preventive Psychology, 7,* 1-26.

Poole, D. A., & White, L. T. (1995). Tell me again and again: Stability and change in the repeated testimonies of children and adults. In M. S. Zaragoza, J. R. Graham, G. C. N. Hall, R. Hirschman, & Y. S. Ben-Porath (Eds.), *Memory and testimony in the child witness* (pp. 24-43). Thousand Oaks, CA: Sage.

Prentky, R. A., Knight, R. A., & Lee, A. F. S. (1997). Risk factors associated with recidivism among extrafamilial child molesters. *Journal of Consulting and Clinical Psychology, 65,* 141-149.

Prince v. Massachusetts, 321 U.S. 158 (1944).

Puttkammer, E. W. (1925). Consent in rape. *Illinois Law Review, 19,* 410-428.

Pynoos, R. S., & Eth, S. (1984). The child witness to homicide. *Journal of Social Issues, 40,* 87-108.

Pynoos, R. S., & Nader, K. (1989). Children's memory and proximity to violence. *Journal of the American Academy of Child and Adolescent Psychiatry, 28,* 236-241.

Quinn, K. M. (1988). The credibility of children's allegations of sexual abuse. *Behavioral Sciences and the Law, 6,* 181-199.

Radbill, S. X. (1987). Children in a world of violence: A history of child abuse. In R. E. Helfer & R. S. Kempe (Eds.), *The battered child* (pp. 3-22). Chicago: University of Chicago Press.

Rainier's Dairies v. Raritan Valley Farms, Inc., 117 A.2d 889 (N.J. 1955).

Ramona v. Superior Court, 66 Cal. Rptr. 2d 766 (Ct. App. 1997).

Random House unabridged dictionary (2nd ed.). (1993). New York: Random House.

Raskin, D. C., & Esplin, P. W. (1991). Assessment of children's statements of sexual abuse. In J. Doris (Ed.), *The suggestibility of children's recollections: Implications for eyewitness testimony* (pp. 153-164). Washington, DC: American Psychological Association.

Read, J. (1997). Child abuse and psychosis: A literature review and implications for professional practice. *Professional Psychology: Research and Practice, 28,* 448-456.

Reece, R. M. (Ed.). (1994). *Child abuse: Medical diagnosis and management.* Malvern, PA: Lea & Febiger.

Reece, R. M. (Ed.). (1997). Review of Fleming, J. (1997). Prevalence of childhood sexual abuse in a community sample of Australian women. *Medical Journal of Australia, 166,* 65-68. (In *Child Abuse Medical Quarterly Manual Update, 4,* 14-15)

Reed, M. L. (1992). Mandated reporting revisited: *Roe v. Superior Court. Law and Policy, 14,* 218-239.

Reeker, J., Ensing, D., & Elliott, R. (1997). A meta-analytic investigation of group treatment outcomes for sexually abused children. *Child Abuse & Neglect, 21,* 669-680.

Reid, T. (1995). *Father-daughter incest in contemporary fiction.* Unpublished manuscript.

Renn v. Garrison, 100 F.3d 344 (4th Cir. 1996).

Renzi v. Morrison, 618 N.E.2d 794 (Ill. Ct. App. 1993).

Reynolds v. United States, 98 U.S. 145 (1878).

Ricketson, M. E. (1991, January). Custody cases and the theory of parental alienation syndrome. *Colorado Lawyer, 20,* 53-56.

Roback, H. B., Moore, R. F., Waterhouse, G. J., & Martin, P. R. (1996). Confidentiality dilemmas in group psychotherapy with substance-dependent physicians. *American Journal of Psychiatry, 153,* 1250-1260.

Roback, H., Ochoa, E., Bloch, F., & Purdon, S. (1992). Guarding confidentiality in clinical groups: The therapist's dilemma. *International Journal of Group Psychotherapy, 42,* 881-903.

Robbing v. Hamburger Home for Girls, 38 Cal. Rptr. 2d 534 (Ct. App. 1995).

Roberts, K. P., & Blades, M. (1996). Children's eyewitness testimony for real-life and fantasy events. *Investigative and Forensic Decision Making, 26,* 52-57.

Robin, R. W., Chester, B., Rasmussen, J. K., Jaranson, J. M., & Goldman, D. (1997). Prevalence, characteristics, and impact of childhood sexual abuse in a southwestern American Indian tribe. *Child Abuse & Neglect, 21,* 769-787.

Rodriguez, N., Ryan, S. W., Vande Kamp, H., & Foy, D. W. (1997). Posttraumatic stress disorder in adult female survivors of childhood sexual abuse: A comparison study. *Journal of Consulting and Clinical Psychology, 65,* 53-59.

Rogers, F., & Barrett, D. (1996). *Daubert v. Merrell Dow* and expert testimony by clinical psychologists: Implications and recommendations for practice. *Professional Psychology: Research and Practice, 27,* 467-474.

Rosenberg, D. A. (1994). Munchausen syndrome by proxy. In R. M. Reece (Ed.), *Child abuse: Medical diagnosis and treatment* (pp. 266-278). Philadelphia: Lea & Febiger.

Rost v. State Board of Psychology, 659 A.2d 626 (Pa. Commonwealth Ct. 1995).

Rotheram-Borus, M. J., Mahler, K. A., Koopman, C., & Lanabeer, K. (1996). Sexual abuse history and associated multiple risk behavior in adolescent runaways. *American Journal of Orthopsychiatry, 66,* 390-400.

Ruby, C. L., & Brigham, J. C. (1997). The usefulness of the criteria-based content analysis technique in distinguishing between truthful and fabricated allegations: A critical review. *Psychology, Public Policy and Law, 3,* 705-737.

Runyan, D. K. (1993). The emotional impact of societal intervention into child abuse. In G. S. Goodman & B. L. Bottoms (Eds.), *Child victims, child witnesses: Understanding and improving testimony* (pp. 263-277). New York: Guilford.

Runyan, D. K., Everson, M. D., Edelsohn, G. A., Hunter, W. M., & Coulter, M. L. (1988). Impact of legal intervention on sexually abused children. *Journal of Pediatrics, 113,* 647-653.

Ruscio, J. (1998). Information integration in child welfare cases: An introduction to statistical decision making. *Child Maltreatment, 3,* 143-156.

Russ, I. (1996, Winter). Parental alienation syndrome does not exist. *CAPSAC Consultant,* pp. 4-5.

Russell, D. E. H. (1983). The incidence and prevalence of intrafamilial and extrafamilial sexual abuse of female children. *Child Abuse & Neglect, 7,* 133-146.

Russell, D. E. H. (1984). *Sexual exploitation: Rape, child sexual abuse and workplace harassment.* Beverly Hills, CA: Sage.

Russell, D. E. H. (1986). *The secret trauma: Incest in the lives of girls and women.* New York: Basic Books.

Russell v. Gregoire, 1997 WL 539074 (9th Cir. 1997).

Sagatun, I. J., & Edwards, L. P. (1995). *Child abuse and the legal system.* Chicago: Nelson-Hall.

Saks, M. J. (1990). Expert witnesses, nonexpert witnesses, and nonwitness experts. *Law and Human Behavior, 14,* 291-313.

Salter, A. C. (1995). *Transforming trauma: A guide to understanding and treating adult survivors of child sexual abuse.* Thousand Oaks, CA: Sage.

Salyer v. Patrick, 874 F.2d 374 (6th Cir. 1989).

Sanders, R. M., & Ladwa-Thomas, U. (1997). Interagency perspectives on child sexual abuse perpetrated by juveniles. *Child Maltreatment, 2,* 264-271.

Sarwer, D. B., Crawford, I., & Durlak, J. A. (1997). The relationship between childhood sexual abuse and adult male sexual dysfunction. *Child Abuse & Neglect, 21,* 649-655.

Saywitz, K. J. (1989). Children's conceptions of the legal system: "Court is a place to play basketball." In S. J. Ceci, D. F. Ross, & M. P. Toglia (Eds.), *Perspectives on children's testimony.* New York: Springer-Verlag.

Saywitz, K. J., & Elliott, D. (1999). *Interviewing children in the forensic context: A developmental approach.* Washington, DC: American Psychological Association.

Saywitz, K. J., & Geiselman, R. E. (1998). Maximizing completeness while minimizing error in children's recall for events. In S. Lynn & K. McConkey (Eds.), *Truth in memory* (pp. 190-223). New York: Guilford.

Saywitz, K. J., Geiselman, R. E., & Bornstein, G. (1992). Effects of cognitive interviewing and practice on children's recall performance. *Journal of Applied Psychology, 77,* 744-756.

Saywitz, K. J., Goodman, G. S., Nicholas, E., & Moan, S. F. (1991). Children's memories of a physical examination involving genital touch: Implications for reports of child sexual abuse. *Journal of Consulting and Clinical Psychology, 59,* 682-691.

Saywitz, K. J., Jaenicke, C., & Camparo, L. (1990). Children's knowledge of legal terminology. *Law and Human Behavior, 14,* 523-535.

Saywitz, K. J., Nathason, R., Snyder, L., & Lamphear, V. (1993). *Preparing children for the investigative and judicial process: Improving communication, memory and emotional resiliency* (Final report to the National Center on Child Abuse and Neglect, Grant No. 90-CA-1179). Los Angeles: University of California, Department of Psychiatry.

Saywitz, K. J., & Snyder, L. (1996). Narrative elaboration: Test of a new procedure for interviewing children. *Journal of Consulting and Clinical Psychology, 64,* 3045-3070.

Saywitz, K. J., Snyder, L., & Lamphear, V. (1996). Helping children tell what happened: A follow-up study of the narrative elaboration procedure. *Child Maltreatment, 1,* 200-212.

Schmitt, B. D. (1987). The child with nonaccidental trauma. In R. E. Helfer & R. S. Kempe (Eds.), *The battered child* (4th ed., pp. 178-196). Chicago: University of Chicago Press.

Shaw, J. S., Garven, S., & Wood, J. M. (1997). Co-witness information can have immediate effects on eyewitness memory reports. *Law and Human Behavior, 21,* 503-523.

Shaw, J. S., & McClure, K. A. (1996). Repeated postevent questioning can lead to elevated levels of eyewitness confidence. *Law and Human Behavior, 20,* 629-653.

Siegal, M., & Peterson, C. C. (1995). Memory and suggestibility in conversations with young children. *Australian Journal of Psychology, 47,* 38-41.

Silberg v. Anderson, 786 P.2d 365 (Cal. 1990).

Simon, W. T., & Schouten, G. W. (1993). The pethysmograph reconsidered: Comments on Barker and Howell. *Bulletin of the American Academy of Psychiatry and Law, 21,* 505-512.

Sims v. State, 311 S.E.2d 161 (Ga. 1984).

Sink, F. (1988). Studies of true and false allegations: A critical review. In E. B. Nicholson & J. Buckley (Eds.), *Sexual abuse allegations in custody and visitation cases* (pp. 37-47). Washington, DC: American Bar Association, National Legal Resource Center for Child Advocacy and Protection.

Slovenko, R. (1996). The duty of therapists to third parties. *Journal of Psychiatry and Law, 23,* 383-410.

Smith, J. T. (1986). *Medical malpractice: Psychiatric care.* New York: McGraw-Hill.

Smith, S. R. (1996). Malpractice liability of mental health professionals and institutions. In B. D. Sales & D. W. Shuman (Eds.), *Law, mental health, and mental disorder.* Pacific Grove, CA: Brooks/Cole.

Smith, S. R., & Meyer, R. G. (1984). Child abuse reporting laws and psychotherapy: A time for reconsideration. *International Journal of Law and Psychiatry, 7,* 351-366.

Sorensen, T., & Snow, B. (1991). How children tell: The process of disclosure in child sexual abuse. *Child Welfare, 70,* 3-15.

Southall, D. P., Plunkett, M. C. B., Banks, M. W., Falkov, A. F., & Samuels, M. P. (1997). Covert video recordings of life-threatening child abuse: Lessons for child protection. *Pediatrics, 100,* 735-760.

Spencer, J. R., & Flin, R. (1993). *The evidence of children: The law and the psychology* (2nd ed.). London: Blackstone.

State ex rel. George B.W. v. Kaufman, 483 S.E.2d 852 (W. Va. 1997).

State v. Alberico, 861 P.2d 192 (N.M. 1993).

State v. Allewalt, 517 A.2d 741 (Md. 1986).

State v. Andring, 342 N.W.2d 128 (Minn. 1984).

State v. Bitman, 13 Iowa 485 (1862).

State v. Black, 745 P.2d 12 (Wash. 1987).

State v. Brodniak, 718 P.2d 322 (Mont. 1986).

State v. Evans, 802 S.W.2d 507 (Mo. 1991).

State v. Graham, 798 P.2d 314 (Wash. Ct. App. 1990).

State v. Hadden, 690 So.2d 573 (Fla. 1997).

State v. Hathorn, 395 So.2d 783 (La. 1981).

State v. Helewa, 537 A.2d 1328 (N.J. Super. App. Div. 1988).

State v. Holden, 414 N.W.2d 516 (Minn. Ct. App. 1987).

State v. Huey, 699 P.2d 1290 (Ariz. 1985).

State v. Hunt, 406 P.2d 208 (Ariz. Ct. App. 1965).

State v. Hurd, 400 N.W.2d 42 (Wis. Ct. App. 1986).

State v. Hutto, 481 S.E.2d 432 (S.C. Sup. Ct. 1997).

State v. Juneau, 59 N.W. 580 (Wis. 1894).

State v. Logan, 806 P.2d 137 (Ore. Ct. App. 1991).

State v. Marks, 647 P.2d 1292 (Kan. 1982).

State v. McCoy, 366 S.E.2d 731 (W. Va. 1988).

State v. Michaels, 642 A.2d 1372 (N.J. 1994).

State v. Milbradt, 756 P.2d 620 (Or. 1988).

State v. Myers, 923 P.2d 1024 (Kan. 1996).

State v. Nations, 354 S.E.2d 510 (N.C. 1987).

State v. P.Z., 703 A.2d 901 (N.J. 1997).

State v. Parkinson, 909 P.2d 647 (Idaho 1996).

State v. Phelps, 696 P.2d 447 (Mont. 1985).

State v. Rimmasch, 775 P.2d 388 (Utah 1989).

State v. Sprouse, 478 S.E.2d 871 (S.C. Ct. App. 1996).

State v. Thorp, 72 N.C. 181 (1875).

State v. Washington, 22 So. 841 (1897)

Stecker v. First Commercial Trust, 1998 WL 66003 (Ark. 1998).

Sternberg, K. J., Lamb, M. E., Hershkowitz, I., Esplin, P. W., Redlich, A., & Sunshine, N. (1996). The relationship between investigative utterance types and the informativeness of child witnesses. *Journal of Applied Developmental Psychology, 17*, 439-451.

Sternberg, K. J., Lamb, M. E., Hershkowitz, I., Yudilevitch, L., Orbach, Y., Esplin, P. W., & Hovav, M. (1997). Effects of introductory style on children's abilities to describe experiences of sexual abuse. *Child Abuse & Neglect, 21*, 1133-1146.

Steinberg, K. L., Levine, M., & Doueck, H. J. (1997). Effects of legally mandated child-abuse reports on the therapeutic relationship. *American Journal of Orthopsychiatry, 67*, 112-122.

Steward, M. S., & Steward, D. S. (1996). Interviewing young children about body touch and handling. *Monographs of the Society for Research in Child Development, 61*, 1-187.

Straus, M. A., & Kantor, G. K. (1994). Corporal punishment of adolescents by parents: A risk factor in the epidemiology of depression, suicide, alcohol abuse, child abuse, and wife beating. *Adolescence, 29*, 543-561.

Styron, T., & Janoff-Bulman, R. (1997). Childhood attachment and abuse: Long-term effects on adult attachment. *Child Abuse & Neglect, 21*, 1015-1023.

Summit, R. C. (1983). The child sexual abuse accommodation syndrome. *Child Abuse & Neglect, 7*, 177-193.

Summit, R. C. (1988). Hidden victims, hidden pain: Societal avoidance of child sexual abuse. In G. E. Wyatt & G. J. Powell (Eds.), *Lasting effects of child sexual abuse* (pp. 39-60). Thousand Oaks, CA: Sage.

Summit, R. C., Olafson, E., & Corwin, D. L. (1993). Modern history of child sexual abuse awareness: Cycles of discovery and suppression. *Child Abuse & Neglect, 17*, 7-24.

Swanston, H. Y., Tebutt, J. S., O'Toole, B. I., & Oates, K. (1997). Sexually abused children 5 years after presentation: A case-control study. *Pediatrics, 100,* 600-608.

Sweaney v. Ada County, Idaho, 119 F.3d 1385 (9th Cir. 1997).

Tarasoff v. Regents of the University of California, 551 P.2d 334 (Ca. 1976).

Tardieu, A. A. (1873). *Etude medicale-legale sur les attentats aux moeurs* [A medico-legal study of assaults on decency] (6th ed.). Paris. (Original work published in 1813)

Taylor, L., & Adelman, H. (1989). Reframing the confidentiality dilemma to work in children's best interests. *Professional Psychology: Research and Practice, 20,* 79-83.

Taylor v. United States, 222 F.2d 398 (D.C. Cir. 1955).

Terr, L. (1991). Childhood traumas: An outline and overview. *American Journal of Psychiatry, 148,* 10-20.

Thoennes, N., & Thaden, P. O. (1990). The extent, nature, and validity of sexual abuse allegations in custody/visitation disputes. *Child Abuse & Neglect, 14,* 151-163.

Thomas v. Chadwick, 274 Cal. Rptr. 128 (Ct. App. 1990).

Thomason v. SCAN Volunteer Services Inc., 85 F.3d 1365 (8th Cir. 1996).

Thompson, W. C., Clarke-Stewart, K. A., & Lepore, S. J. (1997). What did the janitor do? Suggestive interviewing and the accuracy of children's accounts. *Law and Human Behavior, 21,* 405-426.

Thompson v. County of Alameda, 614 P.2d 728 (Cal. Ct. App. 1980).

Thompson-Cooper, I., Fugere, R., & Cormier, B. M. (1993). The child abuse reporting laws: An ethical dilemma for professionals. *Canadian Journal of Psychiatry, 38,* 557-562.

Tiffin, S. (1982). *In whose best interest? Child welfare reform in the Progressive Era.* Westport, CT: Greenwood.

Timmons-Mitchell, J., Chandler-Holtz, D., & Semple, W. E. (1996). Post-traumatic stress symptoms in mothers following children's reports of sexual abuse: An exploratory study. *American Journal of Orthopsychiatry, 66,* 463-467.

Tjaden, P. G., & Anhalt, J. (1994). *The impact of joint law enforcement-child protective services investigations in child maltreatment cases* (Executive Summary for Grant Number 90-CA-1446). Denver, CO: Center for Policy Research.

Tobey, A. E., & Goodman, G. S. (1992). Children's eyewitness memory: Effects of participation and forensic context. *Child Abuse & Neglect, 16,* 779-796.

Tonry, R. A. (1965). Statutory rape: A critique. *Louisiana Law Review, 26,* 105-117.

Tranel, D. (1994). The release of psychological data to nonexperts: Ethical and legal considerations. *Professional Psychology: Research and Practice, 25,* 33-38.

Trent v. State, 20 S.W. 547 (Tex. Crim. App. 1892).

U.S. Advisory Board on Child Abuse and Neglect. (1990). *Child abuse and neglect: Critical first steps in response to a national emergency.* Washington, DC: U.S. Department of Health and Human Services.

United States v. Barnard, 490 F.2d 907 (9th Cir. 1973).

United States v. Carter, 26 M.J. 428 (C.M.A. 1988).

United States v. Ingham, 42 M.J. 218 (C.A.A.F. 1995).

United States v. Iron Shell, 633 F.2d 77 (8th Cir. 1980).

United States v. King, 35 M.J. 337 (C.M.A. 1992).

United States v. Rouse, 111 F.3d 561 (8th Cir. 1997).

Utah Attorney General. (1995). *Ritual crime in the state of Utah.* Salt Lake City: Utah Attorney General's Office.

van der Kolk, B. A., & Fisler, R. (1995). Dissociation and the fragmentary nature of traumatic memories: Overview and exploratory study. *Journal of Traumatic Stress, 8*, 505-525.

Vu v. Singer Co., 538 F. Supp. 26 (D. Cal. 1981).

Wagner, B. M. (1997). Family risk factors for child and adolescent suicidal behavior. *Psychological Bulletin, 121*, 246-298.

Walker, A. G. (1994). *Handbook on questioning children: A linguistic perspective.* Washington, DC: American Bar Association Center on Children and the Law.

Warren, A. R., Hulse-Trotter, K., & Tubbs, E. C. (1991). Inducing resistance to suggestibility in children. *Law and Human Behavior, 15*, 373-385.

Warren, A. R., & Lane, P. (1995). Effects of timing and type of questioning on eyewitness accuracy and suggestibility. In M. S. Zaragoza, J. R. Graham, G. C. N. Hall, R. Hirschman, & Y. S. Ben-Porath (Eds.), *Memory and testimony in the child witness* (pp. 44-60). Thousand Oaks, CA: Sage.

Warren, A. R., & McGough, L. S. (1996). Research on children's suggestibility: Implications for the investigative interview. *Criminal Justice and Behavior, 23*, 269-303.

Warren, A. R., Woodall, C. E., Hunt, J. S., & Perry, N. W. (1996). "It sounds good in theory, but . . .": Do investigative interviewers follow guidelines based on memory research? *Child Maltreatment, 1*, 231-245.

Warren-Leubecker, A. (1991). Commentary: The influence of stress and arousal on the child witness. In J. Dorris (Ed.), *The suggestibility of children's recollections* (pp. 24-26). Washington, DC: American Psychological Association.

Washington State Institute for Public Policy. (1995). *Community notification: A study of offender characteristics and recidivism.* (Prepared by D. D. Schram & C. D. Millor). Seattle, WA: Urban Policy Research.

Watson, J., & Levine, M. (1989). Psychotherapy and mandated reporting of child abuse. *American Journal of Orthopsychiatry, 59*, 246-256.

Watterson v. Page, 987 F.2d 1 (1st Cir. 1993).

Webster's ninth new collegiate dictionary. (1985). Springfield, MA: Merriam-Webster.

Weinberg, K. (1955). *Incest behavior.* New York: Citadel.

Welch, D. (1976). Criminal procedure—instruction to jury that rape is easy to charge and difficult to disprove is no longer to be given. *State v. Feddcroon 280 N.W.2d 610* (Iowa 1975). *Texas Law Review, 7*, 732-737.

Wells, R. D., & Loftus, E. F. (1991). Commentary: Is the child fabricating? Reactions to a new assessment technique. In J. Doris (Ed.), *The suggestibility of children's recollections* (pp. 168-171). Washington, DC: American Psychological Association.

Wells, R. D., McCann, J., Adams, J., Voris, J., & Dahl, B. (1997). A validation study of the Structured Interview of Symptoms Associated With Sexual Abuse (SASA) using three samples of sexually abused, allegedly abused, and nonabused boys. *Child Abuse & Neglect, 21*, 1159-1168.

Wells, R. D., McCann, J., Adams, J., Voris, J., & Ensign, J. (1995). Emotional, behavioral, and physical symptoms reported by parents of sexually abused, nonabused, and allegedly abused prepubescent females. *Child Abuse & Neglect, 19*, 155-163.

Wesolowski, J. J. (1976). Indicia of consent? A proposal for change to the common law rule admitting evidence of a rape victim's character for chastity. *Loyola University Law Journal, 7*, 118-140.

Whipple, E. E., & Richey, C. A. (1997). Crossing the line from physical discipline to child abuse: How much is too much? *Child Abuse & Neglect, 21*, 431-444.

Whipple, G. M. (1911). The psychology of testimony. *Psychological Bulletin, 8*, 307-309.

Whitcomb, D., De Vos, E., Cross, T. P., Peeler, N. A., Runyan, D. K., Hunter, W. M., Everson, M. D., Porter, C. Q., Toth, P., & Cropper, C. (1994). *The child victim as a witness: Research report.* Washington, DC: U.S. Department of Justice, Office of Juvenile Justice and Delinquency Prevention.

Whitcomb, D., Goodman, G. S., Runyan, D. K., & Hoak, S. (1994, April). The emotional effects of testifying on sexually abused children. In U.S. Department of Justice, National Institute of Justice (Ed.), *Research in brief.* Washington, DC: U.S. Department of Justice.

White, S., Strom, G. A., & Quinn, K. M. (1987). *Guidelines for interviewing preschoolers with sexually anatomically detailed dolls.* Unpublished manuscript. Cleveland: Case Western University.

White v. Commonwealth, 28 S.W. 340 (Ky. Ct. App. 1894).

Wicker v. State, 740 S.W.2d 779 (Tex. Crim. App. 1987).

Widom, C. S., & Shepard, R. L. (1996). Accuracy of adult recollections of childhood victimization: Part 1. Childhood physical abuse. *Psychological Assessment, 8,* 412-421.

Wigmore, J. H. (1974). *Evidence in trials at common law.* Boston: Little, Brown. (Original work published 1904)

Williams, G. J. (1980). Cruelty and kindness to children: Documentary of a century, 1874-1974. In G. J. Williams & J. Money (Eds.), *Traumatic abuse and neglect of children at home* (pp. 68-88). Baltimore: Johns Hopkins University Press.

Williams, L. M. (1994). A prospective study of women's memories of child sexual abuse. *Journal of Consulting and Clinical Psychology, 62,* 1167-1176.

Williams, L. M. (1995). Recovered memories of abuse in women with documented child sexual victimization histories. *Journal of Traumatic Stress, 8,* 649-673.

Williams, L. M. (1998). *Trauma and memory.* Thousand Oaks, CA: Sage.

Willman, K. Y., Bank, D. E., Senac, M., & Chadwick, D. L. (1997). Restricting the time of injury in fatal inflicted head injuries. *Child Abuse & Neglect, 21,* 929-940.

Wisconsin v. Yoder, 406 U.S. 205 (1972).

Wojcik v. Town of North Smithfield, 76 F.3d 1 (1st Cir. 1996).

Wood, C. L. (1994). The parental alienation syndrome: A dangerous aura of reliability. *Loyola of Los Angeles Law Review, 27,* 1367-1415.

Wood, J. (1996). Weighing evidence in sexual abuse evaluations: An introduction to Bayes' theorem. *Child Maltreatment, 1,* 25-36.

Wood, J., & Wright, L. (1995). Evaluation of children's sexual behaviors and incorporation of base rates in judgments of sexual abuse. *Child Abuse & Neglect, 19,* 1263-1273.

Wood, P. L. (1973). The victim in a forcible rape case: A feminist view. *American Criminal Law Review, 11,* 335-354.

Woodward v. Weiss, 932 F.Supp. 723 (D.S.C. 1996).

World Book dictionary. (1993). Chicago: World Book.

Wozencraft, T., Wagner, W., & Pellegrin, A. (1991). Depression and suicidal ideation in sexually abused children. *Child Abuse & Neglect, 15,* 505-511.

Wyatt, G. E., & Powell, G. J. (Eds.). (1988). *Lasting effects of child sexual abuse.* Newbury Park, CA: Sage.

Zamstein v. Marvasti, 692 A.2d 781 (Conn. 1997).

Zaragoza, M. S. (1987). Memory, suggestibility, and eyewitness testimony in children and adults. In S. J. Ceci, M. P. Toglia, & D. F. Ross (Eds.), *Children's eyewitness memory* (pp. 53-178). New York: Springer-Verlag.

Zaragoza, M. S., Graham, J. R., Hall, G. C. N., Hirschman, R., & Ben-Porath, Y. S. (Eds.). (1995). *Memory and testimony in the child witness*. Thousand Oaks, CA: Sage.

Zellman, G. L. (1990). Report decision-making patterns among mandated child abuse reporters. *Child Abuse & Neglect, 14*, 325-336.

Zellman, G. L., & Faller, K. C. (1996). Reporting of child maltreatment. In J. Briere, L. Berliner, J. A. Buckley, C. Jenny, & T. Reid (Eds.), *The APSAC handbook on child maltreatment*. Thousand Oaks, CA: Sage.

Zumwalt, R. E., & Hirsch, C. S. (1987). Pathology of fatal child abuse and neglect. In R. E. Helfer & R. S. Kempe (Eds.), *The battered child* (4th ed., pp. 247-285). Chicago: University of Chicago Press.

Index

Abandoning a client, 314
Abandonment, 251
Absolute immunity, 323-330
Accident versus abuse, 242-245
Adult survivors, 56, 15-17, 303-304, 306-308
Adversary system. *See* Legal system
Alcohol abuse, 250
Ambiguous events. *See* Suggestibility
American Academy of Pediatrics, 4-5
American Professional Society on the Abuse of Children, 127, 195, 224-225, 245, 253, Appendix A, Appendix C
Amnesia. *See* Memory
Anatomical dolls, 126-129, 156, 165, 260, Appendix A
Appeal, 66
Attorney:
    Assistant U.S. Attorney, 49
    defense attorney, 60-62, 65, 70, 288-289
    family court, 70-71
    prosecutor, 49, 55-56, 58-59, 61, 69-70, 168
    talking to attorneys, 60-62, 203, 213
    U.S. Attorney 49

Bail. *See* Criminal justice system
Base rates, 254-259, 263, 265
Battered Child Syndrome, 42, 82, 94-95, 229, 242
Bergh, Henry, 39
Bias:
    impeachment in court, 60, 284-286, 292-293
    interviewer, 135
Bill of particulars. *See* Criminal justice system
Bill of Rights, 46, 50, 319-320
Bizarre allegations, 178-190
Blind interviews. *See* Interviewing
Brace, Charles Loring, 38-39

Catchall exception. *See* Hearsay
Character evidence, 273-274, 285
Child abuse:
    difficult to prove, 221
    neglect. *See* Neglect
    physical. *See* Physical abuse
    sexual. *See* Sexual abuse
Child advocacy centers, 169-171
Child custody:
    abuse, 77

alcohol, 77
best interest of child, 74-78
confidentiality, 210, 220
defined, 73
drugs, 77
evaluation, 223, 225
example, 31
fabricated allegations, 25-26, 33-35
immunity for evaluators, 326-330
joint custody, 73
mediation, 75
modification, 73, 78-79
Parental Alienation Syndrome, 276-277
primary caretaker, 75-76
privilege, 210, 220
res judicata, 78-79
skepticism, 78
spousal abuse, 77
tender years presumption, 73-74
types, 73
visitation, 72-73
Child hearsay exception. See Hearsay
Child protection:
    child protective services, 41, 68
    civil commitment of sex offenders, 81
    commitment of sex offenders, 81
    federal law, 47
    government authority, 45-46, 246-248, 320-321
    history, 1, 29, 37-43, 320
    juvenile court, 40
    legal system. See Legal system
    Mary Ellen, 39
    Megan's law, 80-81
    power of government, 45-46, 246-248, 320-321
    reporting abuse. See Reporting law
    registration of sex offenders, 79-80
    sex offender registration, 79-80
Child protective services:
    history, 41
    investigation 53, 68-69, 168-172
Child Sexual Behavior Inventory, 254, 263-264
Child witness:
    accommodations for, 294, 297
    closed-circuit television, 295-297
    coaching, 165, 173

competence, 152
confrontation, 295-297
    expert testimony, 296-297
    face-to-face confrontation, 295-297
    impeachment, 65, 104, 267-269
    lowering suggestibility, 122-123
    most important witness, 104
    rehabilitation, 230, 267-270
    reliability, 119
    preparation, 122-123
    support for child, 294
    testimony, 57, 295, 297
    truthfulness, 269-270
    video testimony, 295-297
Childhood amnesia. See Memory
Christian Scientists, 246
Civil commitment, 81
Civil action, 299
Civil rights, 300, 317-323, 317-323
Clergy member-penitent privilege. See Confidentiality
Coaching, 165, 173
Cognitive interview, 148-150
Common law, 48
Communication between professions, 2, 36, 44-45
Complaint:
    criminal, 56
    divorce, 70
    ethics, 298, 311, 329
Confidentiality:
    asserting privilege, 200-201
    attorneys, talking to, 203
    child client, 203-204, 207, 210, 212
    clergy member-penitent privilege, 198
    client consent, 209-210
    consent of client, 209-210
    court-ordered evaluation, 219
    dangerous clients, 215-218
    defendant's rights, 213-214
    definition, 193-194
    deposition, 202
    disclosure, 198, 202, 209-220
    duty to warn, 215-218
    education records, 214-215
    emergencies, 215, 219
    ethics, 195-198, 200-203, 224
    forensic evaluation, 219, 224

group therapy, 204-206
holder of privilege, 199-200
importance, 194, 196, 204
informed consent, 206-209
liability, 196, 210, 317
limits, 93, 198, 207-220, 224
malpractice, 196, 210
managed care, 209
patient-litigant exception, 219-220
physician-patient privilege, 198, 201-202
privacy, 195-196
privileges, 197-203, 210-212, 219
psychological test results, 208-209
psychotherapist-client privilege, 198-199, 201
psychotherapy, 194
raw test data, 208-209
records, review of, 214
release of confidential information, 198, 202, 209-220
reporting law, 91-93, 208, 215
review of records, 214
school records, 214-215
sexual assault counselor-victim privilege, 199
social worker-client privilege, 199
sources, 194-206
subpoenas, 211-214
talking to attorneys, 60-62
Tarasoff, 215-218
violation, 196, 210, 317
warning potential victims, 215-218
Congress, 46-47
Constitutional law, 46, 49, 59-60, 64, 80-81, 295, 317-323, 338
Corporal punishment, 3-7, 37, 77-78
Courts. See Criminal justice system; Juvenile court; Judicial system
Credibility. See Impeachment
Criminal justice system:
appeal, 66
arrest, 53-54, 56
bail, 56-57
bill of particulars, 59
character evidence, 273-274
child witness. See Child witness
closing argument, 65, 287
communication with defense attorney, 60-62
complaint, 56
confrontation, 295-297
decision to file charges, 55
defense attorney, communication with, 60-62
deliberation, 66
discovery, 59-62
diversion from prosecution, 58
generally, 51-67, 301
grand jury, 57-58
indictment, 57-58
interview of child, 62
investigation, 53
jury, 57-58, 63, 66, 221, 231-234, 265, 269-270, 274, 286, 288-289, 293
motions, 59
magistrate, 49, 51, 54, 56-58
Miranda warning, 54
opening statement, 63-64
petit jury, 58
plea bargaining, 62-63
preliminary hearing, 51, 57-58
probation, 67
prosecutor, 49, 55-56, 58-59, 61, 63-67, 69-70, 168
sentencing, 67
subpoena. See Subpoena
trial, 63-67
warrant, 54
Criteria-based content analysis, 151-152
Cross-examination:
ABCs of coping with cross-examination, Appendix D
children, 65, 104, 267-271
closing argument, 287, 293
coaching, 66, 165, 173
confidential records, 214
control of witness, 287-290
delayed disclosure, 65-66, 267
frontal attack, 286
hiding the ball, 290
hypothetical question, 238, 291
impeachment. See Impeachment
inconsistency, 65, 267
leading questions, 287-288, 290
learned treatises, 292
limiting ability to explain, 288-289

limits on cross-examination, 294
negative cross-examination, 283, 286-287
positive cross-examination, 283, 286-287
preparation, 214, 291, 293
privileged records, 214
purpose, 230, 283, 293
recantation, 267
right to, 65, 230, 282
techniques, 65, 267
undermine expert's assumptions, 290-291
Cued recall. *See* Memory
Custody. *See* Child custody

Damages, 299, 324
Daubert. *See* Scientific evidence
Death from abuse, 3, 7, 85, 244-245
Defense attorney, 60-62
Delayed disclosure, 230, 267-269, 275-276
Deposition, 202, 328
Direct examination, 64-65, 282, 288
Discipline, 95, 196, 212
Disclosure of abuse:
    delayed, 230, 238, 267-269
    distortion, 188
    embarrassment, 139-140
    evidence, 156, 229
    expert testimony, 230, 238, 267-269
    fear, 12
    hearsay, 156, 161, 222
    leading questions. *See* Leading questions
    process, 137-140, 143-144, 192, 222, 267
    threats, 12, 137, 142, 184, 215-218, 297
    reporting law, 89, 98
    videotape, 175-176
Discovery:
    civil, 202
    criminal, 59-62, 213-214
    deposition, 202, 328
Diversion from prosecution. *See* Criminal justice system
Divorce. *See* Family court

Documentation, 98, 153-154, 157, 160-168, 210, 218, 315-316
Dolls, 126-129, 156, 260, Appendix A
Domestic relations. *See* Family court
Drugs, 76, 85, 182, 184, 249-250
Dual relationships, 222-228
Duty, 303-304
Duty to nonclients, 303-304, 306-308

Education records, 214-215
Effects of abuse, 2-7, 10-17
Ethics:
    codes, 311
    complaint, 298, 311, 329
    confidentiality, 195-196
    dual relationships, 222-228
    malpractice, 311
Evidence:
    character
    credibility, 229-230
    defined, 228
    strong, 264-265
    substantive, 229
    weak, 264-265
Exceptions to hearsay rule. *See* Hearsay
Excited utterance. *See* Hearsay
Expert testimony:
    accommodation syndrome, 275
    background information, 238
    basis of expert testimony, 239, 271
    bias, 60, 233, 284-286, 292-293
    Child Sexual Abuse Accommodation Syndrome, 275, 280, 336
    child custody, 223, 225, 265
    child witness, 296-297
    closed circuit television, 296-297
    consistent with, 252-253
    controversy, 252-253
    courts' position on, 265-267
    credibility evidence, 229-230, 267-270, 275, 276
    criminal cases, 229-230, 238, 252-276, 336
    cross-examination, 234-235
    Daubert. *See* Scientific evidence
    delayed disclosure, 230, 238, 278-269, 275-276
    diagnosis, 252

disclosure, 230, 267-269, 275
dual relationships, 222-228
evenhandedness, 232
evidence defined, 228
example, 279-281
family court, 265, 336
form of testimony, 235-238, 252
Frye. See Scientific evidence
guidelines, 268-269
honesty, 232
hypothetical question, 237-238
importance, 221, 251
immunity
juvenile court, 265, 336
limits of expertise, 233, 252
medical neglect, 247
metaprinciples, 231-234
Munchausen Syndrome by Proxy, 244-245
neglect, 245-251
nonabusive parent, 269
noncriminal cases, 231
novel scientific evidence. *See* Scientific evidence
objectivity, 233
opinion, 235, 237, 253
perpetrator, 267, 271-274
physical abuse, 242-245
preparation, 214, 234, 293
profile, 271-274
qualifications, 234-235, 270
Rape Trauma Syndrome, 241, 275-276
reasonable certainty, 236-237
recantation, 138, 146, 173-174, 230-231, 238, 267-269, 275
rehabilitate victim, 230, 267-270, 25-276
relation to lawyers, 62
review of records, 214
records, review of, 214
scientific evidence. *See* Scientific evidence
sexual abuse cases, 230, 251-278
Shaken Baby Syndrome, 244
substantive evidence, 229-230, 238, 252-268, 271-276, 279
symptoms of abuse, 253-264
syndromes. *See* Syndromes

truthfulness, 269-270
video testimony, 296-297
voir dire, 234-235
when allowed, 231, 267
Fabricated allegations:
history, 25-26
reporting law, 97
sexual abuse, 30-35, 186-188
Failure to thrive, 248
False allegations. See Fabricated allegations
Family court:
alienation, 276-277
alimony, 72
attorney, need for, 70-71
CPS involvement, 70
child support, 72
custody, 31-34, 72-79, 326-328
divorce, 71
fabricated allegations, 33-35, 186-188
immunity for evaluators, 326-328
Parental Alienation Syndrome, 276-277
property, 71-72
skepticism, 78
spousal support, 72
visitation, 72-73
Fatal abuse, 3, 7, 85, 244, 245
Federal courts, 49-51
Feminist movement, 29, 42
Ferenczi, Sandor, 20
Fetal Alcohol Syndrome, 85
Finkelhor, David, 10-11, 21
Focused questioning. *See* Interviewing
Forensic practice, 223
Free recall. *See* Memory
Fresh complaint. *See* Hearsay
Freud, Sigmund, 19, 23, 113, 115
Frye. See Scientific evidence

Goodman, Gail S., 105
Grand jury. *See* Criminal justice system
Grooming, 52-53
Group therapy:
confidentiality, 204-206
privilege, 204-206
sexual abuse, 17-18

Hearsay:
    anatomical dolls, 156
    catchall exception, 164-166
    child hearsay exception, 164-166
    conduct as hearsay, 156-157
    definition, 154-155
    documentation, 153-154, 157, 160-168
    exceptions, 157-168
    example, 155-159
    excited utterance 158-161
    fresh complaint, 161
    gathering verbal evidence, 154, 157,
        166
    importance, 154
    medical diagnosis or treatment, 162-
        164
    nonverbal communication as hear-
        say, 156-157
    professional role, 154, 157, 166
    residual exception, 164-166
    rule, 153-156
    state of mind, 161-162
    videotape, 173
History, 18-29, 37-43, 114-115
Hypermnesia, 144
Hypnosis, 307-308
Hypothesis testing. See Interviewing
Hypothetical questions, 237-238, 291

Immunity:
    absolute, 97, 317, 323-330
    qualified, 97, 330-331
    reporting law, 96-97
Investigation:
    bizarre allegations, 178-190
    CPS, 53-68-69
    child advocacy centers, 169-171
    difficult, 102
    hearsay. See Hearsay
    immunity, 330-331
    interviewing. See Interviewing
    law enforcement, 53-54, 168-172
    multidisciplinary investigation, 168-
        172
    multivictim cases, 188, 190-191
    reporting law, 87
    ritual abuse, 178-190

    satanic abuse, 178-190
    videotaped interviews, 172-178
Impeachment:
    bias, 60, 284-286, 292-293
    capacity, 285
    character evidence, 285
    child, 65, 104, 267-271
    Child Sexual Abuse Accommodation
        Syndrome, 275
    closing argument, 287, 293
    coaching, 165, 173
    control, 287-290
    conviction of crime, 285
    credibility, 229-230, 267-270, 283-284
    cross-examination. See Cross-
        examination
    delayed disclosure, 238, 267-270,
        275-276
    developmental differences, 270-271
    doubts raised by, 287
    expert witnesses, 285-293
    expert's own victimization, 293
    frontal attack, 286
    hiding the ball, 287, 290
    inconsistency, 143, 175, 267-270, 284
    lay witness, 284-285
    learned treatise, 292
    nonabusive parent, 269
    observe, opportunity to, 285
    opportunity to observe, 285
    purpose, 230, 293
    raise doubts, 287
    recantation, 238, 267-270, 288
    rehabilitation, 230, 267-270, 275-276
    syndromes. See Syndromes
    undermine expert's assumptions,
        290-291
Inconsistency:
    credibility, 143, 267-269
    developmental reasons, 146-148
    disclosure process, 145-146
    explanation for, 145-148
    impeachment, 143-267-269
    memory, 146
    reasons for, 145-148
    videotape, 175
Indictment. See Criminal justice system
Infantile amnesia. See Memory

Informed consent:
  children, 207, 210
  confidentiality, limits of, 207-208
  elements of, 206-208
  forewarning, 207-208, 311
  generally, 206-209, 307
  malpractice, 207, 307, 311
  managed care, 209
  requirement, 206, 307
  reporting law, 93, 208
  violation, 207
Informed consent:
  children, 207, 210
  confidentiality, limits of, 207-208
  elements, 206-208
  forewarning, 207-208, 311
  generally, 206-209, 307
  malpractice, 207, 307, 311
  managed care, 209
  reporting law, 93, 208
  requirement, 206, 307
  violation, 207
Injunction, 300
Interviewing:
  anatomical dolls, 126-129, Appendix A
  attack on interviewer, 103, 176
  background information, 130
  bad practices, 142-143, 186-187, 191
  bias, 135, 142-143
  blind interview, 130
  child advocacy centers, 169-172
  coercion, 142
  cognitive interview, 148-150
  competence, 152
  compliments, 133
  context reinstatement, 126
  criteria-based content analysis, 151-152
  criticizing child, 142
  difficulty, 102, 108-109
  dilemma for interviewers, 107, 136-141
  disclosure of abuse, 137-140, 143-144, 192, 222, 267
  dolls, 126-129, Appendix A
  early interviews, 112
  flexibility, 129-130
  focused questions, 123-124, 134

  hypothesis testing, 135
  inconsistency. See Inconsistency
  indefensible statements, 117-118, 131-132
  initial questioning, 133-135
  leading questions. See Leading questions
  memory. See Memory
  multidisciplinary investigation, 168-172
  multiple choice questions, 135
  multiple interviews, 143-148, 169
  narrative elaboration, 151
  number of interviews, 143-148, 169-172
  objectivity, 135, 142-143
  open-ended questions, 107-109, 123-124, 133-141, 165
  praise, 133, 142
  preparing children, 122-123, 131-132
  proper practices, 129-141
  props, 126-129
  rapport, 130-131
  reducing interviews, 143-148, 169-172
  repeating questions, 135-136
  specific questions, 124-125, 134
  suggestive questions, 123-124, 134
  supportive atmosphere, 132-133
  terminology, 123-125
  training, 104
  videotaping, 172-178
  "why" questions, 124
  "yes-no" questions, 135
  young children, 107

Jehovah's Witnesses, 246
Joint investigation, 168-172
Judicial immunity, 326-327
Judicial notice, 241-242
Judicial system, 46, 48-51, 68-79, 221, 321
Jury, 57-58, 63, 66, 221, 231-234, 265, 269-270, 274, 286, 288-289, 293, 299
Juvenile court:
  court-ordered treatment, 249-250
  delinquency, 68

expert testimony, 231
generally, 68-70, 321
history, 40-42
immunity for social workers, 325-
    326
jury, 221
medical care, 246
neglect cases, 245-251

Kempe, Henry C., 20, 42, 82, 243

Landeros v. Flood, 94-95
Law enforcement, 53-54, 168-172, 318
Lay witness, 222, 225, 227, 229, 235
Leading questions:
    contamination of memory, 108, 116-
        117, 142-143, 145, 186-187
    cross-examination, 287-288, 290
    danger of, 108-109, 116-117, 142-143,
        145, 186-187
    defined, 125
    example, 125
    excited utterance, 160
    hearsay, 160, 164
    interviewer use of, 104
    justified, 136-141
    need for, 108, 134, 136-141
    See also Memory
Learned professions, 301
Learned treatise, 292
Legal system:
    administrative proceedings, 300-301
    adversary system, 43-45, 65, 75, 232,
        283, 289-290
    common law, 48
    Congress, 47
    constitutional law, 46, 49, 59-60, 64,
        80-81, 295, 317-323
    courts, 46
    criminal cases. *See* Criminal justice
        system
    federal courts, 49-51
    judicial system, 46, 48-51
    magistrate, 49, 51, 54, 56-58
    overview, 45-79
    parens patriae, 45, 247, 321, 338
    parental rights, 46, 319-320
    police power, 45, 321

regulations, 47-48
state courts, 51
Supreme Court, 45-46, 48-51, 246-
    247, 295-297, 319-321
U.S. Attorney, 49
Liability. *See* Malpractice
License to practice:
    action by licensing authorities, 95,
        316
    administrative proceedings, 300-301
    discipline, 95, 196, 212, 300-301, 329

Magistrate, 49, 51, 54, 56-58
Malpractice:
    abandoning a client, 314
    administrative proceedings, 300-301
    bad practice, 181, 301-306
    breach of professional responsibility,
        301-302, 310-311
    civil rights, 300, 317-323, 331-332
    confidentiality, 93, 196
    damages, 299, 324
    dangerous client, 215-218
    documentation, 98, 315-316
    duty, 303-304, 306-308, 310-311
    duty to warn, 215-218
    educational malpractice, 314
    ethics complaints, 298, 311
    example, 331-333
    failure to report abuse, 94-96
    hiring, 313-314
    immunity. *See* Immunity
    informed consent, 93, 207
    Landeros v. Flood, 94-95
    learned professions, 301
    licensing authorities, 95, 316
    managing risk, 315-316
    negligence, 301-306, 309-314
    1983 liability, 313, 317-323, 332
    nonclients, duty to 303-304, 306-308
    parental rights, 318-323, 331-332,
        337-338
    peer review, 315
    psychotherapy, 312-313
    reasonable care, 308-310
    reasonable person, 308-310
    record keeping, 98, 315-316

reducing exposure to liability, 315-
    316
referral, 314
reporting law, 93-96, 316-317
respondeat superior, 313
ritual abuse, 181
settings, 299-301
standard of care, 308-312
state law, 316-317
supervision, 313-314
Tarasoff, 215-218
torts, 302-303, 317
warning potential victims, 215-218
Managed care, 209
Medical diagnosis or treatment
    exception. *See* Hearsay
Medical history, 162
Medical neglect, 246-248
Megan's law, 80-81
Memory:
    accuracy, 105-107, 112-113, 116
    amnesia, 111-113
    anatomical dolls, 126-129
    capacity, 105
    context reinstatement, 126
    cued recall, 108-109
    distortion, 106
    focused questions, 124-124, 134-141
    forgetting, 110-113
    free recall, 106-108, 133, 140-141
    good memory capacity, 105-106, 114
    hypermnesia, 144
    inconsistency, 147-148
    infantile, amnesia, 111-113
    leading questions, 104, 108-109, 116-
        117, 123-125, 134-141
    maturation, 105, 140
    open-ended questions, 107-109, 123-
        124, 133-135-141, 165
    preschool children, 106-107, 112-113,
        126, 140
    props, 126-129
    recognition, 109
    recovered memory, 110-112, 303-304,
        306-308
    reminiscence, 144-145
    repressed memory, 110-112, 303-304,
        306-308

repetition, 144
script memory, 109-110, 146
specific questions, 124-125, 134-141
stress, 113-114, 184-185
suggestibility, relation to, 119-120
suggestive questions, 123-124, 136-
    141
trauma, 113-114, 184-185
videotape, 105
young children, 105-107, 112-113,
    126, 140
Mental retardation, 249
Mentally ill parent, 249
Miranda warnings, 54
MMPI, 271-272
Multidisciplinary investigation, 168-172
Multiple choice questions. *See* Inter-
    viewing
Multiple interviews:
    advantages of, 143, 148
    reducing, 143
Multiple victim cases, 188, 190-191
Munchausen Syndrome by Proxy, 244-
    245, 331

Narrative elaboration, 151
Neglect:
    abandonment, 251
    Christian Scientists, 246
    definition, 83, 243
    drug use, 249-250
    educational neglect, 251
    failure to thrive, 7, 248
    fatal, 3, 7, 245
    filthy home cases, 250
    Jehovah's Witnesses, 246
    medical, 246-248
    mental retardation, 249
    mentally ill parent 249
    Munchausen Syndrome by Proxy,
        244-245, 331
    nonorganic failure to thrive, 7, 248
    physically disabled parent, 249
    psychological neglect, 248
    reactive attachment disorder, 248
    religion, 246-247
    retardation, 249
Negligence. *See* Malpractice

1983 liability, 313, 321-323
Nonabusive parents, 269
Nonclients, duty to, 303-304, 306-308
Nonorganic failure to thrive, 248
Normal sexual behavior, 13

Oath, 64, 232
Open-ended questions. See Memory
Opening statement. See Criminal justice
    system
Opinion, 235-237

Parens patriae, 45, 247, 321, 338
Parental Alienation Syndrome, 276-277
Parental rights, 46, 246, 300, 318-323, 338
Peer review, 315
Penetration. See Sexual abuse
Penile plethysmography, 271-273
Peremptory challenge, 63
Petit jury, 58
Physical abuse:
    accident, 242-243
    Battered Child Syndrome, 42, 82, 94-
        95, 229, 242-244
    cause of injury, 243
    corporal punishment, 2-7
    defenses, 242
    definition, 2, 85
    effects, 2-7
    expert testimony, 242-245
    explanation for injuries, 243
    fatal abuse, 3
    Munchausen Syndrome by Proxy,
        244-245
    prevalence, 2-3
    Shaken Baby Syndrome, 244
Physician-patient privilege. See Confi-
    dentiality
Plea bargaining. See Criminal justice
    system
Plethysmography, 271-273
Police power, 45, 321
Pornography, 260, 321
Posttraumatic stress disorder, 11-12, 14-
    17, 141, 184
Poverty, 6, 37-38, 250
Preliminary hearing. See Criminal
    justice system

Preparation:
    children for interviews, 122-123, 131-
        132
    children for testifying, 122-123
    expert testimony, 214, 234, 293
Prevalence, 2-3, 7-10, 42, 83
Privacy. See Confidentiality
Privilege. See Confidentiality
Probation. See Criminal justice system
Professional defined, 301
Profile evidence, 271-272
Projective tests, 271-272
Props, 126-129
Prosecutor. See Attorney; Criminal
    justice system
Prosecutorial immunity, 325-326
Psychological abuse, 248
Psychological tests:
    anatomical dolls not a test, 127
    Child Sexual Behavior Inventory,
        254, 263-264
    court ordered, 219
    MMPI, 271-272
    no test for trauma of testifying, 297
    penile plethysmography, 271-273
    perpetrator, 271-274
    projective tests, 271-272
    raw test results, 208-209
    Rorschach, 271-272
    sexual abuse, 254
Psychotherapist-client privilege. See
    Confidentiality
Psychotherapy:
    abuse-specific treatment, 17-18
    confidentiality. See Confidentiality
    dangerous clients, 215-218
    dual relationships, 222-228
    duty to nonclients, 303-304, 306-308
    duty to warn, 215-218
    expert testimony, 222-228
    failure to report abuse, 94-96
    forensic evaluation, 222-228
    informed consent, 93, 206-209
    legal implications, 103
    malpractice. See Malpractice
    offenders, 272
    perpetrators, 272

recovered memory, 110-112, 181, 303-304, 306-308
reporting law, 90-91, 96
repressed memory, 110-112, 181, 303-304, 306-308
ritual abuse, 180-181
satanic abuse, 180-181
sexual abuse, 17-18
Tarasoff, 215-218
videotape, 177
PTSD. *See* Posttraumatic Stress Disorder

Qualified immunity, 330-331

Rape, 23-24, 27-29
Rape shield law, 27
Rape Trauma Syndrome, 241,275-276
Rapport. *See* Interviewing
Raw test results, 208-209
Reactive attachment disorder, 248
Reasonable care, 308-309
Reasonable certainty, 236-237
Reasonable person, 308-309
Recall. *See* Memory
Recantation:
    expert testimony, 230-231, 238, 267-269
    rate of, 138
    reasons for, 146
    videotape, 173-174
Recidivism, 81
Recognition. *See* Memory
Record keeping, 98, 157, 160-160, 210, 218, 315-316
Recovered memory. *See* Memory
Redirect examination, 283, 289
Referral, 314
Registration of sex offenders, 78-79
Regulations, 47-48
Rehabilitation. *See* Impeachment
Religion, 246-248
Reminiscence, 145
Reporting law:
    alternatives to mandatory reporting, 98-100
    certainty not required, 86-87
    child's statement, 89
    confidentiality, 91, 93, 208, 215

crime, 95
discretion, 84
drugs, 85
factors influencing, 89-92
failure to report, 88, 94-96, 316-317
forewarning, 93, 208
generally, 82-101
guidelines, 98
history, 42, 82-83
immunity, 96-97
informed consent, 93, 208
investigation, 87
Landeros v. Flood, 94-95
liability for failure to report, 94-96
liability for reporting, 96-97
malpractice, 93-97, 316-317
mandated reporters, 83-84
mandatory, 83-84
reasonable suspicion, 85-88, 96
suspicion, 85-88, 96
when report required, 85-88, 96, 98
who reports, 83-84
Repressed memory. *See* Memory
Repression. *See* Memory
Residual exception. *See* Hearsay
Res judicata, 78-79
Respondeat superior, 313
Retardation, 249
Ritual abuse, 178-190
Rorschach test, 171

Sadistic abuse, 178-190
Satanic abuse, 178-190
Saywitz, Karen J., 105, 151
School records, 214-215
Scientific evidence:
    basis of expert's opinion, 236-237, 240-241
    Daubert, 239, 242, 266-267
    Frye, 239-242, 245, 266-267
    general acceptance test, 239-240
    judicial notice, 241-242
    psychological testimony, 241-242, 266-268
    relevance analysis, 239-242
    sexual abuse, 266-268
Script memory. *See* Memory
Sex Abuse Legitimacy Scale, 277-278

Sexual abuse:
    accommodation syndrome, 275
    adolescent perpetrators, 9-10
    adult survivors, 15-17
    anxiety, 12, 14, 254
    base rates, 254-259, 263, 265
    bizarre allegations, 178-190
    child custody, 31, 33-34, 78
    Child Sexual Abuse Accommodation
        Syndrome, 269, 275, 280, 336
    Child Sexual Behavior Inventory,
        254, 263-264
    clinical interview of alleged
        offender, 271-272
    custody disputes, 31, 33-34, 78
    defined, 85
    depression, 13, 16-17, 254
    developmentally unusual sexual
        knowledge, 13, 252, 259-265
    disbelief, 18-29, 78
    dissociation, 16-17
    duty to warn potential victim, 217
    effects, 10-17
    encopresis, 13
    evidence, 253-278
    expert testimony, 251-278
    fabricated allegations, 25-26, 30-35,
        78
    family court, 31, 33-34, 78
    fear, 12, 14, 16-17, 254
    grooming, 52-53, 279-280, 336
    group therapy, 17-18
    history, 18-29
    interviewing. See Interviewing
    liability for failure to report, 95
    long-term effects, 15-17
    masturbation, 13, 259, 261
    medical evidence, 251
    multiple personality disorder, 16-17
    nightmares, 12, 188, 254-255, 259, 264
    normal sexual behavior, 13, 259
    offender, 271-274
    offender treatment, 10
    PTSD, 11-12, 14-17, 275-276
    penetration, 11, 16, 27
    perpetrator, 271-274
    perpetrator, relation to child, 9, 11
    posttraumatic stress disorder, 11-12,
        14-15, 141, 184, 275-276

    prevalence, 8-9
    prostitution, 12, 17
    psychological evidence, 251-271
    psychotherapy, 17-18
    rape, 23-24, 27-29
    recantation. See Recantation
    recognition of, 8
    recovered memory, 110-112
    regression, 13, 254-256, 264
    rehabilitation of victim, 230, 267-
        270, 275
    relation to perpetrator to child, 9, 11
    repressed memory, 110-112
    ritual abuse, 178-190
    runaways, 12, 17
    satanic abuse, 178-190
    self-concept, 13, 16-18
    sexual behavior, 13, 238, 259-265
    sexual knowledge, 13, 238, 252, 259-
        265
    short-term effects, 11-15
    skepticism, 18-29, 78
    somatic complaints, 15, 17
    statutory rape, 27
    suicide, 13, 17
    syndromes. See Syndromes
    Tarasoff, 217
    theories of harmful effects, 10-11, 275
    treatment, 17-18
    threats, 12, 137, 142, 184, 215-218, 297
    teenage perpetrators, 9-10
Sexual assault counselor-victim
    privilege. See Confidentiality
Sexual knowledge or behavior, 13, 165,
    238, 252, 259-265
Shaken Baby Syndrome, 244
Skepticism about victims, 18-29, 78,
    118, 191
Social worker-client privilege. See
    Confidentiality
Sodium amytal, 307-308
Spanking, 3-7, 37
Specific questions. See Interviewing
Spousal abuse, 77
State action, 322-323
State of mind exception. See Hearsay
State validity analysis, 151-152
Statutory rape, 27
Stress, 113, 254, 275

Subpoenas:
    defense attorney, 60
    generally, 211-213, 219-220
    school records, 214
Suggestibility:
    accusatory atmosphere, 120-121
    adults, 117, 119
    age, 115-117, 119-120, 136
    ambiguous events, 122
    anatomical dolls, 126-129
    authority figures, 120
    bystander, 120
    contamination of memory, 108, 116-
        117
    defined, 114
    fatigue, 187
    generally, 114-123
    history, 114-115, 118
    importance, 106
    indefensible statements, 117-118
    leading questions. See Leading ques-
        tions
    lowering suggestibility, 122-123
    multiple reasons for, 115, 119-120,
        123
    older children, 116
    peripheral details, 117, 119-120
    preschoolers, 116-117, 119-120, 122,
        136
    psychological research, 118-119
    reasons for, 115, 119-120, 123
    resist suggestion, 117
    Sam Stone Study, 121-122
    skepticism, 114-115, 118
    stereotypes, 120-121
    stress, 114
    supportive interviewer, 132-133
    trends in research, 118-119
    young children, 116-117, 122, 136
Suggestive questions. See Interviewing
Summit, Roland, 18, 275
Supreme Court, 45-46, 48-51, 246-247,
    295-297, 319-321
Syndromes:
    Battered Child Syndrome, 42, 82, 94-
        95, 229, 242-244
    Child Sexual Abuse Accommoda-
        tion Syndrome, 269, 275, 280,
        336
    Fetal Alcohol Syndrome, 85
    Munchausen Syndrome by Proxy,
        244-245
    PTSD, 11-12, 14-17, 276, 279
    Parental Alienation Syndrome, 276-
        278
    rehabilitation, 275
    Rape Trauma Syndrome, 241, 275-
        276
    sexual abuse syndrome, 254, 269, 280
    Shaken Baby Syndrome, 244

Talking to attorneys, 60-62, 203, 213
Tarasoff, 215-219
Tardieu, Ambrose, 18-19
Threats, 12, 137, 142, 184, 215-218, 297
Therapy. See Psychotherapy
Torts, 302-303, 317
Trial. See Criminal justice system

U.S. Attorney, 49

Videotape:
    interviews, 172-178
    Munchausen Syndrome by Proxy,
        245
    testimony, 50, 295-297
Visitation. See Child custody

Wigmore, John, 27-28
"Why" questions, 124
Witness immunity, 328-330
Witnesses:
    children, 57, 64-65, 294-297
    credibility. See Impeachment
    expert, 222, 282
    immunity, 328-330
    impeachment. See Impeachment
    lay, 222, 282

About the Author

John E. B. Myers, J.D., Professor of Law at the University of the
Pacific's McGeorge School of Law in Sacramento, California, is
nationally recognized as an expert on investigation and litigation of
child abuse and neglect. He is the author of numerous books and
articles discussing legal issues in child abuse and neglect. His writing
has been cited by more than 140 courts, including the U.S. Supreme
Court and numerous state supreme courts. In addition, he is a regular
speaker at conferences on child abuse.

412